Thank you for your interest in Florida history.

Judy Clements

Legacy of Leadership: Florida Governors and Their Inaugural Speeches

by

Patricia Lasche Clements

Copyright 2005 by Patricia L. Clements

All rights reserved
Manufactured in the United States of America

Designer and Typesetter: Karen Towson Wells
Typeface: Boca Raton and Garamond
Printer and binder: Durraprint Printing Company

Library of Congress Number: 2005922241

ISBN: 1-889574-22-8

Sentry Press
424 East Call Street
Tallahassee, Florida 32301-7693

Dedication

To the two most important men
and the two most important women
In my life . . .

Arthur S. Clements M.D., Ph.D., a man of science
and a dedicated husband
George W. Lasche, a loving father
Claire and Meredith, my beloved daughters

Table of Contents

List of Governor's Wives — vii
Acknowledgments — ix
Introduction — xi

FLORIDA'S GOVERNORS:

William D. Moseley (1845-1849) — 1
Thomas Brown (1849-1853)] — 9
James E. Broome (1853-1857) — 15
Madison Perry (1857-1861) — 23
John Milton (1861-1865) — 31
William Marvin (provisional) (1865-1866) — 35
David Shelby Walker (1866-1868) — 43
Harrison Reed (1868-1873) — 59
Ossian B. Hart (1873-1874) — 63
Macelllus I. Stearns (1874-1877) — 69
George F. Drew (1877-1881) — 71
William D. Bloxham (1881-1885) & (1897-1901) — 75
Edward A. Perry (1885-1889) — 85
Francis P. Fleming (1889-1893) — 89
Henry L. Mitchell (1893-1897) — 93
William Sherman Jennings (1901-1905) — 97
Napoleon B. Broward (1905-1909) — 107
Albert W. Gilchrist (1909-1913) — 119
Park Trammell (1913-1917) — 133
Sidney J. Catts (1917-1921) — 145
Cary A. Hardee (1921-1925) — 183
John W. Martin (1925-1929) — 193
Doyle F. Carlton (1929-1933) — 197
David Sholtz (1933-1937) — 209
Fred P. Cone (1937-1941) — 219
Spessard L. Holland (1941-1945) — 233
Milldard F. Caldwell (1945-1949) — 249
Fuller Warren (1949-1953) — 259

Daniel T. McCarty (1953-1953)	269
Charley E. Johns (1953-1955)	277
LeRoy Collins (1955-1957 and 1957-1961)	279
C. Farris Bryant (1961-1965)	301
W. Haydon Burns (1965-1967)	309
Claude R. Kirk, Jr. (1967-1971)	319
Reuben O'Donovan Askew (1971-1975 & 1975-1979)	329
D. Robert "Bob" Graham (1979-1983 & 1983-1987)	349
Wayne Mixson (1987)	367
Robert "Bob" Martinez (1987-1991)	373
Lawton M. Chiles (1991-1995 and 1995-1999)	383
Kenneth H. "Buddy" MacKay (1999)	401
John Ellis "Jeb" Bush (1999-2003 and 2003-present)	403

Photographs	157
Bibliography	417
Index	421

List of Governors' Wives

March 10-October 6, 1821 Rachel Donelson Robards Jackson (Mrs. Andrew)
1822-1834 Nancy Hynes DuVal (Mrs. William Pope)
1834-1835 Peggy O'Neale Timberlake Eaton (Mrs. John Henry)
1835-1840 Mary Letitia Kirkman Call (Mrs. Richard Keith)
1840-1841 Mary Martha Smith Reid (Mrs. Robert Raymond)
1841-1844 Mary Letitia Kirkman Call (Mrs. Richard Keith)
1844-1845 Elizabeth Foort Branch (Mrs. John)

Statehood:
1845-1849 William Dunn Moseley (Widower)
1849-1853 Elizabeth Simpson Brown (Mrs. Thomas)
1853-1857 Martha Macon Hawkins Broome (Mrs. James Emilius)
1857-1861 Martha Starke Peay Perry (Mrs. Madison Starke)
1861-1865 Caroline Howze Milton (Mrs. John)
April-May 19,1865 Elizabeth S. Coleman Allison (Mrs. Abraham Kurkindolle)
July 13-December 20, 1865 Harriett Newell Marvin (Mrs. William)
1865-1868 Philoclea Alson Walker (Mrs. David Shelby)
1868-1873 Chloe Merrick Reed (Mrs. Harrison)
1873-1874 Catherine Smith Campbell Hart (Mrs. Ossian Bingley)
1874-1877 Marcellus Lovejoy Steams (Bachelor)
1877-1871 Amelia Dickens Drew (Mrs. George Franklin)
1881-1885, 1897-1901 Mary C. Davis Bloxham (Mrs. William Dunnington)
1885-1889 Wathen Herbert Taylor Perry (Mrs. Edward Alysworth)
1889-1893 Floride Lydia Pearson Fleming (Mrs. Francis Philip)
1893-1897 Mary Eugenia Spencer Mitchell (Mrs. Henry Laurens)

1901-1905 May Austin Mann Jennings (Mrs. William Sherman)
1905-1909 Annie Isabell Douglass Broward (Mrs. Napoleon Bonaparte)
1909-1913 Albert Waller Gilchrist (Bachelor)
1913-1917 Virginia Darby Trammell (Mrs. Park)
1917-1921 Alice May Campbell Catts (Mrs. Sidney Johnston)

1921-1925 Maude Randell Hardee (Mrs. Cary Augustus)
1925-1929 Lottie Wilt Pepper Martin (Mrs. John Wellborn)
1929-1933 Nell Ray Carlton (Mrs. Doyle Elam)
1933-1937 Alice May Agee Sholtz (Mrs. David)
1937-1941 Mildred Victoria Thompson Cone (Mrs. Frederick Preston)
1941-1945 Mary Agnes Groover Holland (Mrs. Spessard Lindsey)
1945-1949 Mary Rebecca Harwood Caldwell (Mrs. Millard Fillmore)
1949-1953 Barbara Manning Warren (Mrs. Fuller)
January 6-September 28,1953 Olie Brown McCarty (Mrs. Daniel Thomas)
1953-1955 Thelma Brinson Johns (Mrs. Charley Eugene)
1955-1961 Mary Call Darby Collins (Mrs. Thomas LeRoy)
1961-1965 Julia Burnett Bryant (Mrs. Cecil Farris)
1965-1967 Mildred Carlyon Burns (Mrs. William Haydon)
1967-1971 Erika Mattfeld Kirk (Mrs. Claude Roy, Jr.)
1971-1979 Donna Lou Harper Askew (Mrs. Reubin O'Donovan)
1979-1987 Adele Khoury Graham (Mrs. D. Robert)
January 3-6,1987 Margie Grace Mixson (Mrs. John Wayne)
1987-1991 Mary Jane Marino Martinez (Mrs. Robert)
1991-1998 Rhea Grafton Chiles (Mrs. Lawton Mainor, Jr.)
December 12, 1998-January 5, 1999 Anne Selph MacKay (Mrs. Kenneth Hood)
1999- Columba Garnica Gallo Bush (Mrs. John Ellis)

Acknowledgments

This book would not have been possible without the assistance of many friends and colleagues. I owe a special debt of thanks to Dr. William W. Rogers, Professor Emeritus of History, his encouragement, advice, and expertise were invaluable. I am indebted to archivists Laura Bass and Adam Watson for their commitment to professionalism and a willingness to assist with the excellent resources from the Department of State's State Library and Photo Archive. I appreciate the cooperation of the staff at the Florida State University Library and Dr. Hunt Hawkins and Virgil Suarez of the FSU English Department. In addition, I wish to thank Joan Morris, author, and Joanna K. "Jody" Norman, archive supervisor, as well as Dr. Jeana Brunson and the staff of the Museum of Florida History and all those too numerous to mention whose commitment to the preservation of Florida's history have aided in this project. Finally, a debt of gratitude is owed to Ray Stanyard, photographer extrordinaire.

Introduction

For reasons unknown, there has been no collected version of the inaugural speeches of Florida's governors. Now considered an essential part of the ceremonies attendant to a new governor's taking over, the inaugural speech dates from the first chief executive in 1845. For a considerable time there was not even a consistent record of the addresses, as many governors did not retain copies of what they said, and the only reports appeared in newspapers. The printed record of a governor's speech was dependent upon the accuracy of the journalist reporting it, and the public received as many versions as there were reporters. This book contains the messages of the chief executives and represents the best and truest copies of the varying speeches. Over time, better retention of governors' papers, better records keeping, more accurate reporting, television, and sound recording have made possible the reproduction of exactly what the governor had to say.

Inaugural speeches began after Florida joined the Union as the twenty-seventh state on March 3, 1845, and began its history as an equal partner with her sister states. Of course, Florida had a long period of prehistory and history before it achieved statehood. The elongated peninsula was acquired by the U.S. as a result of the Adams-Onís treaty of 1819. Before that, it had been controlled by Spain beginning April 2, 1513, when the explorer Ponce de León discovered, named, and claimed Florida for his country. Florida remained under Spanish rule despite on-going challenges from colonial rivals England and France in the next centuries. Finally, in 1763 as a result of the Seven Years' War (known in America as the French and Indian War), Spain, an ally of losing power France, surrendered Florida to the victorious English.

Yet, England's control was short-lived, lasting only twenty years.. During the American Revolution Spain supported the rebelling colonies and was able to reclaim Florida in 1783 as a reward for aiding the newly formed and independent U.S. Even so, Spain's power continued to decline as that of the United States rose. Believing in Manifest Destiny, American citizens cast envious eyes toward Florida. Early in the nineteenth century a rough-hewn American general, Andrew Jackson, invaded Florida twice. The American citizenry applauded Old Hickory's military exploits despite his dubious justifications and unclear authority. Jackson's second incursion came during the First Seminole War (1818). It convinced the Spanish monarch to give up Florida under the best terms available. This was accomplished by the Adams-Onís treaty that was ratified by the U.S. Senate in January 1821. None of the preceding seventy governors of Spanish Florida nor any of the eight British governors were elected officials, and none delivered inaugural addresses.

With some reservations about his choice, President James Monroe appointed Jackson governor of the new American acquisition. Jackson was not enthusiastic about the post. He was tired, suffered from a number of health problems, and felt restricted in his authority. Rachel, his beloved wife, dreaded the trials of life in remote Florida. Despite the drawbacks Jackson accepted the post. England had divided the peninsula into West Florida with its capital at Pensacola and East Florida whose capital was St. Augustine. In July 1821, both of the Floridas accepted the transfer of possession with Jackson attending the ceremonies at Pensacola. Robert Butler, one of Jackson's officers and a key figure in early Florida history, carried out a similar exchange at St. Augustine. Jackson resigned his position in early November, and he and his wife returned to their home in Nashville, Tennessee. President Monroe appointed William Pope Duval of Kentucky as governor. In a technical sense, Duval became the first territorial governor because his appointment came after congress passed an act on March 20, 1822, creating the territory of Florida. The law followed the precedent of the Northwest Ordinance of 1787 in outlining the process required to move from territory to state. Jackson deserves credit for expeditiously uniting one Florida and establishing a workable new civil government, including the establishment of counties (Escambia and St. Johns), and the creation of judicial and administrative positions. Although several offices changed from existing appointive positions to popularly elected posts, the office of governor remained appointed throughout the territorial period.

The territorial governors after Jackson were William Pope Duval, who served four three-year terms; John H. Eaton, a Jackson man from Tennessee, who was governor for two years; and Richard Keith Call, born in Virginia but whose career had been in Tennessee, headed territorial government for three years in the 1830s. He was succeeded by Robert Raymond Reid, a South Carolinian who governed the territory two years; then it was Richard Keith Call again for three more years; John Branch, a North Carolinian who had held important offices in his own state and nationally, became the last territorial governor. Because they were appointed by the president and were actually federal officers, none of the territorial governors delivered an inaugural address.

Florida's long territorial period witnessed Indian wars, the firm establishment of slavery, the development of a largely agrarian economy, and a surge in population that was temporarily interrupted by a nationwide economic panic in 1837. There was a new growth in prosperity in Florida during the 1850s. In politics slavery and, early on, the question of a national bank were issues that concerned the emerging political parties, the Democrats and the Whigs. Finally, the Union proved unable to prevent various issues–most importantly that of slavery–from resulting in a four-year Civil War. The triumph of the United States saw the abolition of slavery and the establishment of the federal government's supremacy over individual states.

With few exceptions, usually relating to the untimely death of a sitting governor, the new chief executive has delivered an inaugural speech on the first day of taking office. The speech has either been presented before or after a governor takes the oath of office. The address, unlike taking the oath of office or the presentation of the Great Seal of the State of Florida, is not a formal part of the transfer of power from one governor to another. Even so, the first opportunity to speak as the state's new governor has become an important part of the ceremony and rituals surrounding inauguration day. The inaugural ball and inaugural parade as well as the ceremonial music and the firing of cannons, are included in the tradition accompanying a new four-year administration, Still, none of the events is as significant and personal as the governor's address when he (so far no woman has served as Florida's chief executive) takes control of the highest state office.

Although no formal protocol exists regarding the form or substance of these speeches, it is customary that each governor states the goals or agenda for the new administration. The content of the speech can be reviewed when the gubernatorial term has ended to determine whether the goals were achieved. Yet, there is no constitutional or legislative requirement for such a critique. Since government is at least as much an art as a science, and since the inevitable informal evaluations are partisan politically and given frequently, the results are always mixed about any administration. Besides stating goals, the inaugural speech also addresses the new government's philosophy and summarizes Florida's current status. Properly speaking, it is important as a weapon of propaganda and a barometer of the times, as attested by the following examples:

During the state's first inaugural address, Democratic governor William Moseley, a native North Carolinian who had defeated his Whig opponent by a margin of six hundred votes, discussed what he considered Florida's position within the Union. Emphasizing his state's rights views, Moseley declared that the Federal Government was created by the consent of the individual states. In 1857 Democrat Madison Perry of South Carolina discussed the state's Native American situation: "It gives me great pleasure to announce that there is now a prospect of finally compelling the Indians to migrate, thus relieving the State from a curse which has so long retarded the settlement of a very extensive and interesting portion of our territory." Events changed rapidly, and Perry's successor, John Milton, elected in 1860, was installed as governor after Florida became the third southern state (South Carolina and Mississippi were the first two) to secede on January 10, 1861. At first Milton, born in Georgia, was governor of a state that was an independent republic. Although it joined the Confederacy early in April, official admission came on the 22nd of the month when Florida's Secession Convention ratified the constitution of the Confederate States of America.

    A reading of the various inaugural speeches reveals Florida's role in national history as well as its state imperatives. Certain recurring themes are mentioned by all governors on their inaugural day. These include the state's educational system, the environment, fiduciary responsibility, racial matters, transportation, and public safety. Education has over time been considered by all governors one of their most critical responsibilities. As early as 1849 a native of Virginia, Governor Thomas Brown, Florida's second governor and the only Whig ever hold the office, said, "As we extend the field of education we extend the field of choice." The importance of public education has now become of vital concern. Nor do governors neglect to mention the uniqueness of Florida. Beginning in the twentieth century, the state's warm weather and miles of beaches were recognized as being of enormous economic value, especially with regard to recreation and health. Florida's climate was a natural resource that attracted tourists and contributed to the state's financial growth. The state's geography made possible an agricultural kingdom, as well as a place where livestock, especially cattle, thrived.

By 1845 the institution of slavery was firmly ensconced in Florida. In 1526 the first known African slaves were among the six hundred Spanish settlers brought to North American shores by the Spanish. When Pedro Menéndez de Avilés established St. Augustine in 1565, he found persons of African descent already present from previous European expeditions. Subsequent ownership of Florida by Great Britain and the United States saw the issue of slavery become more complex and necessary to deal with. By 1860 Florida's small population, about 140,000 people, contained almost as many slaves as free persons. Slavery ended with the Civil War and the adoption of the thirteenth amendment in 1865, but the issue of race took a different form and remains vital in the twenty-first century.

There are other minorities in Florida, and post-World War II's rapid growth has seen a large migration of new immigrants, refugees, and exiles from the Caribbean and Latin America. The "Latinization" of Florida was dramatized in 1988 when native Tampan Robert 'Bob" Martinez became not only the second Republican elected in the twentieth century, but the state's first American governor of Hispanic descent.

All women remained second class citizens in Florida until the ratification of the nineteenth amendment on August 26, 1920. They had struggled for the right to vote from the middle of the nineteenth century. Florida's bachelor governor from South Carolina, Albert W. Gilchrist, announced in his inaugural address that, "It is a thing of beauty and a joy forever, to see so many ladies present." Some of the women who were in Tallahassee for the occasion may have been flattered, but the majority of the state's disfranchised female voters wanted (and demanded) much more. Later, in 1941, Spessard Holland became the first governor to acknowledge the role of his wife, Mary Agnes Groover Holland, as first lady. Governor Lawton Chiles, a native son who also was U.S. Senator, used part of his inaugural address to praise his wife, Rhea Grafton Chiles, also Florida born, as his key political advisor, best friend, and closest confidant.

Almost every governor has mentioned religion and invoked God's blessing. Only once has a governor, Sidney J. Catts, narrowly defeated (the decision was made by the State Canvassing board) in the Democratic primary but elected in the general election as the candidate for the Prohibition party, mentioned religion in a negative manner. Catts, a native of Alabama and, among other things, an evangelical minister in the Baptist church, was elected in part because he convinced enough voters that he was the man who could prevent the take over of Florida by the Roman Catholic church. He stated in his inaugural address that "Your [the voters'] triumph is no less this hour in beautiful Florida, for you have withstood the onslaughts of...[the] Roman Catholic hierarchy against you." Jeb Bush, born in Texas, son of a president and brother of an occupant of the Texas governor's mansion and future President, stood in sharp contrast to Catts. Governor Bush dedicated considerable attention in his inaugural speech to asking his audience to focus more attention on the issue of faith and family values. The typical governor's inaugural address mentioned religion and asked for the blessings of divine providence on Florida.

By the twenty-first century Florida had progressed from a small, rural state in 1845 to a multi-cultural, fast-growing complex area that was the fourth most populous state in the nation. It was the South's most urban state and was a microcosm of the nation. It had become an important political battleground that was counted by presidential candidates. Governing Florida was a monumental task. How the chief executives proposed to do it may be seen in their inaugural speeches which offer a panorama of Florida's history.

Governor William D. Moseley
Term: 1845 - 1849

William Dunn Moseley (born February 1, 1795 - died January 4, 1863) was popularly elected and served as Florida's first state governor. A Democrat and native of North Carolina, Moseley graduated from the University of North Carolina at Chapel Hill. After serving as a politician and lawyer in his native state, Moseley moved to Jefferson County, Florida, in 1835.

He became a planter and served in the state legislature before his election as governor, defeating Richard Keith Call, who had served twice as Florida's territorial governor. The no-nonsense chief executive had a wide forehead and was balding. Moseley's sideburns descended almost to the level of his wide, thin mouth. His piercing eyes were his most commanding feature. Down at Shell Point a Democrat gave an agrarian toast to the new chief executive: "His Excellency W. D. Moseley, Chief Ploughman of the State—May he turn his furrows so deep, as to plough up the root of party spirit." As befitted the first governor, Moseley was sworn in with much pageantry, including what became an obligatory parade.

In fact, for weeks Tallahassee and the surrounding countryside had been suffering from a drought. Inauguration day, June 25, was no different. The day dawned bright and clear with still no chance of rain. Gardens were drying up and dying. All week the temperature had ranged between 90 and 100 degrees. Not given to climatic overstatement, the local *Sentinel* described the day as "terribly warm." Less restrained, a correspondent for the St. Augustine *News* informed his readers, "You have no idea how hot it is." Whigs bristled at the new state flag (it was soon abandoned in favor of another) that borrowed from the national banner and also had five horizontal stripes: blue, orange, red, white, and green. In the center was an orange stripe with a white scroll which was inscribed with the motto "Let Us Alone."

Moseley's modest address–hung onto attentively, supporters claimed, scarcely audible from the first row, critics countered–soared on occasion but never achieved eloquence. Still, its 2,250 words were well organized and demonstrated that Governor Moseley was a true believer in state's rights. He beseeched the support of all, and in particular "the aid of the Father of the Universe...."

Inaugural Speech
(Source: Tallahassee *Florida Sentinel*, July 1, 1845)

Senators, Representatives, and Fellow-Citizens:

I should do injustice to the best feelings of my heart were I not, on *this* occasion, to express a becoming sense of gratitude for the *enviable* and *honorable* distinction, so recently conferred upon me, in elevating me to the supreme Executive authority of the State—a distinction the more highly prized from the *flattering* circumstances under which it was conferred. An expression of public sentiment through the suffrages of freemen, for an office within their gift, for which it was my earnest *personal* desire *not* to be a candidate.

I feel, fellow-citizens, a proud consciousness of the truth of the remark, when I assert, in the presence of my assembled countrymen, that this honor I have never sought, nor could it have been acceptable to me, but as the *voluntary offering of freemen*. Under such circumstances, I do not feel myself at liberty to permit this opportunity to pass without adverting to a consciousness on my part of the want of experience, to a satisfactory discharge of a trust, the duties of which are alike arduous and responsible; nor would I do justice to my feelings, if I failed to express the deep sense of painful solicitude which is felt for the performance of them, in a manner at once acceptable to my fellow citizens and to myself. They are entered upon, however, with a confident reliance upon the co-ordinate departments of the government; in the inception and consummation of such measures, as a proper regard for the best interests of the people may suggest, and which, if consummated, may at once insure the happiness, the prosperity, and the glory of our common country. Custom has sanctioned the usage which has ever received my cordial approbation, that public functionaries, entrusted with executive authority, when about to enter upon the discharge of the duties assigned then, should give at least an outline of the leading political principles which may be deemed proper to be observed in the execution of the trust confided to them.

It is now, in obedience to this usage, thus sanctioned by time, and with a becoming respect for public sentiment, that I proceed publicly to declare those principles, so far, at least, as they may be connected with the administration of the national government; or as they may be the basis of measures whose final action may come within the scope of the Executive department of the State Government.

In relation, then, to our Federal Government, I feel myself at liberty to remark that I believe it to be a government of strictly limited powers, a government formed and established through the agency and by the express authority and assent of the States, as independent sovereignties, by ceeding through a written Constitution, portions of that sovereignty for certain enumerated and specified purposes, which could not be so readily and happily effected by the States, as separate, independent communities; that the rights, powers and privileges, *not* thus transferred, were *reserved* as the rights of the States and of the people. That the exercise of any powers by the government thus established, other than those thus enumerated, or of such constructive powers as may be necessary and proper to carry into execution the enumerated powers, would be an usurpation of the rights of the States and of the people: a violation of the letter and spirit of the Constitution, at once subversive of the compact—of the rights of the States and of the people.

That among the most important and highly cherished of the reserve rights, is the right of *State interposition*, under its constitutional authorities, as the *legitimate* remedy for *such* an act of usurpation on the part of the National Government.

The history of the Convention which formed the Federal Constitution, leaves not a reasonable doubt of the fact, that a portion of the members of that distinguished body, advocated a strong central government, of consolidated powers at the expense of State Sovereignty. Such at least was the tendency of their measures. Another portion of the same body was for withholding those constructive powers from the government, *then* about to be established.

"It was the advocating or opposing these measures, in the formation of the constitution, that gave distinctive names to the parties, that then divided the Union; and the principles then avowed, and the measures issuing from them, have, from that to the present time, kept up the *same political* division." The one claiming for the Federal Government the unlimited exercise of the constructive powers, the *other* denying that right, and insisting upon confining it to such matters exclusively, as were of National importance; and in the success of which, the general welfare of the country was immediately and directly concerned. At the head of the former division was Mr. Hamilton, of the latter was Mr. Jefferson.

It was this illegitimate exercise of constructive powers, that established the first National Bank, and gave birth to a system of political log-rolling, under the specious name of Internal Improvement—to a tariff for protection, with revenue as an incident, and to the distribution among the States, of the proceeds of the sales of the Public Domain. All of which measures, I take *this* occasion to declare, as the deliberate convictions of my judgment, to be infractions of the Constitution, as usurpations of the rights of the States; and apart from the Constitutional objection, as unwise, inexpedient and impolitic. The Constitutionality and expediency of these, and kindred measures, I do not, however, deem it proper, nor is it my present purpose, to discuss.

With my regard to the protective policy, however, I feel myself at liberty to remark, (with due deference and a proper respect for the intelligence and patriotism of those who think differently), that if there be *any one* measure, (more than all others), the offspring of constructive powers, which should be met with uncompromising hostility by the advocates of reserved rights and strict construction, it is that odious policy. It is an excresence of the Constitution, maintained at the expense of the day-laborer, the mechanic, the mariner, the merchant, the planter: in fine, at the expense of every species and class of industrial pursuits known to our country, but to the directors of the power-loom, and the lord of the spinning-jenny. It operates upon every other species of industry, as it does upon the agricultural—it raises the price of the *necessaries* of life, and subjects *labor*, which is their capital, to the competition of the rich capitalist. It is a tax upon every species of industry, *not* for the support of the government, *economically administered*; but to administer to the "pageantry of soulless monopolies," and to add to the overgrown fortunes of a favored and haughty aristocracy.

I solemnly believe it to be a violation of the National compact, of the rights of the many for the benefit of the few; and that, too, without the plea of necessity, and, therefore, without even the merit of his plea, whom the cravings of hunger have impelled to an act of larceny. Permit me, in conclusion upon this trite subject, to remark that it would seem that the conclusion is strictly logical; that whenever duties on imports are *not* prohibitory, the *duty* constitutes a part of the price, and is consequently a tax, and unnecessary burthen upon the consumer, *especially* when *such* tax is not required for the support of the government. The conclusion is also equally irresistible, that when such duties *are* prohibitory, foreign competition must cease, commerce must wither, and finally disappear, under its blighting, deadly influence; the sails of our merchantmen that now whiten every ocean, and are unfurled to every breeze will be unfurled no more—an *indirect* revenue will no longer flow into the common treasury. *Direct* taxation, for the support of the government, is then the *only* alternative: a state of things which, I earnestly hope, may never be adopted as the settled policy of our young and still increasing confederacy—

now the pioneer of free government—in its onward move, for the advancement of human rights and human freedom. throughout the world; in opposition to the unjust, oppressive, and iniquitous demands of legislative monopolies, and to the arrogant, impudent, and unblushing extortions of hereditary aristocracies.

In making this public avowal, 'tis hoped that I may not be understood as making an indiscriminate proscription of that portion of my fellow citizens who entertain different views in relation to the powers of the government, and the great national measures that have so long divided our country. Such an opinion, if entertained by any one, would do injustice to every act of my public life. For my political principles, I cherish a lively and abiding attachment and devotion, from the conviction that if honestly administered, they are best calculated to promote successfully our republican form of government. Entertaining this opinion, (as I most certainly do), any abandonment of those principles for selfish purposes, or for an imaginary, *temporary convenience*, would not only be an act of moral treason to *them*, but would properly subject me to the scorn and contempt of all honorable men. The same liberal indulgence for liberty of opinion, however erroneous, and the same charitable construction for honesty of purpose, and purity of motives, which I claim as an act of justice from others, common charity and a generous magnanimity, will always prompt me to extend to them, under similar circumstances.

In relation to our young State, now about to become a member of the great family of states, to you as the representatives of the people, delegated by their authority, as a co-ordinate branch of the Government, now for the first time assembled—to you is confided the important and responsible trust of developing her resources, and of giving character to her institutions, by a liberal, enlightened, and patriotic public policy; and of establishing for her a permanent and enviable rank as one of the members of a confederacy, whose brilliant career and proud preeminence, in all that is great and useful; in the simplicity and purity of its civil institutions; the martial achievements of its heroes; the fervid eloquence of its orators, and the practical wisdom of its statesmen—challenge the wonder, the admiration, and the rivalry of all Christendom: a confederacy whose dominions, increasing with colossal strides, already extend from the Atlantic to the Pacific, and from the sunny regions of the tropics, to the ice-bound possessions of the Autocrat of the north.

To all, therefore, it must be obvious, that upon the policy *now* adopted, depends in a *great* measure, the reputation, the prosperity, the happiness, and the *Glory* of our common country.

With such incentive before them, the patriot, philanthropist and statesman will enter the lists with eager delight, with united energies, a common effort, and a generous emulation and self-devotion, to effect results so desirable.

It is not my purpose on *this* occasion to enter into specific enumeration of all such measures as would, if perfected, effect this attainment of our utmost wishes; but I feel called upon, by a sense of duty, to allude, in an especial manner, to the necessity of a sound constitutional currency; to the preservation of the public credit; to a well regulated system of Common Schools and the School Fund; to the finances of the State, and to the promotion of "virtue, science and knowledge," all of which are deemed *essential* to the purity and preservation of our Republican Institutions, and which cannot be entirely disregarded, without a violation of the injunctions of the Constitution. These subjects, being deemed of vital importance to the ultimate success of our government, and to the happy condition of the people, *individually*, shall, at *all* times, receive such assurances of Executive approbation as may come within the constitutional scope of authority, of that department of the government.

To the same department is entrusted, the high responsibility of seeing that the laws are faithfully and impartially executed; nor is the obligation of this duty in any way lessened by any *supposed* inexpediency of the law, the execution of which he may be required to enforce. This high, important and responsible duty I expect *faithfully* and *promptly* to discharge, from a well-founded and deliberate conviction, that, a few wise laws, faithfully and impartially executed, are the best security for life, liberty and property.

And now, Senators and Representatives, I approach, with a trembling solicitude, the discharge of the duties assigned me, relying upon your *support* in the *discharge* of them, whenever my official conduct may commend itself to your favorable consideration; and invoking the aid of the Father of the Universe in our attempt at self-government, that He would be in the midst of our Councils, guiding and directing them for the common good; and appealing to Him for the sincerity of my motives, and the rectitude of my intentions in the performance of my duty, to my country and to myself; I take upon me the high, responsible and solemn obligations enjoined by the Constitution, with the anxious wish and fervent hope, that my administration may be as successful, in promoting the best interests of our beloved country, as my fellow-citizens have been kind, indulgent, generous and confiding.

Governor Thomas Brown
Term: 1849 - 1853

    Thomas Brown (born October 24, 1785 - died August 24, 1867) was born in Virginia. The active Brown was a veteran of the War of 1812, ran a mercantile store with his brother, and became chief clerk of the Richmond post office (he invented the post office letter box). After serving in the Virginia legislature Brown joined the exodus of other Upper South residents to Florida.

    The second governor settled in Leon County where he operated a plantation until a freeze killed his crop. He next leased a hotel in the territorial capital at Tallahassee, and later built and operated the City Hotel near the capitol building. The longtime Mason entered politics and served as auditor of the territory, president of the Legislative Council, and member of the Constitutional Convention in 1839. A Democrat, Brown was elected to the first House of Representatives under statehood, and later won election and succeeded Moseley. Governor Brown was much concerned with agricultural matters and with internal improvements in the frontier state of Florida.

Inaugural Speech
(Source: Tallahassee *Floridian and Journal*, January 27, 1849)

Gentlemen of the Senate and House of Representatives:

Fellow Citizens:

I respond most heartily to the charge which has been so emphatically and impressively given; and I assure you, fellow-citizens, that my respect and veneration for these books presented to me, containing the Constitution of this State and of the United States, are only surpassed by the deep veneration I feel for that inspired book, used in the solemn ceremony which has just been performed; and the use of which is a public declaration of our faith in the Christian religion, as a nation, and our belief in the over-ruling providence of Almighty God, as well in the affairs of nations as of individuals. I am oppressed with a conscious sense of my insufficiency for so responsible an undertaking, and should shrink from its assumption with fear and trembling, if I did not rely confidently upon the support and assistance of the Supreme Ruler of the Universe, in all my honest efforts to a faithful and zealous discharge of my public duties—with a cordial co-operation or the co-ordinate Departments of the Government, and a kind and a charitable consideration of my fellow-citizens, in regard to all my official acts.

You are now on the eve of separating, gentlemen of the General Assembly, for your respective homes. I trust, in the acts you have passed at the present session of the General Assembly, you have accomplished all that the public good demands at your hands, at this time. There are two subjects to which your labors have been particularly devoted, in which the people are deeply interested; a scheme of internal improvement, and a proper system of education. I hope the bills which you have enacted in regard to railroads will prove ample for those objects; and that, by the time you will again be required, by the Constitution, to assemble here, their effects will be witnessed in the improvement and prosperity of every portion or our beloved State. But, gentlemen, the paramount subject of all others, in this, our happy and favored land, is education. It is upon the education of the youth of our country that depends, not only our pre-eminence as a nation, but its character, happiness and permanence. It is said that money is power—be assured, my fellow-citizens, that knowledge is power. By the principles of our glorious institutions, the field of office is open and free for every citizen, and as we extend the scheme of education, we extend the field of choice. You witness today a practical illustration of our simple, equal and Republican institutions, in the elevation, by the free choice of the people, of one of the most humble and unpretending of their citizens to the highest office in the State. Therefore, cherish education as the palladium of our liberties.

Fellow-Citizens, I might close here; but having solemnly pledged before you, and in the presence of God, who holds the destines of nations in his hand, to support the Constitution of the United States, I should not permit this occasion to pass without the expression of an opinion in regard to the crisis now impending over the Southern portion of our Union.

There is no public officer who will defend the sovereignty of the States, the rights, of the South, and the compromises of the Constitution with more firmness and devotion that I will. I would say to all who would be disposed to violate those sacred rights, "thus far shalt thou go, and no further." But there is a wide difference, I humbly conceive, between a firm and manly resistance to unjust encroachments, and the empty vapouring and gasconade which has become so common, in the form of stereotyped resolutions, that we remember, the fable of the Boy and the Wolf; and should danger actually come, the sober and discreet would hardly regard our cries. There was a time, fellow-citizens, when there was no man, however high his standing and influence with the people might have been, who would have dared "to calculate the value of the Union," or could have spoken lightly of its permanence, without bringing down upon his head the indignation of the People. But in these days, partisan politicians, apparently unrebuked, can "calculate the value of the Union," and flippantly discourse of the "capacity of the people," when their own selfish, ends are to be advanced, (while quite as ready to deny it, when they are disappointed,) and the talk of the dissolution of the Union has become almost as familiar as household words.

Fellow-citizens, there was a time, under this Constitution, when the opinions of that great man, so justly called the Father of his Country, whose portrait is now before me, were revered and respected by every statesman in this nation—when his *Farewell Address* to the people of the United States was regarded as the promptings of inspiration.—But where are the *politicians* now to be found "so poor as to do him reverence?" Who regards his admonition, "indignantly to frown upon the first dawning of every attempt to alienate any portion of our country from the rest?" We have witnessed the attempt to make the question of our Southern institutions—the question upon which the destinies of this Union hang—peculiarly a *party* question. Failing in that most signally, by the election of General Taylor—a Southern man, educated in the South, and deeply interested in *Southern institutions*—by Northern support, we now see the attempt to make this—the most delicate of all questions, upon which our liberties hang—a mere sectional question. I believe fellow-citizens, that the Northern fanatics have done much to weaken the attachment and reverence of the people for the Union; and I fear as much has been done by Southern demagogues as Northern fanatics. But I have full confidence in the soundness of the great body of the people, North and South. They know, and they appreciate, the value of this Union—they will not permit it to be put in jeopardy, either by Northern fanatics or by Southern demagogues. The election of the first officer of the Federal Government from the South is the strongest evidence that could be given of the desire of the North to do ample justice to the South, and to regard her rights—and of not a less import, is the election of a statesman for the second office in the Government, who is liberal, enlightened, and above sectional prejudices, and destined, I trust by Providence, to occupy a large space among the statesman who are to be instrumental in the preservation of this Union, won by the valor, and erected by the wisdom of our Fathers. And now is the period when the *Farewell Address* of Washington ought to be published by every patriot editor, and caused to be read in the family of every patriot father.—It comes to us now as the warning voice of the Father of his Country, from the spirit land.

Fellow-citizens, no patriot, no statesman, should countenance the intimation, for one moment, that this glorious, this free and happy Government, secured by the union of these States: this model of human wisdom and greatness—can be destroyed. When its influence is now being felt and imitated by all the nations of Europe, it is not a matter of speculation just now to be tested, that the people of the United States are "capable of self-government,"—or that the arch, which binds together the glorious Confederation, is strong enough to bear the pressure of war in defense of rights, our national honor, or our liberty. The recent successes in Mexico were not necessary to establish that position. The war of 1812, justly called the second war of the revolution, settled these questions, and no sound statesman has since entertained a doubt upon these subjects. But there were giants in the land in those days—giants at the head of the Government—giants at the head of our army, and at the head of our navy; and men who believed we were a chosen people of God, and that, in his Providence, we would be guarded and protected. I believe now, that his overruling Providence will preserve our union, against the designs of all the fanatics, and the gasconading of all the partisan demagogues in the land.

In the discharge of duty, my humble efforts shall be directed to a firm and unyielding support of the rights of the South, and the cultivation of a good understanding with our Northern brethren, praying for the aid of a beneficent Creator to support me in an honest discharge of my official duties.

Governor James E. Broome
Term: 1853 - 1857

Florida's third governor was James Emilius Broome (born December 15, 1808 – died November 23, 1883) was born in South Carolina, he migrated to Leon County in 1837 and ran a mercantile store until he retired in 1841. Broome also became one of the state's largest planters. He was appointed probate judge of Leon County in 1843 and held that position until 1848. As the local judge Broome administered the oath of office to Governor Brown. Although the election year of 1852 saw the Whigs win numerous offices, Democrat Broome used his oratorical skills well. He managed to capture the governorship in a narrow victory over Whig candidate George T. Ward who was a popular Leon County planter.

Over the course of his 75 year life, Broome had five wives. He governed the state during the troubled 1850s when the bitter sectional controversy, especially the issue of slavery, moved the nation toward the Civil War. Broome was well known as an early and ardent advocate of states rights, and was serving as a state senator from Nassau County when the war began. After the war he moved to New York City.

Inaugural Speech
(Source: Tallahassee *Floridian and Journal*, October 8, 1853)

Fellow Citizens:

Called to preside for a season over the Executive Department of our State Government, and about to pledge myself by the solemn sanctions of an oath to the discharge of its duties, I avail myself of your presence to acknowledge my gratitude to my fellow citizens for this mark of their confidence, and to declare that, when I survey my own feeble powers, and then the delicate and important duties before me, there arises unbidden a distrust and anxiety, which causes me to humble myself before the magnitude of the trust committed to me.

Our State Government is yet in its infancy, and there are great questions of State policy, with which the Executive office will identify me, that are but partially settled. The discussion of these on an occasion like the present, would be manifestly improper; and yet there are several of them so overshadowing in their consequences, that I may be permitted briefly to express the opinions I entertain, and to indicate the policy which will govern me in my connection with them.

The first of these to which I will allude, is the subject of Common Schools. This is an interest of paramount importance, and to make it what every patriot desires to see it—a blessing to the generations who are to succeed us—two things are necessary: First, a revenue sufficient to place a plain English education within the reach of every child in the State; and second, a proper and convenient system for the equitable distribution of the money. As we progress with the sale of our Sixteenth Sections, we may expect annual increase of revenue for this purpose; but without important additions, it is not likely ever to equal the wants of our population. The increase of the School Fund should be looked to as a measure of State policy, and such additions made from time to time as a due regard for other interests would justify. Of our present school system but little can be said. It is yet in its infancy, and there has not been money enough for distribution to test its efficiency. Experience may and probably will suggest modifications of the law, calculated to adapt it more perfectly to the wants of the people. This subject, in all its bearings, will receive my careful consideration, and it will give me pleasure to cooperate with the Legislative Department of the Government in such measures as may be proper for increasing the fund, or improving the system for its proper application.

The removal of the Seminole Indians from our State is another of these questions of which I may briefly speak. They are here, a blight to our prosperity, in violation of their treaty obligations, and in open defiance of the power, authority and importunity of the Federal Government. Their presence prevents the influx of population, which the salubrity of our climate and fertility of our soil would invite—depresses the price and retards the sale of large bodies of State lands, the proceeds of which are wanted for purposes of education and internal improvements.—Their treachery renders insecure the lives and property of our frontier population—keeps them in a continual state of anxiety and alarm—prevents the organization of Schools, and forbids the employment of capital in useful enterprises. They occupy a part of our territory which, if opened to settlement, would soon become one of our richest and most densely populated sections. Its superior adaptation to the culture of Sugar, Spanish Tobacco, Sisal Hemp, with a great variety of tropical fruits, would make it an inviting field for the investment of capital and the employment of labor. Under such circumstances, the State, can never sanction, and I hope will never submit to a policy which looks to anything short of their removal.

With a view to facilitate so desirable an object, the General Assembly, at its last session, passed a law entitled "An Act to provide for the final removal of the Indians of this State, and for other purposes." This law devolves on the Executive important trusts, and the conflict of opinion in reference to his duties under it, may justify me in saying more on this subject than, under other circumstances, would perhaps be proper.

The 16th Section of the 3d article of the Constitution of this State, fixes the law making power, and prescribes the manner in which laws shall be passed, and a reference to the Journals shows that the law under consideration was passed in the manner prescribed by that section.—The 10th section of the same article of the Constitution prescribes, as one of the duties of the Executive, that "'He shall take care that the laws be faithfully executed,'" and one of the obligations which I am about to assume, under the solemn sanctions of an oath, is to "protect and defend the Constitution of this State." I need hardly say to you, fellow citizens, that I shall consider it a part of my constitutional duty to see that this law is "faithfully executed."

In connection with this declaration, it is perhaps due to the anxiety prevailing on this subject that I shall speak briefly of the general requirements of this law.

First, the Governor is required to raise one Brigade of volunteers, commission the officers, and tender the Brigade to the Federal Government for the removal of the Indians. These duties are purely executory, and will be promptly discharged. Second, should the General Government decline to accept the services of the Brigade, the Governor is required to secure the frontier settlers, and employ the Brigade in carrying out the provisions of the law in that part of the Peninsula now occupied by the Indians, and is authorized, under certain restrictions, to borrow money on the faith of the State, for their subsistence, transportations, pay, etc. These latter duties, however, the law requires to be discharged under the proviso contained in the 11th section of the act, which is in these words:

> <u>Provided</u>, That the Governor shall not commence actual operations within the Indian boundary until the 4th day of May next, and not until he is satisfied that the General Government has determined not to remove said Indians, by force or otherwise: <u>Provided further</u>, That if actual hostilities shall be commenced by the Indians before that time, the foregoing proviso shall be of no force or effect.

Thus it is seen that there are two contingencies, and only two, upon the happening of either of which the Executive is authorized to order the Brigade into actual service. One of these is that the <u>Indians shall commence actual hostilities</u>, and the other is that he shall be satisfied that <u>the General Government has determined not to remove said Indians, by force or otherwise</u>. To decide whether the General Government has so determined, may prove one of the most delicate and difficult of all the duties imposed by the law; but it is a duty, and I pledge myself to discharge it to the best of my ability. In doing so, I may commit errors of judgment, but none, I hope, which will compromise the interests or dignity of our commonwealth.

Another of these great questions, of which I may speak briefly, is that of Internal Improvements in our State. On this subject, we are not without examples worthy of our imitation. If we look to our next neighbor, (our sister State of Georgia,) we see her stretching out her iron arms, scaling a mountain here and tunneling another there—penetrating her interior—enlarging the field for her commercial enterprise opening new markets for her agricultural productions—increasing her prosperity and augmenting her wealth with a rapidity which we can scarcely credit; and the same may be said of many other of our sister States. Why are we not of the number? We have a geographical position, in a commercial point of view, superior perhaps to any of them. We are on one of the great highways of the world's commerce and the use of our ports is almost a commercial necessity. —We have, too, a fund of great value, the judicious investment of which, aided by such private subscriptions as could be readily obtained, would be an ample security in the markets of the world for such additional amounts as might be required to consummate the great State enterprise of connecting with bands of iron our Western, Eastern and Southern section. The consummation of this great work would develope agricultural, commercial and manufacturing resources in our State which would astonish the most sanguine. Our population would be rapidly increased—our rich lands would be reduced to cultivation—our pine forests would furnish inexhaustible supplies of lumber and naval stores for export—cities would spring up where villages are now but feebly sustained—a prosperity hitherto unknown amongst us would visit every interest—we should become a great and influential commonwealth, and should occupy the proud position among our sister States to which our advantages would entitle us. Shall we as a State give confidence to this great enterprise, by engaging in it with an energy equal to its magnitude? Or shall we, by pursuing a timid and inefficient policy postpone its consummation until others have built up rival routes and rival interests, which will prove fatal to our success? These are questions which interest alike every section of the State, and the people of the State must answer them. For myself, I may say that I am for action—judicious, but prompt energetic and efficient action—and shall take pleasure in co-operating with the Legislative department of the Government in all proper measures for securing it.

These are great questions of State policy yet to be settled, and if I have devoted more time to their consideration than the occasion seems to justify, my apology will be found in the overshadowing importance and the general anxiety with which they have inspired the public mind.

While we should guard with unceasing watchfulness the administration of our State Government, and require of every department and agent an honest and faithful discharge of their duties, we should remember that we have another great interest which should receive a share of our attention. As one of the sovereign States of the Union, our relations to the Federal Government forbid us to feel indifferent to the manner of its administration. That Government was created by the States, as their common agent for certain specified purposes, limited by the Constitution to the exercise of certain expressly delegated powers, and such as were necessary to carry them into execution. Conflicts of opinion have arisen in reference to the extent of the powers thus delegated, the discussion of which would be improper on an occasion like this. I may, however, be permitted to say that in the triumphant election of Gen. Pierce to the Presidency of the United States, I understand the people to have decided in favor of the time honored doctrine of strict construction, and I cannot doubt that he will firmly and faithfully enforce their decision. In doing so, he will be true to his past history, true to the imperishable sentiments of his inaugural address, and will make his administration one of the most valuable in his country's history. I need hardly say to you, fellow citizens, that such an administration will receive my cordial and hearty support.

In conclusion, I will say that the powers with which the Executive Office will invest me are derived from the Constitution, and shall neither be enlarged by assumptions of those reserved by the people, or by encroachments on those delegated to the other departments of the Government. My purpose shall be honestly to administer the Executive Department, with a view to the best interest of the State, and of the whole State. That a defective judgment will often lead me into error, I have too much reason to fear; but conscious of the rectitude of my purpose, I may ask your indulgence for my errors for they will never be intentional.. And now, with an humble reliance, (as I hope) upon the Supreme Ruler of the Universe, for that wisdom which will enable me to discharge my duty in such a manner as to promote your interest and His glory, I am ready to take the oath of office.

Governor Madison S. Perry
Term: 1857 - 1861

Holding office at the end of the 1850s, the South Carolina born Democrat Madison Stark Perry (born in 1814 – died March, 1865) first settled in Alachua County where he became a leader in the broadcloth ranks of planters. Perry became a state Senator in 1850, and the nominee of his party for governor in 1856. The Whig party had been largely destroyed in the South over the slavery issue. Its members joined other groups, including the American party, more popularly known as the "Know Nothing" party (its platform of Unionism appealed to former Whigs who otherwise professed to "know nothing" about its anti-slavery, anti-Catholic, and anti-foreigner proclivities).

Perry strongly advocated the economic development of Florida, and his administration witnessed the extension of existing railroad lines and the building of new ones. He also oversaw the end of a contentious and drawn out boundary dispute with Georgia. National affairs soon assumed a dominant role, as Perry, realizing that war was probable, urged the legislature to reestablish the state militia as more than a token force. The governor prophetically warned the legislature that the election of Abraham Lincoln as president meant the ascendancy of the Republican party. That, he predicted, would be followed by the disruption of the Union, and conflict was inevitable. After his tenure ended, the fifty-three-year-old Perry entered the Confederate military ranks. He served as colonel of the Seventh Florida Regiment until forced to retire by illness. Perry never saw the complete collapse of the Confederacy and never experienced Reconstruction: he died in 1865 at his Alachua County plantation

Inaugural Speech
(Source: Tallahassee *Floridian*, October 10, 1857)

Fellow Citizens:

I appear before you to take the oath of office as Chief Executive of the State and to make a grateful tender of my sincere thanks for the distinction conferred. The fact that the position was unsought determines me the more to merit in some degree the confidence so generously bestowed. When properly estimating the magnitude of the trust confided to me, and seriously distrusting my ability to discharge satisfactorily the duties imposed, I almost shrink from the task. I enter upon the duties of my station with already good will to devote all my powers to the service of the State, and pledge you, that I will maintain, to the utmost of my ability, unimpaired and untarnished, its interests, its dignity and honor. I am unwilling to depart from the established custom of my worthy predecessors, and will sketch, therefore, briefly the outline of policy to be pursued during my administration of the State Government, promising however, that the absence of the Legislature would seem both to render such a course unnecessary, and to detract much from the imposing solemnity of the occasion.

I will endeavor clearly to understand the powers confided to me by the Constitution, and by a rigid adherence to this sacred instrument, carefully avoid the slightest infringement of other departments upon whose intelligence and experience I will reply for co-operation in the discharge of my duties. It will be my constant care to have the laws faithfully executed.

As the rights, liberty and happiness of a people depend in a great measure upon their capacity to understand and appreciate them, everything calculated to promote and diffuse knowledge among our citizens will receive my constant care and attention. If we cannot boast as many or as renowned institutions of learning as some of the older States, and if we have not advanced in our School System as rapidly as could have been desired, we have in the past sufficient incentive to greater exertions in future. In addition to the Academies and High Schools within our State, the State Seminaries give promise of extended usefulness. That at Ocala is now in a flourishing condition, and the one situated at Tallahassee as at present endowed, and under the management of the present able and efficient Board of Instruction, bolster to take high rank—a consummation to be devoutly wished for—for then no longer will there exist a necessity for sending our sons abroad to educate them, especially to those States hostile to our institutions, from whence they too frequently return tinctured with sentiments of a baleful character, impressed by surrounding circumstances on the youthful mind, incapable of detecting the insidious approaches of the designing hypocrite, who intentionally seeks confidence but to abuse it.

It is gratifying to state that the various Railroads in course of construction within our State are progressing steadily and in some instances rapidly, giving promise of certain completion at an early date, which when completed, will form an important era in our sea-girt yet to a certain extent, land locked State. Much of the best land in our State is situated from thirty to eighty miles from the coast or navigable streams, and the projected Roads pass through the most fertile portions, and will greatly appreciate the value of real estate for many miles on either hand, invite emigration, and contribute largely to the wealth and importance of our State. Possessing as it does, a climate which in the opinion of intelligent observers, is unsurpassed by any in the world, classed as the third State in the Union in point of health as shown by the last census, with a fertile, generous soil producing abundantly Indian Corn, Sea Island and Upland Cottons, Sugar, Rice, Spanish tobacco, and most of the Tropical Fruits; abounding in valuable Timber and Naval Stores, indeed in all the elements of greatness—a brilliant era is dawning upon us soon to be realized in the enjoyment of unexampled prosperity. Every lawful aid will be given to these enterprises. Another, and no inconsiderable reason why these Roads should receive our fostering care, is the facility of intercourse afforded our citizens, and which must tend to annihilate all geographical and sectional feeling.

The chief support that these Roads are to receive from the State arises from the sales of lands placed in trust by the General Assembly in the Board of Trustees of the Internal Improvement fund. As a member of the Board, it will be my constant care to have the trust faithfully executed for the benefits of the system and the advancement of the interest of our State, and will advocate the appraising of these lands at such prices as will induce immigration and actual settlement.

It gives me pleasure to announce that there is now a prospect of finally compelling the Indians to migrate, thus relieving the State from a curse which has so long retarded the settlement of a very extensive and interesting portion of our Territory. The adoption of volunteers instead of regulars for this service, as urged upon the present administration by my illustrious predecessor, has thus far demonstrated that our hope of forcing this enemy to leave the borders of our State or end in extermination depends on our native swords and native ranks.

It is unnecessary for me on this occasion to enumerate minutely all the measures that I may deem important. Suffice it to say that all measures calculated to increase the knowledge, happiness and prosperity of our citizens; to promote agriculture, commerce and mechanics, or redound to the interest and honor of our State, will receive the fostering care of the Executive department, to the full extent of the powers intrusted. Such are my views on the internal policy of our State affairs. But there is a question of vital importance to us as a constituent portion of the National Confederacy that merits and must receive some expressions of my views, lest a silence at this time might be construed into indifference or acquiescence. The policy of the present Governor of Kansas in attempting to dictate to the Convention selected by the legal voters of the Territory what kind of constitution it must form to gain admission into this Union, has seriously disturbed the minds of patriotic men at the South, causing much anxiety for the safety of our institution, and producing excitement where before had prevailed good feeling and faith in the settled principles of non-intervention on the part of Congress, or other national powers in the domestic affairs of the territories. It affords me no pleasure to animadvert upon his course, but I would be recreant to the trust confided to me, were I to fail to notice in becoming terms, his wanton violation of this principle. Upon the faithful enforcement of the principles of the Kansas-Nebraska act the existence of the Union may depend, and it is impossible, therefore, to over-estimate the importance of the policy inaugurated by Governor Walker, fraught as it is, (if successful) with such mischievous consequences. —The systematic effort for years on the part of the anti-slavery men at the North to cripple Southern institutions, by preventing further expansion of slave territory, was defeated by the legislation of 1854, known as the Kansas-Nebraska act, by which the question of slavery was removed from the control of the General Government and left with the people of the Territories. A portion of the act is in these words: "It being the true intent and meaning of this act, not to legislative slavery into any Territory, nor to exclude it therefrom, but to leave to the people thereof perfectly free to form and regulate their domestic institutions in their own way, subject to the provisions of the Constitution of the United States."

The South by this act gained no advantage over the North, desired none. An acknowledgement of the equal rights of all the States to a fair participation in the public domain, and the recognition of the principle of non-intervention, was all that was desired. With a fair field, the South enters the contest fully alive to the importance of the issue, determined if possible to regain her equality in the Senate, and prevent Missouri's being hugged in by free States. The struggle was an arduous one, and success would be attended by very different results to the contending parties. To the North defeat would only bring with it disappointment at the failure of a favorite measure, and the expenditure of only a few thousand dollars, whilst to the South the pecuniary loss would be the least consideration. A hopeless inequality in the

Senate, the almost certainty that no slave state that might be hereafter formed would ever be admitted into the Union, are some of the evils that would follow in the train of defeat. To the South it was a vital struggle, and success favored her efforts—the Legislature, all the principle officers in the Territory, everything indeed, necessary to make Kansas a slave state, was secured. Suddenly a change takes place, Governor Walker arrives and marks out a line of policy calculated to make Kansas a free State. He tells the people that the laws of climate *forbid* its being a slave State, indicates the kind of Constitution that would be acceptable to him, dictates the mode of perfecting it—prescribes the qualifications of voters by declaring that all the inhabitants should have the privilege of voting, and says emphatically, if any other formula is followed, "I will join you, (the Black Republicans) and have no doubt one greater than I, the President of the United States, will join you in rejecting it." It would be difficult, if not impossible, to force a parallel outside of an absolute monarchy, to this high-handed, dictatorial course of Gov. Walker. At one stride, he overleaps the organic law of Kansas, the action of her Territorial Legislature, violates the principle of non-intervention, and the pledges of his own party platform. The power to prescribe the qualifications of voters certainly belonged to the Legislature, and was exercised by them. While it had been doubted by many whether the Convention itself, without the authority of the legislature would have the legal right to submit the Constitution for a vote of ratification, or to prescribe the qualification of voters, Gov. Walker ventures to *order* such submission, and fix such qualifications.

The question of slavery was taken from the control of Congress, as clearly shown by the above extract from the Kansas-Nebraska act, and left with the people of the Territory "to form and regulate their domestic institutions in their own way, subject only to the provisions of the Constitution of the United States," and any interference on the part of Gov. Walker was a gross and wanton violation. —If Kansas shall choose to draft a Constitution prohibiting slavery, that is a different question, and if she so elects, untrammeled, we must submit to her will, but the palpable and flagrant violation of the principle of non-intervention, and the rights of the South by Gov. Walker, will continue to excite the virtuous indignation of the friends of justice, equality and the Constitution, throughout the land. —But it is said the people of Kansas are satisfied with Gov. Walker's policy, and all other should be. This statement needs confirmation, and that its truth is far from being established cannot be denied. If so, however, such satisfaction has been secured by a wanton violation of a principle vital to the whole South, and requires at our hands a *signal rebuke, should every man in Kansas,* constrained or otherwise, *acquiesce* in such executive policy.

It is asserted by Gov. Walker, that he is sustained in his views and positions by the President of the United States; and such a declaration from a source so distinguished, sustaining so intimate a relation to the President, caused many patriotic men to distrust him on the great, and to us, vital question of non-intervention. I am free to confess, that I shared largely in that distrust. His recent letter, however, to the New England preachers gives hope that there is a difference of opinion on this subject, and that he will be found true to the organic act, to the pledges of his party platform, the principles of his inaugural address, and the great and vital principle of non-intervention on the question of slavery in the Territories. But fellow citizens, should this hope prove delusive, I now declare to you that I have denounced Gov. Walker for his faithlessness, so I will denounce Mr. Buchanan, should he show himself untrue on this vital question.

I will not make war on the National Democratic party, because of the treachery of one of its agents. If we cannot maintain our rights I see no prospect of maintaining them through any other present organization. When some act violative of our rights has been perpetuated by that party then, and not until then, will I agree to repudiate and destroy that national organization. —Regarding that as the last hope for the preservation of Southern Rights in the Union—should its Northern wing, unmindful of their constitutional obligations desert us and unite with our enemies in their fanatical crusade against our equality and institutions, I shall be among the first to advocate a dissolution of every national tie, and the taking of our destiny in our own hands.

In conclusion, I humbly invoke the protecting care of that power whose providence has so often manifested an especial interest in our country from its infancy and devoutly supplicate, that the threatening clouds may be speedily dispelled from the political horizon, and our Government preserved in its purity.

Governor John Milton
Term: 1861 - 1865

    Florida's Civil War governor John Milton (born April 20, 1807 – died April 1, 1865), served during a tragic time, and the end of his life was a tragic microcosm of the fate of the Confederate States of America. Yet, Milton was an exceptionally able governor who served his state and Jefferson Davis with a dedication rare among other southern heads of state. John Milton, descended from the English writer John Milton who followed Oliver Cromwell in the English Civil War, was born in South Carolina. Milton's father was a general and bore the classical name of Virgil Homer Milton. Before he became governor Milton lived a varied and controversial life. He was a lawyer who resided variously in Georgia, Alabama, and Louisiana and served as a captain in the Florida militia during the Second Seminole War. Before coming to Florida permanently in 1846 (he bought "Sylvania" plantation in Jackson County and was a Democratic presidential elector in 1848 and a state representative in 1850), he killed a man in Columbus, Georgia..

As an outspoken States Rights Democrat, Milton advocated the seizure of United States military forts and installations in Florida and was an outright secessionist who helped make Florida the third state to secede (January 10, 1861). The governor's election proved extremely close. Milton defeated Edward A. Hopkins, the Constitutional Unionist candidate, by only 1,746 votes. The narrow victory indicated that Florida voters were divided over the question of withdrawing from the Union. The Civil War had begun when Milton took office in October 1861. Despite the confusion of the times, Milton delivered an inaugural address, and there is documentary evidence that he did. Even so, a copy of the speech has not been found.

Governor Milton was a strong advocate of defending Florida, but he supported the larger Confederate effort conceived in the capitals at Montgomery and Richmond. He delicately balanced a small state's efforts to serve both state and nation, but in the end Florida and the Confederacy could not stand against the superior Union forces who held advantages of manpower, industry, and war materiel. Knowing that the result would be defeat and not wishing to live once more under the U.S. flag, Milton went to his plantation, Sylvania, and on April 1, 1865, took his own life by shooting himself with a shotgun.

The death of Milton created the need for an acting governor, and it was filled by Democrat AK. (Abraham Kurkindolle) Allison (April 1, 1865-May 19, 1865), the senate president. Allison (born December 10, 1810 – died July 8, 1893) was a native of Georgia, had some schooling and early on was a merchant in Columbus, Georgia, and Henry County in Alabama.. Later, he moved to Apalachicola where he entered politics and served as the town's first mayor, the first county judge of Franklin County, clerk of the U.S. Court, and member of the territorial legislature. Moving to Quincy, Allison represented Gadsden County in both the territorial legislature and later in both the house and the senate. As speaker of the house, Allison proclaimed himself acting governor when both the governor (Thomas Brown) and the senate president were temporarily out of Florida–he served less than three weeks.

He was a member of Florida's constitutional convention of 1860, and saw military action during the Civil War at Macon, Georgia, and Natural Bridge, Florida. He resumed his political career, took over as governor at the time General Edward McCook and his Union troops were formally occupying Tallahassee. In the meantime Allison attempted to resume normal relations with the federal government. He notified General McCook that he had appointed a five man commission to go to Washington and enter negotiations with the government. Further, he summoned the legislature to meet early in June and set June 5, to elect a governor. Such independent maneuvering forced President Andrew Johnson to order McCook not to recognize Allison's action. The general placed Florida under martial law on May 22, and Allison, along with other Confederate authorities, was arrested and charged with treason. Allison was never indicted, although he was imprisoned by federal authorities at Fort Pulaski, Georgia, for approximately six months. The former acting governor returned to Quincy and was later convicted of intimidating blacks. His sentence was a fine and six months in the Tallahassee jail.

Governor William Marvin
Term: 1865 - 1866

William Marvin (born April 14, 1808 – died July 9, 1902) was appointed by President Andrew Johnson as provisional governor and held office for only a little more than five moths. Born in New York, Marvin was busily practicing law in his home state when he was appointed by President Andrew Jackson to the post of U.S. District Attorney at Key West. From there he was appointed and reappointed a federal district judge, and used his geographical location and factual knowledge to write an authoritative and widely used textbook *Law of the Wreck and Salvage*. He was a member of the territorial legislative council and a delegate to Florida's first constitutional convention. Although he was sympathetic toward the South, Marvin opposed secession and was defeated as a candidate to what became Florida's secessionist convention. He was part of a large minority that did not incur any lasting enmity from other Confederate Floridians. The pro-southern president Andrew Johnson, anxious for the South to resume its former relations with the national government, appointed him provisional governor to reestablish Florida's state government.

As new governor he shared authority with General John G. Foster because the state was still under martial law. Governor Marvin called for a constitutional convention which met in October. All white males who were twenty-one who took the oath of allegiance and those with presidential pardons were eligible to register and vote. Marvin campaigned in the interest of moderation and also spoke to the freedmen about their responsibilities in their new status. He showed nonpartisanship in restoring the property of Union men confiscated by the Confederacy and stopping the sale of property belonging to native Floridians that had been commandeered by the Federal authorities. Since President Johnson did not require that African American men be given the vote in order for Florida to rejoin the Union, nothing was done, and many prewar and wartime Democratic leaders were elected. The constitution as adopted proscribed blacks as voters and imposed harsh "Black Codes" of racial discrimination. Marvin correctly predicted that if white Floridians restricted blacks from their voting rights, congress might well refuse to let them and other southerner states rejoin the Union. The Florida constitution of 1866 was unacceptable to northern politicians and many northern citizens. When Marvin went out of office, the state was still not an equal partner in the Union. Later, Marvin was elected as a Democrat to the US Senate, but the Republican-controlled national senate refused to seat him. Marvin dropped out of politics and returned to New York where he died.

Inaugural Speech
(Source: Gainesville New Era, August 12, 1865)

Fellow Citizens:

I am happy to meet this large audience and discuss the important subjects which are claiming the attention of every one. I have the right to address you, because I am one of the oldest citizens of Florida. I came here whilst we were yet a territory, and assisted in the organization of State Government. Florida is my state by adoption and affection. Her prosperity and happiness are linked with my own. I have a right, also, to address you, because I have been appointed by the President of the United States to aid you in the reconstruction of your State government. I shall make known to you the plan of the President and call your attention to the subjects which are [illegible] to your welfare. I trust [illegible] you will give me on this occasion [your patient?] attention.

At the outbreak of [illegible] so-called Confederate Government confiscated the property of all Union people, and had the insurgents been successful in the war, the property of such citizens would have been confiscated and lost [to them?]. The United States, also, as a means of strengthening the government, and crippling the rebellion, confiscated the property of its most guilty instigators and adherents. In this category was embraced a large class—for nearly all were rebellious. The action of government in this matter, was in accordance with the usual practice of nations under similar circumstances. By the failure of the rebellion the property of Union people is restored to them, and that of the insurgents is forfeited. We are [utterly helpless?] and [illegible] in the hands of the victors. However humiliating it may be to confess it, we are nevertheless a conquered people, and at the mercy of the Government. In this condition of affairs what does the government propose to do? Still press on with its armies? Glut its sword of vengeance with our blood? Appropriate all our property? Not at all. Its majesty and might are no greater than its clemency and mercy. It comes to us as the Father went to his prodigal son. It says lay down your arms and return to the peaceable pursuits of life. Nearly all of you I freely pardon, [illegible] you your property, and civil and political rights. The cases exemplified from this general amnesty, are Generals, Judges, Governors, members of Congress and a few others. You may ask why pardon was not extended to those who were worth over $20,000 of taxable property. Several reasons may be given. Their presumed superior intelligence, their ability to take some pains to secure pardon, their responsibility and obligations to the State, may have been among the reasons which led the President to make the exception. But, though these wealthier persons stand unpardoned, their case is by no means hopeless. The are in the same category as the Generals, the Judges and others exempted from the general amnesty. Many of these classes will, I have no doubt, receive executive clemency. It may be necessary to make examples of a few of the most wicked and malignant persons, and confiscate their property. In my official position, I shall take pleasure in [re-establishing?] to the favorable consideration of the President all who are truly penitent and give good evidence of a determination to be good citizens in the future.

Having presented these general remarks—I wish to make an application of them to a case in hand in which many of you are personally interested. While the war was still raging, many of the inhabitants of this part of the State were within the Rebel lines, a District Court of the United States was held at St. Augustine, then and now occupied by Union [illegible] and a large number of decrees of confiscation of lands and houses were [entered?] up in the absence of the owners and without their appearing. They were, in many and perhaps most instances, in the rebel country, where, perhaps, they ought not to have been, but where they, in fact, were. The owners of these lands and houses, in many instances, are now as well-disposed to become loyal and good citizens as any in the state. Since these decrees were passed, they have been embraced with the Amnesty Proclamation. Under these circumstances, it appeared desirable, that they should have an opportunity to be heard—that the sales advertised for the 7th of August should be suspended, and the decrees opened, and the owners allowed to make such explanations, and set up such defenses as they should be advised by their counsel and proper to be made—in other words, that they should have a full hearing on the merits—and plead their pardon, if such plea should be deemed admissible in their cases. I accordingly wrote to the Attorney General on the subject. And his answer was so prompt, so ready, as to give full assurances that the Government of Washington, does not desire to confiscate any person's lands without giving him *every possible* opportunity to be heard. The Attorney General ordered the sales to be suspended until the [action] of the department, and he directed the District Attorney to [counsel?] to the opening of the decrees in these cases. By means of these orders, time and opportunity is now given to the owners, after the country is quieted, to cast about, look up their testimony, take advice and counsel, and see what defense they can make. It is possible the houses and lands of some may be confiscated. In other cases explanations will be made or defenses established. Besides, Congress may deem it wise before long to repeal this confiscation law. Accept, Fellow Citizens, this prompt and cheerful series of the Attorney General in response to my application, as an omen of good—the olive branch held out by the civil authorities to all persons who are now sincerely willing to do right, however much they may have erred in the past.

I have heard some censures cast upon the Judge, the District Attorney, and the Marshal for executing these confiscation laws. I have listened to all complaints from every person who had anything to say, and so far as I can now judge, I think these censures are unjust, these complaints unreasonable. So far as I can learn, these officers have done their duty under the law, and according to the law. If they have committed mistakes or errors, it is not so much their fault as the owners or [illegible] of the property, who, had they not in many [instances?] left their homes and gone within the rebel lines, would have been present in court and would have interposed their claims and [illegible] the court from committing any errors or mistakes. The Judge, the District Attorney, and Marshal, it must be presumed, throughout all this business have done their duty according to law unless the contrary is plainly proved. I have heard of no such proof, and you, instead of indulging a spirit of criticism and censure, should be thankful, that the Attorney General has been able to give you all the relief desired, and at the same time has [cast no censure?] upon the proceedings of the Judge, the District Attorney, and the Marshal.

[Illegible] of the results of the great rebellion, slavery has ceased to exist. With the fall of the Confederacy, its corner stone crumbled to dust, and the winds have scattered it. The war which was commenced among other reasons, for perpetuating the black man's bondage, has, [in?] the providence of [illegible] brought him freedom. He can never be enslaved again, [the?] great shout among the colored people. No form of slavery can ever be established again in this country. From all I can learn, I think too, that the people of this Negro not only realize this fact, but they are now generally becoming glad of it. The constitution which you will be called upon to form will [illegible] the order of things, and secure [illegible] for all alike.

With slavery out of the way, there will be nothing to hinder a restoration of our constitutional relationship with the general government, and our becoming a great, prosperous, homogenous and happy people. In the U. S. Senate, Florida will be the peer of New York, and in the lower houses she will be duly represented. The restoration of civil government will be through a convention to be called at [a distant?] day to alter or amend the State constitution. No time should be lost in becoming qualified to vote for members of the convention.

In the meantime the preservation of peace and order will continue in the hands of military authorities. [Illegible] of affairs here as far as I have [able?] to learn has been so wise and so mild, that there will be no impatient and [illegible] for a change. But some will ask "why don't you [illegible, 3 words] [once?] of the civil administration as we prefer civil rule?" I answer that no authority to [reinstate?] the [illegible, 2 words] or to [illegible, 4-5 words] what is necessary to the [calling of a convention?]. My [business?] is to assist you in organizing a government. I trust you will cheerfully [acquiesce?] in this arrangement.

But what will be your conduct when the wheels of civil government are not in motion, and the strength of the military forces is greatly reduced in the State. Will we behave better than formerly? I remember the organization called [Regulators?] and the terrorism exercised by them, and the lynching and the murders which occurred in some parts of the state. I trust when the civil authorities are once more established, that you will yield to them and [illegible] the heartiest support. The spirit of malice and revenge must be banished from among us, and every one of us must embark on a mission of peace and good will. If you would see your fair land happy, inviting capital ad good citizens to come among you, you must see to it that Judge Lynch and his infernal cohorts are never allowed to scourge the country again. Let every one yield supreme obedience to the laws and prosperity will follow.

And you, Freedmen, have now exchanged masters—you must now make law your master, for it is the law which is to protect you in your freedom [illegible] other [illegible] leads to happiness and [illegible]. Will you stand by me and where officers who may be in authority and obey the laws? Obedience to the law is freedom. My knowledge of the past makes me earnest in this matter.

We are about to enter upon a new [era?]. Between the two races a good understanding must be created and continued. Some persons, disappointed and vexed, will not have any faith in the colored man. They will not [illegible, 2 words] of him with [illegible] now that he has become free. They have an anxiety to see him socially and morally elevated because they have no faith in his [illegible]. Let me say in all plainness to each, try him. Give him a fair chance. Teach and encourage him [illegible] our happiness and prosperity are now [illegible] connected with the welfare of this people. Their elevation will add to the power and prosperity of the state. They cannot remain [illegible, 3 words]. Their movement must be separate or they will become [illegible, 3 words], the [illegible] vagabond, and rest like an [illegible] upon the country. In many respects the white man is superior to the to the colored man and his responsibility is [illegible] accordingly increased. We want the colored people here. In their [illegible] and [illegible] the State has immense wealth; but that they may be made available we must trust them blindly, give them an education and make them an [illegible] part of the body politic. And you, my colored friends, must not be idle or lazy. Labor is the law which [illegible] has imposed upon us all. I have been and [choose?] to be one of the most [illegible] men in Florida. If you are respectful to all and industrious, you will be protected by the law in the enjoyment of all the rights of humanity. You must keep away from [illegible] and try to [illegible] your children in the [illegible] of the Lord. Send them to the Sunday schools. The while man, [illegible, 3 words] himself to this new order of things. His responsibilities and duties are of the [illegible, 3 words]. He must [illegible, 2 words] like a [illegible], or the worst of consequences will follow to himself and family. Schools must be established over the land. Northern teachers must be welcomed—some of them have their peculiarities, but what of that, let them come among us—you must also send out missionaries and teachers from among yourselves and [illegible] yourselves in promoting the intelligence, virtue, and general elevation of all the people of the State. The Ministers of the chapel have a heavy responsibility in this matter. They should be instant in [illegible] and [set of season?] in exhorting and rebuking with all long suffering and patience, and in teaching and instructing the ignorant and the wayward in a knowledge of their moral and religious duties, and in promoting peace on earth and good will to men. Let every man, woman, and child throughout the State cease to murmur or complain against the [dispensations?] of Providence, but cheerfully and hopefully accept the new order of things, as coming from Him whose ways are not as man's ways, and whose thoughts are not as man's thoughts. There is a bright prospect in the future for our beautiful State. The rainbow of promise is seen in the dissolving clouds. Let each man do his own duty and God will bless us.

Governor David S. Walker
Term: 1866 - 1868

David Shelby Walker (born May 2, 1815 – died July 20 1891) was born in Kentucky and schooled in that state and Tennessee. He studied law and moved to Leon County in 1837 and successfully entered politics, serving in the first state legislature's house and later in the senate and again in the house. From 1859 to 1854 Walker was the Register of Public Lands and, by virtue of that office, was also State Superintendent of Public Instruction. Walker's interest in education led to the establishment of a free school in the capital supported by city taxes. Other offices that he held included mayor of Tallahassee and associate justice of the State Supreme Court. Although he was a slaveholder, Walker was a former Whig and Constitutional Unionist who opposed breaking up the Union. Still, once Florida left the US he supported the state.

Florida's constitutional convention met in November to vote on the new document and to elect state and local officials. In a greatly reduced vote of about 4,000 votes, Walker was elected governor, although no blacks cast ballots. Walker had the difficult task of serving as governor and restoring civil government during a period of military occupation. Congress reacted sharply to Florida and the South's black codes and other discriminatory legislation aimed against the freedmen, substituted Congressional Reconstruction for Presidential Reconstruction, and enacted the Fourteenth Amendment which made African Americans US citizens . Governor Walker and President Johnson advised Florida voters to reject the amendment , and across the South only Tennessee approved it. Congress refused to seat the newly elected congressional delegations from Florida and the other southern states, and imposed Military Rule. Colonel John T. Sprague established the District of Florida and proclaimed martial law on April 8. The Republican party was soon established in opposition to Walker and the Democrats, and, although torn by bitter internecine warfare, established a decade of political rule. Walker, returning to the practice of law, was appointed Circuit Court Judge in 1876. He held the post until his death.

Inaugural Speech

(Source: Jacksonville *Florida Times Union*, December 30, 1865)

Gentlemen of the Senate and House of Representatives:

From the beginning it has been the custom in the States of our Union for the Governor elect to improve the occasion of his inauguration by making such remarks as existing circumstances might suggest, and by recommending the adoption of such measures as the good of the country might require.

In compliance with this time-honored custom, I now address you.

By failing to regard the disinterested warnings of the "Father of his country" against "the baneful effects of the spirit of party," and particularly "when founded on geographical discriminations"—by omitting, as he advised, to remember that "the jealousy of a free people ought to be *constantly* awake against the insidious wiles of foreign influence," and by neglecting, as he recommended, "to frown indignantly upon the first dawning of every attempt to alienate any portion of our country from the rest, or to enfeeble the sacred ties which now link together the various parts"—the people of the United States, nearly five years ago, became involved in the terrific civil strife which has but recently ended. We now hope that by a strict adherence to his advice, "the unity of government which constitutes us one people" will again become "dear to us," and that in all future time, we will regard it as "a main pillar in the edifice of our real independence, the support of our tranquility at home, our peace abroad, of our safety, of our prosperity, of that very liberty we so highly prize."

To repair the waste of war; to restore the States to their proper relations with the Union; to bring about an era of good feeling and fraternity; to re establish the government on the principles of the Constitution, and to perpetuate our unity by securing all that makes it desirable, are now objects of primary desire with all patriotic and honest men, North and South, East and West.

But it is more particularly of our duties as citizens of Florida, that I would speak.

And, in the first place, as we are now renewing our relations of friendship and union with the States of the North, let us be particular to abolish all points of difference among ourselves. During the late unhappy conflict, some of us were known as Union men, some as Constitutional Secessionists, and others as Revolutionists. A glorious opportunity is now afforded to fling away these names, and with them the strifes they have engendered, and to meet, as brethren ought to meet, upon the platform of the Constitution which our fathers made for us in 1787. If I shall be permitted to administer the government, I shall know no distinctions between citizens on account of past political differences.

I will not condemn the Union men, because I know from experience how completely the love of the Union becomes a part of our very existence, and how it is endeared to us by a thousand glorious recollections, and as many brilliant anticipations. I know that the heart of Florida's greatest and most renowned citizen was literally broken by the severance of the Union.

Nor will I condemn the Constitutional Secessionist, because I know that, though he differed from me, his side of the question was supported by arguments, if not unanswerable, yet of great plausibility, and by the authority of many of the greatest names that this country has ever produced.

Nor yet will I condemn the Revolutionist, for I know that he, though originally opposed to secession, went into the war, after the fact was done, upon the conviction that it was no longer an open question, and that it was the duty of every man to stand or fall with his own section.

In fact, the great questions connected with the integrity of the Union were, before the war, so unsettled, and the opinions of great men so varied, that it required a man greatly superior to myself to say with certainty who was right and who was wrong. Seeing the different luminaries which guided our people, I am not astonished that the very best men in our land were found arrayed in opposing ranks.

I need not enumerate the host of great men who stood with the immortal [Henry] Clay for the integrity of the Union and against the doctrine of secession.

The logic of events has proved that they were right. But among those who held the contrary doctrine, that a State might secede from the Union without an infraction of the Federal Constitution, we find the names of such men as Mr. Rawle, a distinguished lawyer of Pennsylvania, to whom Gen. Washington more than once tendered the office of Attorney General of the United States, John Randolph, of Roanoke, Nathaniel Macon, of North Carolina, Mr. Calhoun, of South Carolina, P.P. Barbour, a late Justice of the Supreme Court of the United Sates, and Judge McKean, a late Chief Justice of the Supreme Court of Pennsylvania.

Those who advocated the right of revolution quoted the remark of Mr. [Daniel] Webster, that "a bargain broken on one side was broken on all sides, and that if the North should not obey the Constitution in regard to the rendition of fugitive slaves, the South would no longer be bound by the *compact*.." Mr. [Horace] Greeley, then, as now, a great leader of Northern sentiment, had said that "he could not see how twenty millions of people could rightfully hold ten, or even five, in a Union with them, by military force"; and again, "that if seven or eight States should send agents to Washington to say 'we want to get out of the Union,' he should feel constrained by his devotion to human rights to say, let them go." In this connection he also quoted the Declaration of Independence, that "Governments are instituted for the benefit of the governed; and that when any form of Government becomes destructive of these ends, it is the right of the people to alter or abolish it, and to institute a new Government," &c.

Mr. Lincoln, prior to his first election, had acknowledged this principle, with the addition, that not only a people, but any part of a people, being sufficient in numbers to make a respectable government, might set up for themselves. Mr. Tyler, a later President of the United States, held to the doctrine of secession, and Mr. Buchanan, the then President of the United States, said, just before the commencement of the war, that while he thought a State had no right to leave the Union, yet if she should leave it, the remaining States would have no right to coerce her return.

Amidst these various and conflicting views, all supported by the highest authority, it is no wonder that our people should have become bewildered, or that, being forbidden by the stress of events to remain neutral, some should have adhered to the Union and others to the State.

For these reasons, I repeat, that if I shall be permitted to administer the Government, I shall know no distinction between citizens on account of past political differences. I shall take it for granted that all have done what they conceived to be their duty under the circumstances, and the only question I shall ask concerning any one presented to me for position, will be, "Is he honest, is he capable, is he attached to the principles of the Constitution of the United States and the Constitution of the State of Florida?" All shall have the equal benefit of the laws, and, as Heaven is my judge, all shall equally suffer the keenest penalty of the laws for any infraction thereof. Law and order shall be maintained.

I am happy to believe that this declaration meets with the general approbation of our people. Already they have given the most gratifying indications that they hold the same opinion with myself on this subject. All over the State I hear of citizens, who were recently in hostility, now forming business associations, and getting along most harmoniously; and in our Constitutional Convention, just adjourned, I saw gentlemen who had served in the army of the United States, and gentlemen who had served in the army of the Confederate States, sitting side by side, consulting only for the good of the Union, and the State as one of its members.

Having spoken of the relations which ought to exist, and which, for the most part, do exist among the white people of the State, I now naturally come to speak of the feelings which ought to be cherished, and the policy which ought to be pursued, towards our colored population.

I think we are bound by every consideration of duty, gratitude, and interest, to make these people as enlightened, prosperous and happy as their new situation will admit.—For generations past they have been our faithful, contented and happy slaves. They have been attached to our persons and our fortunes, sharing with us all our feelings—rejoicing with us in our prosperity, mourning with us in our adversity. If there were exceptions to this general rule, they were only individual exceptions. Every Southern man who hears me knows that what I say is literally true in regard to the vast mass of our colored population. The world has never before seen such a body of slaves. For, not only peace, but in war, they have been faithful to us. During much of the time of the late unhappy difficulties, Florida had a greater number of men in the army, beyond her limits, than constituted her entire voting population. This of course stripped many districts of their entire arms-bearing inhabitants, and left our females and infant children almost exclusively to the protection of our slaves. They proved true to their trust. Not one instance of insult, outrages, or indignity, has ever come to my knowledge. They remained at home and made provisions for our army. Many of them went with our sons to the army, and there, too, proved their fidelity, attending them when well, nursing and caring for them when sick and wounded. We all know that many of them were willing, and some of them anxious, to take up arms in our cause. Although, for several years, within sound of the guns of the vessels of the United States, for six hundred miles along our seaboard, yet scarcely one in a thousand voluntarily left our agricultural service to take shelter and freedom under the flag of the Union. It is not their fault that they are free—they had nothing to do with it; that was brought about by "the results and operations of the war."

But they are free. They are no longer our contented and happy slaves, with an abundant supply of food and clothing for themselves and families, and the intelligence of a superior race to look ahead and make all necessary arrangements for their comfort. They are now a discontented and unhappy people, many of them houseless and homeless, roaming about in gangs over the land, not knowing one day where the supplies for the next are to come from—exposed to the ravages of disease and famine—exposed to the temptations of theft and robbery, by which they are too often overcome—without the intelligence to provide for themselves when well, or to care for themselves when sick, and doomed to untold sufferings and ultimate extinction, unless we intervene for their protection and preservation. Will we do it? I repeat, we are bound to do it by every consideration of duty, gratitude and interest.

Much has been said of late about the importation of white labor from Germany, Ireland, Italy, and other countries, and with proper limitations and restrictions I am in favor of it; but let us always remember that we have a laboring class of our own which is entitled to the preference. It is not sufficient to say that white labor is cheaper. I trust we are not yet so far degraded as to consult interest alone. But interest alone would dictate that it is better to give these people employment, and enable them to support themselves, than have them remain upon our hands as a pauper race; for there they are, and here, for weal or woe, they are obliged to stay. We must remember that these black people are natives of this country, and have a pre-emption right to be the recipients of whatever favors we may have to bestow. – We must protect them, if not against the competition, at any rate against the exactions of white immigrants. They will expect our black laborers to do as much work in this climate as they have been accustomed to see white ones perform in more Northern latitudes. We know that they cannot do it. They never did it for us as slaves, and the experience of the last six months shows that they will do no better as freedmen. Our fathers of 1783 knew that it takes five black men to do the work of three white ones, and consequently, in adjusting the apportionment of taxes upon the basis of the labor and industry of the country, eleven of the thirteen States of the old Confederation recommended that every five blacks be counted as only three. The same rule was afterwards adopted in the Constitution of 1787, in regard to representation. But I fear those who may migrate hither from Europe or elsewhere, will be unmindful of this fact. We ought not to forget it, and between foreign and black labor we ought always to give the preference to the latter when we can possibly make it available. And if we can offer sufficient inducements, I am included to think that the black man, as a field laborer, *in our climate*, will prove more efficient than the imported white.

We ought to encourage our colored people to virtue and industry, by all the means in our power. We ought to protect them in all their rights, both of person and property, as fully as we do the whites.

This is the view taken by our recent State Convention. After recognizing the fact that they are free, and declaring that slavery shall never hereafter exist in this State, they proceed to open to them all the Courts of Justice, and admit them as witnesses "in all criminal proceedings founded upon an injury to a colored person, and in all cases affecting the rights and remedies of a colored person."

I trust, gentlemen, that this action meets your approbation, and that you will take great care, not only not to discriminate in your legislation against the colored race, but that you will so shape your enactments as to promote their welfare and happiness to the fullest possible extent.

Considering their ignorance and liability to be imposed upon, I think it would be well for you to provide that they shall be bound by no contract to labor, unless the same be reduced to writing and acknowledged before some judicial officer, that a speedy remedy be given them to collect their wages, and that they recover damages when dismissed without good cause. And on the other hand, considering how essential it is to the successful cultivation of our great staples, that those who engage as laborers should remain throughout the whole period of service contracted for, I recommend that a violation, without good cause, of any contract once fairly entered into, either by black or white laborers, be made a misdemeanor, and punishable with such penalties as will prevent the evil.

I now invite your attention to our relations with the Federal Government.

Thus far our people have manifested their loyalty and desire to return to the Union, by doing all that the Government was understood to desire. They have taken the oath prescribed in the proclamation of the President, "to support the Constitution of the United States, and the union of the States thereunder, and to abide by and faithfully support all laws and proclamations which have been made during the existing rebellion with reference to the emancipation of slaves." They have held an election, under the proclamation of the Provisional Governor, for members of a State Convention. That Convention has annulled the ordinance of secession. It has repudiated all debts contracted by the States since the date of the secession. It has declared that all those who were slaves are now free. It has opened to them all the Courts. It has admitted them as witnesses in all cases in which they are interested. And in short, they have left nothing undone which they understood the Government to desire.

At the conclusion of the session of the Convention, our much esteemed Provisional Governor, who represents the President, and so deservedly possesses his confidence as well as that of our people, appeared before that body and said:

> I congratulate you upon the termination of your labors. The result of them merits and receives my entire approbation as Provisional Governor. As a citizen of the State, I approve of *nearly* all that you have done. Speaking, however, merely as any other *citizen*, I confess that some of your action I could have preferred to have been different. But, as *Provisional Governor, I am entirely satisfied with what you have done.* You have done everything that in my official capacity I asked you to do. I asked nothing but what was right. You have done it all, and in the right spirit. Your action in regard to negro testimony receives my especial commendation. You have met the issue fairly and fully, and have done all that could have been desired. The Conventions of other States have evaded it by transferring it to their legislatures. I hope they will be successful and prosperous, but feel that the action of Florida, so fully in accordance

with the wishes of the President, will place her in a better situation than their's. With such a Constitution as you have adopted, there can be no reason to doubt the admission of your Representative and Senators into the Congress of the United States.

Thus we have the endorsement of the Government itself upon the action of our Convention, that "they have done all that could have been desired, and in the right spirit."

Yes, gentlemen, the Convention did all that *it* could do. And now one thing remains for the Legislature to do, which the Convention could not do, and that is to ratify the proposed amendment to the Constitution of the United States, which reads as follows:

> First. Neither slavery nor involuntary servitude, except as a punishment for crime, whereof the party shall have been duly convicted, shall exist within the United States, or any place subject to their jurisdiction. Second. And Congress shall have power to enforce this article by appropriate legislation.

I cannot better give you the reasons why this amendment should be adopted, and, at the same time, the true meaning of the second clause thereof, than by repeating to you a portion of the correspondence which recently took place between the President and the Provisional Governor of South Carolina.

On the 28th of October last, the President telegraphed to the Governor as follows:

> I hope your Legislature will have no hesitation in adopting the amendment to the Constitution of the United States abolishing slavery. It will set an example which will no doubt be followed by the other States, and place South Carolina in a most favorable attitude before the nation. I trust in God that it will be done. The nation and State will then be left free and untrammeled to take that course which sound policy, wisdom and humanity may suggest.

Three days subsequently the President telegraphed to the Governor as follows:

> There is deep interest felt as to what course the Legislature will take in regard to the adoption of the amendment of the Constitution of the United States abolishing slavery, and the assumption of debt created to aid in the rebellion against the government of the United States. I trust in God that the restoration of the Union will not be defeated and all that has so far been well done, thrown away. I still have faith that all will come out right yet. This opportunity ought to be understood and appreciated by the people of the Southern States. If I know my own heart, and every passion which enters it, it is my desire to restore the blessings of the Union, and tie up and heal every bleeding wound which has been caused by the fratricidal war. Let us be guided by love and wisdom from on high, and union and peace will once more reign throughout the land.

To these telegraphic dispatches the Provisional Governor replied, among other things, that

> There was no objection to the adoption of the proposed amendment to the Federal Constitution, except an apprehension that Congress might, under the second section of that amendment, claim the right to legislate for the negro after slavery was abolished.

To this the Secretary of State replied on the 6th of November, stating, among other things, as follows:

> The objection which you mention to the last clause of the constitutional amendment is regarded as querulous and unreasonable, because that clause is really restraining in its effects instead of enlarging to the

power of Congress. The President considers the acceptance of the amendment by South Carolina as indispensable to a restoration of her relations with the other States of the Union.

The President of the United States, the Attorney General, and the Secretary of State, are all understood to concur in this obvious meaning of the proposed amendment, and with this understanding, I earnestly recommend it to your adoption. Congress can only enforce, "by appropriate legislation," the non-existence of slavery. This being done, their power is exhausted, and "the apprehension that Congress might, under the second section of the amendment, claim the right to legislate for the negro after slavery was abolished," "is regarded as querulous and unreasonable, because that clause is really restraining in its effects instead of enlarging the powers of Congress."

The only other objection I have heard to the adoption of this amendment, is that its adoption may only be opening the door to a demand for new concessions. My answer is, that we have no reason to believe that this will be so. It is unfair and ungenerous to suppose that the Government is endeavoring to inveigle us into the adoption of certain measures, with a promise of a restoration of our rights in the Union, when in fact it does not mean to admit us upon the adoption of those measures, but intends to make further demands after the first shall have been acquiesced in. Such a suspicion is entirely unworthy of the course which the President of the United States has pursued towards us since the cessation of hostilities. He told us frankly from the beginning what would be required of us. I know that he told me in July last the adoption of this amendment would be expected. Our Provisional Governor told us so in his speech in Quincy, and on other occasions. All the action of the convention was had with a full knowledge of that expectation, and in the adoption of the amendment you will but be completing a series of measures which they knew must be completed to secure to the State all her rights as a member of the Union.

The new demand, I am informed, some fear will be made is that of negro suffrage. I am satisfied that this demand will never be made by the President. If there is any one thing that he is more pledged to than another, it is that of allowing each State to prescribe the qualifications of electors and eligibility of persons to hold office under the Constitution and laws of the State—a power, (which he says,) the people of the several States composing the Federal Union have rightfully exercised from the origin of the Government to the present time.

This is the language used and the position taken by him in his proclamation organizing the first Provisional Government in North Carolina. On the third of October last, he said, "Our only safety lies in allowing each State to control the right of voting by its own laws," and in his message to Congress, which we have just received, he stands firmly, fairly, and squarely up to his original position.

Nor do I think that this unjust demand will ever be made by Congress. I think the position of the President will be sustained. The recent vote in Connecticut and Wisconsin, expressly repudiating negro suffrage—together with the fact that it is allowed in only a few States of the Union, and in those few only with qualifications, renders it highly improbable that a Congress of Northern men will compel us to admit it while they reject it themselves. To do so would be to assert that many generations of freedom have not qualified the few negroes, in their midst, to vote, while as many generations of slavery have qualified our millions.

But suppose, for the sake of the argument, that Congress should make this demand—what then? Still I say we will be in a better position by having adopted the amendment. We will have done all that the President desired us to do, and so far as the Executive Department is concerned, we may be considered as in the Union and entitled to the enjoyment of all its blessings, for the President most feelingly says, "If I know my own heart and every passion which enters it, it is my desire to restore the blessings of the Union, and tie up and heal every bleeding wound which has been caused by the fratricidal war." We may then reasonably hope that ere long martial law will cease to prevail in our State, that civil law will be fully restored and the authority and jurisdiction of the State Government entirely reinstated.

If Congress shall unexpectedly refuse to admit our Senators and Representative, because we have not allowed negro suffrage, we must then, without manifesting any undue impatience, wait until Congress shall think better of the matter. The justice of our cause, the influence of the President, and the good sense and patriotism of the nation, cannot fail to give us our representation in the end.

Of course we could never accede to the demand for negro suffrage, should it be made.

We have manifested that our loyalty and desire to renew our relations with the Union are so great that to do so we are willing to yield every thing but our honor and our consciences. We have all lost much—many of us our all—all but our honor. Let us preserve that, though we lose every thing else. We have been able to give an honest and conscientious consent to all that has been done, but each one of us knows that we could not give either an honest or a conscientious assent to negro suffrage. There is not one of us that would not feel that he was doing wrong, and bartering his self-respect, his conscience, and his duty to his country and to the Union itself, for the benefits he might hope to obtain by getting back into the Union. Much as I have worshipped the Union, and much as I would rejoice to see my State once more a recognized member thereof, yet it is better, a thousand times better, that she should remain out of the Union, even as one of her subjugated provinces, than go back "eviscerated of her manhood," despoiled of her honor, recreant to her duty—without her self-respect, and of course without the respect of the balance of mankind—a miserable thing, with the seeds of moral and political death in herself, soon to be communicated to all her associates.

If time allowed, I would like, now, to speak of what provision ought to be made for our poor and for those who have been disabled in, or made widows and orphans by the late war, and upon our financial, educational and internal improvement systems. But to do so, would protract my remarks to an inconvenient length. I must, therefore, make what I have to say on these and other points, the subjects of special messages. I shall at all times seek a free interchange of opinions with you, deeming it important to the welfare of the State that a good understanding and cordial relations shall exist between the Executive and Legislative Departments of the Government.

And in this connexion, it is proper to say, that I shall deem it my duty, as the representative of the State, and it will be in perfect accord with my feelings, to cultivate the friendship and invite the confidence and co-operation of the Provisional Governor and of the gentlemen of the army of the United States, who are stationed amongst us. They are our fellow-citizens and the officers of our government, on duty here, not to irritate and oppress us, but to assist in preserving order during our transition state, and to conciliate and soothe. With few exceptions, they all have filled their delicate mission with credit to themselves and satisfaction to us. To Maj. Gen. Foster, commanding in this State, our thanks are due for the general justice and mildness with which he has exercised his great authority, and particularly for the facilities he has afforded to the members of the Convention and of this Legislature in assembling at the Capitol.

In conclusion, I beg that you will excuse a few words in regard to myself.

Twenty-eight years ago, I was a pennyless stranger, from a far distant State, seeking in this bright land a place where, by close attention to business, I might earn an honest living, I found it here. The people took me by the hand, and ever since, whether in prosperity or adversity, peace or war, have held me in the embrace of their confidence. As a Lawyer, Representative, Senator, Register of Public Lands, and Judge of the Supreme Court, they have always stood by, encouraged, sustained, and, with their approbation, more precious than the gold of Ophir, rewarded me.

Six years ago, when they placed me upon the Bench of the Supreme Court, I fondly hoped my political days were numbered, and that the residue of my life was to be spent in the calmer labors of judicial investigation. But now, the tornado of civil discord having swept over the land, prostrating every interest, entirely destroying our labor system, and uprooting the very foundations of our political edifice, they have called me, with a unanimous voice, to preside as Grand Master at the re-building of the temple.

My obligations are the more sensibly felt from the fact that this honor has been conferred without one word of solicitation, without the writing of a single letter, or the making of a single speech—without a pledge, a platform or a party.

For this extraordinary manifestation of kindness and confidence, I wish thus publicly to acknowledge my great indebtedness to the masses of the people.

But it is not in words that I will attempt to express my gratitude. The unremitting and utmost efforts of whatever powers a merciful God may bestow, to secure to our State, as one of the co-equal members of the Federal Union, all the benefits and blessings of wise laws and good government, must attest the depth and sincerity of my thankfulness.

And now, gentlemen, requesting all the pious people of the States to join me in prayer to Almighty God that He will convert the weakness and inadequacy I so painfully feel, into strength and competency for the good of my country, and that He will, of His abundant mercy, bless our State and our whole land, I bring these remarks to a close.

Governor Harrison Reed
Term: 1868 - 1873

A native of Massachusetts, Harrison Reed (born August 26, 1813 – died May 25, 1899) was Florida's ninth and one of the state's most controversial chief executives. He was Florida's first Republican governor. During Reed's candidacy and administration Republicans engaged in various political machinations. A minority of blacks and their white supporters developed a bitter rivalry with the majority of blacks and their white cadre. Florida's new political party was made up of native whites, pejoratively called Scalawags; northern whites, dismissed as Carpetbaggers; and the former bondsmen. The Republicans wound up nominating Harrison Reed for governor. Reed had come to Florida from Wisconsin as a treasury agent. The conservative white Democrats named George W. Scott, a former Confederate colonel, as their candidate. In the voting the new "Radical" constitution of 1868 which enfranchised black male voters of twenty-one was ratified, and Reed defeated Scott. The constitution of 1868 further set the governor's term at four years, provided for meaningful state support of public education, and., importantly, democratized state government.

Reed's tenure was tumultuous. Even so, he was inaugurated on June 8, 1868, and on July 4, civil government was resumed in Florida. On July 25, Congress declared that the state of Florida was once more in the Union. The wily governor courted Conservative Democrats by appointing some of them to high office, but was spurned by them. Naturally, his actions alienated the other Republican factions. Beyond that, native whites attempted to drive him from office with acts of violence, as the North Florida counties unleashed a deadly campaign by the Ku Klux Klan. Reed constantly contended with both parties, and fought off four unsuccessful attempts to impeach and remove him from office. Reed's latter years were spent as editor of a magazine that promoted southern development, serving a single term as a house member from Duval County, and, in a political appointment, being postmaster at Tallahassee.

On separate occasions during Reed's time in office there were two pretenders, William H. Gleason (born circa 1830 – died November 9, 1902) and Samuel T. Day, who claimed to be the legitimate governor of Florida. Neither was, but their attempts to usurp Reed are given below.

Inaugural Speech
(Source: Tallahassee *Weekly Floridian*, June 8, 1868)

Fellow Citizens of Florida:

In entering upon the high trust which your partiality has conferred, in deference to time honored custom, it becomes my duty to briefly indicate the policy of my administration as Chief Magistrate of the State.

In November, 1860, the constitutional rights of the people of Florida were subverted and its civil government was overthrown. Since then the State has been without a constitutional government and subject to military law.

In March, 1867, the Congress of the United States, in obedience to its obligations to "guarantee to every State a Republican form of government," prepared a plan by which the State could regain its forfeited rights and its people be restored to the benefits of constitutional government.

Under this plan, you have framed a government which we are here today to inaugurate and prepare to make effective. You have formed and adopted a Constitution based upon the great theory of American government, that *all men are by nature free and endowed with equal rights.* You have laid deep and broad the foundations of the State upon the principle of universal freedom.

Bred to freedom and under Republican institutions; believing slavery an unmitigated curse, as well as a violation of human rights—a moral, political, and physical evil, wherever tolerated, I most cordially congratulate you that it no longer exists to blight the fair heritage which God has given us here, and that the Constitution which you have adopted contains no germ of despotism to generate future discord.

I congratulate you also that no spirit of malevolence or bitterness, growing out of the wrongs and conflicts of the past, has been suffered to mar your organic law, but that in a spirit of magnanimity and forbearance worthy of the highest commendation, those who have forfeited their citizenship are welcomed back to the benefits and privileges of the government upon the sole condition of fealty and adherence to the Constitution and laws.

Amid the ruins of a government embodying antagonistic principles, you have laid the foundations of a government insuring harmony, stability, security, and peace. The conflicting elements and interests of the past may now all unite in a homogeneous system, all yielding obedience to a common law, which respects alike the interests of all. Time alone can heal the social disorders and dissensions created by the disruption of society and the radical change in the system of government consequent upon the war. We will patiently await its mollifying influence, interposing no obstacles to a speedy restoration.

All classes of society and all the interests of the State demand peace and good government, and if the spirit of our Constitution is appreciated and reciprocated, every citizen may realize these advantages, and the State may arise from its prostrate condition to a measure of prosperity unknown in the past, and become one of the brightest luminaries in the galaxy of our glorious Union.

Fellow Citizens! I accept the high responsibility of the Chief Magistracy under your new Constitution, believing firmly in its principles, and unqualifiedly endorsing its policy and that of the Congress under whose clemency we are permitted to inaugurate anew a civil government for the State. I enter upon this high trust with the firm purpose of executing the laws in the spirit of liberality in which they are conceived, and in view of the highest interests of the State and the people. Relying upon your loyalty and patriotism, and the favor and guidance of that Divine Power which sways the destinies of all, I shall do what within me lies to render effective the Government, and to command for it the respect and obedience of all classes of our citizens.

Governor Ossian B. Hart
Term: 1873 - 1874

Ossian Bingley Hart (born January 17, 1821 – died March 18, 1874) was a Republican and Florida's first native-born governor. He was born in Jacksonville, and his father, Isaiah David Hart, was one of the city's founders. Ocean Street in the North Florida city was named for Ossian. The future governor practiced law in his home town. Moving to a farm near Fort Pierce in 1843, Hart represented St. Lucie County in the state house of representatives (1845). He established himself in Key West in 1846 and resumed the practice of law. In 1856 he moved once again, this time to Tampa..

Although raised in the environment of his father's plantation, Hart opposed slavery and secession and suffered disapproval by the native white population. As a Republican he participated in the reconstruction of state government both at the state level and in Jacksonville. He was appointed to the Florida Supreme Court in 1868, but in 1870 when he sought a house seat in the national congress he lost a contested election. Even so, the able Hart was elected governor in 1870 defeating William D. Bloxham, a native Floridian. During the strenuous winter campaign Hart became ill with pneumonia. The physically overextended governor paid a heavy price: he died less than three months into his administration.

Inaugural Speech
(Source: Tallahassee *Weekly Floridan*, January 7, 1873)

Fellow citizens:

Upon the taking of the oath of office by a newly elected Governor, custom seems to require an inaugural address. I am not aware that it prescribes what it shall contain. It is difficult for any man to determine with reasonable accuracy what he will do in any given capacity for four years. There are, however, some subjects of a general character that we can expect to act upon with tolerable certainty. I have just now sworn to support, protect and defend the Constitution of the United States, and of the State of Florida against all enemies, domestic or foreign, and that I will bear true faith, loyalty and allegiance to the same, and faithfully perform the duties of the office; and praying for the help of God I mean to do so.

These Constitutions and governments are now in perfect political harmony, and it is of the highest importance that they should never be otherwise. Indeed they cannot be otherwise: their relation cannot be severed. The government of the United States, with that of the State, constitute the grandest and most perfect system of government that the world has ever known. If unexampled success in government affords any proof of the sanctions of Providence, it is proven that our government of the United States, our National government, has that sanction, for it rose to the grade of a first class nation in eighty-five years, an eminence that no other nation ever reached under hundreds of years. The theories calculated to disturb the permanence intended and expressed by its founders, have been made to undergo the severest test—*that of being submitted to the event of rebellion* and civil war. They were signally overthrown, and, it is believed, will never again to insisted upon to the extent of any disturbance of the system. Thus the prospect is rendered more brilliant.

From conditions of distant colonies and provinces of European monarchies, of Indian wars, of territorial dependence, of slavery, of civil war, and of the unavoidable ascerbities of reconstruction, Florida emerges into the present comforting, soul-inspiring prospect, staunch, safe, free, well equipped, and manned; the old flag, with all its glories ever radiating from it, as her guide, the great patriotic united people constituting her officers and crew, and ever enveloped in the fairest clime, freighted with the most inviting products, there is nothing in the war, nothing worth a serious thought, to prevent common sense from making her always eminently peaceful and prosperous.

Official duties, correctly understood, are generally simple, and when diligently and honestly performed, are under our system of government, sure to effect its great object "the greatest good to the greatest number." Public officers should be not only diligent and honest, but zealous for the reputation of the State, and at the same time so circumspect as that the keen scrutiny of opposing aspirants can find no ground even of suspicion.

There is much to be done for the public good. To punish crime, so that perfect safety under the law alone shall everywhere prevail; to stimulate education until it shall, as it ought to do, be universally known as one of the first necessities; to husband all our resources and use them only for the public good; to cancel useless paper; to raise money with which to pay all of the State debts with the interest promptly when due; to pay the outstanding and fearfully increasing warrants, and current expenses in cash. I trust that my fellow-citizens everywhere in the State will cheerfully make the efforts so pressingly necessary in order to acomplish these great objects fraught with untold benefits to Florida. The ordinary expenses of government are more than double what they would be under prompt cash payments, and during the continuance of the present system the situation is growing worse daily. There is remedy with the people, who are our masters to instruct their public servants, the makers of statutes, what to do with this great evil, and how to do it. It matters not who is to blame, the Scrip system in one form or another, has long existed here, and never effected any good. The evil is upon the people, upon us all, in terrible earnest, and must be overcome and prevented for the future.

In the affairs of the State, of the counties, and of the cities, extravagance, venality and neglect should be stopped short by the voice of the people. Resolutions of public meetings concerning the particular duties of County Commissioners, Road Commissioners, Justices of the Peace, Sheriffs, Clerks, Public Attorneys, Tax Assessors and Collectors, Treasurers, School Commissioners, and any other officers, demanding punishment for neglect or misconduct, insisting upon necessary legislation, and the effectual correction of any abuses, followed up by other meetings, showing determination by the people that their public servants shall be vigilant and faithful, will more surely effect needful reforms than any course we have yet pursued. The people are sovereign masters to whom we, their servants, must ever look for examples of public virtue and instructions in official duties. If in all parts of the State the people will move in these matters and show their determination and power, the unfaithful will tremble, better men will displace them, and improvement soon be every where visible. The Executive Department will exert itself continuously in behalf of these important reforms, but will every day need the countenance and support of the people.

The law, the voice, the deliberate mandate of the people will be the guide of the Executive in all his acts, and his unbounded trust in the great sovereign people is that they will set him the example of perfect, cheerful obedience to the aggregate command. Whenever it may be so despised as to be disregarded and violated, its command that examples shall be made will surely be obeyed by the officer when it directs to see that the laws shall be faithfully executed. Abundant power of two kinds is bestowed for that purpose, and must be used whenever really necessary in order to preserve perfect safety or persons everywhere.

I feel already impressed to state that in selecting men to fill the "Cabinet of Administrative Officers" provided by the constitution to aid the Governor, he must of course be permitted by his friends to make his own selections, or else he ought not to be, as he is, held responsible to the great people for all the acts of his administration. If other, if his friends, select them, they will not be his selections, and it would be unjust to hold him responsible for any of their acts. –He must, however, be so responsible, and hence the Constitution, which we are sworn to support, provides that they shall be appointed by the Governor and confirmed by the Senate. –Their counsels will be needed daily. Each should be perfectly competent to fill his position thoroughly, without the aid of clerks, were it possible for one person to perform all the labor. He must be able to instruct, direct, and control the clerks in his office and keep its important affairs finished up every day, and all the documents and records of his office safe, perfectly safe, for he is and must be held responsible for their acts.

Praying to the Divine Creator of us all for aid to enable me to act wisely and do right, I enter with cheerful confidence upon the discharge of the duties of the high office to which the sovereign people of our beloved State have elevated me.

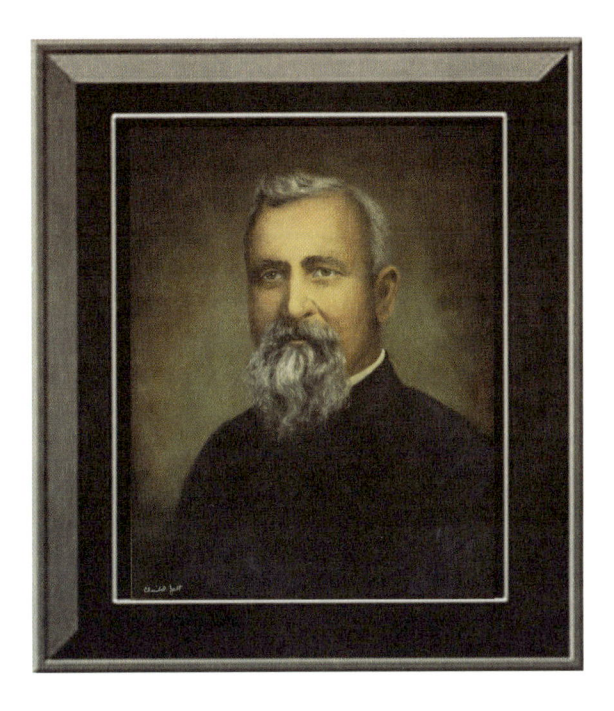

Governor Marcellus I. Stearns
Term: 1874 - 1877

Governor Hart was succeeded by Lieutenant Governor Marcellus Lovejoy Stearns (born April 29, 1839 – died December 8, 1891). He was born and educated in Maine, attending Waterville (now Colby) College. During his junior year he enlisted and wore the Union blue. Stearns rose to the rank of lieutenant, and lost an arm in combat. Transferred to the Freedmen's Bureau, he wound up in Quincy and remained there until being mustered out.

The one-armed veteran's political interests led him to seek and win membership in the constitutional convention of 1868 and in the state house of representatives representing Gadsden County. He held the latter position from 1868 through 1872. At the age of thirty-four Hart was elected lieutenant governor in 1872. Succeeding to the governorship on March 18, 1874, Stearns did not deliver an inaugural address. He sought reelection in 1876 but was defeated by the

Democrat and redeemer governor George Franklin Drew whereupon his term officially ended January 2, 1877. In short order Stearns was appointed United States commissioner at Hot Springs, Arkansas. He held the position until 1880 and died in New York state in 1891.

Governor George F. Drew
Term: 1877 - 1881

Curiously enough, the man who restored Florida to Democratic control, George Franklin Drew (born August 6, 1827 – died September 26, 1900) was born in New York. He migrated to the South in 1847 settling in Columbus, Georgia, and engaging in the lumbering industry. After living in various Georgia counties Drew finally came to Florida at the end of the Civil War. He established the state's largest saw mill at Ellaville in Madison County on the east bank of the Suwannee River.

After ending the hegemony of the Republican party, Drew helped reconfigure the state's political system. His major role was his acceptability to Conservative Democrats, soon known as Bourbon Democrats (after the ruling house in France which resumed control in 1815 after the defeat of Napoleon). In effect, Drew was a compromise candidate (he was known as a Unionist during the Civil War) who could attract and, more importantly, not alienate voters. He won the contested race for governor, although Florida's electoral votes in the presidential race, also contested, went to Rutherford B. Hayes, the Republican candidate. Florida's votes along with those of South Carolina and Louisiana decided that Hayes, not Samuel J. Tilden, the Democratic candidate, would be the next president. In a similar way, Florida's vote in the election of 2000 would decide the presidency. The tumultuous election of 1876 saw the restoration of the Democrats at the state level in Florida and the continuation of Republican rule at the national level.

Inaugural Speech
(Source: Tallahassee *Weekly Floridian*, January 2, 1877)

Fellow-Citizens:

Having taken the oath of office as prescribed by the Constitution, I am about to enter upon the grave and responsible duties appertaining to the position of Chief Magistrate of the State of Florida.

The will of the people, as legally expressed at the ballot-box, has been enforced by the mandate of our highest judicial tribunal, and it must be a source of supreme gratification for every citizen to feel that, whatever results may flow from the excitements of political contests, he has the broad shield and protecting arm of an impartial judiciary as the final arbiter of his rights. And the quiet and entire submission of citizens of all parties to the decision of the Supreme Court is the surest guarantee that we are a law-abiding people, resolved to perpetuate free institutions, and to transmit to our posterity the blessings of constitutional government.

As the contest is over, let us hope that the animosities engendered thereby have died away, and that, as your chosen Executive, I may be able to rise to the true and broad statesmanship of occupying the position of the Governor of the State of Florida, and not the head of a political party. Our immense territorial dimensions demand a population commensurate with its capacity. Let us demonstrate by wise measures that our feelings and interests combine to generously invite an immigration that will promote this most desirable result.

Reflecting upon the past only as a guide for the future, let us endeavor to bring about an era of good feeling between all classes, and build up the prosperity of Florida by the combined efforts of her entire population. A large portion of that population, recently enfranchised, have been taught to feel solicitous of the continuance of their newly-acquired rights, if the party of which I have been the honored candidate came into possession of our State Government. Their fears are groundless, and our colored fellow-citizens may finally rest assured that their rights, as guaranteed by the Constitution, will be fully sustained. It is both our wish and our interest to protect them in all their rights and to bring about the kindest feelings between the races. As the Executive of this State, I shall exhaust every legal and constitutional remedy for the protection of the rights, the life and the liberty of every citizen—feeling that such a course is my highest duty and most conducive to the prosperity of the State.

A Northern man by birth and a Union man from principle, I recognize that the Democracy of Florida, in placing me in this position, demonstrate their desire for a true and fraternal union of all sections of our common country. That such a union may be firmly established, and ever remain peaceful, prosperous and happy, is the hope of every patriot. At a period in our country's history when the theory of Republican government is undergoing a severe test, it is the duty of every law-abiding citizen to use his earnest efforts for the promotion of harmony and the security of those institutions. I hope and believe that the political contest now waging in the Federal arena will be peacefully settled, and that the chosen constitutional agents of the people will be quietly inaugurated with the full sanctions of the honest masses of all parties.

When I have received and considered the reports of the various Heads of Departments I shall, in accordance with duty and usage, transmit them to the Legislature with such suggestions as I may deem appropriate. Then I can more appropriately refer to details affecting the political and material interests of the State.

Returning my heartfelt thanks to the people of the State of Florida for their confidence and support in elevating me to this position, and hoping that I may be able to meet all their just expectations, I ask their kind indulgence upon my administration of public affairs, and in my earnest efforts for their welfare and prosperity I invoke the assistance of an over-ruling Providence.

Governor William D. Bloxham
First Term: 1881 - 1885
Second Term: 1897 - 1901

A native of Leon County, William Dunnington Bloxham (born July 9, 1835 – died March 15, 1911), a two-term governor, was Florida's only governor to serve split terms. He earned a law degree from William and Mary College, but like many other southerners Bloxham found the attractions of being a planter compelling. With the additional reason of poor health, he devoted his labors to the soil rather than following Blackstone's profession. Yet, politics and the military were not precluded from his activities, and Bloxham was elected to the Florida House of Representatives 1861. He also organized an infantry company which he commanded through the war.

During Reconstruction he became even more involved in politics. He was the apparent winner in the race for lieutenant governor in 1870, but lost due to the machinations of the Republican controlled State Canvassing Board. He ran for governor in 1872 but was defeated by Hart. As a native son and by personal political philosophy, Bloxham was a quintessential Bourbon Democrat. Party loyalty and service paid off in 1877 with his appointment as secretary of state in the Drew administration. Then in 1888 he won the governor's chair, defeating the Republican candidate Simon B. Conover, a former state senator. Although a true Bourbon, Bloxham did not stress the tenets of retrenchment and reform. Instead, in his inaugural address he described the need for transportation, immigrants, and a better educational system.

The most outstanding single act of Bloxham's first administration was the Disston Land Purchase. Hamilton Disston, member of a wealthy tool making family in Philadelphia, was introduced to Florida by Henry S. Sanford with whom he fished. Florida's Internal Improvement Fund (IIF), established to manage Florida's public land, was practically insolvent when the Bloxham government negotiated the sale of approximately four million acres in the Everglades to the Disston interests for $1,000,000, or twenty-five cents an acre. The draining of the Everglades was made possible, and, importantly, the sale saved the IIF. It performed the further service of giving momentum to the development of South Florida, especially with the coming of railroads and the opening of large hotels by economic titans Henry M. Flager and Henry B. Plant.

After his term ended, Bloxham was still vigorous. Although he declined appointment to be minister to Bolivia in 1885, he accepted the post of United States Surveyor-General for Florida. In 1890 Bloxham was appointed state comptroller, and in the next general election ran successfully for the post. In the last governor's election in the nineteenth century Bloxham again sought the governor's seat, and defeated the Republican candidate Edward R. Gunby of Tampa and the Populist standard bearer William W. Weeks.

In his second administration Bloxham became Florida's first governor in the twentieth century. Taking office in 1897 he had to confront financial problems that plagued his entire term. In 1894 and 1895 severe freezes damaged the state's citrus crop destroying not only trees but also other tax-producing property. Florida also suffered physically and financially from a hurricane in 1896. Bloxham had to deal with the aftermath.

Bloxham, as Florida's "war governor," was confronted by the conflict between Spain and the US. The Spanish-American War, although brief (lasting only from the late spring of 1898 until the early summer), began as the US aided the Cuban revolutionaries in their struggle to become independent from Spain. It ended with that objective achieved and the addition of Pacific territory and the beginning of an American empire. As the closest state to Cuba, Florida became the focus of attention for the rest of the country. Tampa became the debarkation port of American forces, which were composed of regular soldiers and volunteers. US military headquarters was at the Tampa Bay Hotel. Despite the confusion of inadequate planning excessive heat, heavy rain, mud, dust, and sand, General William Shafter and the invasion fleet sailed for Cuba on June 14, 1898.

Ten regiments of volunteers were authorized by the War Department, and among them was the First Florida. Governor Bloxham had twenty companies of Florida troops, but finally chose twelve from various counties and cities. He appointed Colonel William F. Williams as their commander, although none of the volunteers was selected to go to Cuba. Despite all of the difficulties, including the Plant Railroad system's transportation failures, Tampa managed to make a major contribution to the war effort. When he retired in 1901, Bloxham had provided his state with more than twenty-five years of public service.

Inaugural Speech
First Term: 1881 - 1885
(Source: Fernandina *Florida Mirror*, January 4, 1881)

Fellow Citizens, Ladies and Gentlemen:

In response to the summons of the people as officially announced, I have come to take the oath prescribed by the Constitution, preparatory to entering upon the duties appertaining to the position of Governor of Florida. Fully appreciating the importance of these duties I ask the indulgence and seek the assistance of all lovers of the State in their proper and faithful discharge.

Looking alone to the interest, welfare and prosperity of our State, it will be my pleasure as well as my duty to bend every energy to promote her further progress and growth. That future rests to a large extent with her people. To secure its full fruits to ourselves and our posterity, we must invite a healthy immigration; develop our internal resources by securing proper transportation; and educate the rising generation. These are the three great links in the grand chain of progress upon which we can confidently rely for our future growth and prosperity.

Immigrants come where the blessing of good government secure to them the protection of life, liberty and property; and it is a source of profound gratification to know that the faithful enforcement of the laws has secured that protection in Florida, as fully as in any State of the Union, and she is reaping her just reward, not only in the general prosperity of her varied industries, but in the constantly increasing tide of immigration that seeks her shores. And it is due to the State that all patriotic citizens, and all public associations, and the public press, that great lever that makes and moves public sentiment, should unite in allaying the misapprehensions sought to be created for partisan purposes during the late political campaign, and by all proper means afford assurances to capital and industry of safe and profitable investment. Yes, let us invite and encourage immigration by every legitimate means at our command. And I feel that I but utter the sentiments of the entire people—from Escambia's beautiful bay to the magnificent St. Johns, from our northern limits to the bright Key of the gulf, where the lone exile rests in conscious security under the broad aegis of our flag, whilst weeping over the fate of the beautiful Queen of the Antilles—when I extend a hearty welcome to all visitors and a Godspeed to every settler who desires to become a citizen of Florida. We question neither their nativity, their political views, nor religious sentiments. All that we can desire is, that they be honor-loving and law-abiding.

Owing to our geographical and semi-tropical position, we possess advantages claimed by no other State of the Union. To utilize these advantages to their full extent it is not only necessary to secure immigration, but also that handmaid of progress, transportation. With the Peninsula of our State furnished with proper transportation and railroad facilities secured to the West, with their magnificent lands and virgin forests, who can predict our future? Owing to the embarrassed condition of our internal improvement Fund, all may not be accomplished at once that is desirable, but let us work unitedly and unceasingly to the success of these grand objects. Florida, indeed, stands but upon the threshold of her greatness. With her climate and soil, and her varied productions, her future is full of hope and full of promise. An intelligent and enterprising people blessed with such resources can but build up a great and prosperous Commonwealth. Let us then devote ourselves to these great objects, worthy of the consideration of the leading minds of our State.

Let us hope that the asperities engendered by the heated discussions of the canvass have died away, and that as American citizens, proud of our country, we will cherish our republican institutions and lend a hearty acquiescence and cordial support to those placed in power by the people. With true loyalty and devotion to an "indissoluable union of indestructible States," we will cherish and obey, without mental reservation, the Constitution of our country, with all of its amendments, believing that a strict adherence to all of its provisions will prove the prophet's rod which is to sweeten the waters from which have flown the bitter strifes of the past. Knowing no sectional lines, and fostering no sectional animosities, let our patriotic impulses be as broad as the Union itself, and as pure as the inspiration that gave to us the Divine injunction of "peace on earth, good will towards men."

As to our colored population, I can but assure them that their rights and liberties are secured by the great fundamental law of the Union as well as that of the State: and that they need entertain no fears of their violation. Their equal rights before the legal tribunals will be maintained; equal justice fully meted out, and their future prosperity left to their own industry and thrift, assisted and encouraged by good government as the result of equal and just laws.

To you, Governor Drew, allow me to say that in laying aside your official robes, you carry with you the affections and esteem of the people of Florida, whom you have so faithfully, so honorably and so efficiently served. And it is a source of great pleasure to me, having been officially and intimately associated with you for nearly four years, to bear willing testimony to your devotion to the State's best interests. May your years be long, peaceful, and prosperous to wear the laurels so freely placed by the people of your State upon your honored brow.

And now, fellow-citizens, animated alone by a desire to promote the best interests of our beloved State, I crave your confidence and support. Remembering that it is impossible to satisfy and gratify the wishes of all—particularly in the unpleasant duty placed by the Constitution upon the Executive of selecting officers—I shall go forward in the discharge of my duty strengthened by the purity of my motives and trusting to time and the good judgment and patriotism of the people for proper vindication. And in the discharge of these duties I ask the protecting and guiding hand of the Supreme Ruler of the Universe to the end that Florida may be free, prosperous, and happy.

And now, sir, I am prepared to take the solemn oath to support, protect and defend the Constitution and Government of the United States and of the State of Florida, and bear true faith, loyalty and allegiance to the same.

Second Term: 1897 - 1901
(Source: Pensacola *Daily News*, January 8, 1897)

Fellow Citizens—by the suffrages of the electors of our state, I have been called to a second term as chief magistrate of Florida. The call not only carries with it duties of the most delicate and responsible character, but it is the highest honor that the people of the state can bestow.

I know of no means more appropriate to attest my appreciation than by an earnest effort to exercise the high functions of the position solely for the purpose of securing an honorable, economical, just and progressive administration.

It is proper, however, to remember that the best state government can do little directly in promoting individual success or individual prosperity.

The evils of bad government can more readily mar those desirable results than good government can secure them.

Vicious government, in fettering the hopes, efforts, and energies of individuals, spreads its baleful influence over all classes and tends strongly to the disorganization of society.

Good government, while shielding us from such destructive agencies, can act affirmatively only in giving the undisturbed opportunity of securing the rich resulting fruits of well directed individual efforts.

The true function of government is to protect us in our natural and inalienable rights.

Those rights are defined by our constitution as enjoying and defending life and liberty; acquiring, possessing, and protecting property, and pursuing happiness and obtaining safety.

The best government is that which interferes the least with the legitimate business vocations of its citizens and imposes the lightest burdens upon property and labor; which administers prompt justice to all, regardless of station and without discrimination; which throws the protecting shield of its sovereign power over every inhabitant and secures the greatest liberty consistent with the public good which leaves personal prowess and personal effort free to accomplish legitimate results, untrammelled by governmental interference: which avoids paternalism and stimulates individualism as the true philosophy of a democracy.

Fellow citizens: With our climatic conditions secured by geographical position: with our varied and fertile soils, admitting a range of production without a rival in our great sisterhood of states and suited to both temperate and tropical climates: with our forests studded with natural contributions to commercial and manufacturing wealth; with thousands of miles of waterways where myriads of food-producing fish; cut with golden oar, the silvery steam: with extensive herds grazing alone upon nature's bounty with vast phosphatic deposits necessary to enrich the world's worn soils; with remunerative and increasing manufacturing interests; with admirable transportation facilities, and unrivaled seaports; with a generous and law-abiding people, we can confidently invite immigration and claim profitable remuneration for capital.

Immigration and capital are two of the necessary factors to invigorate the growth of a state and we should give our earnest and best efforts in securing for Florida those unrivaled motive powers of development. With them, will come transportation facilities to those sections of the state still requiring it and the development of our varied, vast and valuable resources.

Recognizing that an intelligent suffrage is the best safeguard of constitutional liberty, we should fully sustain the paramount claim of public education and not rest content with surpassing our neighboring sisters, but press forward to a still higher goal.

Our commercial growth should be blocked by no improper impediments while our enviable health record should be sustained by proper quarantine and municipal hygiene, to be enforced through the channels of our legally constituted health authorities in accordance with the most advanced scientific thought.

It is the exclusive perogative of the state to redress wrong and to execute justice. An unrelenting opposition should be given to any effort to stain our state's fair name by the assumption of those duties by individuals.

Let our people see that no charge of blood guiltiness can be truthfully brought against their loyalty to law. Society's only safety rests with just laws, vigorously and impartially administered.

We must give no excuse for individual redress of wrong by allowing criminals to be encouraged to crime from hope of immunity.

Mercy is of divine origin, but it should walk the path-way of our civilization hand in hand with justice—justice to the living as well as to the dead.

Mercy to the bad is often times cruelty to the good.

The sovereigns of our social fabric are law and justice. Let us crown them and keep them enthroned as the only security to society, the only means of perpetuating government.

Fellow citizens: in the language of Mr. Jefferson: "I shall often go wrong through defect of judgment. When right, I shall often be thought wrong by those whose positions will not command a view of the whole ground. I ask your indulgence for my errors which will never be intentional; and your support against the errors of others, who may condemn what they would not if seen in all its parts."

I have no interest that can be served that will not be the same to all; and claim no higher honor than to share the future with the people of my native state.

Our hearts, our hopes, our love, our prayers go out together to our beloved Florida. May every sunbeam kiss her fair brow with the kiss of peace and prosperity. May the guardian angels of love and humanity hover over her people. May the God of truths and justice guide and direct them.

Governor Edward A. Perry
Term: 1885 - 1889

Edward Aylsworth Perry (born March 15, 1831 – died October 15, 1889) was born in Massachusetts. He attended Yale before coming South to teach briefly in Alabama. Perry moved to Pensacola where in 1883 he began his law practice. In a remarkable Civil War career, Perry was wounded twice and went through the ranks from private to brigadier general. As a military hero and a Bourbon he was the ideal candidate, although poor economic times had caused much dissatisfaction among some Democrats. A group of angry dissident Democrats nominated an Independent named Frank Polk of Madison County. The Republicans, who were saddled by the Bourbons with being responsible for the excesses of Reconstruction and "Negro Rule," endorsed Polk but did not nominate him. The vote was close, and, ultimately, the disgruntled white Democrats went back to their party. The issues remained, and the way was paved for the Populist party of the 1890s.

The full-bearded Perry saw his administration advocate and the legislature establish the State Board of Education and there was a resulting improvement in the state's system of schooling. The Bourbons moved to solidify their control by eliminating all vestiges of Republican rule. This was accomplished with the constitution of 1885. The document curbed the power of the governor, eliminated the office of lieutenant governor, and made the six-man cabinet elective. Salaries and taxes were reduced and biennial legislative sessions were continued. The constitution made possible the first steps toward eliminating black (and later poor whites) voters by enabling the legislature to make the payment of poll taxes a prerequisite for voting. It was made more palatable by requiring that the revenue raised would become part of the school funds. The legislature of 1889 passed the multiple ballot law calling for separate ballot boxes and causing much confusion among illiterate blacks and whites. In the elections of 1890 there was a dramatic drop in the number of black voters. The poll tax remained in effect until 1937.

Six new counties were created under Perry, but natural disasters hurt his administration. The worst cold wave since 1835 caused ruin within the citrus industry. A crippling yellow fever epidemic occurred in 1887 at Tampa, Manatee, and Plant City, and in 1888 at Jacksonville. Perry died in 1889.

Inaugural Speech

(Source: Jacksonville *Florida Times-Union*, January 8, 1885)

My Fellow Citizens:

In thanking you, as I most heartily do, for the honor of the high office to which you have chosen me, I take this occasion to express also my profound gratitude for the flattering reception and uniform kindness extended to me by every portion of the State during the late campaign. Gratitude, as well as a sense of duty, and the obligation just taken, will exact my utmost endeavors to discharge the duties of the office for the best interests of the whole State. Realizing the great importance of the trust and my want of experience in civil office in the past, I shall enter upon the duties with no few misgivings, but I am encouraged by the hope that there is throughout the State a sincere and earnest purpose to work for the advancement of and progress of Florida, which will have the hearty co-operation of the people as well as the different departments of the government.

Our country, like our State, has been excited by a heated political contest, but that excitement will soon pass away and the groundless fears entertained by some of our colored citizens that their constitutional right are endangered by the result are fast subsiding. Such apprehensions will soon give place to a general rejoicing that the result of that contest instead of threatening the rights of any will demonstrate that such rights or the rights and interest of an particular class or section in our common country are in no wise to be better secured or advanced by keeping alive bitterness between the sections or political discord and enmity between classes or races.

In our own State let us hope that any and all asperities engendered in the heart of the political canvass may be buried by united and cordial determination to work together that our many resources may be developed, our vacant lands utilized by every legitimate encouragement to immigration, investment and labor, that our educational facilities may be every succeeding year increased and all the moral and material interests of our State advanced. In view of the expressed will of the people to revise our organic law, I shall not upon this occasion or in my subsequent communications to the legislature at its present session attempt to point our particular ways and means to be adopted under the existing constitution by which these great purposes can be best accomplished. It is evident that much will depend upon the people, more indeed than upon any contemplated methods or acts of the public agents today vested with temporary power under a mandate soon to be reversed.

It is my earnest hope that until the people in their sovereignty shall meet; we may in every department study the strictest economy consistent with our duty to conserve the interests of the State.

Whatever may be our political views, whatever our position in the State, and whether our duty be to make or execute the laws, let us not forget that the great end and object of constitutions, laws and government should be to secure the peace, promote the happiness, and advance the prosperity of the people.

Governor Francis P. Fleming
Term: 1889 - 1893

Francis Philip Fleming (born September 28, 1841 – died December 20, 1908) was born in Duval County and was descended from two families dating to Florida's English period (1763-1789). Educated at home by private tutors, Fleming did not follow his father's agricultural interest, and entered the business world. During the Civil War he was a member of Florida's famous Second Regiment, earning a battle field promotion to first lieutenant. He was at home on sick leave in 1865, when, ironically for him, the Battle of Natural Bridge occurred, and he commanded a company of volunteers in the fighting. The battle had no influence on the war's outcome, but it was a rare Confederate victory that late in the conflict.

In the post-war period Fleming studied law and earned a statewide reputation for his abilities. His fame gained the soulful-eyed and elaborately mustashioed Fleming (he looked something like an actor in a Gilbert and Sullivan opera) the nomination. The process took forty ballots, although Fleming easily defeated his Republican opponent V. J. Shipman and the candidates of the Labor party and the Prohibition party. The Democratic platform did not mention the emerging Farmers' Alliance which was headed for political action as the Populist party or the problems of Florida's black and white farmers. The decade of the 1890s was partly colored by a nation wide economic depression. Yet, politics continued, even though in Florida they were confused and confusing. Even so, Governor Fleming called for a special session of the legislature to establish a State Board of Health. This important act was prompted by the yellow fever epidemic, and the board's creation had lasting and beneficial effects.

Inaugural Speech

(Source: Jacksonville *Florida Times-Union*, January 9, 1889)

Fellow Citizens of Florida:

The wisdom of those statesmen and patriots, who were the architects of the admirable system of Republican government which obtains in our country, located in the people the fountain of power, and the source of all governmental authority, based upon the principle that that government which best insures the happiness of a people must rest upon the consent of the governed. In harmony with the system thus marked out, and in the exercise of that right guaranteed by the Constitution, the people of our State have chosen by ballot those who will exercise the functions of government for the next four years.

As the chosen head of the next Administration, with a grateful appreciation of the honor conferred upon me standing upon the threshold of my official career, I cannot but be profoundly impressed with the responsibilities and difficulties which confront me, all the more so by reason of my inexperience in official life, never before having held a civil office. And when I glance back at the wise and able administrations of my predecessors, I have indeed misgivings as to my ability to satisfactorily discharge the duties of the high office to which I have been chosen. Well may I supplicate the Great Ruler of the universe in the humble language of the mighty sovereign of His chosen people: "Give therefore Thy servant an understanding heart to judge Thy people, that I may discern between good and bad." Relying upon His aid and guidance, I shall earnestly endeavor to discharge those duties faithfully and impartially, with fidelity to the people and in the interest of the whole State.

Having visited every section of Florida within the past few months, my pride and admiration of my native State are, if possible, increased by a more extended acquaintance with her people and a better knowledge of her resources, industries and attractions, which are unsurpassed in variety, and have drawn within her borders a valued immigration and large capital for their development. Within the past decade she has made rapid strides in material prosperity, and is destined to advance to the front rank of the great sisterhood of the Union.

Her prosperity, however, has been temporarily retarded by the visitation of yellow fever to our eastern metropolis, and some other places, which has cost the State the loss of some of her most valued and esteemed citizens, brought affliction and sorrow to the hearts of many of our people; and has seriously interrupted business and travel. But while we extend our sympathy to those who have suffered personal bereavements or pecuniary loss, let us thank Almighty God for the bright spot in that dark cloud which overshadowed us, as presented by the example of that noble band of heroes, who, facing pestilence and death, swerved not from the path of duty in their labors of love and mercy, ministering to the cause of suffering humanity. The State should ever cherish them in grateful memory among the heroes who have shed lustre upon her name. Well did those martyrs who fell at the post of duty illustrate the true that

> Whether on the scaffold high,
> Or in the battle's van—
> The noblest place for man to die
> Is where he dies for man.

And we have indeed much to be thankful for in the exemption of all but a small portion of the State from the dread disease, for the almost unprecedentedly small death rate, where the fever prevailed and the entire abatement of the disease at this time, as well as for the revival of business and the bright prospect of the future.

I feel that a sacred duty rests upon me, as well as upon every good citizen, that nothing be left undone which may contribute to guard us from a visitation of epidemic disease in the future, and especially to prevent its recurrence during the year upon which we have entered. Being so impressed I shall carefully consider the expediency of convening the Legislature in extra session earlier than the time appointed for its regular meetings, to provide such further legislation for the preservation of the public health as to them may seem best.

I take pleasure on this occasion extending to the people of Florida my sincere thanks for the uniform kindness and hospitality which I received, and the flattering demonstrations which greeted me on my recent tour of the State, made, as it was, under many unpropitious conditions. I shall ever look back to their kindness as among the most grateful memories of the past.

To you, my friends, fair daughters, and gallant sons of Florida, who in these imposing ceremonies and this grand demonstrations attending the inauguration of the incoming administration do honor to your State, in her name, permit me to extend my thanks.

I congratulate our citizen soldiers on this admirable military display, of which any State might feel justly proud. A well organized volunteer soldiery is a safeguard in the preservation of liberty and the perpetuation of peace. I sincerely hope that you may never be called on to engage in the deadly occupation of war. But, with the record of the Florida soldiers in the war, some of whom, my old comrades, I see around me, should your country need your services, I am sure you would prove as valiant in battle as you are handsome in parade. [Great applause, and one lady behind the Governor said, in a staccato voice: "I see the new Governor knows how to flatter," which provoked great laughter].

In conclusion I earnestly ask of all our people their sustaining aid to the administration in the discharge of the duties which devolve upon it. Let us all, with unselfish devotion to our beloved State, and with a purpose single to her prosperity, strive to continue to her the blessings which flow from good government.

Governor Henry L. Mitchell
Term:1893 - 1897

Henry Laurens Mitchell (born September 3, 1831 – died October 14, 1903) was born in Alabama, but at the age of fifteen went to Tampa. He studied law and was admitted to the bar in 1849. Mitchell resigned as state attorney when the Civil War began. He was a lieutenant and was promoted to captain. After the Vicksburg siege in 1863, he was elected to the Florida house and resigned his commission to represent his home county of Hillsborough. Mitchell served again in the sessions of 1873 and 1875, and, as a hard working representative, helped the port city of Tampa emerge as an important part of the Plant railroad system. In 1888 he was appointed an associate justice on the Florida Supreme Court. Rugged looking and with a full head of hair, Judge Mitchell inspired confidence.

He was elected on a platform that endorsed Alliance and Populist demands for reform, but Mitchell retained the confidence of Democrats. His election was assured. Hard economic times and natural disasters such as the destructive hurricane at Cedar Key in 1896 made it impossible to enact agrarian demands even if Mitchell had wanted to. By then he became interested in judicial matters once more. He ran for and won the far lesser office (especially when compared to his positions as supreme court judge and governor) of clerk for the sixth judicial circuit. When still governor, he signed his own commission for the office.

Inaugural Speech
(Source: Jacksonville *Florida Times-Union*, January 4, 1893)

Fellow Citizens:

You are gathered here today on this historic spot in the shadow of this ancient building that reaches back in its memories to the days when this grand commonwealth was but a territory of the national government, not dignified with the name of state; when her present smiling fields, busy cities and villages were parts of an unknown wilderness: that building which has seen the advancement of our state and people go on year by year, fostered by our free, democratic government, until today Florida occupies the proud position that she does amid the cluster of sovereign states that form the United States of America.

You are gathered here for the purpose of witnessing a fellow-citizen taking the oath of office before entering upon the performance of his duties as governor of the state. It is useless for me to say that this vast assemblage and these imposing ceremonies add naught to the solemnity of the occasion, for they do; and there has not passed a moment since I first learned that the suffrages of the people of the state had elected me governor, down to the present time, but that there has ever been present in my mind the responsibilities of the office and the magnitude of the duties imposed upon me. But right here I would say that one thought has always buoyed me up, and that thought is that the burden of responsibility is not borne by me alone, but that each one of you, my fellow-citizens, no matter in what capacity you serve the state, whether as office-holder or private citizen, alike shares the responsibility. The oath of office which I am about to take is but a renewal of the oath I have taken as a private citizen, and has been taken by each of you.

The induction into office, while it widens the field of employment and brings more before the public one's acts, in truth and in fact adds no new obligations as it is always his duty to serve the state faithfully.

Here in the sight of the people of this state I pledge that in all the acts of my public life I shall ever keep in mind the obligations of the oath of office, and only ask of you, fellow-citizens: that you too shall keep with you an abiding sense of the obligations of your oaths as citizens. If this be done nothing can prevent the full realization of all the benefits guaranteed by our free and democratic form of government, the grandest form of government ever conceived by the brain of man. The selection of the chief magistrate of our state is made amid the strife of partisans, but after the selection has been made it is the highest duty of the citizen to sink that feeling of partisanship and help with every effort to work out the glorious destiny of our common state. Partisanship in its place is necessary for the preservation of our republican institutions, but it is just as essential that proper limits should be marked out beyond which partisanship should not go.

The constitution of our state has wisely provided that sometime shall elapse between the inauguration of the governor and the meeting of the Legislature, so that the incoming governor may have the necessary time within which to familiarize himself with the workings of the various departments of the government, and fully mature the details of the measures that, in his opinion, are best for the welfare of the people. It is not fitting, nor would it be proper for me at this time to detail the policy of the incoming administration, but it is my pleasure, as well as my duty to say what shall be the controlling spirit of the policy of the new administration. The people have a right to know at this time how the public interests entrusted to me shall be cared for. The expression that the "revenue of the government shall be limited to the necessary expenses of the government economically administered" has been reiterated in party platforms and from the stump so often, that it has become trite, and the people are too apt to consider it a mere sounding phrase with no meaning. I consider it fraught with deepest meaning; the truth therein contained is the foundation of republican institutions, yea, the corner-stone of our liberties, and I hereby pledge myself, as far as in my constitutional power lies to see that this principle of government is carried out to its fullest extent, not only in letter but in spirit. With the aid of the legislature I mean to see that every unnecessary expense of the state government is stopped as far as possible, and that the state take by taxation from her citizens no money that it is not necessary for the purposes of obtaining those benefits, the fruition of which is the very object of the state itself.

I have at all times favored the public school systems of our state. The guarantee of the constitution of a common school education is one of the most sacred of all its guarantees. I consider the result of this guarantee one of the greatest blessings of our land, and one of the grandest forces in the advancement and progress of our state; and it shall be my aim not only to keep up all the common school we now have but to widen and increase their usefulness. But the laws of the state in regard to the expenditures and accounting of money collected for this purpose are too lax, and it shall be my endeavor to have them so remedied that the people shall get the value of every dollar collected for this purpose, and the office expending this money shall be required to make full and accurate account thereof, so that the people may see and know that they are receiving every benefit thereof.

There are various other matters affecting the interests of the state which I have not time to mention at the present, but will call to the attention of the Legislature at the next session.

In conclusion, I desire, and hope I will not be considered presumptuous in doing so, to thank the citizens of Tallahassee, in the name of all the people of Florida, for the grand exhibition of their hospitality and patriotism shown on this occasion and I also desire to thank them for the many acts of kindness I have individually received at their hands.

Governor William S. Jennings
Term: 1901 - 1905

William Sherman Jennings (born March 24, 1863 – died February 27, 1920) was born in Illinois. He came to Florida in 1885, completed his law degree, and began his practice in Brooksville (Hernando County). Aside from his own talents, the distinguished looking Jennings had two important assets: he was married to the remarkable May Mann Jennings, the state's most prominent woman during the twentieth century's early decades, and secondly, he was a cousin of William Jennings Bryan who ran for president in 1896, 1900, and 1908, and was the most powerful politician in the Democratic party. Bryan himself moved to the Miami area and would participate in the land boom of the 1920s. After Jennings secured the Democratic nomination for governor in 1900, he faced Matthew B.

Macfarlane who represented the Republicans. McFarlane received 6,357 votes, which was considerably more than the 631 than A. B. Morton got as the candidate for the moribund Populists, but he could not overcome the Jennings's 29,251 (81 percent of the popular vote).

Because of its geography, Florida was widely affected by flood control and the issue of reclamation of flooded lands. Overflow was a danger to much of the state. Napoleon Bonaparte Broward, deservedly gets credit for the state's drainage of hundreds of thousands of acres near Miami. Yet, it was Governor Jennings who first established the state's claim to land for reclamation. He employed Fred G. Eliott of the US Department to Agriculture to survey and begin attacking the problem. Thus, Jennings merits a share of the credit for Florida's role in the Progressive Movement, a vast reform movement which swept across the land beginning about 1900. Progressivism included private institutions and every aspect of government. Jennings gave Florida a progressive voice and worked to utilize the state to protect it from unscrupulous land developers and railroad owners.

Inaugural Speech
(Source:Jacksonville *Florida Times-Union*, January 9, 1901)

Friends and Fellow-Citizens:

Before entering upon the duties of the first executive office of our State, to which I have been elected by the deliberate and tranquil suffrages of the electors of Florida, it is meet that I should avail myself of this occasion to express my gratitude to my fellow-citizens for so distinguished a mark of confidence. It is impossible to express this gratitude in mere words, and I can best reflect my sense of the honor and its obligations by pledging to the people of our State my most sincere purpose to perform the duties of the office of Governor of Florida with all the abilities that I possess, to the end that the people may enjoy the best possible administration of the laws of the State.

I recognize with pride the presence of the Florida State Troops, who have so generously enlisted and stand ready to defend the State and its citizenship and enforce the law, and I bespeak a liberal policy toward this organization, as well as to the Florida Naval Militia, during my administration. This great and growing State spreads over a territory greater than that of any other State east of the Mississippi River; its shores are washed by the great Gulf and the mighty Atlantic, with a coast line of nearly 1,200 miles, with navigable rivers aggregating over 1,000 miles; with the rich production of their industry; discovered four hundred years ago, it has been occupied by colonies from European countries at different times; it has been the scene of war and massacres and contention between Spanish, French, English and Americans, as well as terrible conflicts with the savage races which once inhabited it; a remnant of whom still remains within its southern borders. For more than 250 years the territory was in the grasp of a power far away; a monarch despotic and cruel; hence we find that the early history of Florida was not one of rapid and encouraging development.

In 1823 Congress established a Territorial government (the census of 1830 shows a population of 34,730), which continued until 1845, when Florida was admitted to Statehood. The census of 1840 shows a population of 54,477; that of 1850 a population of 87,445; that of 1860 a population of 141,424; that of 1870 a population of 189,995, at which time our beloved State was just emerging from the effects of a terrible war, without funds, and its population reduced to poverty, which condition was aggravated and made more desperate by the reckless bonding of the State, and the extravagant and wasteful expenditures of the people's money extorted by Republican Administrations, which condition was ended in 1876 by the election of a Democratic Chief Magistrate of Florida. Since then our State has grown and prospered in population and in wealth as but one other— Texas—has done. During the past three decades our population has increased from 189,995 to 528,543; our assessed valuations have increased from less than thirty millions to upwards of eighty-five millions, on the tax books, besides more than two hundred millions not on the tax books, with exports from fields, gardens, mines manufactures, forests, lakes, and rivers, amounting to millions of dollars annually.

Three thousand miles of railroads and great ports have been constructed, as monuments of our progress.

Our educational facilities have grown during this period to accommodate the enrolled scholarship of more than one hundred thousand students. Churches have been erected in every city and hamlet as monuments of the people's generosity and of the high civilization attained.

Much credit is due to my immediate predecessors, and it is proper that I should express the well-nigh universal sentiment of appreciation of their faithful performance of duty. We congratulate ourselves that Providence has given us wise, able and judicious Governors.

And to Governor Bloxham I express the sincere hope that after his retirement from the office of chief executive of Florida he may live long to enjoy the delightful memories that cluster thickly around his public life. His services, which have been pre-eminent, entitle him to the love, admiration and veneration of every Floridian.

With assumption of high responsibilities on this occasion, it might become me better to be silent. Yet, standing as we do on the threshold of a new century, closing the door of the old one, with the historian reveling in its wonderful achievements; opening the door of the new, the imagination can see a century whose possibilities are yet unparalleled in history, and we appreciate and realize that there are "other steps to climb"; we see the steps leading upward, but the topmost one is far beyond our view. We can but look up and press onward, striving as we go to do our whole duty to God and to our fellow man.

As some expression of purpose is expected of me on this occasion, I venture to express some views based on observation of a general character, with the hope that I shall be enabled to more specifically set forth my views in messages to the Legislature. In contemplating the exercise of duties, which comprehend every thing dear and valuable to the people of Florida, it is proper you should understand what I deem essential principles of our State government, and, consequently those that ought to shape its administration for you; retain the sovereign power and guard your rights with jealous care. Our declaration of rights, our fundamental law, declare that:

All men are equal before the law, and have certain inalienable rights, among which are those of enjoying and defending life and liberty, acquiring, possessing and protecting property, and pursuing happiness and obtaining safety; that all political power is inherent in the people

that

The right of trial by jury shall be secured to all, and remain inviolate forever; that all courts in this State shall be open, so that every person, for any injury done him in his lands, goods, person or reputation shall have remedy by due course of law, and right and justice shall be administered without sale, denial or delay.

These I deem essential principles of our State government. The judiciary is a subject I consider of first importance.

The platform adopted by the dominant party, assembled in State convention, "declares the present condition of the Supreme Court docket to be intolerable, the long delays in getting decisions amounting to practical denial of justice." The Supreme Court was established by the Constitution of 1845; no change was made in the Constitution of 1868, nor in the Constitution of 1885. The Supreme Court as first constituted is the Supreme Court of today. From 1845 to 1891—forty-six years—the court issued twenty-six volumes of reports, at which time (1891) the court was six and one-half years behind with its work. During the past nine years the court has issued sixteen volumes of reports, containing more matter than the former twenty-six volumes, and yet the court is five years behind with its work. That the people of Florida are entitled to the enforcement of this declaration of rights no one can deny; that this condition of the court's docket has been correctly stated we must admit; that the sixteen volumes issued by this court during the past nine years testify to the energetic efforts of the learned Justices, and should convince all reasonable men that it is impossible for these Judges to perform the duties devolving upon this court under the existing circumstances and our complex system of practice.

A comparison of the conditions, the wealth and population of Florida when this court was created with that of the population, development and wealth of today should appeal to the law-making power for its best thought and action, which I beg to urge to the end that a temporary commission may be created to adjudicate and dispose of certain cases to be allotted to it by the Justices, to enable the court to dispose of accumulated cases and clear the docket speedily; and to provide by constitutional amendment for the establishment of another division of the Supreme Court.

The Circuit Judges are likewise unable to perform the duties devolving upon their courts in several of the counties. These courts were established by the Constitution of 1868 and although our population has more than quadrupled and the business of these courts more than six times as great, we have the same number of Judges that we had in 1868. We have faithful, able, energetic Judges, but they cannot perform the duties of these courts. The criminal dockets in several of the counties require all the term period, thus depriving litigants on the civil side of their rights and leaving them without a remedy. These conditions demand correction, and must appeal to every patriotic legislator to provide a constitutional amendment creating additional circuits or judgeships. County Courts and Criminal Courts of Record have been established in several of the counties of the State from time to time, but as a rule they have been abolished. That these courts have been found unsatisfactory is evidence of a demand for a court of higher jurisdiction. Hence the greater necessity for a provision for additional circuits and circuit judges. It has occurred to me that perhaps the establishment of a county court in every county of the State, to be maintained at the expense of litigants by fees to be prescribed, would bring immediate partial relief, and the suggestion is submitted for investigation and consideration.

From the great increase in homicide and other cases of felony appearing on the dockets of our Circuit Courts, the time of the State's Attorney being required in court work, it appears to be impossible for a State's Attorney to acquaint himself with all the cases in a circuit and prepare for the prosecution as the interest of the State demands. The lawmakers having the power to bring about a correction of these evils, I suggest that the subject be investigated by them, with a view of providing by constitutional amendment for a State's

Attorney for each Senatorial district to be paid out of fees to be prescribed by law.

Section 1, Article 9, of the Constitution reads: "The Legislature shall provide for a uniform and equal rate of taxation, and shall prescribe such regulations as shall secure a just valuation of all property, both real and personal," exempted property excepted. This is a subject that has perplexed the most experienced minds from time immemorial, and will continue to do so while the subject lasts. It has been ascertained that under our present system of valuations, property in some counties is assessed at 90 per cent. of its value, while in other counties the assessment is as low as 20 per cent. of its value. In 1871, the Legislature created a State Board of Equalization to determine the relative value of the real estate in the different counties, resulting in a policy of local depression of valuations, which has placed our State in the awkward position of maintaining an uneven burden of government, and a higher rate of taxation than would have otherwise been required. That a remedy should be provided to relieve those who are bearing an unjust burden, and to provide for a uniform and equal rate of taxation, must be apparent. I am convinced that such is the wish and will of the people and suggest the creation of a State Board of Equalization, whose powers shall be prescribed by law.

I heartily approve the State Board of Health as constituted, and believe that our safely lies in our retaining supreme sanitary control.

Since the enactment of the law establishing our State Board of Health, the employment of a competent State Health Officer ten years ago, and the enforcement of the law, our State has been immune from yellow fever epidemics, save during the year 1899, when our State control was practically suspended by Federal authority. Our State being immune during the entire period of the operation of our State control, enabling our port cities to increase in population and in wealth during this period over 50 per cent and our State to increase under adverse circumstances more in population in the past decade than any other State in the Union, convinces me that we should sustain our health laws.

I am in favor of the most liberal support and development of the public school system, and contemplate with pride the record made in our State, and hope to see an advance commensurate with the necessities before us, extending, if necessary to the establishment of night schools in such places as are found advisable to meet a growing demand, and the adoption of the free school book system in each of the counties of the State.

These, and other important matters that I shall not undertake to further discuss on this occasion, I will submit to the people for consideration, discussion and action.

When I contemplate the magnitude of the duties that I am about to enter upon I shrink from the undertaking. Indeed, I should despair, if unaided I should be forced to assume all the great responsibilities that are part and parcel of the position.

But by the will and the wisdom of the people who have placed me here, I am surrounded by some of the ablest and most experienced statesmen of Florida, in whose good judgment I have an abiding faith.

And in addition to these, the presence of many whom I see here reminds me that in other high authorities provided by our Constitution, I shall find sources of wisdom, of virtue and of zeal on which to rely in all vicissitudes. To you, gentlemen, who are charged with the sovereign functions of legislation, and the other State and county officers, I look with confidence for that guidance and support necessary to maintain, as Jefferson says,

> A wise and frugal government which shall restrain one from injuring another; shall leave them otherwise free to regulate their own pursuit of industry and improvement; and shall not take from the mouth of labor the bread it has earned. This is the sum of good government, and this is necessary to close the circle of our felicities.

Assuring myself that under every difficulty the determined spirit and united councils of the State will be safeguards to its honor and essential interests, I repair to the post assigned me with no other discouragement than that which springs form my own inadequacy to its demands.

If an attachment to the Constitution and a conscientious determination to support it; if an equal and impartial regard for the rights, interests, honor and happiness of the whole people of Florida; if a love for knowledge and a wish to encourage schools, colleges, universities, and every institution for its attainment; if a veneration for religion among all classes of the people, not only for their good and the happiness of life in all its stages, and of society in all its forms, as a means of sustaining a better State government; if a love of equal rights to all and special privileges to none; a love of justice and humanity in its enforcement; if a desire to improve agriculture, commerce and manufacture; if an inflexible determination to maintain peace and to take care that our laws are faithfully executed; if an earnest endeavor to investigate every just cause and remove every colorable pretense of complaint; if a regard for a well-disciplined militia under competent officers and the control of civil authority; strict economy in public expenditures; the diffusion of information and the arraignment of all abuses at the bar of public reason; freedom of religion; freedom of the press; a liberal provision for our disabled soldiers and sailors; if an energetic support of the State and its institutions; if an unshaken confidence in the honor, spirit and resources of the people of Florida; if a perfect realization of the terrible losses that have fallen to the lot of those of our fellow-citizens that have sustained severe losses by freezes, storms, fires and failures; if a continuing sympathy with them in their brave and self-reliant efforts, many of whom were thrown from the couches of luxury into the lap of poverty, and yet have sustained themselves; if elevated ideas of the high destinies of this State and of my own duties toward it; if an humble reverence to that infinite power which rules the destinies of the States can enable me to comply with your wishes, it shall be my strenuous endeavor to perform the duties before me as directed by your will.

And may that Being who is supreme over all, the fountain of justice, the protector of liberty and dispenser of right continue his blessing upon this State and give it all possible success consistent with the ends of his providence.

Governor Napoleon B. Broward
Term: 1905 - 1909

Napoleon Bonaparte Broward (born April 19, 1857 - died October 1, 1910) was a flamboyant governor who is considered the prototype of a southern progressive. He was born on a Duval County farm and became the only governor who had also served as a sheriff. After losing his parents at the age of twelve, Broward worked variously as a logger, farm hand, seaman, steamboat roustabout, woodyard operator, gunrunner for Cuban revolutionaries, phosphate development, and owner of a steam tug. Georgiana Carolina "Carrie" Kempt, his wife, became his partner in operating steamboats on the Saint Johns River. Broward entered Jacksonville politics serving as a city commissioner, member of the Florida House of Representatives, and member of the Florida State Board of Health.

Bringing an honest sheriff's administration to Duval county, Broward won many local constituents. He used the sheriff's office to attract statewide attention especially with his attempt in 1894 to thwart the holding of a heavyweight champion fight in Jacksonville. The fight, won by heavyweight champion John L. Sullivan over the British challenger Henry Mitchell, was held in violation of a legislative statute. Broward became known as a defender of law and order. The energetic sheriff parlayed his fame into winning the governor's nomination. Broward had added to his reputation with his performance as a member of the house and senate and service on the Florida State Board of Health. With the aid of outgoing Governor William Sherman Jennings, he defeated a powerful group of Democratic rivals, and in the general election beat his Republican opponent, M. B. McFarlane, over four to one.

Broward's inaugural speech was a model of progressive idealism, and set the stage for what was to come. As governor, Broward continued the progressive record he had built in the legislature and as a member of the health board. He became known for his advocacy of trust regulation, Everglades drainage, aid to public education, and statewide prohibition (considered a part of the reform movement). His legacy included the creation of the Board of Control, the purpose of which was to coordinate the state's institutions of higher education. During his administration, the Buckman Act of 1905 reorganized and consolidated higher education in Florida, and, among other things, located Florida Agricultural and Mechanical College at Tallahassee. Broward's influence was so great that his term in office was later referred to as the "Broward Era". In 1907, two years after he took office and sixty-two years after Florida became a state, the Broward family moved into a states provided official Governor's Mansion at 700 North Adams Street, Tallahassee. While still governor, Broward ran unsuccessfully for the US Senate in 1908, but won the election in 1910. He died before he was able to serve.

Inagural Speech
(Source: Jacksonville *Florida Times-Union*, January 4, 1905)

My Fellow Citizens of Florida:

Chosen by the citizens of this great State to administer for a time the high office of Governor, profoundly grateful for the honor conferred and conscious to some degree, I trust, of the manifold duties and responsibilities imposed, I come in their name to enter upon their service. Thus made the central figure on this occasion by that interest which the people manifest in the one who is to fill the office of Chief Executive of their State, I am profoundly impressed by the confidence bestowed and deeply grateful, not only for this splendid proof of confidence in me but also sincerely appreciate the demonstration made on this occasion by the State troops of Florida here present, the visiting distinguished citizens and the gracious hospitality by the courteous people of the capital city.

Were it not for the fact that I am to be surrounded and aided by a patriotic and intelligent Cabinet and painstaking, wise and conscientious judiciary I would feel overawed by the responsibility that I am this day to assume. I fully recognize that to fill the position, the duties of which have been so ably discharged by the many illustrious Chief Executives of Florida in the past, who have done so much to make its people happy, law-abiding and prosperous, will require not only my own best efforts, but the united wisdom of the efficient Cabinet officers who are this day inducted into office with me. I here see about me those high authorities provided by the Constitution, in whom I shall find recourse to wisdom, virtue and zeal to put into effect all that is within our power for the good of the people. Under our Constitution, our officials are elected by a majority of the people, but let us all bear in mind the sacred principle that though the will of the majority is in all cases to prevail, in order to be just we must recognize that the minority possess their equal rights which equal law must protect, and to violate would be oppression. Then, fellow-citizens, united with one heart and mind, working for the good of all, let us extend the right hand of fellowship to all honest, liberty-loving people who desire to make their homes among us, and offer to them the opportunity of participating in all of the privileges vouchsafed to any of us.

It is not my purpose to, on this occasion, specifically make reference to all the policies of this administration, but merely at this time to refer to some of the most important in a general way.

Governments are created by the people for the protection and benefit of the people who created them and those who are to come after them. How to keep a Government in touch with the people at all times, has been the burden of the most devoted statesmen of our country. How to make the Government do that work which is best for the great majority of the people is the work that we have to do, as the tendency of most Governments of the world is to drift away from the people and to develop into a machine that oppresses them.

The primary system was inaugurated in this State for the purpose of destroying this growing evil. In my judgment it tends to do that as it brings the people and the Government nearer together, and makes government indeed the act of the people. It deepens the gratitude of the chosen official to feel that he has received his honor and his trust directly from the body of the sovereign people, and that to them individually, as well as collectively, he is responsible for the faithful and conscientious discharge of his every duty.

The success of the system impresses on my mind a firmer belief that our future depends upon the untrammeled expression of the voice of the people themselves. It can scarcely be doubted that the light now gained by its practical operation will enable the law-making body without difficulty to remove from statute whatever defects may yet remain.

Appreciating as I do the suffrages of this free and enlightened people, I also appreciate the fact that I was nominated in a primary election, in which almost all of the white people of Florida participated, that each of those running for this high office, as candidates before the people for a nomination, made declarations of principles and submitted them to the people, declaring that if elected he would carry out the principles as set forth by him. The sovereign people of this State elected me, and as I declared that I would carry out, if elected, those principles of policies advocated by me in the primaries, I believe it proper for me to mention them briefly at this time. Although the fiat of the people of Florida has gone forth proclaiming me the Chief Executive of the State of Florida, nothing on their part remaining to be done, some of our people conscious of the fact that men do not always make any great effort to carry out the principles and policies after election that they advocated to obtain election, may suspect avoidance on my part of the work necessary to effectuate the results that were advocated by me. Therefore, I feel that it is proper on this occasion to reiterate the pledge made by me to the people, which, in brief, are as follows:

> That I favor the primary election system, that I believe it to be on trial, that I will oppose to the utmost of my ability any measure to weaken or repeal this law, unless it has first been submitted to a vote of the people and received their approval, and I further pledge the people that I will do my utmost to strengthen and perfect the system, and that I will cheerfully approve any bill tending in that direction.

In recent years Florida has made rapid advance in material progress and prosperity, but in my judgment, she has only fairly begun to enjoy the rich heritage justly hers by reason of vast resources in field and grove, factory and mine. I believe that no agency has had more to do with this progress and prosperity than the wise and conservative administration of our Railroad Commission laws, I believe that the department of State institutions should give every encouragement to the development and construction of transportation lines, and thereby facilitate and cheapen transportation, an achievement working both for the benefit of the people in affording a larger and readier market for the numerous products of field, farm and grove, as well as to the transportation companies, in the increased amount of business that they will handle. In my canvass of this State, I put myself upon record as being in favor of doing all within my power as Governor to strengthen and protect the laws creating the Railroad Commission, I also promised to recommend to the Legislature that a resolution amending the Constitution, so as to make the Railroad Commission a constitutional part of the Government, be passed.

I also declared that a good education was the most valuable heritage that we could leave our children, and, therefore, I believed in a longer school term for children attending our free schools, and that I favored large appropriations for our colleges. Few States have been more liberal in recent years than ours in the matter of education. Not only have we an excellent public school system, but also well equipped and endowed higher institutions of learning supported at public expense, and it is now inexcusable that the children of our State should grow up in ignorance.

Our Government is the outgrowth of public opinion. This Government was established by and must be administered for the good of the people regardless of personal and local surroundings. The policy of the Government is your creation and your dictates must be obeyed. It cannot be perfect, but it will be just what its citizens make it. Its excellencies and efficiency of those you elect to administer its affairs will always depend upon the virtue and good sense of the people who make it and uphold it. This emphasizes the importance of education and of a general interest of affairs of States. Our continued success, our prosperity, our power rests on the intelligence of the people. The common school is the cornerstone of our political structure. If we have a state Government intelligently administered, we must educate our children that they may be able to understandingly consider all questions of public interest with broad and enlightened views. From the doors of our common schools must come our officials, our lawmakers, our businessmen, our farmers and all who help to build up and maintain the State, consequently, I shall do all that I have the power to do to uphold and extend the common school system. I do not wish to be understood as opposing "higher education"; on the contrary, I believe in colleges and universities and the many advantages they confer, but the great mass of the youth cannot hope for the advantages of a college education, and it is upon this great majority, that the hope of success under our form of government always has and always must rest.

It is not now my purpose to do more than attempt to impress upon your mind the importance of general education, of the development of higher ambitions and of broad and liberal views on each and every subject in every walk of life. The man who has advanced to the period that I have feels more keenly than those of fewer years the lack of what the youth of today have at their command, and the increasing advantages that the youth of tomorrow will enjoy. Thus can public opinion be best enforced in government. Therefore, this public opinion should be enlightened and the youth of the State educated by the State to the fullest extent possible. It was Washington who said: "In proportion as the structure of a Government gives to public opinion it is essential that public opinion should be enlightened."

I also declare that the patriotic service and self-sacrifice of our soldiers and sailors in the Civil War should guarantee to the needy ones of their widows such reasonable pensions as an appreciative people are over ready to pay. We can see the remnant of that army returning, battle scarred, dust covered and poorly clad, overwhelmed by force of numbers. Their homes destroyed, conditions under which to make a living for their brave mothers, wives and sisters changed, yet they did not falter, but took up the battle for bread under these changed conditions and have caused a country so developed that it is the envy of the world.

I also declared that the manifest patriotism of our Florida State troops and Florida Naval Militia should be encouraged by the most liberal support commensurate with a reasonably economical administration of our State government. We must all grant that in reliance on the self-sacrificing patriotism of our State militia depends the safety of our institutions in times of trouble.

I also declared that I would favor the passage of such laws as would best tend to the improvement of our system of public roads, hard surface or otherwise, as may be most practicable, and I believe that a system of good roads in every county would contribute more to the prosperity, comfort, and enjoyment of the people than any other one improvement that is now engaging the attention of the public.

I also declared that I would, so far as it was in my power, protect the people in the ownership of their public lands, that I believed that the Everglades of Florida, or as much of them as possible should be drained and made fit for cultivation, as it is the most productive land in Florida should it once be protected against overflow by proper canals. The State owns in the Everglades several million acres of unreclaimed lands as fertile as any in the world. It is my hope and purpose to secure their reclamation and convert what is now unsurveyed waste land into a State asset more valuable than all the lands now under cultivation within her borders.

All of these pledges I again renew to the people, and I promise them that I will do my best to make good these pledges.

As some of our laws, if not universally favored, are at least conceded to be a part of our government system, so others are opposed or upheld according to environment and interest. A citizen should not violate any law. The Executive should enforce all laws, and this is shall be my purpose to do in order that the enjoyment of life, liberty, and property may be secure to all. I, therefore, earnestly solicit the cooperation of all our people in the enforcement of the law. No one citizen can expect to enjoy the blessings vouchsafed to him by the Bill of Rights, or that part even which pledged the nation to protect every individual in the employment of life, liberty and the pursuit of happiness, unless the law be equally enforced. To this end I ask the generous aid of the fair-minded people of Florida—for with their aid much can be accomplished—and I do this with confidence, as the people of Florida have never yet deserted a public servant honestly striving to execute a trust they had reposed in him.

I can never forget, and I certainly shall not ignore the many kind and loyal friends throughout the State, to whom I owe my nomination and election. I should be unworthy of your confidence if I could forget these friends, but I should be equally unworthy of that confidence if I could, in this devotion of my friends forget or neglect the interests of the whole people, whose servant I am and must be until I hand over to my successor the Great Seal of the State and relinquish to him the high trusts you have confided to my care.

We look back upon the achievements of our predecessors and our hearts beat with pride. Let us look forward and hope for even greater achievements in the near future. Is this an unreasonable hope? I think not. We have the recorded worth of our predecessors before us, may we not hope to profit by their experience, thereby achieving more in the future?

Finally, I wish to congratulate the people of this State upon the most excellent condition of all the administrative departments of

State government. Her finances are in a most creditable condition and she has no floating debt. Too much credit cannot be given to the most efficient and capable Governor whom I am about to succeed in this office. So faithfully and wisely have the administration of the various departments been affected, that the people are on the whole happy, contented, prosperous and law-abiding.

Indeed, we possess a great State. With a surface area of thirty-five million acres, bounded on the south, east and west by eleven hundred miles of seacoast, that if unwound and turned south and east, then north, would lap the gulf of St. Lawrence, this entire stretch of seacoast, besides many inlets, bays and rivers abounding with fish, oysters, and sponges. The fish, oyster and sponge business may be developed in value to our people many times their present proportions, which even now are not at all insignificant.

I find that reports obtained by our statistical department, for the year 1903 show that the number of men engaged in the fish business is 9,116; number of vessels and boats engaged, 4,318; value of vessels and apparatus, $553,890l; cash capital invested, $608,000; total value of investment, $1,160,890; fish caught of all kinds, exclusive of home consumption, 61,136,795 pounds; value of above, $1,414,314.

Besides this, we have oyster beds more extensive than are to be found in any half dozen States of the Union. This industry is in its infancy, and the same report shows that in 1903 there were caught and sold 888,656 bushels, valued at $161,296; this is exclusive of home consumption, as well as the many thousand wagon loads annually caught and hauled into Georgia from our Gulf coast.

From this same report we find that the quantity of sponges caught for 1903 was 365,899 pounds, of the value of $367,450. So it is seen that there is at present, derived from the sale of fish, oysters, and sponges for that year in round numbers, $2,000,000.

There are under cultivation in this State less than one million acres of land. From reports obtained by our Agricultural Department we find for the year 1903, the follow values:

Value of farm products, $11,800,064; value of vegetable and garden products, $2,400,368; value of fruit crops, $4,187,280; value of livestock, $10,382,368; value of poultry, $350,485; value of dairy products, $1,036,115; value of miscellaneous products, $127,674; total value of agricultural products, $30,904,365.

Our commerce for the year 1903, combining these items with lumber, naval stores, phosphate and other items, so far as reported, amounted to $99,840,000.

We have millions of acres of fertile lands in Florida that will produce crops of great value long after our forests have become things of the past, besides that vast acreage of the most fertile lands in the world, to be drained and reclaimed for our people. I refer to the overflowed lands of the Everglades and Lake Okeechobee, where there are several million acres of land especially adapted for the cultivation of sugarcane. There is now imported into the United States annually, 2,400,000 tons of sugar upon which duty is paid. With the best climatic conditions to be found in the United States, and this vast amount of fertile lands so fully suitable for its cultivation, from this one crop alone, there could be produced every pound of sugar imported in this country, at a value to the producers of this State of $300,000,000 annually.

Besides our extensive and rapidly growing system of railway transportation, there is in this State, approximately, 3,000 miles of navigable waters, by the improvements of which, our transportation facilities may be vastly increased and benefited.

From a view of the figures shown by this partial date, it is seen that Florida is a State of great natural resources, which only await our development. Let us enter upon this great work without delay, and carry it to a successful conclusion.

I cannot do better than close with the words of the immortal Jefferson—"I shall often go wrong through defect of judgment. When right I shall often be thought wrong by those whose position will not command a view of the whole ground. I ask your indulgence for my errors, which will never be intentional, and your support against the errors of others, who may condemn what they would not if seen in all its parts. The approbation implied by your suffrage is a great consolation to me, and my future solicitude will be to retain the good opinion of those who have bestowed it in advance, to conciliate that of others by doing them all the good in my power, and to be instrumental to the happiness and freedom of all."

Relying, then, on the patronage of your good will, I advance with obedience to the work before me, and may that Infinite Power which rules the destinies of the universe lead our councils to what is best and give them a favorable issue for your peace and prosperity.

Governor Albert W. Gilchrist
Term: 1909 - 1913

Albert Waller Gilchrist (born January 15, 1858 – died May 15, 1926) was born in Greenwood, South Carolina, and was descended from families directly related to George Washington and James Madison. He graduated from Carolina Military Institute and was a member of the US Military Academy at West Point (class of 1882), although he did not graduate, failing to pass experimental philosophy. Years later he returned to West Point as a member of the Board of Visitors. Among his civilian activities Gilchrist was a civil engineer, dealt in real estate, and grew oranges at Punta Gorda. As a military man, he was appointed Inspector General of the Militia and was made a brigadier general of the Florida military. In 1898 he gave up the rank to enlist as a private in the Third Volunteer Infantry. He served in Cuba during the Spanish-American War and rose to the rank of captain.

Returning to Puna Gorda, Gilchrist became a house member from DeSoto County for the 1893-1895 session and returned to serve from 1902-1905, and was house speaker. He became well versed in the workings of state government. In the governor's race of 1908 Gilchrist campaigned on a middle of the road platform and easily defeated his Republican opponent, John M. Cheney, and the Socialist candidate, A.J. Pettigrew.

As governor he lacked the personal flair of Broward and had no desire to alter radically Florida's politics, declining to engage in controversial ventures. Even so, the bachelor governor (Mrs. J. B. Gibbs, his mother, acted as his official hostess) was intelligent, creative, and charming. He proved indefatigable as a promoter and advertiser for Florida, traveling extensively to carry out that mission. While not in the front rank of progressive governors, Gilchrist was a far cry from arch conservatives who still promoted old Bourbon programs. He took the lead in promoting health programs for citizens and approved legislation to improve Florida livestock.

Inaugural Speech
(Source: Jacksonville *Florida Times-Union*, January 6, 1909)

Ladies and Gentlemen:

The great distinction conferred on me by the people in electing me governor of Florida is highly appreciated. Some one will say that the "great honor" is highly appreciated. It has long since been learned that "Honor and shame from no condition rise, act, well your part, there all honor lies." The French put it "Noblesse oblige." meaning nobility imposes obligations. The position of governor imposes the obligation of being true to all the people in the state and to all the industries in the state. It requires labor and attention and executive ability, to manage successfully the affairs of any business, of any nature whatever. Much more labor, and attention, and executive ability is required in the executive office of a great and growing state like ours.

One might shrink from assuming the obligation if he were not mindful of the fact that they were not thrust upon him. It has been said that some men are born great, some achieve greatness, and some have greatness thrust upon them. The office of governor was not born to me; the office of governor was not thrust upon me; the office of governor was just wanted by me and the people gave it to me; that's all. Besides, governors of this and other states have assumed these obligations and are still alive. There are gentlemen who would like to assume these obligations and they still live. It is therefore natural for me to think these obligations can well be assumed by myself. Besides, the governor is far from being the whole thing. There will be associated with me experienced gentlemen who have filled various offices. Like myself, they have at heart the best interests of the people.

Your attention is invited to the fact that in many states the governor is inaugurated coincident with the assembling of the legislature. His remarks at the inaugural partake largely of the nature of a message to the legislature. In our state, the constitution provides for the inauguration on the first Tuesday after the first Monday in January, being three months prior to the convening of the legislature, on the first Tuesday after the first Monday in April. This is a wise provision as it gives the governor an opportunity to become better posted as to his specific recommendations.

No one unless he has been governor or has been elected governor can possibly imagine the great diversity of opinions, and the diversity of subjects on which the diversified opinions are expressed. Riding on trains, in letters, in every and from every portion of the state come some expressions on numerous subjects. A governor is fortunate in having obtained these various expressions. They manifest, however, an absolute impossibility of any one carrying out the many divergent views expressed.

But a few of the subjects will be touched upon.

Many are specially interested in good roads. Everybody should favor good roads. They would all favor them if they did not cost money. The following data, completed from information obtained from the clerk of the circuit courts of the various counties will convey some idea of the interest taken in good roads by the people of some of the counties:

Counties	Miles Graded Road	Miles Clayed Road	Miles Hard Road
Alachua	.....	.....	.....
Baker	None	None	None
Bradford	50	None	None
Brevard	.....	.....	.....
Calhoun	None	None	None
Citrus	None	None	6
Clay	None	None	6
Columbia	.....	.....	.....
Dade	None	None	203
DeSoto	286	None	18
Duval	.....	.....	.....
Escambia	115	None	85
Franklin	None	None	None
Gadsden	None	100	None
Hamilton	18	None	None
Hernando	.....	.....	.....
Hillsborough	None	None	None
Holmes	.....	.....	.....
Jackson	None	None	None
Jefferson	None	None	None
Lafayette	.....	.....	.....
Lake	None	60	88
Lee	13	None	30
Leon	.....	.....	.....
Levy	None	None	4
Liberty	.....	.....	.....
Madison	22	8	20 or 25
Manatee	......	......	......
Monroe	None	None	4
Marion	None	50	450
Nassau	None	None	15

Orange	300	**135	None
Osceola	30	6	None
Pasco	.....	.....	.....
Polk	None	150	None
Putnam	10	12	13
St. Johns	.....	.....	.....
St. Lucie	.....	.....	.....
Santa Rosa	100	40	None
Sumter	.....	20	*5
Suwannee	.....	.....	.....
Taylor	None	None	None
Volusia	None	C25	B60
Wakulla	None	None	None
Walton	None	1-3/4	None
Washington	None	None	None
n			

None - *indicates miles strawed: **clay or marl; a, rock; b, shell; c, pine straw.

Some clerks failed to respond to the letter sent to them. This information proves that many of our counties are interested in good roads and are willing to pay for them. It shows that these counties would hardly consider it just to pay state taxes to build state roads through other counties.

Whilst speaking en the subject of roads, it might be well to refer to the convict question. You know that of our people would like for the state convicts to be worked on the roads. On account of recent action of the Georgia legislature, the county commissioners of some of the Georgia counties met, with the view of determining how many state convicts could be used by their respective counties, in building good roads. Our state is very responsive to any action taken by our great neighboring state. This is due to proximity, and, among other reasons, to the fact that so many of our good citizens come from Georgia. Some think that in using the convicts on the roads, the work will be done for nothing. They forget that in so doing the county loses its part of the hire of the convicts and will in addition pay its cost of maintenance of the convicts. There is another reason, humanitarian, which would operate against the use of long term convicts, in the temporary camps afforded by the counties. The convicts camps are now fitted up with iron beds, springs, mattresses, blankets, pillows and sheets, baths, and sanitary arrangements, and comfortable houses. The Hon. B.E. McLin, commissioner of agriculture, has kindly furnished me the following information: The number of state prisoners handled during the year 1907 was 1,736. The number of women handled during the year was 43. Of this number of women prisoners, there are three white women, for both the years 1907 and 1908. They are at the headquarters hospital, two being at Quincy and one at Ocala. The report about white women state convicts being sent out indiscriminately with Negro prisoners is therefore a mistake. Of the total number of prisoners handled, during 1907, there were twenty-nine deaths. Of these, five were killed in attempting to escape, one was killed by a falling wall; twenty-three died natural deaths. It thus appears that 1.13 per cent or 13.35 in every thousand died from natural causes. In most cases the prisoners died from the effect of diseases contracted prior co entering the state prison. This death rate is less than what it is in some insurance companies, in which, of course, they pick their members. United States census for 1900, vol. 3, page 56, registration area U.S., being that part in which the statistics are based upon registration records, death , rate is 17.8 per 1,000. The registration area embraces the New England states. New York, New Jersey, Michigan, and the District of Columbia. In the registration area, as a whole, the death rate of the native white is about 13 per 1,000 and that of the foreign white about 10 per 1,000, 13 less than that of the colored. Then considered that a large per cent of the prisoners are colored, and that the death rate from natural causes is only 13.25 per 1,000.

With the inconveniences necessarily incident to the camps used by counties in building roads, there would be no such small, death rate. Humanity would prevent long term convicts from being used permanently in temporary camps. On page 30 of the admirable report of the commissioner of agriculture for the years 1906 and 1905, the commissioner invites attention to the fact that "we stand solitary and alone in trading women, black and white, for a monied consideration" and "we again stand alone among the states in leasing the aged, the decrepit, and the young."

The commissioner recommends that some provision be made for the detention of the women and the infirm on some farm, owned by the state. It is to be hoped that his recommendation may sooner or later prevail. Attention is invited more particularly to the convict question, because it is liable to be a subject of legislative action at the coming session. As before mentioned our state is very responsive to any action taken by our neighboring great state of Georgia. This state having recently acted on this subject, many Floridians think that it will necessarily be a subject of legislative enactment by our own state. It is to be hoped that the various newspaper men of the state will read the able report of the commissioner of agriculture for the years 1905-06, or as much, at least, as concerns the subject of convicts. In discussing the subject, they ought to make a distinction between the state system and the county system, as regards the management of convicts. There are many humanitarians and sentimentalists who know very little about the material facts on which their humanitarian sentiments and their sentimental humanitarianism is based. The convicts are prisoners sentenced to hard labor as a punishment, yet they are wards of the state and are human beings. There is not a member of the board who is not anxious to have them properly treated. It is desirable that every member of the next legislature and at least some of the newspaper men, and other public spirited citizens visit the convict camps within their respective counties. While a member of the legislature, such an examination was not made by myself. The natural assumption is that many other legislators will fail to make such examinations unless his attention is especially invited to the same. It is my intention to follow my own advice by citing some of the camps, prior to the convening of the next legislature.

The attorney general is now a member of the board of pardons. It might be well to relieve him of the duties so that he could represent the state, in cases of parties seeking pardons before the board. In some cases the States Attorney should appear before the board.

Notice is hereby given, with all possible emphasis, that no person need apply for pardon who has been convicted of any degree or form of robbing the public. Stealing from individuals is reprehensible enough, but stealing from the public by officials, high or low, will, under no circumstances be tolerated or pardoned.

In our courts the technicalities of "due process of law" often prevail over the justice and real merits of the case at issue.

Much has been said about the state is "honor bound" to drain the Everglades. Florida received these lands under the act of Congress, by which other states received theirs. Our neighboring state of Alabama gave hers to her insane asylum. Iowa gave hers to her counties. California sold hers. It is unknown to me if the officers of any other state have taken the position of "in honor bound." The matter of the drainage of the lands of the state is simply a business proposition, to be executed as the conditions warrant. In this connection, there should be considered section 4, article xii, of the State constitution, "twenty five per cent of the sales of all public lands now owned by the state, or may be hereafter owned by the state, shall constitute a part of the state school fund, the interest of which shall be exclusively applied to the support and maintenance of public free schools." Recurring to the drainage question, several years since the trustees of the internal improvement fund agreed to give an acre for every 25 cents expended in drainage—2,000,000 acres were set aside. Of this, 1,652,712 acres were deeded to the Atlantic Gulf Coast Canal and Okeechobee Land Company. The assignees of this company sued for the remainder, 347,288 acres. The trustees of the internal improvement fund have advantageously settled this claim. How much land was actually drained is unknown. The lands in the Everglades have recently been sold generally at $1.25 to $2.00 per acre. The trustees now hold a little over 2,000,000 acres—about 90 per cent of which is in the Everglades. How much it will cost to drain them is unknown. This entire matter is simply a business proposition. The State Superintendent, Hon. W.M. Holloway, informs me that $8,324.94 was paid to the school fund in November, 1908, on account of the constitutional provision of 25 per cent on all sales of public lands. This is the first and last payment on such account. How much is due the school fund on such account will require Investigation.

The recent administration has settled some compromises as to legal suits brought against the internal improvement fund. The trustees made a good compromise and for the best interest of the state.

Eight or nine months since one of the dredges operating near Fort Lauderdale was visited by myself. The land through which one of the canals is being cut was examined. The quality of the remaining lands of the Everglades is unknown to myself. The land on this canal as far as it was then cut, about one and a half miles, will surely produce. They can be cleared for $2 to $3 per acre. Other lands cost to clear $25, $50 to $100 per acre. If the reclaimed lands will produce only vegetables, the present markets could be overstocked. Their productiveness would be limited to a limited market. If the lands will successfully produce sugar as many believe, their value or productiveness will be greatly increased. In that event their reclamation would lead to the first double tracking of a railroad in Florida, the East Coast system.

The most of our people are deeply interested in the advancement of our schools and in the education of our people. The United States, census for 1900 shows that the illiterates of the states are rapidly decreasing. To the total population, the per cent of the illiterates in Florida was for 1880, 43.4: for 1890, 27.8: for 1900, 21.9. This compares favorably with the percentage of illiteracy in the following southern states for 1900: In Georgia 30.5, South Carolina, 35.9, North Carolina 28.7, Virginia 22.9, Alabama 34.0, Mississippi 32.0, Louisiana 38.5. The illiterate native white population of Florida shows a great decrease for 1890, the illiteracy was 20.7 per cent. This compares favorably with the illiterate native white of the above mentioned states: for the year 1900, Georgia 11.9, South Carolina 13.6, North Carolina 19.5, Virginia 11.1, Alabama 14.8, Mississippi 8.0, Louisiana 17.3. The percentage of the illiteracy for the negro population for 1900 shows favorably also: for Florida 38.4 per cent, for Georgia 52.4, South Carolina 52.8, North Carolina 47.6, Virginia 44.6, Alabama 57.4, Mississippi 49.1, Louisiana 61.14. There is no state in the Union in which more money, in proportion to the taxable property, is collected for school purposes than in our state. There is the one-mill tax for the public schools, the state appropriations for the higher institutions of learning, and the state appropriation for the high schools. Then there is the one dollar capitation tax, all of which goes to the free schools. Then the constitution provides that no county shall assess less than three or more than seven mills for free schools. This was limited to five mills, until an amendment to the constitution raised it to seven. It also provides for school sub-districts, in which a special tax of not more than three mills may be levied. In many counties, these school sub-districts embrace the entire county. In addition to the foregoing, there is the "net proceeds of all fines collected under the penal laws of the state" and the interest on the state school fund. All this would represent a millage of between eleven and twelve mills, in many of the counties of the state for educational purposes. There is no people in the world who so willingly assess themselves for school purposes as they do in Florida. There has been quoted statistics showing that beneficial results are being obtained.

We have, as other states, two races, the white and colored. Weverever thrown in any number with other races the white race rules. A handful of our forefathers thought it was right to rule the country, when it was owned by the "noble red, man." A handful govern South Africa. A handful govern the teeming millions of India. We are mighty apt to govern this country. Whilst governing it we are under obligations to "be fair" and to be just. In our state, the relationship between the two races is harmonious. It is to be hoped that it will continue. There is a cement of kindliness between the two races which may be best understood from the following extract from a letter recently received by myself: "When I tell you that my father and mother were the slaves of your father and mother in the days of slavery, you can readily see why I take the liberty of addressing this humble epistle to you. For there is a tie, unseen and inexpressible between the master and the slave that death only can sever. My father and mother are still alive, and enjoy the high hope of seeing you when you take your seat at Tallahassee. From the time they heard that you were running for governor of the state of Florida, they prayed for you, asking God to give you the victory. And when they heard that you had been successful, they wept, laughed and shouted, so full was their joy that their young master was governor of the state of Florida. I advocated your cause fearlessly through my paper, and thank God that you have been elected."

In this connection occurs the suggestion that the three greatest men whom the greatest nation on earth has produced are George Washington, Robert E. Lee and Abraham Lincoln. The anniversaries of the birthday of Washington and Lee have been by legislative enactment made legal holidays. It is high time for our state to recognize the patriotism and true greatness of Abraham Lincoln by declaring February 12, the anniversary of his birth, a legal holiday.

Nothing illustrates the growth of the state more than is shown by the United States census of 1900 as relates in increase of population. From 1890 to 1900 this census shows the following increase: Florida 35 per cent, Georgia 20.6 per cent, South. Carolina 16.4 per cent, North Carolina 17.4 per cent, Virginia 12.0 per cent, Alabama 20.8 per cent, Mississippi 20.3 per cent, Louisiana 23.5 per cent. The percentage of increase for these states has been quoted because references have been made to them for other comparison. No other states have shown a greater increase of percentage in population, except North Dakota, Wyoming, Idaho, Oklahoma, Washington, and Texas. The latter state, Texas, shows an increase of 36.4 per cent, as against 35 per cent for Florida.

Our state has made great growth in transportation facilities, in commerce, in manufactures, horticulture, in the products of the field, the farm, the forest and of the mine. But a few years since we mined nothing. Now we mine more than one-half of the phosphate of the United States and more than one-third of the phosphate of the world. We mine Fuller's earth and clay for fine pottery. There is nothing like being a prophet or the son of a prophet: we will yet be one of the great oil producing states.

We are living in an age of great progress. Men are beginning to understand some of the forces with which the earth was made and are beginning to know how to handle these forces. In this latest period in the development of man, one of the great engineering feats of the world is now being completed within the borders of our own state. The binding of the island of Key West to the mainland with bars of steel, and cementing it to the continent with arches of masonry. Such great works can only be accomplished through aggregations of capital and combinations of men. The natural man dies. The artificial man known as the corporation lives on. The natural and artificial man are both necessary. Both have certain rights. Both have certain duties Neither should be allowed to suppress the other. Shakespeare says: "It is nice to have a saint's strength, but it is villainous to use it as a giant." The state has a giant's strength, the corporations have a giant's strength. It would be villainous for the state to use its strength as a giant against the corporations. It would be villainous for the corporations to use their strength as a giant against the people. The corporations should be regulated but should not be regulated out of their boots.

Many of our people advocate changes, all of which cost money, yet they all want a reduction of taxation.

My observation has been that at the beginning of the session the newspapers say, "Behold the brightest and smartest set of legislators ever assembled in Tallahassee." Towards the end of the session the same sea of men, who could not possibly enact with laws all the various projects proposed, and who would bankrupt the state if they did, are usually, according to these same papers, about the worst set of men ever assembled. In spite of all this, legislatures are elected, and are convened, governors are elected and are inaugurated. In each case there is usually but the satisfaction of having done the best you could. In many instances, those with whom you do not agree can see the good in you. Happy is the man in either case who feels that he has done the best the circumstances allowed. It has been said, "Angels could do no more."

Suggestions will be gladly received from anyone, from the humblest to the most pretentious, always reserving to myself to do as it seems just and proper to be done.

The people have selected me governor of Florida, without my having made any promises, as to say special policy, other than what is embodied in the platform published in the campaign and in the various speeches made during the same. It would be my wish for the public to know of every move made by the administration. There should be no secrets as between the administrators and the people. There should be no greater policy for any governor to have than his administration should be run on business principles, free from graft and free from personal glorification. Although no claim is made as to being stronger than the generality of men, yet strength is hoped for to be good enough, strong enough and true enough to perform my duties without thought of personal gain or future political preferment.

The welfare of the people or the state should mark the lines of whatever power is given a governor. The very channels in which the governor moves should be bounded by the constitution and the laws. The beacon light should be the best brightest of the people at large.

In the filling of vacancies in office, the recommendations of the primaries will be respected. Where no primary elections are held, the filing of vacancies in county offices will be referred to the Democratic executive committees of the respective counties. Whether the officers recommended are friends of mine, or belong to the same political party, is of small moment. They should be competent, sober, and honest.

Permit me to say to the people of Tallahassee and Leon county that the royal manner in which you supported me, at the trying moment, is highly gratifying. It makes me feel as though you really wanted me to live with you for four years. On my part this feeling is surely reciprocal. My infancy, boyhood, and childhood days were spent in the neighboring city of Quincy, amid the grand oaks, the strong, true hickories, the sturdy pines and the sweet magnolias of middle Florida. Middle Florida is associated with many delightful recollections. It is also associated with privations and hardships, which undoubtedly did me good. Many a pleasant moment has been spent by me in old Tallahassee, pleasure from pleasant associations with pleasant people and pleasure from the pleasure derived from hard work. Any state would be fortunate in having at its capital such cultured and highclass citizens. Profound gratitude is felt toward the people of this city and vicinity for the many courtesies and attentions shown me.

The attendance of some of the state troops adds much to the interest of the occasion. But few of our people realize the real value to the state in simply having well organized state troops. The mere knowledge of there being such organizations acts often as a conservative force in preventing riots and bloodshed. The state troops are of inestimable value to the state.

The presence of so many of our fellow citizens from various parts of the state is exceeding gratifying.

"It is a thing of beauty and a joy forever" to see so many ladies present. It is to be hoped that their good wishes and the good wishes of their husbands, their fathers, their uncles, and their cousins will always attend me. With the women on my side, success will surely be with me.

Much has been said about being a bachelor governor. The Pensacola *Journal* comes to the rescue saying: "A bachelor governor: Good thing. He will look after the affairs of state and will not be worried looking after any other state of affairs."

Although a bachelor governor, yet if the men are as easy to please as some of the women are with their governors, you will find me the best governor Florida has ever had.

Now ladies and fellow citizens my sincere and heartfelt thanks are extended to you one and all. May we all strive to do our duty as best we can, "Heart within and God overhead."

Governor Park M. Trammell
Term: 1913 - 1917

Park Trammell (born April 9, 1876 – died May 8, 1936) was born in Macon County, Alabama. As a small child he moved with his family to Florida, and attended grade school in Polk County. Coming up, Trammell worked on the farm and for a newspaper. He served in the quartermaster service at Tampa during the Spanish-American War. After studying law at Vanderbilt in Nashville and graduating from the Cumberland Law School in Tennessee, Trammell began his law practice in Lakeland. He also became a citrus grower and returned to journalism by becoming a newspaper owner-editor.

He served two terms as mayor of Lakeland and, coming up through the Democratic ranks, was elected to the Florida House of Representatives from Polk County, and in 1905 he was president of the Florida Senate. He adapted well to state politics, being elected Attorney General in 1908 and governor in 1912.

The presidential race in 1912 drew most of the state's attention because it marked the return of the Democrats to the White House for the first time since Grover Cleveland in 1892 and the election of a southerner: Woodrow Wilson. Florida's Republican party, small in number and lacking unity, became even more factionalized in 1912 as the party's black voters formed two groups and opposed the mainstream white Republicans who supported the reelection of William Howard Taft. The dissenters were among those who formed the Progressive party that nominated former Republican president Theodore Roosevelt. When Roosevelt recognized his white Republican supporters, some of the African-American Florida dissenters even supported Wilson. Trammell's election was so overwhelming that his 38,977 votes dwarfed the 3,467 votes that went to the Socialist candidate Thomas W. Cox. Republicans had fallen on such bad times that William R. O'Neal, their nominee, got only 2, 646 which was 1,221 fewer votes than the Socialist.

As governor, Trammell spearheaded the successful enactment of a law regulating campaign spending. He also obtained the creation of a State Tax Commission, a body that equalized property assessments among the state's counties. His program as governor reflected the best parts of both the Populists and the Progressives' programs. He advocated such constructive policies as repealing the railroad land grant law, abolishing the convict lease system, and he favored a graduated tax on inheritances and corporate profits, strengthening the railroad commission, providing for absentee voting, and introducing the initiative referendum, and recall of elected officials. Other measures that had his backing were the passage of progressive banking laws, establishing a state agricultural station in the Everglades, taking official action to eradicate cattle ticks, and encouraging home building with a tax exemption law. Under Trammell, Florida got a law establishing a State Highway Commission. Trammell was elected to the US Senate in 1916, and retained his seat in that body until he died in 1936.

Inaugural Speech

(Source: Tallahassee *Semi-Weekly True Democrat*, January 7, 1913)

Ladies and Fellow Citizens:

In the breath and in the spirit of the solemn oath which has just been administered to me by the state's highest judicial officer, I desire now, not in any empty sense of formality, but with all the sincerity and earnestness which I possess, to pledge my time, my best services and whatever of ability I have, to the cause of Florida; her moral advancement, her material growth, the betterment of her institutions, the happiness of her citizens, and to the administering of all the affairs of government in a manner which will protect, promote and foster the interest and welfare of the people of this great state.

From the moment it was decreed by the sovereign will of the people of Florida that upon this day I should succeed to the office of governor, I have been filled, I assure you, with the keenest and most sincere gratitude for the honor conferred upon me, and have prized more than anything beneath the Heavens the token of confidence recorded by my fellow citizens. I am profoundly thankful for this opportunity at the very threshold of the administration upon which we are about to enter, to say that, come what may, I shall always stand a debtor to the people of Florida, and it shall be both my pleasure and my constant purpose, by a proper regard for my fellowman, by an unanswering fidelity and loyalty to every public trust, to manifest my gratitude and heartfelt appreciation for the honor of having been called to the chief magistracy of our state.

I enter upon the duties of this important office fully mindful that to the man who has the right conception of his duty, the ambition to serve in a public capacity is not for the purpose of enriching himself, the punishment of enemies or rewarding at the public expense his friends, nor that he may extend any special privilege to any person or class; but he is moved by the higher and nobler purpose of rendering the greatest service of which he is capable to the whole people. So far as human limitations and my own capacity will permit,

I now assure you that my official conduct during the next four years shall be ever guided and governed by this high conception of public duty.

I have been gratified and pleased to note the satisfaction with which the people of Florida generally seemed to accept the result of our recent primary and the general election following; and I hope and believe that whatever feeling my have arisen in the heat of the campaign for the governorship has now given place to good will; and this happy condition fills me with the confident hope that Florida is now preparing to enjoy a most beneficial period of good feeling and harmony—a period in which political controversy will give way to the state's advancement in which rivalries and jealousies of whatever nature will be subordinated to hearty and healthy promotion of the general welfare.

No state is richer in its history, its traditions, or in romance than ours. None has a past more glorious, nor a future fraught with greater promise. Surely, there are unerring indications that Florida is now entering upon a new, brilliant and most fruitful period of industrial development. It is impossible for the keenest prophetic vision to forecast her progress within the next decade. With our state alive in every field of endeavor, necessarily the duties and responsibilities of those who are charged and entrusted with the conduct of the public business are greatly augmented and the public demands broadened and enlarged. The times demand aggression and progress in public affairs. Government should keep abreast with the time, and it is my earnest hope that Florida's public interests during the administration now beginning, and throughout the future, shall be fully responsive to the industrial and social progress of her people.

Politically, we are at the dawn of a new era in the history of this great nation—an era marked by an unparalleled awakening of the public conscience upon the problems of the age and in the matter of demanding the highest standards of service from public officials. The masses have grasped a full realization of the fact that the foundation of free government rests upon the consent and should be guided by the will of the people. Government is for the general good, and that public servant who fails to exert honestly all his energies towards assuring the greatest possible benefits for his constituents has fallen short of fulfilling the just and reasonable demands which should be expected of those called to positions of public trust. Nothing short of the most constant devotion to duty is going to satisfy the people under the happy, new conditions of popular concern about political affairs—and I believe nothing should satisfy them.

For about a score of years the contest has waged heavily in this country—as it has indeed, throughout the civilized world—between the old order of special privilege and the reformed idea of equal opportunity and fair play for all. We marvel at the progress being made by the various professions and sciences and crafts; but as I see it, one of the most significant evolutions in history, which the world has made in our own generation, has been the real awakening of the people to the glorious realizations that they are in fact their own rulers.

With this revolution in political thought the citizens of Florida are largely in sympathy. They are well forward in the movement to secure and perpetuate genuine popular government. It shall be my earnest endeavor, my fellow citizens, to assist in securing legislation and in following policies which will firmly intrench the people in the control of their government—national, state, county and municipal. There seems today to be a greater unanimity of popular sentiment and a clearer recognition of popular power and rights in support of the idea of a government meaning justice to all and special privileges to none than at any time during the last half century—and upon this happy condition I most heartily congratulate our state and the nation.

Today, as I look to the future with a desire to do, and build hopes for accomplishing something worth while for those whom I have been called to serve, and whose happiness, contentment and welfare weighs heavily upon my heart, I realize as you must, that the extent of my accomplishments and achievements as a public servant rests largely upon the degree of cooperation and sympathy which shall be accorded me by the citizens of this state.

I believe the people should take an active, militant and discriminating interest in the conduct of the business of the commonwealth; that they should scrutinize the acts of their officials and at all times feel free to exercise their right and priviledge to make known their needs and the public demands. He can best serve who is most familiar with the conditions and the problems which surround those he represents. While I shall do all in my power to keep in touch with the requirements of the citizens of my state, and to accomplish all possible in their behalf, I appeal for the sympathy and the aid of the people of Florida, and urge that they lend their influence toward the inauguration of every policy necessary for the public good.

We gather from our own experience and from the lessons of history that the basic strength and stability of government is lodged in the people. So long as they are safe in their freedom and liberty, protected in their property and secure in their rights, prosperity and happiness will abound; but when their rights are infringed, their function in government trampled upon, such conditions unless soon checked lead to decay and the final decline of the erring nation.

We point with pride to the increasing wealth of our state; we are justly proud of our untold resources; we rejoice in thoughts of the limitless value of the material wealth of our nation, and every American citizen feels proud of his country and hopeful for its destiny; but when we look behind all of these evidences of the magnificence and the grandeur—of state and nation, we find the citizen to be the foundation of good government, the architect and builder of all our material wealth.

Some months ago I visited our national capital. As I called in the various departments and beheld their magnitude, splendor and magnificence, I was thrilled with pride and inspired with even greater love for my country. I was impressed with the tremendous powers assembled there, with the great responsibilities there centered—the nation's president, its congress, its courts, its navy, its army and its gathered treasure; and as I meditated upon all of these evidences of my country's greatness and the wealth there represented, I thought for a time that the very prosperity and the destiny of the American people found lodgment in those headquarters of our great government. But, my friends, a little later, in my own state it was my good fortune to visit for a night in the home of one of my country friends. His was a modest, simple house, sheltered by great trees and encircled by field and grove, rich in harvest and laden with fruit of golden hue. The next day, as I journeyed homeward, I found myself absorbed in meditation upon the vivid picture of my country's capitol presented but a few weeks before, and upon the impress and the inspirations gathered in the home of my country friend; and as I thought of the happiness that prevailed in that home, of the nobility of purpose that pervaded its occupants, of the influence of that stalwart citizen in his community and his part, as well as that of every citizen, in shaping the destiny of the nation, the glittering picture of our capitol, its splendor and its treasure faded from my mind, and I said surely here, here, in the homes of the people is lodged the destiny of my country—here is found its majesty and strength—here is the beginning of its power and the end of its responsibilities.

The Florida legislature will meet here in regular session three months hence. The governor is directed by the constitution to communicate to that body information concerning the condition of the state and recommend such measures as he may deem expedient. Details as to the public policies which are contemplated to be followed can more appropriately be discussed in the message to the legislature than upon this occasion; therefore, I will not now occupy your attention at length upon the question of specific policies. I made certain campaign pledges as to principles, and I assure you that I shall live up to those promises, and shall further endeavor, as far as is within my power, to inaugurate all other policies which it is felt will contribute to popular government and be for the good of the state.

As some of the essential parts of the program which I have in mind the following may be mentioned.

The primary and general election laws should be so perfected that all opportunity for fraud and trickery in elections shall be removed and campaign expenses reduced to the minimum. I believe 90 per cent of the people of this state are heartily in accord with the idea that the man and not the dollar should triumph, and will welcome for all time to come a law that will stamp out the idea entertained by a few, that public office is a chattel to be sold at public outcry to the highest bidder.

Florida is well advanced in its public school system, yet our present day progress calls for its further improvement, and I shall advocate the raising of the standard of our common schools. In these practical times, I believe we should give great importance to the agricultural, the mechanical, and domestic science features of school work.

It is my purpose to labor for a greater agricultural and farm activity. I consider it wise that we enlarge the work of the agricultural experiment station at the university, in disseminating information to the farmers, the truckers and the fruit growers, in conducting farmers' institutes, organizing corn clubs, tomato clubs and otherwise stimulating farm, grove, and rural development. Public aid should be given to stamp out pests that may become a public menace by injuring our farm or grove products.

The 1910 census credits Florida with about 800,000 head of cattle, valued at about eight million dollars. It is estimated that about three per cent of these die annually from cow ticks, causing a loss in deaths from this source alone of about $25,000 a year. The federal government in co-operation with certain of the state governments has accomplished splendid results in the eradication of the pests; and I believe our state, with the aid of the federal government, should inaugurate, under the direction of the state board of health, a movement in this behalf.

Court procedure should be simplified and provisions made for more speedy trial in both civil and criminal cases. The time allowed for perfecting appeals should be shortened and other measures enacted to protect the citizen in his rights and secure justice without reasonable delay or excessive cost.

Practically every citizen of our state who is familiar with the Florida Everglades realizes that it is one of the state's most valuable assets. Under more or less financial embarrassment, a very marked progress has been made towards the reclamation of this territory within the past six years, and your officials are now pushing that undertaking as rapidly as the finances available will permit. I have great faith in this enormous enterprise and will, with my co-laborers, do everything possible to accomplish the drainage and reclamation of this vast area of rich and fertile land.

I believe one of the needs in connection with the project is the establishment of one or two experimental farms.

Within a short time we should endeavor to have the federal government assume the maintenance and care of certain of the drainage canals for water transportation across the state.

The time is ripe, in my opinion, for a change in our plan of handling the state convicts. With the great demand for labor upon our roads and in road building, we can utilize the convict labor to an advantage upon the roads, and I think that the necessary steps should be taken providing upon the expiration of the present convict-lease, on January 1, 1914, for the withdrawal of the prisoners from the lease system in such reasonable installments as may be advisable to safeguard the state's finances in making the change from the present plan of hiring them out to placing them on the roads.

In my study of public problems for the past ten years I have given more or less thought to the subject of good roads and the advisability of governmental activity along this line. From my interest in this subject and its study, I am firmly convinced that a thorough system of good roads in each county in Florida will add more to the material advancement of our varied resources, to the upbuilding of our state, to property enhancement, and to the comfort and convenience of our rural citizens and to the people generally of the state then any other one step that can be taken.

One of the greatest factors in our state's growth and development is the laboring interests. I believe it would be of benefit to the state to have a labor commissioner to compile labor statistics, to aid in the enforcement of the child labor law and otherwise promote the labor interests.

The railroad commission has proven of value to the state and should be clothed with such further power as is required to make more efficient its work in requiring of common carriers good service and reasonable passenger, freight and express rates.

Our laws governing the formation of corporations for profit are too lax and should be amended so as to give better protection to the public against those who take advantage of the weakness of the law to carry on wild cat schemes.

Every county in Florida has a large quantity of rich, fertile land, and there is no reason why there should be any land frauds in our state. To check the few who are disposed to defraud and deceive land purchasers, I think we should have a law providing for all literature relative to lands to be sold under the colonization or kindred plans to be first approved by the Department of Agriculture—the expense incident to this requirement to be paid by the party selling the land.

Much of the time of each session of the legislature is consumed in the consideration of city charter measurers. To relieve the legislature of this work and in order that the people of the towns and cities may have authority to make their own charters and alter same, a constitutional amendment removing this authority from the legislature and vesting it in the towns and cities should be submitted.

It is my opinion that a constitutional amendment granting to the people the right by petition to initiate legislation, and the right by petition to vote upon laws enacted by the legislature when desired and expressed by a reasonable percentage of the qualified votes, should be submitted. Another and separate constitutional amendment giving the electors the right, upon demand of a reasonable percentage of the qualified voters, to vote upon the recall of public officers, should be submitted.

I favor the fullest publicity in the administration of the public business. The people are entitled to know what their officers are doing. A law is needed requiring that the biennial reports of the state officers, with complete and detailed information, be printed and distributed among the legislature, the press and the public at least thirty days prior to the regular sessions of the legislature. This would place the information contained in these reports in the hands of the legislators and the public in time to be of service and benefit when the legislature convenes.

Prior to the last three years the principal of the state school fund was invested exclusively in state bonds, paying an average of about 3½ per cent interest. This fund as it becomes available is now being invested in Florida county and city bonds bearing an average of about 4½ per cent interest. I think we can get as much as 6 or 7 per cent interest upon this fund by investing it in county warrants when needed laws are enacted to make such investments safe, and thereby increase the state income from this source materially.

It is the policy of insurance companies to invest their surplus funds in interest bearing securities. This being true, it is my opinion that they should be required by law to invest in Florida securities a reasonable percentage of their net surplus from Florida earnings.

At present interest is required on state funds on deposit, the state receiving 2½ per cent on daily balances. The law should also require banks to pay interest on deposits of county funds. It should also provide for the state and counties receiving bids from the banks of the state for the deposit of the funds. This policy, in my opinion, would produce much more interest on state funds, and will result in the counties deriving an income of from $50,000 to $75,000 annually from a source now producing no revenue.

Upon constitutional questions, I think the state should have the right of appeal in criminal cases so that the points involved may be passed upon by the supreme court and not finally settled by the lower courts, as under our present system. A law so providing should be enacted.

I favor such changes in our laws applicable to juvenile offenders as may be necessary for the proper care and maintenance and training of this class of offenders. We should make a real reform school of our present institution known as the state reform school.

Possibly no subject is more difficult of solution than the tax problem. We should have the tax burden bear equally upon all. There should be absolutely no favoritism, either by the tax laws or by the assessing officers. A long step towards equalizing of taxes, in my opinion, could be accomplished by changing our system so as to provide for the discontinuance of the levy of an ad valorem state tax, and have the state government supported exclusively by the license and franchise taxes. This would remove the necessity of state uniformity in assessments, leaving uniformity necessary only in the counties.

The heroism, the bravery, the love of country and devotion in duty of our Confederate heroes is a heritage of which our state and the South is justly proud. Every homage and tribute should be paid these veterans by our state and her people. Ample provision should be made for the Confederate Home, and a liberal pension policy followed by the state.

One of the elementary principles of efficient Democratic government is that the public business shall be conducted with the strictest economy consistent with the public needs and welfare. I feel confident that I can promise the people both for myself and for those who are to be associated with me in the state government, that rigid economy will be followed in the conduct of all the business entrusted to us. I deem it appropriate, however, to offer the suggestion that the greatest portion of the tax burden which has to be borne by the people of Florida consists in the expenditures made by their county and municipal governments. Eternal vigilance on the part of the people as to all public disbursements, whether state, county or municipal, will be, I am sure, the greatest possible preventive of extravagance, and I earnestly recommend such vigilance on the part of the people of Florida.

More or less extravagance has at times been permitted by our legislatures in the employment of large numbers of clerks and attaches. This should be discontinued. The legislature should, of course, have all the clerical assistance required to expedite business, but the public funds should not be wasted merely to provide salaries for persons whose services are not actually needed, and who will not perform any actual service further than signing the pay roll.

It has been my pleasure and good fortune, ladies and gentlemen, to serve for the past four years as attorney general in the administration of the able, clean, honorable and patriotic governor who is today retiring from office. Governor Gilchrist, your able and painstaking conduct of office of governor during the quadrenniem ending today reflects great credit both upon you and upon the state of Florida. I feel fortunate in having been in a position to observe your devotion to duty and your many manifestations of manliness and moral courage. You retire, Sir, with the respect and best wishes of the people of your state, and I gladly join my fellow citizens in wishing you a long life full of happiness and prosperity.

In conclusion, my friends, permit me to say that I am deeply grateful for both the past and present opportunities afforded me to engage in the public service. It has offered a field of usefulness which I hope has borne some fruit. While I have remained poor in purse, I have rejoiced at each opportunity to be of benefit to the good people who have honored me. Conscious of my own limitations and of my aptness to err in judgment, as all mortals err, still I have been filled with the earnest desire to give to the people of my state the most enlightened and capable service within my power and relying upon Divine guidance of Him who rules over the nations, upon the moral support of the men and women of Florida, upon the promptings of virtues instilled into me in youth by a sainted mother and noble father and upon the inspirations and strength gathered daily from the counsel and the love of a devoted wife, after expressing my warm thanks for your presence here and for all that has been done to make this occasion such a delightful one, with a strong realization of duty and responsibility, I proceed now to the discharge of the high trust which has been accorded to me.

Governor Sidney J. Catts
Term: 1917 - 1921

Sidney Johnston Catts, like Trammell, was a native Alabamaian and also got his LL.B. from Cumberland University, but the two men could not have been more different. Catts (born July 31, 1863 – died March 9, 1936) was ordained a Baptist minister in 1886, and preached at several places in Alabama until 1903, a year that saw him mix politics with religion. He made an unsuccessful race for a seat in the national House of Representatives from the state's Fifth Congrssional District. Soundly defeated by the incumbent demagogue J. Howell Heflin, Catts picked up some campaign tricks that he would use later in Florida.

He moved to DeFuniak Springs in 1911 as minister of the First Baptist church there. An excellent speaker, Catts became well known for his fundamentalist theology which saw the Roman Catholic church as a threat to southern Protestantism and to the South itself. In 1914 he resigned. Becoming state representative of a fraternal insurance company, he traveled the state promoting the firm and continuing to speak. Convinced that he could best defend Florida from the papal menace (although the state had less than twenty-five thousand Catholics) by entering politics, he ran for governor in 1916, campaigning in a Model-T Ford.

Catts pulled an astounding upset and emerged victorious in the primary. His closest competitor was State Comptroller William V. Knott, Taking advantage of Florida's state election law that permitted second choice voting, Knott's forces challenged Catts's victory and in a recount the State Canvassing Board ruled that the comptroller had won by 21 votes. At that, Catts accepted the nomination of the Prohibition party and campaigned in the regular election as the people's candidate in opposition to the evil forces of bureaucracy. He easily defeated the Democrat Knott, the Republican, George W. Allen, and the Socialist and Independent candidates.

As governor Catts's bark was far worse than his bite. His was an "average" administration, one not marked by persecutions of religious groups. He did feature his campaign Ford in the ceremonies of his swearing in and used his inaugural address as the occasion to gloat over his opponents and to feature himself as the champion of the people. He appropriated Andrew Jackson's "spoils system" to appoint relatives and friends to positions for which they had limited qualifications. To his credit he promoted public roads, fairer appointment of the state legislature, and championed improvements in education. During his administration statewide and national prohibition went into effect and Florida did its part in providing soldiers and supplies to the successful prosecution of World War I. Florida did not aid the cause of giving the vote to women. Although the Nineteenth Amendment was added to the constitution in 1920, Florida did not ratify the amendment until 1969.

Catts failed to in his effort to win a seat in the US Senate in 1920 and in the governor's races of 1924 and 1928. He died in 1936 at Defuniak Springs.

Inaugural Speech
(Source: Tallahassee *Daily Democrat*, January 3, 1917)

Citizens of Florida:

This is the supreme hour of your triumph, to have gained this victory over all the forces of opposition so masterful and strong as were those that stood arrayed against you; and to have withstood them and conquered them, places this hour of your success with the historic ones, when the people of England raised Cromwell to peer, or when the citizens of France desolated the feudal system in the rejection of the Catholic hierarchy, and the kind craft of that age, by the French revolution, or when the colonies of America stood by Thomas Jefferson as he gave to the world the supremist bill of man's rights, the Declaration of Independence.

Your triumph is no less in this good hour in beautiful Florida, for you have withstood the onslaughts of the county and state political rings, the vast corporations, and the railroads, the fierce opposition of the daily and weekly press, and organization of the negro voters of the state against you, the judiciary of the state partisan to your needs, and the power of the Roman Catholic hierarchy against you. Yet over all these the common people of Florida, the everyday masses of the cracker people, have triumphed, and the day of your apotheosis has arrived, and you can say, as said the ancient Hebrew devotee, "Lift up your gates, and be ye lifted up, ye everlasting doors, and let the Lord of Glory in, Who is this Lord of Glory, The Lord God of Hosts, He is the King of Glory."

In my days of fervid youthful imagination I have often wondered what could be the crowning achievement of a human ambition, and have pictured some things which might satiate human power, or crown ambition's desire. I have imagined that to be a great Rothschild of finance and hold the riches of a hemisphere in my hands, or to be a Morgan and listen to the monetary praise of the Americas, while crowned heads and potentates of the old world bowed to my financial requests, would be the meed of human endeavor, or the goal of man's distinction. I have dreamed that to be a great preacher like John the Baptist, Christmas Evans, John Knox, and Charles Wesley, or the superb Talmage and sway the masses of mankind to repentance and to tears before the Christ, and the throne of the supernal, would be the supremest achievement of the race, and the crowning event of man's lofty ambitions. I have sometimes thought that to be a great traveler and stand on Sahara's scorching borders or amid the arctic's polar snows and hear the cry of the gaunt wolf far-flung on Alaska's barren shore, or stand on ship deck beneath the equator's lurid touch and gaze at night upon the splendor of the Southern cross, or rest at noonday upon the lofty heights of the Andes or the snow-crowned peaks of the Himalayas, or

> Sail upon the Rhine and Rhone
> And view Mount Aetna's fiery side,
> And see the Italian sunset sky,
> Blend with the Adriatic Sea,
> And hear the shout of fishermen
> Along the shores of Galilee.

could crown every ambition as a noted traveler and satisfy the desire of the soul.

I have thought that to be a great warrior, and like Alexander, Caesar, Anthony, Cromwell, Napoleon, Washington, Grant or Lee, lead the charging squadrons of earth to noble battle for the right, and read one's history in a people's praise and gratitude, would be the lordliest of human anticipations. But my ideal has changed, and I stand to tell you, comrades and fellow citizens, that to triumph with my people in an hour like this is grander far, than all else on earth to me. To be under God and my noble constituents an apostle of a new and nation sweeping tenet and a political doctrine, which doctrine is "nothing in Florida above the nation's flag." The little red school house to stand as an emblem of the nation's liberty. No money ever to be given for any sectarian schools from our treasury forever; the freedom of speech, conscience, and press, and entire separation of church and state forever; to vote for no man for any office, nor appoint any, who owes his allegiance to a foreign national potentate, or foreign ecclesiastical power on American soil; the suppression of the whiskey traffic for state and nation, and the crowning political dogma for all "American for Americans throughout eternity." Here is to my mind all the greatness that any man should carve, and you, my comrades, have given to me this victory today, and in it I am supremely happy and blessed. With my hat off, and as Jacob of old, facing Bethel, I stand in mute and silent gratitude to you and God, my fellow citizens, and comrades, and thank you for this glad hour, the hour of your political triumph and power.

I had rather stand here today as your apostle of victory and success in these great political doctrines than to live in any other age of the world's great history. If only the God of our fathers will give me the grace, wisdom and judgment to serve you and Him, and make you the governor I desire to be, and like Solomon of old I lift my voice to the Supreme Architect of the universe today for theses great gifts that I so much desire and need, and as he said so say I, "Master I am only a little child before Thee. I know not how to rule this great people, which is like the dust of the earth in number. Give me, O, Lord God, I pray Thee, wisdom and knowledge, that I may judge this Thy people and rule them aright."

Citizens of my beloved and adopted state, there are many problems to confront us in the next four years, and with your help and confidence, and with the mutual respect and consideration for each other by the legislature, the senate and the chief executive, we hope to master many of these perplexing conditions.

The most important thing facing Florida today is the drainage of the Everglades, and if the incoming administration can succeed in doing this in the next four years, an event of as much moment will have transpired in the history of Florida as the opening of the Panama canal was to the world. The first step in this direction, as I see it, would be an awakening of the people of Florida to the greatness of the project. I have recently returned from a trip through the Everglades and Lake Okeechobe, which showed me the immense richness of the section to be drained. To my mind, this is now the richest section undeveloped on earth today, and so rich is the land, and so fertile its quality, that the land itself might be taken up and shipped just as it is as a fertilizer to the poorer sections of the state and the Union. This rich black much land runs six or eight feet deep throughout nearly the extent of the millions of acres, and produces the greatest crops I have seen anywhere in all my travels. One trouble about the matter is, the people living in other sections of the state are not in sympathy with the drainage of the Everglades as they should be. This we desire to develop by a speaking tour through the state at not distant future, so that a spirit of cooperation and enlistment may be awakened everywhere. The first great project after this will be the floating of the first (about) $3,000,000 worth of bonds, and after that $3,000,000 more, which should put the whole section largely in a condition of cultivation, and after the first crop is made on this land you may look for prices to soar until the fabulous prices of California will be nothing to what this, the richest land on earth, will bring. I guess I had better stop before you call me a prophet.

The next thing that will claim out attention will be the cutting out of all waste in the administration of state institutions and industries. It is an established fact that when the same officers continue too long at their jobs, that they let in extravagances, here and there, until by and by great methods of waste are established, and the state loses many thousands of dollars per year because of lack of system upon the part of those whose business it is to see after her affairs. Our ideas will be to effect changes in these matters by rotation in office and putting in new men as far as we can do so practically; and in case these men do not make good, put them out and put others in until we find the right men.

The next thing that will claim our attention will be giving the board of equalization of taxes more power, so that they shall not only have the right to equalize large and vast estates of private persons and corporations, but their privileges shall be extended to the vast systems of railways now penetrating our state. We notice that they have already effected great good in St. Johns county in the matter of the Flagler estate, whose taxes they raised from $75,000 to a tax on $16,000,000 which increased the taxes of St. Johns county $107,000, state and county, and decreased the millage from ten mills to five. This will pay their salaries for many years, and shows what they would do were they adequately equipped with legal authority and had the right kind of men on the board. It will be our pleasure to try to get the legislature to see that this body should be given full and competent power to equalize the taxes of all property lying within our domain.

The primary law will also come in for its change, as the recent election muddle proved conclusively that it is very deficient in regard to second choice votes. Just what the changes are to be cannot yet be said, but we notice that many newspapers of the state are taking this matter up, and are insisting upon it that the law shall be simplified and the second choice vote cut out entirely. Our suggestion will be that not only this change be wrought, but that others also shall be effected which will materially change conditions of collusion and fraud, and which will simplify the ballot to such an extent that "the way faring man, though a fool, need not err therein."

Many of our sober and best thinking men also think that the time has come in the history of our state when the initiative, referendum and recall laws shall be put upon our statute books and become a corporate part of the laws of the land. They also think that, with proper provisions of protection, these laws should run the gauntlet from constable to the highest officers of the state and thus insure in times of danger that no czar-like procedure shall ever be taken part in by any official or set of officials.

Another problem that will come up for solution upon the initiative of the house and senate, will be the matter of prohibition. This is a question which, like Banquo's ghost, will not down until it shall be finally settled for what is best to the greatest masses of mankind. The whiskey men of the state all feel that it is a question which will ultimately go against them, not only in Florida, but in the nation.

The next question that will come before us for solution will be the opening of all closed institutions within the state of Florida for police inspections, such as convents, parochial schools and other institutions of like nature. The taxing of all church property, with the exception of the pastoral homes and the churches themselves, and the same universal examinations for all teachers, whether they be in public or parochial or denominational schools. This possibility will have some disquieting effects upon legislation, but like the great question of prohibition will never down until it is settled upon a basis of Americanism.

Another question which will claim the best thought and attention of our house and senate is the matter of industrial schools and training for boys and girls of Florida. As Senator Williams says, the time is past when boys and girls know all about Latin, Greek, French, Hebrew, Sanskrit and all the dead languages, and yet when they go to sell goods know nothing about how to be polite to people, to cut the goods right or to retain their positions, and when they go to farm "it will take two years to make their sugarcane grow big enough to chew." If we desire to retain the respect of ourselves and the nations of the earth we must educate the hand as well as the brain. This is one of the great schemes which we hope to see instituted in Florida in the next four years.

Another question of vital importance will be to get cooperation between the people and the railroads of the state, by a system of properly regulated freight rates which will insure to them the early shipping of their commodities, vegetables and fruit, no discrimination against them and such through cooperation as shall put the magnificent productions of Florida into the Eastern markets on the same basis of railroad cooperation as California now enjoys. To do this we must have the attention of the railroads to such an extent that they must attend to the wants of Florida with no less avidity, by having plenty of cars always on hand, rapid transportation, low freight rates, etc., as now marks the shipping facilities from the wheat and corn regions of the West, and from the fruit regions of California. Such conditions as these will make Florida the golden state of the Union.

Standing as we do today, without the pale of specific knowledge it is impossible for us to tell of many evils that should be corrected. Suffice it to say that with the help and cooperation of all the forces involved in these matters, we shall strive as best we can to correct each and every one of them as they may present themselves. One cannot but feel how helpless he is until faced with such grave responsibilities as will confront him as the chief executive of the state, and in such an hour as this we feel that we may well say with the consecrated poet of old, with his faith fixed in the Almighty and his fellow creatures:

> I know not where his islands lift
> Their fronded palms in air;

I only know we cannot drift
Beyond his love and care.
I know not what the future hath
Of marvel or surprise,
Assured alone that life and death
His mercy underlies.

This age of ours is marked by a revival of patriotism upon the part of the states and the nation. In most of the Southern states conditions have grown into the same mould as in the antebellum days, with the exception of slavery. Therefore society in its crudescences is fixed and firmly established in grooves which cannot be changed or molested. In Florida conditions are very dissimilar on account of the cosmopolitan nature of our population. Here the new world and the old grapple for power. Here the old South, with its settled habits of society, is thrown together with the restless forces of the East, while the miner from Arizona or Alaska comes in contact with the Cuban, Spaniard or inhabitant of the old world. These conditions of mingled society, forces of habit, trend of thought and variation of citizenship has not yet reached its fruition, nor has the settled character of inhabitant and citizenship yet been wrought. This is necessarily bound to cause much thought on the part of us all and while we look at our allegiance to our state from many angles, can we not say, with Tallahassee's splendid young poet laureat, Prof. Benjamin Benson Lane:

Florida, thou matchless state,
Of all thy sons the ready toast,
Around thy thousand miles of coast.
The south seas toss, and toss and wait
The day, when from harbor-bar and strait,
Shall sally forth the nation's fleets,
And make thy gulf a sea of streets,
That lead to Pacific's gate,
'Tis here that Fate with Purpose meets,
That Chance and Will may harmonize;
Today the tale of time completes
Hither the world shall turn its eyes,
North, East and West shall mingle here:
Arouse thy sons—their day draws near!

> Their day draws near! Arouse them then;
> Give them the mastery of this wealth
> A climate rare, exuding health,
> A perfect land beyond men's ken.
> Let not the welcomed stranger, when
> He cometh, find himself more fit,
> Nor better trained his native wit;
> This is the land to grow true men.
> Floridians all, this land is ours,
> And we that love it love to serve.
> God strengthen every heart and nerve
> Whene'er a danger near us lowers.
> Alert, courageous, ready—all
> Answer the throbbing future's call!

In conclusion, there is but one thought further that I desire to bring to your notice. Our state is so rich in all that makes for material wealth that as a people we may be prone to forget the benign hand of Him who has given it all to us. When we contemplate the millions of forest lands, teeming with its turpentine, rosin and lumber, our lakes, estuaries, bays, gulfs and rivers thronging with fish, and the crustaceans of every tribe; the splendid muck lands of the Everglades, the acres of yellow gem citrus fruits; the millions of sheep, hogs and cattle; the rolling prairies of the southern peninsula; the thriving villages, hamlets, towns and cities; the soaring prices of our land, the magnificent climate, and the teeming trains bearing their hundreds of thousands to the state, we as a people are prone to forget that the one aim of life is, not to acquire knowledge of how to obtain wealth, but that there is a higher, a grander, a nobler principle of living and that is the same thought expressed in Kipling's great Recessional where the people, drunk with the tumult of England's mighty glory in the jubilee of their splendid queen, caused him to repeat with prayerful consideration this wonderful hymn, bringing the people back to a knowledge of God and the consciousness of the fact that it was His hand that had given them all this wonderful glory, and with this poem as a prayer to our ever-to-be-adored and conquering God, we will close.

God of our fathers know of old—
Lord of our far flung battle line—
Beneath whose awful hand we hold
Dominion over palm and pine—
Lord God of hosts, be with us yet,
Lest we forget—lest we forget!

The tumult and the shouting dies—
The captains and the kings depart—
Still stands Thine ancient sacrifice,
An humble and a contrite heart.
Lord God of Hosts, be with us yet,
Lest we forget—lest we forget!

Far-called, our navies melt away—
On dune and headland sinks the fire—
Lo, all our pomp of yesterday
Is one with Nineveh and Tyre!
Judge of the Nations, pare us yet
Lest we forget—lest we forget!

If, drunk with sight of power, we lose
Wild tongues that have not Thee in awe—
Such boasting as the Gentiles use,
Or lesser breeds without the Law—
Lord God of Hosts, be with us yet,
Lest we forget—lest we forget!

For heathen heart that puts her trust
In reeking tube and iron shard—
All valiant dust that builds on dust,
And guarding, calls not Thee to guard—
For frantic boast and foolish word,
Thy mercy on Thy people. Lord.

Legacy of Leadership   157   Patricia L. Clements

Governor Collins holding up a bass at mansion on inaguration day, 1955. Photo courtesy Department of Commerce Collection, Tallahassee, Florida.

In 1957, the second governor's mansion was built at a cost of $350,000. This sum included the furnishings as well as an $80,000 design and furniture procurement fee. A large Florida room was added in 1985, at a cost of approximately $200,000. One half of the funds ($100,000) for this space were raised from private donations, the other half of the cost was provided by the state. The addition remains a much used and favorite venue for state related gatherings. Photo courtesy Florida State Archives, R.A. Gray Building, Tallahassee, Florida.

Legacy of Leadership 158 Patricia L. Clements

Governor Napoleon Bonaparte Broward inauguration, 1905. Photo courtesy Florida State Archives, R.A. Gray Building, Tallahassee, Florida.

Governor Cone leaving the mansion with future governor Spessard Lindsey Holland, 1941. Photo courtesy Florida State Archives, R.A. Gray Building, Tallahassee, Florida.

Legacy of Leadership 159 Patricia L. Clements

Governor and Mrs. Holland with Governor-elect and Mrs. Caldwell leaving the mansion, 1945. Photo courtesy Florida State Archives, R.A. Gray Building, Tallahassee, Florida.

Governor Dan McCarty's inaugural parade, 1953. Photo courtesy Florida State Archives, R.A. Gray Building, Tallahassee, Florida.

Airplane supporting Fuller Warren for governor, 1948. Photo courtesy Florida State Archives, R.A. Gray Building, Tallahassee, Florida.

Governor-elect and Mrs. Burns (left) and Governor and Mrs. Bryant in Capitol awaiting march to inaugural platform, 1965. Photo courtesy Florida State Archives, R.A. Gray Building, Tallahassee, Florida.

Governor-elect John W. Martin, Governor Cary A. Hardee and third man during Florida's centennial celebration, 1924. Photo courtesy Florida State Archives, R.A. Gray Building, Tallahassee, Florida.

Governor Reubin Askew taking the oath of office, 1971. Photo courtesy Florida State Archives, R.A. Gray Building, Tallahassee, Florida.

Governor Claude Kirk about to deliver his inaugural address, 1967. Photo courtesy Florida State Archives, R.A. Gray Building, Tallahassee, Florida.

Florida Governor Bob Graham and Lieutenant Governor Wayne Mixson, 1982. Photo courtesy Florida State Archives, R.A. Gray Building, Tallahassee, Florida.

Legacy of Leadership 163 Patricia L. Clements

First inauguration ceremony of Governor Jeb Bush, 1999. First lady Columba Bush observes as the oath of office is administered. Photo courtesy Florida State Archives, R.A. Gray Building, Tallahassee, Florida.

Inauguration of Wayne Mixson as governor of Florida for three days, 1987. Photo courtesy Florida State Archives, R.A. Gray Building, Tallahassee, Florida.

Legacy of Leadership   164   Patricia L. Clements

In 1985, the state of Florida purchased "The Grove" from Governor and Mrs. Collins for approximately $2,300,000. Under the terms of the purchase, Governor and Mrs. Collins maintained life estates. The historic furnishings were not included in the purchase. Currently, and for the past 20 years, Mrs. Collins has resided at the Grove. The property is immediately adjacent to the Governor's mansion. Photo courtesy Florida State Archives, R.A. Gray Building, Tallahassee, Florida.

Inauguration of Governor William S. Jennings, 1901. Photo courtesy Florida State Archives, R.A. Gray Building, Tallahassee, Florida.

Legacy of Leadership   165   Patricia L. Clements

The Reverend Billy Graham, President George Bush, and Mrs. Barbara Bush arriving at prayer breakfast before first inauguration of Governor Jeb Bush, 1999. Photo courtesy Florida State Archives, R.A. Gray Building, Tallahassee, Florida.

Governor Farris Bryant taking the oath of office from Justice B.K. Roberts, 1961. Photo courtesy Florida State Archives, R.A. Gray Building, Tallahassee, Florida.

Legacy of Leadership   166   Patricia L. Clements

Inaugural address of Governor Sidney J. Catts, 1917. Photo courtesy Florida State Archives, R.A. Gray Building, Tallahassee, Florida.

Governor Warren cutting 250 pound cake during his inauguration in 1949. Photo courtesy Florida State Archives, R.A. Gray Building, Tallahassee, Florida.

Inaugural address of Governor William S. Jennings, 1901. Photo courtesy Florida State Archives, R.A. Gray Building, Tallahassee, Florida.

Built in 1907, the original Florida governor's mansion cost $21,242. The Florida legislature allotted $4,444.75 to furnish the 14 rooms. Governor Broward and his family were the first family to occupy this state building. In 1955, amid protests to restore the mansion, it was demolished. The original furnishings were sold at public auction. Photo courtesy Florida State Archives, R.A. Gray Building, Tallahassee, Florida.

Inauguration of Governor Spessard L. Holland, 1941. Photo courtesy Florida State Archives, R.A. Gray Building, Tallahassee, Florida.

An opening day of the Florida legislature, mid-1950s. Photo courtesy Florida State Archives, R.A. Gray Building, Tallahassee, Florida.

Governor Graham taking oath of office from Chief Justice James Alderman, 1983. Photo courtesy Florida State Archives, R.A. Gray Building, Tallahassee, Florida.

Governor Claude R. Kirk dancing with "Madame X" (the future Mrs. Kirk, Erica Mattfield) at the inaugural ball, 1967. Photo courtesy Florida State Archives, R.A. Gray Building, Tallahassee, Florida.

Legacy of Leadership 170 Patricia L. Clements

Charley E. Johns taking the oath of acting governor after the death of Governor McCarty, 1953. Photo courtesy Florida State Archives, R.A. Gray Building, Tallahassee, Florida.

Governor Millard F. Caldwell delivering farewell address, 1949. Photo courtesy Florida State Archives, R.A. Gray Building, Tallahassee, Florida.

Legacy of Leadership   171   Patricia L. Clements

The third State Capitol was completed in 1845, the same year that Florida entered statehood. Presently, it is a museum. It was saved from demolition through the efforts of Senator Pat Thomas of Quincy and Representative Herbert Morgan of Tallahassee, as well as a local citizens group headed by Dr. Christie Koontz. Behind it stands the fourth Capitol, completed in 1977. Photo courtesy Florida State Archives, R.A. Gray Building, Tallahassee, Florida.

Governor Frederick Preston Cone taking the oath of office, 1937. Photo courtesy Florida State Archives, R.A. Gray Building, Tallahassee, Florida.

Governor Cary Augustus Hardee speaking at Governor John Martin's inauguration, 1925. Photo courtesy Florida State Archives, R.A. Gray Building, Tallahassee, Florida.

Legacy of Leadership   173   Patricia L. Clements

Governor Reubin Askew and first lady-elect Donna Lou Askew sit on the inaugural platform, 1971. Photo courtesy Florida State Archives, R.A. Gray Building, Tallahassee, Florida.

First lady Rhea Chiles observes as Governor Lawton Chiles is sworn in by Justice Leander Shaw, 1991. Photo courtesy Florida State Archives, R.A. Gray Building, Tallahassee, Florida.

Inaugural parade for Governor Sidney Johnston Catts, 1917. Photo courtesy Florida State Archives, R.A. Gray Building, Tallahassee, Florida.

Jan Garber and his orchestra going to Governor Martin's inauguration, 1925. Photo courtesy Florida State Archives, R.A. Gray Building, Tallahassee, Florida.

Legacy of Leadership 175 Patricia L. Clements

Governor McCarty and family members in the grand march at the inaugural ball, 1953. Mrs. McCarty's gown is housed in the Museum of Florida History as part of the Inaugural Gown Collection. Photo courtesy Florida State Archives, R.A. Gray Building, Tallahassee, Florida.

Governor-elect Dan McCarty leaving the mansion with Governor Fuller Warren and Mrs. Ollie Warren, 1953. Photo courtesy Florida State Archives, R.A. Gray Building, Tallahassee, Florida.

Legacy of Leadership 176 *Patricia L. Clements*

Governor Dan McCarty delivers inaugural address, 1953. Photo courtesy Florida State Archives, R.A. Gray Building, Tallahassee, Florida.

Lt. Governor Wayne Mixon and Mrs. Margie Mixon at inaugural ball of Governor Bob Graham. Mrs. Mixson's gown is housed at the Museum of Florida History as part of the Inaugural Gown Collection. Photo courtesy Florida State Archives, R.A. Gray Building, Tallahassee, Florida.

Legacy of Leadership 177 *Patricia L. Clements*

Governor-elect and Mrs. Haydon Burns leaving mansion for inauguration, 1965. Photo courtesy Florida State Archives, R.A. Gray Building, Tallahassee, Florida.

Looking west towards the Supreme Court building during Governor Kirk's inauguration, 1967. Photo courtesy Florida State Archives, R.A. Gray Building, Tallahassee, Florida.

Gubernatorial candidate Millard Caldwell and Mrs. Mary Harwood Caldwell, 1940s. Photo courtesy Florida State Archives, R.A. Gray Building, Tallahassee, Florida.

Governor Bob Martinez and first lady Mary Jane Martinez waving to the crowd during his inauguration, 1987. Photo courtesy Florida State Archives, R.A. Gray Building, Tallahassee, Florida.

Legacy of Leadership   179   *Patricia L. Clements*

Seminole Chief Billy Osceola riding in Governor Kirk's inaugural parade on Monroe Street, 1967. Photo courtesy Florida State Archives, R.A. Gray Building, Tallahassee, Florida.

Governor-elect Bob Graham delivering his inaugural address at the west side of the Capitol, 1979. Photo courtesy Florida State Archives, R.A. Gray Building, Tallahassee, Florida.

Governor Martinez delivering inaugural address, 1987. Photo courtesy Florida State Archives, R.A. Gray Building, Tallahassee, Florida.

Florida Governors Forum, convened and moderated by Patricia L. Clements. Standing, left to right: Dr. Patricia L. Clements, Governor Claude Kirk, Governor Jeb Bush, Governor Bob Martinez, Secretary of State Katherine Harris. Seated, left to right: Governor Wayne Mixson, Governor Reubin Askew, and Governor Farris Bryant, April 4, 2000. Photo courtesy Florida State Archives, R.A. Gray Building, Tallahassee, Florida.

First ladies participating in political forum entitled, Political Partners. Left to right: First ladies Adele Graham, Margie Mixon, Donna Lou Askew, Mary Call Collins, Columba Bush, Mary Jane Martinez, and moderator, Dr. Patricia L. Clements, 1999. Photo courtesy Florida State Archives, R.A. Gray Building, Tallahassee, Florida.

Florida Governor-elect Bob Graham and Mrs. Adele Graham leaving for morning prayer, 1979. Photo courtesy Florida State Archives, R.A. Gray Building, Tallahassee, Florida. Special appreciation to Ray Stanyard.

Florida House, located in the District of Columbia, is Florida's embassy in the nation's capitol. Purchased with monies from private donations, the building and exquisite furnishings were a remarkable gift to the people of Florida. This project was conceived and executed by Mrs. Rhea Chiles, the wife of Governor Lawton Chiles. The historic building (constructed in 1887) is maintained by private funds and has a current value of millions of dollars. Florida is the only state to have such a property in Washington, D.C. Photo courtesy Florida State Archives, R.A. Gray Building, Tallahassee, Florida. Special appreciation to Ray Stanyard.

Governor Cary A. Hardee
Term: 1921 - 1925

Cary Augustus Hardee (born November 13, 1876 – died November 21, 1957) was a native Floridian who was born in Taylor County. He was educated in the public schools, later becoming a teacher. He was admitted to the bar in 1890 and practiced law in Live Oak. Hardee was state's attorney 1905-1913, and served in the house where he was the speaker for two sessions. He became a Live Oak banker and in 1920 sought the Democratic nomination for governor as a conservative. His primary opponents were Van C. Swearingen, who was in the Catts tradition, and Lincoln Hulley, president of Stetson University. He defeated Sweringen by over twenty thousand votes, while only 5,591 citizens cast ballots for the erudite Hulley. In the general election he won going away from his major Republican opponent George E. Gay. This was the first gubernatorial election in

Florida which allowed women the right to vote. The ratification of the Nineteenth Amendment was achieved on August 26, 1920 thus granting all women the right to suffrage. This same right was granted to all African-American men in 1868 by the ratification of the Fourteenth Amendment some fifty-two years earlier.

Florida outgrew its sister southern states in the Booming Twenties. It led in the number of miles of hard surfaced roads, but experienced natural disasters in the form of three hurricanes and manmade debacles that included unregulated real estate sales and the catastrophic collapse of banks, the overexpansion of railroad lines, and, finally, the crippling nationwide Great Depression.

Hardee's administration was hampered by the effects of the hurricane of 1923, although progress toward improving the quality of the state's livestock was accomplished with a law requiring cattle owners to dip their cattle with an insecticide solution that killed ticks. There was much opposition to the law because small owners objected to the difficulties and the expense. The open range did not end in Florida until 1949 when a law required owners to fence in their livestock. A major improvement came with the end of the infamous convict lease system in 1923. Education was improved with a law allowing school districts to levy up to ten mills for school purposes. The previous limited had been three mills.

Governor Hardee ran for chief executive again in 1932 but was defeated. He died at Live Oak in 1957.

Inaugural Speech
(Source: Jacksonville *Florida Times Union*, January 5, 1921)

My Fellow Citizens:

A very wise provision in our state constitution has placed a limit of time in which one may serve continuously as chief executive of Florida. That he may not succeed himself finds hearty approval from thoughtful men and women. The inauguration of a chief executive becomes a frequently recurring event, marking the close of one administration and the beginning of another. In this representative government they who shall administer the affairs of the state must first be called to service by the sovereign voice of the people, and so today having been thus called, and in obedience to the will of the people of Florida, I am about to assume the high and responsible duties appertaining to the great office to which they have called me. It is my desire and it seems quite appropriate that I should avail myself o the occasion now presented to pay grateful acknowledgement of my indebtedness to the people of our state for the confidence reposed in me, as evidenced by my election to such exalted station. I am not unmindful of the great honor conferred, and am not lacking, I trust, in the fine sense of gratitude which fills my heart today. As I read the fundamental and statutory laws of Florida wherein are prescribed the duties and obligations of the chief executive, any possible sense of self sufficiency seems to grow less and my feeling of dependence upon the patient good will of the people and upon the cooperation and assistance of my associates in office more pronounced.

I seriously question if the present is propitious for one to assume the governorship of the state, if perchance, he expects to bask thereafter in popular favor. We are today in the wake of a great world conflict which taxed to the utmost the productive forces of the nation. During its continuance and immediately following the armistice which marked its conclusion, private business and public affairs have been administered in keeping with such profligacy of expenditures as was never before known. Individual thrift and frugality have been largely discarded, and erstwhile luxuries are now being classed as necessities. Thoughtful men have known that such an orgy of inflation and expenditure could not continue, and with prophetic voice have all along wooed the people back to safer ground. Unfortunately we have not listened to more conservative counsels, and as a result we are in the midst of a period of industrial deflation which in magnitude, our country has never experienced before. There is rapidly accumulating a vast army of unemployed and the farms and manufactories find difficulty in disposing of their products.

If the people of Florida, forced by stress of circumstances, need to take stock of themselves and learn again the lesson forgotten during the great war, even so must the state "set its house in order" against the perils of changing conditions. I desire to call upon the people to exercise a spirit of charity towards us, who shall attempt to lead during the critical period of readjustment and likewise I call upon them to practice individually those wholesome principles—perseverance, industry, economy and sober thinking.

We have no cause for gloomy foreboding, no reason for discontent if only we are filled with a consciousness of our inherent power, and a realization of the matchless resources which a kind of providence has bestowed upon us. The future is big with promise, and Florida may, if she will, come into her own. Ours is a rising state. Her people are not lacking in vision, and in natural resources she is rich indeed. The sturdy character of American citizenship is a result of the admixture of virile elements of varied nationalities. In a similar sense the amalgamation of those every increasing streams of population, coming to us from every section of this broad land, must mean a citizenship of spiritual power and material achievement.

The courageous spirit of the people given fair opportunity and materials with which to work, will make Florida one of the greatest states of the Union. Do I need to call your attention to the vast resources granted us by a beneficient Creator? Nearly 1,500 miles of sea coast, dotted here and there by splendid harbors. The commerce of the world finds facilities for trade and the wealth of the waters of the sea belongs to us. Millions of acres of splendid agricultural lands rich and fertile, specially adapted to agriculture, horticulture and live stock development, with little more than five per cent of it under cultivation. The wealth of our timber supply upon the face of the land and the hidden treasures beneath its surface speak of potential wealth of untold millions, and above all God's eternal sunshine affords us a climate which is attracting the peoples of less favored climes. I am tempted, perhaps, to speak too much at length while contemplating the greatness of Florida. Let us set ourselves resolutely to the task of utilizing the proffered opportunities and building here on this heaven favored peninsula a commonwealth whose laws and institutions shall be so just and so efficiently administered that men everywhere will be attracted to us.

In its distribution of powers, the constitution has divided our government into three departments. As the head of the executive department, I shall not forget the intent of the fathers who wrote and published that great instrument and who saw therein each of said departments free and coordinate. A free, untrammeled and independent judiciary must ever remain the bulwark of individual liberty. An enlightened and incorruptible legislature is the absolute essential in governmental progress. By reason of supposed particular knowledge of our laws and policies, acquired through the administration and execution of them, it is made the duty of the governor to cooperate with the legislature and assist, if possible, in its law-making functions. I shall propose measures and policies but shall not attempt to influence their adoption through the improper use of executive power.

We are to be congratulated in that men of experience, ability, and patriotic consecration to the public good have been chosen as head of the constitutional departments of our state government. For my part I am greatly pleased to be associated with them in the work ahead of us and can but feel that the official family, which I may with propriety call the cabinet, will, from the abundance of their experience contribute much towards the success of our administration. The occasion is quite opportune for me to bring them assurance that executive interference will not be indulged. And only in keeping with the spirit of the law shall I concern myself with their departmental affairs.

I wish to welcome, as co-partners, the men and women who have been chosen to fill their respective positions incident to the administration of the law. There should exist between such officials and the chief executive a spirit of cooperation and mutual helpfulness. Each of us may well feel honored that we have been called to service. That our fellows have such confidence in our fitness that they trust their business in our hands. We can best repay them by a conscientious regard for the important duties of our respective offices.

The laws of Florida must be enforced. Private property must be respected. The rights of the individual safeguarded in his legitimate aspirations, but at no time and under no circumstances must the individual, whether in a personal or in a corporate capacity, be allowed to assert himself to the detriment of the superior rights of the public. The obligation of law enforcement is upon the executive department. I trust that all of us who may be thus associated will somehow hear the call of the people for real service and for high ideals in the administration of the law. Permit me further to indulge in the hope that it will not be necessary for me as chief executive to resort to that instrumentality of the constitution, carrying the power of removal of subordinate officers, in order to force a proper execution of the laws. The incorporation of this high prerogative in the hands of the governor contemplates, however, a necessity at times for its use. I would have every one clearly understand that I shall not hesitate to use it when there appears wanton disregard of the oath of office or gross incompetency in the performance of official duties.

Perhaps no great service can be performed than that of caring for our state institutions. Florida has not been backward in making provisions for her unfortunate, who by reason of infirmity of mind and body have become legitimate charges upon the state. She has also provided institutions corrective in character for those who have violated the laws, the state hospital for the insane in Chattahoochee and the institution at Gainesville for the epileptic and feeble minded. Adequate provision for their maintenance and humane treatment of the inmates must always be observed. The industrial school for boys at Marianna and the school of like character for girls at Ocala, while incarcerating wayward youths, must somehow lead them back to a respect for constituted authority and obedience to law, and especially at these two institutions, the application of effective methods and humane treatment upon plastic minds will largely redeem and reform them. Our prison farm at Raiford should be operated only by that class of convicts not physically able to work upon the public roads. I am in sympathy with every practicable humane method used in handling the convicts of the state. He who would mistreat them, or who would lose sight of a possible reformation is utterly unfit to deal with the problem, but I am unwilling for an ultra-humanitarianism to dictate our policy to that extent that we lose sight of the economic and disciplinary questions involved in incarcerations. I believe the farm should at least be self-sustaining and that the people should be relieved of taxes for its maintenance. The convicts physically fit must work. That was "the judgment of the law and the sentence of the court." Our system of working them upon the public roads must be maintained, and we will never I trust, go back to the private lease. As a prudent business man would handle his own affairs even so should we endeavor to manage the various state institutions, remembering always that economy as well as efficiency must be kept constantly in mind.

What should be our aim for the future? Speaking very generally, because this is not the time or place for very specific treatment of existing problems, I would suggest that we begin to give care to the conservation of our natural resources. The timber supply upon which the state is so dependent, must be intelligently conserved; not only conserved, but made sufficient for all times through reforestation. The fish and game of the state, now quite plentiful, must be preserved, and propagated. This, to my mind, will be most effectively done, when we have taken the matter of enforcement of our fish and game laws away from local influences. And inasmuch as those resources belong to all the people there should accrue to the people a fair and reasonable revenue through the operation of the laws. Conservation of resources is not enough. We must build up and develop. That great tract of fertile land known as the Everglades is a potential empire within itself. The very important work of drainage and reclamation, undertaken years ago must go on. Utilizing the funds derived from the sale of public lands after paying to the school fund the amount as required by the Constitution, we will, I trust, continue the task until completed.

We must cooperate with the national government in the construction of roads and highways. We must match the federal appropriation, always with an adequate state appropriation. A system of public roads connecting every county site in Florida should be laid out, and eventually, I believe, the state should actually take over, construct and maintain, without assistance from the counties, main thoroughfares connecting different sections of the state as distinguished from localities. We have dreamed and planned sufficiently long. Now has the time arrived for actual work and construction. It is our great problem today. I trust that the highway commission for the next four years may set themselves to the task of actually building roads.

Our aim for the future should be to give to the people of other states some conception of the greatness, the attractiveness and beauty of Florida through truthful advertising. To keep in mind and foster every movement which will develop and benefit our agricultural, horticultural and livestock interests. The development of our marketing bureau, and the encouragement of cooperative movements to the end that the farmers and producers may receive the highest possible prices for their products.

Our aim for the future should express itself in improved methods in assessment and collection of revenue. An amendment to the Constitution permitting the assessment at proper rates of the great class of intangible properties; a more equitable assessment of property as between the different counties; coordination of the various departments of the state; an elimination of expense incident to duplication of work, and finally the systematizing of our work so that many positions now hardly necessary may be abolished.

It is essentially the part of good government, insofar as laws and government regulations can do so, to create the highest possible type of citizenship, having due regard for the physical and spiritual welfare of all the people. The work, of a well organized and efficient health department cannot be dispensed with. Improved sanitation and general health conditions result always in increased capacity for efficient labor, giving to every one a clearer conception of life's duties, and the ability to perform them.

As a component part of this great republic we must give serious consideration to educational problems, if we would preserve for all time the democracy of our institutions. In a country whose government "derives its just powers from the consent of the governed," a country where the voice of the people directly, and through chosen representatives, become the real law of the land, the necessity for an educated citizenship is more pronounced. I feel that we are to be congratulated upon an awakened interest in the great cause of popular education. Our national legislature is now considering the question of national aid to our public schools and acting on the same principle our state must eventually aid the counties in a similar manner. The day for provincialism is past, the time for larger conception of our obligation is upon us. The richer sections of our country have drawn their wealth, not only from the immediate surroundings, but from every state in the Union. The more affluent communities in Florida, having done the same thing, cannot say that the education of the people in less forward communities is no concern of theirs. We have recognized this principle in the one-mill constitutional school tax and we should more adequately observe it in the future.

Let us adequately support our institutions of higher learning. I glory in the great work they are doing and am much impressed with the ever widening fields of activity which they are opening up to the lasting good of the state. I hope the time may soon come when we shall hear no more that inadequate facilities must be pleaded as an excuse for turning away from their doors so many of the youths of the state knocking for admission. Our real educational problem today, however, is with our rural schools. The overwhelming percentage of our future citizenship is now attending the country school trying as best they can to equip themselves for life's duties in a school whose term is, in many counties, not more than four months a year, and ofttimes presided over by poorly paid incompetent teachers. It is the rural school problem which is beginning to attract the attention of our national government and whatever plan may be undertaken must find in our state a responsible partner in the great work.

And finally we should aim to maintain our democratic institutions and a government that is jealous of all the rights of the state but at the same time is broad enough to realize that the federal constitution must also be given ready obedience and respect. A government that guarantees to every citizen, the weakest and the strongest alike, equal and exact justice before the law and that stands always ready to make good that guarantee; a government, too, that offers to every citizen, the weakest and the strongest alike, a fair and impartial opportunity to exercise his inalienable rights of life, liberty and the pursuit of happiness circumscribed only by a just consideration for the rights of his fellow-men. A government that is strong enough, fearless and fair enough to make every citizen, the strongest and the weakest alike, obey the law and respect the constitution under which he lives. Without this obedience to law and order and this sort of respect for constituted authority, the fairest and strongest government that human intelligence could conceive and human energy direct, must ultimately fall a prey to its own internal anarchistic tendencies.

I have spoken perhaps too much at length, but now that the obligation of a great office is mine, I find much difficulty in giving full expression to my views on so many important questions within a given time. In trying to serve you for the next four years, I am sure that I shall make many mistakes. In making them, however, am indulging in the hope that you will credit me with worthy motives and ascribe my errors to that frailty of human foresight and judgment so seriously afflicting us all. When right I court your commendations, when wrong, I pray your forgiveness and sympathetic counsel. Ofttimes when right men will say I am wrong, because the judgments of men are not always made with full possession of all the facts and only too often their view fails to cover all of the ground. At this the beginning I have been made to feel supremely conscious that the people are with me now, and as the days lengthening into the years may come and go, my constant prayer to the Divine Ruler shall be so to prepare me, so to lead me, that they will be with me to the end.

Governor John W. Martin
Term: 1925 - 1929

John Wellborn Martin (born June 21, 1884 – died February 22, 1958), a native Floridian, was born at Plainfield in Marion County. Admitted to the bar in 1914–he had attended school for four years and then completed his education by studying at night—Martin practiced law in Jacksonville. Entering local politics, he served three terms as Jacksonville's mayor and turned the experience and the reputation he had earned into a successful race to garner the Democratic nomination for governor in 1924. Martin swamped William R. O'Neal, his Republican opponent, who had run against Trammell in 1912, in the general election.

Martin's administration presided over Florida's boom and bust during the 1920s, attracting both national and statewide acclaim and derision. Beyond the dramatic events of the decade (spectacular land deals and growth, expansion of building, more and more banks that made more and more loans, thousands of investors, permanent settlers, and tourists, both the "the tin can" variety and the affluent), the Martin administration rates good marks for its progressive program. The boom's end was underscored and italicized by the banking crisis and the hurricane of 1926 (in the Miami area it claimed 392 lives and adversely affected thousands of families). Then in 1928 another hurricane caused Lake Okeechobee to overflow and may have cost at least 2,000 deaths. Late in the year a disastrous freeze caused damage of Biblical proportions.

Despite the writ large disasters, Martin could claim credit for free textbooks for students in the first through six grades, direct state appropriations for public education; and the building of highways across the state. Martin was defeated for a US Senate seat in 1928 and for reelection to the governor's chair in 1932. In his later career, Martin was trustee of the Florida East Coast railroad.

Inaugural Address

(Source: Jacksonville *Florida Times-Union*, January 7, 1925)

To my fellow citizens of Florida:

In this hour, on this impressive occasion, I have taken the solemn oath of the office of Governor of Florida as prescribed by the constitution and the law. Thus, the mandate of the people as expressed in the Democratic primary and confirmed in the general election has been fully executed and sealed. It was your wish and decision to place in the hands of your fellow-citizen who addresses you, this great responsibility and trust. I have accepted it. In return, I pledge you the use of my best talents and consecrate myself on the altar of duty to honest, courageous service.

Let us today bury and forget political differences and animosities and abandon sectional distrusts. The well-being and prosperity of the state can mean only happiness and benefits to the people. Every citizen is an integral part of the state government and has his share in its operation. This responsibility should not be shirked. Loyalty to the state does away with misunderstanding, often the breeder of discontent and prejudice. It behooves us, therefore, to have honest confidence in one another. In this way and through harmonious effort and co-operation, the best results can be accomplished.

The growth and advancement of the state depends upon the proper development and utilization of the state's diversified and magnificent resources. In keeping with this, it shall be my steadfast purpose to devote and direct my energy and ability to aid in affording the people of this great commonwealth an honest and efficient administration of governmental affairs, with the least possible burden. It shall be my pleasure and earnest effort to co-operate with the other departments of the government in securing for the people a reduction and equalization of taxes, economy and efficiency in office, the building and maintenance of good roads, the improvement of the public school and its facilities, prompt and impartial administration of the law, the safe-guarding of the public health, encouragement to the agricultural, citrus, horticultural, and mining industries of the state, the conservation of the oyster and fish resources of the state, drainage of the Everglades, justice to labor and capital and all other interests that tend to the welfare and happiness of the people. But above everything, let us constantly remember that the greatest need to the security of good government and to its perpetuity is the training for good citizenship—the youth of the state. And in so doing the democratic principles of "government of the people, by the people and for the people," will be forever sustained.

My fellow-citizens, permit me to express my deep appreciation and gratitude for the great honor you have so generously conferred upon me. It is a great responsibility and task. I realize the weakness of human nature and my own limitations and you may expect me to commit errors but I ask your counsel and indulgence. I go into office wholly free and unhampered to serve. The office belongs to you. It shall be conducted as yours. It will not be necessary for the people to speak to me indirectly, through any agency, individual, or group of men, and I shall not speak to them in any other but a direct manner. The office shall be open to all of the people. With the aid of the patriotic law-abiding citizens and with full and implicit faith in Him the supreme ruler of the destinies of all governments and men, I look to the future with hope and confidence.

Governor Doyle E. Carlton
Term: 1929 - 1933

Doyle Elam Carlton (born July 6, 1887 – died October 25, 1972), another native Floridian, began a law practice at Tampa in 1912 with impressive educational credentials: undergraduate degrees from Stetson and the University of Chicago and a law degree from Columbia University. His was the dubious distinction of dealing with the first years of the Great Depression. Before that he served as state senator from the district of Pinellas and Hillsborough counties. In the Democratic primary Governor Carlton defeated four opponents including a strong race by former governor Catts. In the general election Carlton beat his GOP opponent W. J. Howey by over 53,000 votes.

Carlton faced the aftermath of the 1920s plus new problems of economic depression and the unexpected destruction caused by the

Mediterranean fruit fly. As governor he trimmed state services, backed governmental streamlining, urged paving roads on a pay-as-you-go basis, and supported the restriction of local government bonding. He backed a sales tax to raise money but opposed levying a state income tax, and, on moral grounds, opposed legalized gambling. He lost on the latter issue: in 1931 the legislature created a State Racing Commission, legalized pari-mutual betting, and taxed the proceeds. Cities cut budgets and reduced tax millages, "Buy Now" campaigns were launched, and municipal and county relief efforts, although inadequate, did more than the Board of Public Welfare which lacked resources. President Hoover's philosophy of self-sufficiency proved inadequate as Florida was hard hit by the large number of transients, many of them young who flocked to the state, although some relief came with the Republican president's extension of the Reconstruction Finance Corporation's powers. Governor Carlton asked for $500,000 and Florida got its' first relief funds in September 1932.

Carlton remained active after he left the governor's chair, resuming his Tampa law practice. In 1936 he tried to reenter politics by contesting for the Democratic party's nomination for US Senator but lost in an extremely close election to Charles O. Andrews. He served as special attorney for the state and was president of the Florida State Chamber of Commerce in 1951-1952.

Inaugural Address
(Source: Jacksonville *Florida Times-Union*, January 9, 1929)

I am grateful beyond expression for the honor which is mine by the vote of the people. I accept it as a call to service, and shall, in patriotism as well as gratitude dedicate my talents to the happiness of our people and the welfare of the state of Florida.

This day marks the beginning of another ear in the history of Florida, with problems great but possibilities greater. The next few years as no other period in our history will determine the destiny of the state. My share of responsibility is accepted in a spirit of deep humility and with an abiding sense of my dependence upon a wisdom greater than mine. In the fulfillment, therefore, of the task to which I am called, I earnestly invite the counsel of my fellow countrymen and invoke the gracious favor of Almighty God.

Before dealing with the fundamental principles of government, the proper conception of public service, a constructive program for the building of the state, I call attention to the problem of finance and taxation so intimately interwoven with this as to involve the very structure of our government. This problem must be solved as a condition to our future progress.

The duties and powers of the chief executive are measured by the fundamental law of the land—our constitution, to which I must ever resort,, and which I swear to preserve, protect and defend. All public officers, with me, must find in this the chart and compass of our official conduct—the greatest safeguard of stable government.

Perhaps the greatest menace to the purpose of the constitution is the evil of "over-government" where each new ill seems to seek its remedy in some new bureau, commission or public office, until our government is rapidly passing from the hands of the people to the office-holding class. In the interest, therefore, of economy, efficiency and democracy, we must keep our government as simple and direct as possible, with every branch of the state's activity directly accountable to some constitutional officer, who, in turn, is directly accountable to the people through the ballot. Useless offices should be abolished; kindred functions should be consolidated; all to avoid overlapping, confusing, and interrupting activities.

The passage of local legislation without notice is false to the spirit and purpose of our constitution. Measures suddenly conceived and hastily passed do thus become the edict of a minority rather than an expression of the will of the people. The results are iniquitous in many cases and unfair in all where unexpected burdens are voted on unsuspecting people. Provision is made in our state for passing local measures upon giving proper notice. That provision is plain, positive, and generous. It is to protect rights that are sacred. I shall, therefore, at the opening session of our legislature, bring the subject before our lawmakers with the belief that they will join me in defeating every local measure not offered in accordance with constitutional requirements. Wherever, therefore, we have wandered away from the constitution, let us return to the house of our fathers, thus carrying our government back to the people and the people back to our government.

Speaking nationally, as well as state-wide, we are becoming the most legislated and worse regulated people on earth. Our goal should ever be: Fewer laws and better observance; the lowest reasonable number of public officers; the highest possible conception of public service.

A perfect machinery of government, however, will prove futile, unless administered by faithful public servants who find in office their highest reward, not in the material compensation it brings, but in the honor and glory which come from a noble and upright public service.

Among the duties of the chief executive, there is none more important than the choice of subordinates. In the nature of things, with the change of an administration, there are frequent changes in personnel, to meet the requirements of the new administration. In our change, however, no one will be displaced for personal reasons; none appointed for political purposes; no one denied a place but with regret. I shall share the grief of all those who may be disappointed in their aspirations for public service. It must be remembered that positions are few—they will be fewer. Applications are many—they will increase. Regardless of our personal feeling, we must think of each public office in terms of service to the people, rather than favor for the individual.

Those so fortunate as to find employment should remember that these are days when the people have a right to expect more of their public servants than in times of ease and great prosperity. The burden of the taxpayers should be an inspiration to greater service by public officers. Those who may be tempted to use their office for unholy gain, to withhold service for which they are paid, to greedily absorb excessive fees or cling to moneys belonging to the people must catch a new vision of public service.

In the work which lies before us, I shall ask no more of the lowliest servant than, as your chief executive, I must give to the state. I shall, at all times, be on the front lines of service and, if need be, sacrifice, and shall withhold no executive power in helping public officers to discharge their full duty under the law.

Florida has been blessed by a host of faithful public servants, ever loyal to her honor. Let us, at the beginning of this new year, renew our vows at the shrine of our country and with pride in our task and devotion to duty, write across the life of this state, in letters that will never die. "public office is a public trust and a true public officer is a servant of all the people."

It is well, on a day like this, that we pause to seriously measure not only our political, but economic strength and security. We have had an era of unparalleled, we might say, unbridled prosperity, and while great permanent progress has been made, much that is transient has already passed away. Abnormal conditions have left their mark on public as well as private life to such an extent as to endanger the fine reputation of the state for a sane conservatism.

For this we blame no one. It is a logical outcome of the spirit of the times just passed. But the results are evident. We now find ourselves in a time of peace, burdened with a wartime equipment. We have made triumphal advances on every front but at a cost which must now be paid. Weak spots have developed in our financial structure. Public expenditures—and I speak of county and municipal as well as state—have become excessive. Our disbursements have exceeded our receipts to an alarming degree, with taxes far too high.

To make ends meet our general revenue fund has had to borrow from the pension fund $50,000, from the general inspection fund $400,000, from the text book fund $150,000, from the fire insurance fund $50,000, from the motor vehicle license maintenance fund $150,000, from the permanent building fund $100,000, from banks $535,964.65 and it owes a tax collectors in unpaid commissions $71,301.03. In addition to this we have an outstanding indebtedness to meet of $600,000 for public buildings making a total of more than $2,000,000 owed by the general revenue fund. Our first responsibility then is either bring our receipts up to our expenditures or our expenditures down to our receipts. This gap cannot continue to widen without disaster. There is, my friends, a deadline of cost in government which, when reached by the taxing power, marks the decline of a state's prosperity. We are approaching too dangerously close to that deadline now.

It is, therefore, plain to see that a sound fiscal and a sane economic policy lie at the base of our future development. We face this at every turn. Let us deceive ourselves no longer, but meet with vigor and courage the problem which will determine the destiny of our state. This issue is even more vital to counties and cities than to the state, for state obligations are small compared with those of counties, districts, and municipalities. Our interests, however, are so bound together that weakness of one endangers the other; a default in one discredits all. Ours must be a policy of rigid retrenchment and never dishonorable repudiation.

Every branch of government activity must begin the new year with a strict accounting—a rigid budgeting and organization from the standpoint of economy, efficiency and service. Unnecessary expenditures must be eliminated; useless offices must be abolished. Men must be employed as needed, because of their fitness for the task to which they are called and their willingness to give the state the service for which they are paid.

Responsibility does not rest upon public officials alone. Private citizens must carry their share of the burden and interest themselves in the affairs of their government, either with or without the approval of their officers. Investigation, counsel, co-operation on the part of the private citizens will stimulate efficient public service. Too often our interest in public affairs ends with an election. Moreover, taxpayers can now best serve themselves and aid the state by discharging as promptly as possible their obligations to the government. Florida expects every citizen—public and private—to answer the call in one common spirit with one common purpose. Our patriotism must be exalted and applied to the problems of peace as well as the trials of war.

The uppermost problem—finance and taxation—must be met with wisdom and caution. The fact that nearly 25% of our lands are off the tax books for non-payment of taxes; that collections have fallen off 10, 20, and in some cases 50 per cent in counties and municipalities in the last two years that the state paid out $707,380 for costs in making tax sales, show that the problem is serious. Investigations further discloses that the default is not wholly due to inability to pay, but to the weakness of our collection system. A reasonable tax, equitably distributed, with a collection law that is simple and certain is a necessary condition to the financial stability of the state.

We must next restrict the power by which counties and districts burden themselves with financial obligations. In one county, ten citizens by a vote of eight to two, bonded their community for many thousands. In other places, bonded indebtedness almost equals the assessed valuation. The multiplication of bonding districts is a menace to the financial security of the state. The duties now discharged by bond trustees should be headed up in some county officer required to keep proper records and make regular reports to some state authority. Today, in the majority of counties, there is no central authority where one can find the obligations of the counties and their districts. Authority must be centralized and responsibility must be fixed.

There are three parties at interest in the fiscal soundness of the state. First, organized government which cannot survive except by taxes, promptly paid; second, the taxpayer, who in many cases is overburdened; third, the investor in Florida securities who has a right to expect prompt payment of obligations.

These interests must be protected. This, however, is not the time for a detailed outline of program. Information is being gathered along all lines affecting the outlook of the state and will be furnished legislators and other public officers to guide them in their councils.

Let me warn you that relief cannot come in a day. Miracles are not performed by man. We, as a people, cannot in a moment repair the imprudence of years. We shall meet, however, the emergency as it exists, and then with patience and fortitude, with confidence and wisdom, build for the coming years. Our path is clear. The solution of our problems is certain. Never was there such intelligent interest, such oneness of sentiment, such readiness to act on the part of our people. Never were the prospects brighter for a progress that is permanent. From our experience of the past we have caught the vision of values that will endure.

Fundamentally, our state is as sound as the Rock of Gibraltar. Our climate, which is a commodity that cannot be carried away, is the dream of the multitudes.

Our location, once considered a handicap, is now by improved railways, highway, waterways and airways, brought into the center of the nation's activities and lying in the very path of the future trade and travel of America.

More miles of railway were, in one recent year, built in Florida than in all the other states taken together. Some of these lines are of a pioneering nature, but they are prepared for a great advance. By rail we are within forty-eight hours of 75 per cent of the wealth and population of our country; not more than one-half to one-third the distance from our centers of population as is our nearest competitor.

Great progress has been made in highways. The road work will go on, but in keeping with our ability to pay as we go.

Our federal government has spent in excess of $38,000,000 to improve the harbors and waterways of Florida. These present an advantage of immeasurable significance to industry and commerce.

Travel by air now leads in point of progress and promises untold value to the state. It is easier to foresee great airliners with cargoes of passengers or freight flying between Florida and distant points that it was thirty years ago to foresee the Wright brothers making their initial flight of a few hundred feet. We must be on the alert to take advantage of this great movement.

Our public improvements in the way of schools, other public buildings, highways and the like have increased far beyond 1000 per cent in the last ten years. Some of these improvements are in advance of our needs, but have prepared us for the future.

Certain public utilities starting with the social population of 1900, estimate that by 1940, Florida will be home of over 3,000,000 persons.

The insurance companies, twenty years ago, found their premium income in Florida to be less than $5,000,000. Last year it was $51,000,000 or 1,000 per cent increase.

The banks twenty years ago showed a total financial strength of $51,000,000. In December of last year, their strength was ten times greater, or over $518,000,000. But as I stated in my platform: We must improve our banking laws and practices with provisions for adequate examination and strict supervision for the protection of depositors and stockholders.

Our school population, twenty years ago, was only 130,000; now it is nearly 400,000—an increase of nearly 300 per cent. Our school facilities twenty years ago were valued at about $2,000,000 now at over $70,000,000, an increase of 3,500 per cent.

Great wealth has rapidly arisen in the state. We paid into our national treasury in 1972—the last complete report as much and almost half as much again inheritance tax as all the other southern states combined. We were fifth in the United States. Fairness on the part of the federal government, prudence on the part of the state, will make this the investment home of untold millions. If, however, the federal inheritance tax is not repealed and the discrimination heretofore done to Florida rectified, we should, through our delegations in congress, call upon our federal government to return 80 per cent of the inheritance tax paid by our state into the federal treasury. There is no reason or justice in punishing our state and requiring us to divide our tax monies with other states of the Union simply because we do not see fit to pass laws like theirs. With our boom over, opportunities for profitable investments are now such as to bring in capital as rapidly as we prepare the way.

Our Everglades constitute an area of immeasurable wealth, and must be reclaimed in a wise engineering and a sound economic manner, with regard to the future as well as to the immediate present.

The state is rich in her forestry possibilities. At one time our lumber and naval stores produced one third of the state's income, business and payrolls. We must, however, guard against exhausting this resource with no adequate effort for its replenishment, give more attention to those resources which can never reproduce and by human supervision, never become exhausted.

I wonder if we too often think of our state as a place where wealth is found, rather than created. The ease with which it comes, sometimes misleads. There is no land so responsive to labor, so suggestive to enterprise and capital as Florida. It is essentially a land of industry, agriculture and forest products. It makes its appeal to the man who works. Our future lies in production and not in promotion. Our reward must come through labor—"The curse of Earth's morning is the blessing of its noon." Work—physical, mental, spiritual, continuous—is the warrant of our expectation. To me, the greatest material blessing the Son of Man ever gave to the world was when He came, not in the pomp and pride of a king, but as an humble child of toil and thereby lifted labor from the level of serfdom and crowned it with glory and honor. Let us talk in our homes, let us teach in our schools, let us proclaim from every platform of this great commonwealth, the dignity of industry and effort as an inescapable condition to the future glory of the state. By the sweat of our face, shall we build Florida.

But, in the last analysis, the strength of a state is not all found in its form of government or economic resources. Lowell reminds us that the value of a nation is weighed in scales more delicate than the balance of trade, as much as to say, that it is the manpower linked with the soul that gives strength to a people—that manpower which must be developed through our common schools and institutions of higher learning, in the building of physical, mental and spiritual values. The education of our young citizenship is the path to permanent progress. Proper training is more vital to the defense of a nation than armies, forts and implements of war. Skip one generation in education and our people would lapse into servitude. Organized society performs no function so vital to its perpetuity as the education of the youth who, in a few short years, will arbitrate the destinies of the world. With millions expended, our schools are crowded and facilities are inadequate. What shall the program be? Shall we admit some and close the doors to others? If so, whose son or daughter shall be left out? Shall our schools continue—or for lack of funds be compelled to close? As we prize the higher values of life, so shall material things survive and prosper.

> We are blind until we see
> That in the human plan
> Nothing is worth the making
> That doesn't make the man.
>
> Why build these cities glorious
> If man unbuilded goes?
> In vain we build the world
> Unless the builder grows.

When we contemplate the problems of the present, the possibilities of the future, when we find the honor, happiness and hopes of our people involved in the issues of this hour we might be tempted to despair. Yet there is not distrust of the future. The wisdom of our potential greatness is clear.

Our strength has been tested by storm as well as calm; by misguided friends and malicious enemies; by abnormal prosperity and abnormal adversity. We are wiser and stronger by the experience and stand now at the dawn of a new day on a new land, not a land of reckless speculation but a land of safe investment; not a land of wild promotion, but a land of sound production; not a land of dreams where fairies dwell but a land of reality where strong men work, achieve and build.

I shall enter my path of duty strong in the experience of my official comrades; inspired by a trust in the patriotism of our people; sustained by my faith in the Father of Light who presides over the destinies of states as well as of men.

Governor David Sholtz
Term: 1933 - 1937

David Sholtz (born October 6, 1891 – died March 21, 1953) was a New Yorker born in Brooklyn. His undergraduate degree was from Yale and his law degree was from Stetson University. He served as an ensign in the navy during World War I. Sholtz practiced law in Daytona Beach and entered Volusia County politics. His first elected position was as a member of the Florida State House of Representatives in 1917. He was state's attorney from 1919 to 1921 the year he became city judge. In the 1932 gubernatorial contest Sholtz faced seven Democrats, including two former governors, Hardee and Martin, who were expected to lead the party's primary election ticket. In the voting Martin got the most votes but Sholtz was in second place and well within striking range. In the run off election he won by a wide margin of 70,000 votes. Sholtz had become president of Florida's Chamber of Commerce in 1927 and had many contacts across the state. Promising the voters a business-like administration, he offered solid proposals for action. Just as Franklin D. Roosevelt would be swept into national office by promising a New Deal, Sholtz had his "Little" New Deal for Florida. Sholtz almost doubled the Republican E. E. Callaway's voting total in the general election. The prohibition issue provoked some cynics to say that Sholtz's victory came because voters confused him with Schlitz, and thought they were voting to bring back beer. Repeal came with the ratification of the Twenty-First Amendment on December 5, 1933.

Florida felt the impact of the Great Depression by the time Roosevelt took over in Washington and Sholtz assumed the leadership of Florida. FDR's New Deal profoundly affected all Floridians. The various federal agencies—the Works Progress Administration, National Youth Administration, Civilian Conservation Corps, federal aid to agriculture, the National Recovery Administration, and others—left permanent imprints. Sholtz had major difficulties raising sufficient money to pay the state's share of administering the programs. New state tax policies were enacted, the State Welfare Board became active, and various economic groups became dissatisfied. Overall, the program was a success. The city of Key West fell into financial chaos, and Governor Sholtz declared a state of emergency. The community was turned over to the Federal Emergency Relief Administration (FERA). Great progress was made until the Labor Day hurricane of 1935 hit and claimed at least 500 lives in the Florida Keys. Yet, rebuilding took place and the a new highway was opened in 1938 connecting Key West to the mainland. World War II and wartime prosperity completed the rebirth. Apalachicola and Franklin County experienced less dramatic changes but benefitted from the results of federal and state agencies working together. In the long run the New Deal's contribution as well as that of Governor Sholtz were more realistically felt, but in the short run there was some displeasure in Florida with both. Neither of their programs pulled Florida out of the Great Depression. Still, they galvanized Floridians and stopped the sharp economic slide.

Inaugural Speech
(Source: Tallahassee *Daily Democrat*, January 3, 1933)

My Fellow Floridians and my Good Friends: The Constitution of the state prescribes the oath of office for your chief executive. It in itself constitutes perhaps all that need be said in an inaugural address.

Were I not to consider my oath of office as a serious and binding one, I would be totally unfit for the trust and confidence that you have reposed in me. I solemnly assure you that in my efforts during the next four years to serve you as I feel a public servant should serve you, the mandates of my oath of office shall at all times be my guiding star.

Nothing that I can say on this occasion will be of value whatsoever or will be long remembered if my oath of office be lightly regarded or easily forgotten. The people rightfully should and will judge us more by what we do during the next four years, than by what we may say or may leave unsaid on this occasion.

I am grateful, and take this opportunity to thank the people of Florida for the confidence they have manifested in me by giving me the extraordinarily large majorities at the primary and general election. I believe and am confident that these majorities are definite evidence of the fact that the people will give me their support.

And may I express my grateful appreciation and thanks to the Chamber of Commerce of the city, their officials, the various committees, the citizenship generally, and particularly the official committee chairman and his committee for their hospitality, their courtesy and their expression of good-will in their efforts to stage a gala and proper recognition of the occasion and which has been so ably done.

I am also grateful that you have not only honored me by elevating me to the high and noble and the distinguished position of your Governor; but you have likewise given me the opportunity to render a service to a great State and to its distinguished citizenry. It is through your gracious benificence that mine is the honor to become not only your chief executive, but likewise your co-worker in all worthy efforts.

I am soberly conscious of the responsibility which I assume on this occasion, and I do humbly realize that mine is the obligation to respond with all of the industry and ability that God has given me to the trust and confidence, you have reposed in me.

It is my earnest desire and purpose to so conduct the affairs and responsibilities of the office of chief executive as to secure the greatest good for the greatest number.

Having embarked upon this mission of high governmental responsibility, I. shall train my sails not according to political advantage but rather according to the things I believe are right.

Today you are an expectant people because you feel, and I believe you have a right to feel, that the future of this State holds much promise of just reward for industry, enterprise and frugality.

You are and always have been a patriotic people, always willing to forget and forego petty differences when the welfare of the State or the Nation is imperiled or involved.

You are a progressive people, and no one can compare what we have in Florida today with what we had a decade ago and but realize that the progress that has been made in educational, spiritual and material development is second to none among our sister states of this great nation. Certain it is that for Florida the curfew has not yet tolled the knell of parting day.

You are a patient people because you have borne disappointments and hardships that always attended a national and world-wide depression with fortitude and with hope.

The people of Florida as a whole have the right to feel every degree of confidence and of optimism that an industrious people in a State of great opportunities, many of which are partially developed and many of which are largely undeveloped, should feel.

We have the blessings of sunshine, and a matchless climate, of fertile soil, and perhaps the greatest variety of resources of any State in the Union. Our population and our wealth have increased many fold in the last generation, and there need be no fear but that such increase will continue in the succeeding generation.

However magnificent our climate, our soil and our natural advantages in Florida may be, unless we have wise, sane, conservative and economical administration of affairs, there will be no influx or capital here until men with financial means are assured of such administration.

It is true that in times of plenty all peoples are prone to anticipate that plenty will always prevail, and in this we people of Florida have been no exception. Thus it is that in portions of our State we have burdened our present and we have magnified the problem of our future by having contracted debts which in the more mature light of the present we would have contracted. It is folly to state that in many instances and in restricted areas these debts have not precipitated a. troublesome and most perplexing problem.

The ultimate solution in some instances may be far from clear to the minds of any of us; but with courage, fortitude and determination the situation is being met by those of our people directly affected. With God's help I am confident of ultimate success. At any and all times whatever service, counsel, and advice your chief executive can give, will be willingly and eagerly rendered.

The unfortunate financial and economic condition in which many of our counties, municipalities and tax districts now find themselves is, to some extent, a result of the indifference of our people to governmental matters. If you question this, go to your public records and investigate for yourselves the manner in which this indebtedness was incurred. Consider well the fact that in many instances less than 25 per cent of the qualified electors were sufficiently interested even to go to the polls and vote upon the proposed expenditure.

A similar lack of interest in political matters has, to some extent, impaired the efficiency of our national, state, county and municipal governments and has caused you and me to labor and suffer under some tax burdens and governmental restrictions that seem unnecessary and unwise. The responsibility for this is ours and we must see that it does not again occur.

I say to you that a Democratic and free government for the people must be of the people and by the people, we cannot have the privileges without the responsibilities. You cannot successfully apply the principles of absent treatment to a Democratic form of government.

The vote in our State and Nation in November clearly and positively indicates to me that the people at last have awakened and fully realized this; they have taken their government back into their hands—may it remain there forever more!

I urge that you maintain that interest and that each citizen in this Stare familiarize himself or herself with the affairs of the Nation, State, county and city, so that we may never revert to that dangerous condition, or state of indifference to government from which we are now emerging.

Let every citizen be cognizant of the responsibilities and privileges of citizenship and be zealous in the performance and enjoyment of each.

If I can arouse and maintain your interest in the affairs of your government so that you will actively and energetically consider and participate therein, I shall feel that my term of office has had a most encouraging and worthwhile inauguration.

Assuming the office of governor as I do, without previous commitment or obligations of any political nature, things will of necessity be done in the setting of our house in order that will arouse the anger of any selfish interests, of professional politicians and political racketeers. Regardless of their chicanery, their conniving and their attacks, I. shall as governor hew to the line, letting the chips fall where they may, without regard for anything but the general good.

This is a fitting occasion to impress upon the minds of our people the priceless heritage of citizenship in our great country. Many millions of people of other countries consider as greatest luxuries the very things that we consider necessities, such as the automobile, radio, telephone, good roads and other things.

There are radical communists in our very midst who would literally destroy our great country. They would deprive us of the three fundamental American rights that we have: That of worshiping God as we see fit; that of maintaining our homes and raising our children in our own way; and the right to have orderly government. It is high time that the citizenship of the United States began to think in terms of the United States, to trade at home, to buy American produced products, and to realize that we owe an obligation of brotherhood and friendship each to the other. It is time we began to think Florida and buy Florida, think United States and buy United States.

There has been a gradual inculcation of radical communistic ideas, particularly in these times. It has spread so that many many instructors in American colleges and public schools have become and are becoming inbued with such ideas and are secretly imparting them to students and citizens.

The situation in Florida is no exception. There is great danger in American liberty and institutions just so long as there is a careless disregard and lack of appreciation for the priceless heritage and inheritance that we enjoy. No student should be graduated from our public schools or universities unless able to pass satisfactory examinations covering fundamental principles of Federal and State Constitutions.

Be Americans, be Floridians, proud of our country and proud of our State, militantly aggressive in the cause of good, decent, clean government.

This occasion is neither the time nor the place for your governor to discuss in detail new laws or changes in existing laws which he feels would be of common benefit to the people or Florida. Your public servants, chosen by you as your legislators, will assemble in April, and then, I shall make such specific recommendations as I believe to be beneficial for our orderly development and for our common welfare.

I ask for cooperation by the legislative and administrative department in enforcing strict economy in every governmental function. I here and now put all on notice that efficiency and economy shall be the unvarying rule of my administration.

It is however not amiss for me to say on this occasion that you have bestowed upon me this honor and have chosen me your public servant only after a campaign in which I promised you an economical administration, and urged that your expenses of government should be reduced as much as would be consistent with the orderly development of the State and the retention of our constitutional form of government.

My friends, such promises made by me were not for the purpose of charming an imagination to the end that political preferment should be bestowed upon me. I meant what I said then and I mean it today.

The determining factor in dealing with most of our State affairs can be clearly outlined by asking ourselves three questions: 1.

Can the State afford it? 2. Does the State have money to pay for it? 3. Can I the State get along without it?

The same questions can well apply to our city and county governments. Naturally I intend to do all that is humanly possible and in my power to see to it that intelligent economy is effected in every branch of the State government. If extravagance or waste can be found in times particularly such as these, they must be rooted out.

The business of Florida is the biggest business of Florida. It will require constant uninterrupted and undivided attention on the part of your chief executive. Aided by the drafted loyalty, unselfishness and patriotism of Florida's best citizens, virtually every requirement of sound governmental practices should be sure of accomplishment.

It is my expectation during the next three months to devote myself to a continuation of a study of Florida's problems. I expect, first, to ascertain just what the State's condition is financially. I look upon Florida as a great corporation, the people in it as its stockholders and myself as its chief executive.

You, the people of Florida, are entitled to know just how the State stands financially. Just as soon as I ascertain what the financial condition of the State is, I expect to give that information through the press to the people, so that they may know what the situation is, thereby enabling them to manifest their representatives in the legislature as well as the chief executive what is desired.

I expect the detailed audits of the different departments to show that funds appropriated for some departments have been diverted under the law to the use of other departments, and that the probabilities are that the funds so diverted cannot be replaced for some time to come.

I expect the detailed audit further to show that the State of Florida is having great difficulty in meeting the actual costs of government, not only on account of shortages of funds but also on account of the high cost of operating the State government.

Some reduction in the expenses of our governmental machinery can come through executive order. Many reductions must come through legislative sanction. We all know that today most businesses are required to merely survive. Profits, if any, are small. Many of our people are today continuing their struggle with unprofitable ventures solely by reason of the hope that the future holds for a brighter is promise.

The Federal Government in its effort to perpetuate itself, as sovereignty must at all times try to do, is laying a heavy hand in the form of additional taxes upon industry. Men who have today adjusted their businesses to meet the present demands are necessarily anxious to know whether the State of Florida is going to make additional and increasing demands upon them.

When human activity as a whole is showing so small a margin of profit, or loss, as the case may be, it is clear to be seen that if new and additional taxes are imposed, they can only be met at the expense of further reduction in wages of the employed, or in the further curtailment of activities now going on, thereby increasing the number of our unemployed.

Florida needs to encourage instead of discourage her payrolls, Florida needs to encourage instead of discourage her citizens who now constitute her economic and industrial life.

For these reasons, I have heretofore, said and I now again say that the welfare of Florida will be best subserved by discouraging all efforts for new and additional sources of revenue and by conducting as economical a movement as is consistent with the ideals herein expressed. Such a program cannot help but restore confidence and that before long.

I shall not be unconscious of the fact that within constitutional and legal limitations I am your leader and your mouthpiece, and I shall at all times and on all occasions feel and know that the greatest leader and the best leader must at all times humbly and honorably serve you.

I sincerely pray that the efforts which I shall make as your Governor will meet with your approbation and approval. To this end I pledge you my every effort and my every devotion. I cannot do more. I would be unfaithful and untrue if I consciously did less.

And so in conclusion, may I repeat the words that immortal leader expressed in the first inaugural address:

> This is not a day of triumph, it is a day of dedication. Here muster not the forces of party, but the forces of humanity. Men's hearts wait upon us; men's

lives hang in the balance, men's hopes call upon us to say what we will do. Who dares fail to try? I summon all honest men, all patriotic, all forwardlooking men, to my side. God helping me, I will not fail them, if they will but counsel and sustain me.

Governor Fred P. Cone
Term: 1937 - 1941

Frederick Preston Cone (born September 28, 1871 – died July 28, 1948) was as plain, southern, and rural as Sholtz had been fast-spoken, Yankee, and urban. Cone had the weathered look of an outdoorsman, and, with his hair parted down the middle, gave the impression of what he was: a totally unpretentious man. In 1938 Governor Cone not only appointed Florida's first woman sheriff, Eugenia Simmons, who filled out her husband Claude's term (he died of pneumonia), he also, in the same year, after Walton County Sheriff D.C. Adkinson was fatally shot, appointed Adkinson's wife, Celia, as the second woman sheriff. Senator Claude Pepper appraised Cone accurately in his diary: "He is a grand fellow...an old cracker with the cunning of an Indian and a heart of gold." The folksy governor delivered an inaugural address without notes, and told Florida's lawmen,

"You sheriffs, when you deal with bandits and criminals, don't be too particular how you handle them, for the governor will be back of you."

Born in Florida's Columbia County, Cone attended Florida Agricultural College and Jasper Normal College, and began practicing law in Lake City after being admitted to the bar. He was also a banker and successful politician. From 1907-1913 he served in the Florida State Senate, and was president of that body in 1911.

Well known because of his long career, Cone entered the governor's race in 1936, which even by Florida's unusual electioneering practices, had a "crowded field" of fourteen candidates, including former governor Martin. No one received a majority in the first primary. A Tampa lawyer and judge, Raleigh W. Petteway led the field, although he received only sixteen percent of the vote. Cone was a close second. In the runoff primary Cone attracted enough votes from the defeated candidates to beat Petteway by a vote of 184,540 to 129,150. In the general election Elvery. E. ("E. E.") Callaway was the Republican nominee, but was embarrassingly defeated by Cone 253,638 to 59,832,.

Despite Roosevelt's popularity, Cone was no New Dealer. In his campaign he called for "lowering the budget to balance taxes instead of raising taxes to balance the budget." Although Florida voters gave Roosevelt a large majority in the same election, they demonstrated their independence by backing Cone. As governor the informal chief executive was known as "Old Swanee," and fought to reduce the budget and lower taxes. He firmly believed that individual Floridians should be relieved of indirect and hidden taxes. The legislature fought him, passing increased appropriations for public schools and a general appropriations bill almost a million dollars higher than in 1935. The chief executive and the legislature refused to consider income tax and inheritance tax proposals. Additional revenue came from the sale of tax-delinquent property that was put back on the tax rolls and from increased taxes on occupational licenses and higher liquor taxes. Cone took justifiable pride in Florida's state sponsored exhibit at the New York World's Fair in 1939. It was considered one of the best, and drew long lines of admiring crowds.

Inaugural Speech
(Source: Jacksonville *Florida Times Union*, January 6, 1937)

My Friends and fellow citizens of Florida. You have no idea how glad I am to be present here upon this occasion. You have no idea how much I appreciate all of you good people coming here to see me enjoy this occasion and I want to thank you all, one and all, for being present here today, and I want to thank the good people of this State, especially the people that voted for me in the first primary, and the thousands of other good people that supported me in the second primary, and for the overwhelming vote that you gave me as an endorsement, in the general election, and I want to tell you good people today, feeble as I may be, and I want to do by my acts during my four years as Governor of this State so that you good people won't be sorry that you voted for me.

Now, my friends, I want to say this in the beginning—I can't give everybody a job in this State. In fact, we are not going to have as many jobs as they have had heretofore, but I want all of you good people to know that if I don't give them to you, that I want to give them to you awful bad, but I just won't have them to give, and I hope you will take that for granted.

I am proud to have the confidence of the good people of this State, as has been shown to me, and I want to tell you that I recognize my inability to perform the many things that are going to be expected. I hope that you people will endure with me. I know that I am going to make a great many mistakes. Anyone who tries to do anything makes mistakes, but if I do make mistakes, they are going to be mistakes of the head and not of the heart, and they are going to be made in trying to do something for the best interests of the entire State.

We should all be proud that we live in Florida. We should be proud that we call ourselves citizens of this State, that has been blessed with practically every known natural resource. We have a balmy climate; we have almost perpetual sunshine; we have natural resources abounding in every part of this State; we have food in our lakes and rivers and along our seacoast, to feed all of our people in case of famine, and a great part of our Nation itself. We have so many advantages that other people do not have. I hope, my friends, that when I have served my four years as your Governor that you good people will still be proud to call yourselves citizens of this State.

My friends, we should all be happy indeed that we live under a democracy and a democratic form of government:, absolutely controlled by the people, so that the people themselves can change their government at will. No faction or clique or anything of that kind can control the vote and the actions of the people of this great country of ours.

You know a democracy is managed and controlled by representatives elected by direct vote of the people, and whenever the people take an interest in the affairs of their government, by going out and voting and participating in the management and control of their government—whenever they do that my friends, they can always control that government, but if, on the other hand, you do not look after your government and you take no interest in its affairs, it just gets in the hands of a few, in the minority, and then we do not have good government. I want to say to you good people here today that if anything ever happens to this government of ours, if it ever decays and crumbles into dust, and that dust is blown to the four corners of the world, it will be due to the indifference of our people.

If we want to continue this government of ours, so that our children, after we are passed and gone, may have a better government to live under; it is our business to look after the affairs of our government today. Our forefathers have handed you down a good government. They didn't look at the present; they looked to the future. They built the greatest democracy that has ever been thought of by human minds, and passed down from generation to generation to our people here today, and we should, if we think anything about prosperity and want to pass along a good government, look after the affairs of our government, and if, my friends, we look after the affairs of our good government and take an interest in its affairs, we can pass this great government down to the end of time, so that our children and our children's children can enjoy the blessings of good government.

We should be happy that we have a great democratic leader at the head of our Nation in the government at Washington—that great humanitarian whose every heartbeat is for mankind, a man who believes in that greatest of the principles of democracy—the greatest good to the greatest number; who can look over the faces of the special interests and the dollar, and into the faces of the American people, and say that everybody can enjoy some of the blessings of a free government. We should be happy, and are happy and fortunate in knowing that we have a man at the helm of our government now who will look after the interests of all of our people, and that we will have peace on earth and good will towards men.

I have no fear of war as long as Franklin D. Roosevelt is President of the United States.

I am confident that not only the people of this Nation, but the entire masses of all the entire world have confidence in Franklin D. Roosevelt's judgment, and that they will stand loyally by him in his efforts to maintain peace all over the world. I believe as firmly as I have ever believed anything in my life, that for the next four years we will have peace all over this world: that all of these difficulties will be peacefully settled, and that we will be a happy, contented and prosperous people.

My friends, I have not tried to make a prepared speech. I have never read a speech in my life. Every time I write one and try to say it, I always think of so much better things that I want to say, that I decided not to write one today. So I decided to give you people a short message, not everything, but just a few things that I am going to try to do. From time to time I am going to say other things to the good people of this State about what I am going to try to do for the benefit of all of the people, and I hope and believe that I will have the co-operation of the Legislature, and that I will have the moral support of all of the people of this State.

My friends, there are two questions that are foremost in the minds of the people of every democratic form of government—they are two simple words when you tell them, but they affect practically everything that has to do with any democratic form. of government. One of them is finance and the other is taxation.

There has [sic] always been disputes and always will be disputes about the question of finance and taxation, as long as we have free governments, and it is well that it should be, and my friends I am going to give you my idea of what should be done in regard to the finance and taxation situation in this State.

My friends, in every department of this State the income is increasing every month; it is increasing so fast, to wit: The gasoline tax money increases at the rate of a million and a quarter dollars a year, and every other department is increasing; so that if we would take our financial system in this State and our expenses, and bring it down to a level, good, honest, straight business basis, and hold it still for a few years, we would have all of the money in this State to do any thing with, that we needed.

The unfortunate thing has happened that every time we get new money we have new expenses, and with all of the millions of dollars that we have increased our income in the last few years, that have been stated by the previous governor, such as extra liquor taxes, increases in gasoline taxes, racing and other taxes, the expenses have increased right along with all of those extra things.

I don't know what would have happened if these taxes hadn't increased the income. I don't know whether the expenses would have stayed stationary or not. Take two years ago, our income was about thirty-five million dollars, and the expenses about the same thing. Now our income has increased to about forty-three or forty-four million dollars, in two years, and our expenses have kept pace with the increase. All of this increase, now, has been wrung out of the taxpayers of this State.

There is no way to get a dollar in the State Treasury, to be used for expenses, except for some taxpayer to pay it, in some form or another. My policy will be to go slow and follow one of the old principles of democracy that are as old as the Nation itself, and that is, the best government with the least amount of taxation.

If we do that we will be following one of the oldest principles of democracy that we have in the Democratic Party from its adoption and birth, and it is as old as the Nation itself.

The Democratic Party has always been an enemy of taxation, and when you follow Democratic principles, they have always been the enemy of every tax on earth.

A tax is nothing in the world but a penalty or fine for our living in a free government, because you cannot run a government without finances, and you cannot get finances without taxation.

I find that in the last few years we have collected a great deal more money that we did in the few years before, but we find that some of our departments of government and some people, instead of becoming tax-minded are what you call spending-minded, or whatever you call it, and have got in the habit of thoughtlessly and carelessly spending and wasting the people's money, and practically all of these so-called boards; and commissions have increased their expenses to such an extent that it is almost a disgrace to our State.

Take the State Road Department—the money that has been wasted in that Road Department would take care of practically any other want that we should have. Our State Racing Commission ban spent enough money uselessly to give every county in this State from two to three thousand dollars extra money, to help out with their expenses.

Things of this kind I am going to try to eliminate if I possibly can do it, and I believe that the Legislature will be 100 per cent with me. They have assured me, practically 75 or 80 per cent of them, that they are with me in this program 100 per cent, and if they do, then we will put this State on a Democratic, business basis, and when we do, we will have all of the money that we need for every purpose whatsoever.

The hardest time I am going to have is going to be in the next 18 months or two years. We have coming up now some extra things that we did not all expect, out of the ordinary, that we have got to look into and take care of. One of them is the old age pension voted by a mandate of the people, and we have got to provide this fund from five or six or maybe seven million dollars extra money, in order to carry out this mandate. What is going to worry me more than anything else is how we will raise that money without extra taxation and without putting any more taxes on the back of the people of this State, but I tell you right now, that if the Legislature will do it, and I believe they will with the moral backing of the citizens of this State we will take care of this extra item, without putting any more taxation on the people of the State.

All we can do, my friends, is to give the best government with the least amount of taxation.

It is not my idea to cut people's salaries. I do not believe in paying niggardly salaries. That is false economy and it could be a bad thing to come in here and cut people's salaries, because the laborer is always worthy of his hire, but I am not going to put 10 or 15 or 20 men on the payroll, when we don't need but five. That has been the trouble with our Government today, putting people of the payroll when we didn't need them, because somebody else pays the bill. I believe the minds of the people of this State are already made up on that question, and I am not going to put a single man on the payroll unless I am satisfied that he is absolutely needed.

Some of the salaries paid in this State are very inadequate. You take some of the highest elective officers in this State, the Cabinet officers, are the most poorly paid, and I think that while the past legislatures were increasing some of the big salaries, and furnishing free cars to ride in, and almost unlimited expense accounts, that they might have thought something about some of our constitutional officers here.

It is going to be my idea to pay people a living salary, but I do not believe in packing the payroll with hundreds of people that we don't need.

Then we have our schools and educational system to take care of. That is the most important department of our government because our boys and girls will be the future men and women we will leave in charge of our government a few years from now, and our government will be theirs, and how it will be will depend on what we do for them now. If we can, we should avoid any neglect in the education of our children, for the foundation of the government itself depends on them, for no government is better than its citizens. I am going to give the schools every dollar that we can give, commensurate with a business and economical government, and I hope the school people will co-operate with us, because our hearts will be with the boys and girls of this State, and every dollar that we can legitimately spare, taking into consideration the needs of this government, I am going to give to the schools. I want them to get a certain amount of money that they can count on, and not depend on collecting any particular taxation.

There is one thing specially that I believe causes us more trouble in this State than any other one thing, and that is the tax powers that are given certain boards and commissions that are not responsible to the State, or anyone else. We look at the picture of the State collecting forty-three or forty-four million dollars and the Legislature only appropriating nine or ten million dollars of that amount, expended by them. In other words, I believe that the constitutional branch of this government, the Legislature, should appropriate every dollar spent by this Government, whereas it really appropriates about 25 per cent of the money that is spent in this State. Yes, I contend that every dollar that is expended in this State should be passed on by the Legislature, after these different departments have been properly budgeted, and I shall contend that all of the money collected in this State, by whatever means, shall first be put in the treasury of the State, where it belongs, and appropriated out by the Legislature, and that every one of these commissions and boards be budgeted by the Legislature itself, the only constitutional power that we have in this State for that purpose, and when we do that we will begin to have orderly government in this State.

I am proud of a lot of our boards and commissions, if we can afford that luxury. I am proud of the board of patrol that we have here that rides up and down the road and looks after the filling stations and one thing and another. I am proud of them, but my friends, they should have been authorized by the Legislature, and not be put on by the State Road Department.

It is very nice for us to have an airplane to be used by the State, but if they want to go around in one, the Legislature should be in favor of it and appropriate the money lawfully and orderly, to pay the expenses for the aviation department of this State, and not just let the State Road Department go into the aviation business. If these things can be done we may have some submarines running around in the lakes for the pleasure and amusement of some people.

I think and believe that the citizenship of this great State desires that the lawful branch of our government, to wit, the Legislature, should have the power to do all of these things, and I am going to say right now, whilst I am here, that I am not going to try to interfere with the lawful powers of the Legislature, but I am going to try to the best of my ability to look after the executive department of this government and let the Legislature look after their part. I am going to try to co-operate with them and want them to co-operate with me, but we have three branches of government in this State, the legislative, executive and judicial, but they are separate branches and each of then should manage its own affairs, and not go and try to dictate what the Legislature should do. I am going to recommend to them in a lawful way what I. think should be done, and leave them free to carry out the mandates of their people back home, and then, my friends, I believe, we will have more orderly government in this State.

We are coming into what is known as a humane age, the time that we must think more about humanity and less about the almighty dollar. For 150 years the American people have used up the natural resources of this country, that nature gave to everybody, and they have passed into the hands of a few, and there have been built up colossal fortunes that can hardly be measured by figures, and while they have been doing that, millions of people have been made paupers. We have seen them walking the streets, looking for something to do, because they had nothing to eat. We have got to, in this government, if we expect to survive as a democratic government, keep looking after the great mass of human beings that makes up our government, because no government can be better than its citizenship, and, my friends, we have got to look on the human side of things.

Our great President has taught us and has led the way, for this great agitation is going on all over the country in behalf of human beings and the preservation of our free government, and unless we do this we will not have a free government, because government is no better than its citizenship.

I don't care who a man is, he might be the leading churchman of his city or the leading business man of his State, his character might be as pure and perfect as possible to attain and surrounded by pearls of brilliant lustre, but if his heart does not beat for mankind he is not the proper man to rule over the destinies of a free people. You have got to have that human touch, where you can look over the dollar like Roosevelt has done, and look into the faces or the masses of the American people and say that they shall not starve, but shall get some of the good things that are handed out in this Nation of ours.

That is the great democratic principle that we get back to, of the greatest good for the greatest number of people.

That is democracy, and when it ceases, then democracy ceases. That is the reason why I have always tried to be fair to the labouring man and the farmer and classes of that kind, because they need help and the others can look out for themselves.

That is what the great masses of the people need today, is to be helped until they get a start. The people that are already started and have plenty don't need help. The others, the great masses of the people, need help, end everybody must share in what prosperity we have or we won't have any democracy.

We must have in this country law enforcement if our government is to exist. We must say to the vicious criminal, the murderer and the robber, that we don't need them in the State of Florida. We need our State free and safe so our people can transact their business without having a gun stuck under their nose and somebody telling than what they have got to do. So far as I am concerned, so long as I am Governor of the State of Florida, I am going to hold up the hands of the law enforcement officers, and I will tell all the sheriffs and police officers, "when you deal with criminal, don't be too particular how you handle them, because the Governor of your State is behind you, and our people must be protected in this State."

My friends, the expenses of government must come down. Because we increase taxes and raise money is not any excuse for raising the expenses of this State. So far as I am concerned, I am going to see that every dollar, as near as I can, that is spent for the State is spent like every other dollar is spent, because tax money is the hardest money that is spent, and no more money should be wrung out of the taxpayers of this State than is absolutely necessary to run an efficient government, economically administered.

I want to say again, our State needs advertising. Any State that has a whole lot to show should tell the people about it, but I want to say to you good people here today that there are two kinds of advertising. One is the kind that we put in the newspapers and magazines and on the billboards. The other one is the government that we have here, and the citizenship that we have here in Florida, which are the best advertisements that we can have.

If the people of this Nation find out, and they soon will find out, that we have good, straight, honest, business administration in our government in this State, where their property will be safe when they move down among us, and will not be confiscated by high taxes and unreasonable assessments, and that when their families drive up and down our highways they will not be held up by highwaymen and their property taken away from them, and that they will be safe, then that is the best advertisement Florida can have.

I want to appeal to the people of this State to assist the enforcement officers every way you can, and to help them to put down crime instead of criticizing them every time they shoot a bank robber jumping out of the window with the money in his hands. This sort of sub stuff in this State is one of the things that we have to contend with, and has made crime what it is now.

I would like to see good, orderly government, so that not a dollar would be raised except for something that we had need for, and for efficient government. I would like to see our school system of this State stand out at the head of all of the educational and school systems.

I would like to see sectionalism forever wiped out of this State. I would like to see one end of this State strong for every enterprise that was started in the other end. I am going to be for every section of this State, and for any great enterprise that comes to Florida, whether at Pensacola or Miami or Fort Myers or Key West. There will be nothing in my part of the Government that will show sectionalism.

I would like to see our people united and happy and prosperous. I would like to see that old-fashioned, neighborly spirit return, so that when an enterprise is proposed in one end of this State, that the other end will be for it too. I would like to see an end to this jealousy and suspicion, and envy of one section for the other wiped out of this State, forever, and if my actions would have anything to do with it, I am going to try to get everybody to shake hands, and be one, united people, all for Florida, and Florida for all. That is the slogan that we should have in Florida and if we adopt that slogan we will go on to prosperity that nothing can stop a united people from having.

An old saying is that "United we stand, and divided we fall," and that should be the slogan of our people here, and when we have done that, our children and our children's children will thank us for wiping out all of this feeling from one end of the State to the other.

My actions and tenets during the time I am your Governor are going to be along that line. I would like to see our people get together and think more of each other. I would like to see them be kind and neighborly, like they used to be in the old days. I would like to see them build a monument of service, a monument of good will, a monument for the benefit of all of the people. I would like to see this monument built so high that it would shine like a guiding star to the other nations of the world and all or the States of this Union. I would like to see the monument so high that the morning sunbeam would cast its first light upon it, and that the dying rays of the evening sunset would rest upon it. I would like to see a permanent monument, permanent in its construction as it is beneficial in its application, so permanent that it would for ages defy the everlasting and corroding touch of time, and that after centuries and centuries its majestic silence would eloquently proclaim to future generations in this State that our mission in life was not the quest and search for gold, but was patriotic and loyal service to mankind, inspiring patriots of this or any other age. When we have done that, my friends, we have done something worthwhile.

I want us to follow the dictates of the Democratic Party and its principles that are as old as the Nation itself and will die when this Nation ceases to exist, one, equal opportunity, so that everybody can have an equal chance in life; equal rights to all and special privileges to none; best government, with the least amount of taxes. And when we have done that we will have pure democratic government, and all our people will be happy and prosperous and contented.

Let our lives be likened to the morning sunshine, clothing the earth, and as we lie down to sleep, ask not only for the forgiveness of our iniquities, but also of our neighbors, then, my friends, we will have a sure enough democracy, and we will have universal peace on earth and good will toward men, and toward all. I thank you and I thank you again.

Governor Spessard I. Holland
Term: 1941 - 1945

Spessard Lindsey Holland (born July 10, 1892 – died November 6, 1971), a native son and product of "Imperial Polk" County, held the reins of power during much of World War II. Educated at Georgia's Emory College and the University of Florida, Holland practiced law in his home town of Bartow. At the outbreak of World War I and was commissioned a second lieutenant. At his request Holland was transferred from the coast artillery to military assignment in France. He participated in heavy action with the Twenty-Fourth Flying Squadron (including the Meuse-Argonne campaign) and was awarded the Distinguished Service Cross for valor.

After leaving the army in 1919, Holland resumed his lawyer's profession in Bartow, and, on entering politics, served as Polk County Prosecuting Attorney and in 1920 was elected Polk County Judge, holding office for eight years. The handsome Holland (he had alert and piercing eyes) won election to the Florida State Senate in 1932 and served Polk County in that role until he was elected governor. A young Fuller Warren made an impression by finishing third in the eleven-man field. Second place was won by Francis P. Whitehair, but Holland won the run off by a comfortable margin. Unable to mount a strong front, the Republicans did not offer any opposition in the general election, and Holland received 334,152 votes.

During the war Florida was a major area for military training of all kinds, and there was activity throughout the peninsula. Tourist facilities were converted to meet wartime needs. Shipyards and many other civilian administered, war-oriented industries and activities brought prosperity to Florida and ended the bitter years of the Great Depression. The state grew in population, and many of those who came to the state to work or were stationed at military installations either stayed or moved back once the war ended. They brought their families and enticed others to come as well, and Florida exploded with people. The process continues into the Twenty-First Century.

A number of important matters took place during the Holland administration: increased appropriations for highway improvement and construction; the Game and Fresh Water Fish Commission became an independent agency; the committee study that initiated the Minimum Foundation Program for school financing was begun; the bonded debt of the Everglades National Park Drainage District was adjusted; teachers' pay was dramatically increased; there was a large increase in grants for old age assistance and for the blind and to dependent children; and the Everglades National Park was established.

When US Senator Charles O. Andrews did not seek reelection, the popular Holland was appointed to the Senate in 1946 by Governor Millard Caldwell. Subsequently, Holland served four full terms and retired from office in 1971.

Inaugural Speech
(Source: Jacksonville *Florida Times-Union*, January 8, 1941)

Mr. Secretary of State, Governor and Mrs. Cone, Members of the Cabinet, Members of the Supreme Court, Members of the Legislature, fellow citizens of Florida, and distinguished guests:

The people of Florida, by naming me as their Governor for the term of four years, which begins today, have, in my opinion, conferred upon me the highest honor which it is within their power to give to one of their citizens. And so in the beginning I must say that I am literally overwhelmed today by gratitude which I could never adequately express. I am grateful to those thousands of friends who, throughout the length and breadth of Florida, worked so untiringly in my behalf in the Democratic primaries. Without their never-ceasing efforts a successful outcome would, of course, have been wholly impossible. I am grateful to the press, the radio and the newsreels which have shown me such uniform kindness. I am grateful to that large part of the public of Florida which, realizing the critical times confronting our State and Nation, has shown such unmistakable evidence of its willingness to lay aside political and personal differences and to work together in united effort for the public good, with me and with its other officials of all the branches of government. I am particularly grateful to the grand crowd here, civilians and active members and veterans of the military and naval services, coming from every part of our great State, whose very presence hear speaks louder than any mere words of its awakened concern in government and of its love of State and Nation. I shall show my appreciation by working unceasingly in the effort to justify the confidence which you have manifested in me and to do my part in realizing your hopes and expectations.

In a more personal vein may I express my deep gratitude, and that of Mrs. Holland and our family to Governor Cone and Mrs. Cone for the true courtesy and kindness which they have shown us in assisting us to move in and get pleasantly established both at the mansion and in the offices of the Governor. I am sure that I speak not only for us, but also for the people of Florida, as a whole when I express our joy at the fact that Governor Cone has so fully regained his health and our sincere wishes that good health, happiness and prosperity may attend him and his as he retires with the knowledge that his years of courageous service to the State have earned for him a permanent place in the affection and esteem of his fellow citizens. Likewise, may I assure the two members of the Cabinet who retire today, State Treasurer Knot and Attorney General Gibbs, that they too, carry with them the affect and esteem of the people of Florida for good service ably rendered. Lastly, on this point of the overwhelming sense of gratitude which I feel today, I wish to express to the good people of Tallahassee our appreciation for the most hospitable welcome which they have given us and for the splendid way which they, through their efficient committees, have planned and are carrying out the details of this inaugural celebration.

But, though I have mentioned first the gratitude which I feel, I am just as mindful of the heavy responsibility which must weigh on me as your Governor in these four years. Under our form of government the Governor is a trustee for the entire people in administering the executive powers which are entrusted to him. He represents not just his close friends, political or otherwise, not just those who supported him in his candidacy but all the people. If representative government, as it prevails in America, means anything at all, it means just that, and I recognize this trust and will observe it scrupulously and continuously. Even in ordinary times and under normal circumstances this responsibility of serving the people is most heavy. But, under present conditions when many pressing internal problems of this growing, progressive State must be faced and solved and when the critical international situation confronting our Nation as a whole imposes many new and added responsibilities on us as a State, it is very clear that no man can hope to discharge the high duties of Governor satisfactorily to the people or to himself unless he has the confidence, the active interest and the sympathetic support of State, County and local officials and of the entire body of citizens who are the State of Florida. It is just such confidence, interest and support that I shall strive to merit and hope to have, for I know that without it my administration cannot possibly fulfill your expectations and my earnest desires

And, so let me first say that in carrying out my trust as your Governor, and in seeking to maintain a government in which you will have confidence and which will command your respect and enlist your active support, I shall consider myself bound in every way to carry out, to the limit of my ability, and the extent of my official power, the objectives which I announced in my campaign. You will recall that while I did not make a great number of specific promises I did make certain general commitments binding my conduct as your Governor, which I feel should be repeated and renewed to you now on this solemn occasion.

First: I said then, and I say now, that I shall do my utmost to establish and maintain cordial working relations with the Cabinet, the Legislature and the other public officials of this State. The job to be done requires harmony and team work and can be done on no other basis.

Second: I shall appoint to public office only men and women who are qualified by character, training and ability to do the job.

Third: I shall insist on keeping clear from political control and manipulation all those service branches of government which are so vital to the satisfactory serving of our people and for whose proper handling we need our ablest citizens who will not assume the heavy burdens unless they are at least allowed, in their own judgment and under their own consciences to do the job which they feel should be done. In this connection I am thinking of the State Welfare Agencies, the State Board of Health, the Board of Control, the Florida Citrus Commission, the educational system and many other similar service activities of the highest importance. We must keep them out of politics.

Fourth: I can and will lead the way to economy by actually practicing economy in those activities under my control, and using my strongest efforts to obtain economy in every other State activity.

Fifth: I shall be your Governor. I shall not be controlled by any machine, or group, or clique. I recognize no obligation to any individual or interest or group which conflicts with my obligation to the public. The public interest will remain, with me, the dominant consideration in all matters.

I want to now go clearly on record as being committed, during my administration, to maintain those positions in the various fields of public activity on which I stood in my platform. I do not regard a candidate's platform as something to be adhered to conveniently only for the duration of the race, but, rather as a sincere declaration of convictions on important questions of government on which the people have a right to rely after the candidate has been elected by their vote. This is no time or place to restate the details of my platform, but I would not be content without confirming here the various positions which I took in my platform.

In my messages to the legislature I shall, no doubt, find occasion to develop in greater detail the means of fulfilling various platform commitments. At this time I content myself with assuring the Florida public that on such vital matters as the support of public education, increased assistance for our aged citizens, as well as for the blind and for dependent children, the development of our agricultural and livestock industries, the conservation of our natural resources, including game, fish, forests, soil, and water, the improved protection of public health, the attraction and entertainment of tourists, the development of the Everglades national park and of the state park system, the better serving of both labor and industry, the progressive handling of problems of taxation and the building and maintenance of an adequate system of public roads, I shall adhere to my positions as stated in my platform and as discussed by me throughout the state in the course of my campaign. And, I think it only fair and proper to say to the people of Florida that many fields coveted by my platform diligent work is already underway to prepare a legislative program for submission to the 1941 session of the state legislature. For instance, in such important matters, among others, as taxation, fish and game conservation, old age assistance, and the better serving labor and industry, through equitable amendment and strengthening of the unemployment compensation act, as well as on the important question of what kind of a parole system will be best suited in our State to carry out the provisions of the constitutional amendment adopted last November; a vast amount of study and work has been already done throughout the summer and fall by many citizens and by me in an effort to have ready a constructive program for recommendation to the approaching legislature. I hardly think it necessary to add that the legislative program which I shall submit to the Legislature will simply be my sincere recommendations, based upon all of the facts which I can discover, and will not be an effort to dominate the will of the Legislature but rather, an effort to assist its members in every possible way. I shall always keep in mind the fact that our State, the fastest growing in the Nation, must go ahead as rapidly as possible with its internal development and that there exist many varied problems which must be met which are not covered in my platform, such as preparing for the proper observance in 1945 of the centennial celebration of the admission of Florida to the Union, the readjustment and refunding of the Everglades Drainage Bonds, the authentic restoration of a part of the ancient city of St. Augustine, the enlargement of our program to encourage civilian aviation and other similar matters of great importance to the State as a whole. Our program must be kept progressive and we must always look ahead to the creation of an ever greater and more beautiful State so that we may realize the glowing opportunities which lie ahead of us in every field. Likewise our program must always put human values first—material values in second position.

To the subject of finance and taxation I must devote more than mere passing mention. The most critical internal problems facing our State lie in this field and they must be solved to allow orderly government to continue. The existence of these problems is not chargeable to any person or to any administration, but rather to the fact that we have, as a State, been pursuing for years an aimless tax policy, patching and temporizing here and there from time to time, but making no serious, sustained effort to discover the basic ills and to constructively cure them. I wish to make it wholly clear that in what I am about to say I am in no sense reflecting upon the distinguished outgoing Governor or the members of his Cabinet. I believe they have all done a good job. I have no doubt, that everything within their power, individually and collectively, to meet the state's pressing financial problems has been done. After all they could use only those tools and that machinery which has been supplied to them by the Legislature through its enactments and by the people, themselves, through the State Constitution, which the people alone have the right to change. And the undeniable fact is that the popular will, both through constitutional amendments adopted in recent years and through the action of the Legislature, has been the principle responsible cause for the situation which exists. As a member of the Legislature for the last eight years and a life-long citizen of Florida, I. cheerfully accept my share of the responsibility for the existing condition, but I firmly believe that the people of Florida do not wish to longer tolerate the continuation of this course of drifting and temporizing and I know that they cannot hope to continue the governmental functions which they have regarded as necessary without now facing the facts and adjusting our tax structure to meet them. And so, in order that this vital matter may be clearly called to the attention of our people, I shall state the facts which in my judgment reflect the tremendous gravity of the public financial situation in this State.

In the first place our people adopted in 1934 the constitutional amendment exempting from taxation homes up to the value of $5000, and the courts properly held that this amendment exempted homes from the payment of operating taxes for State and local government. The amendment has become a part of the permanent tax policy of our State, but the large losses of operating revenue, particularly to the schools and to the municipalities, have never been replaced. During the present rapid growth of our State these problems are growing more acute, particularly for the cities, and relief has to be given.

In the second place special groups of all kinds have been active for many years in earmarking revenue for their exclusive use and the result has been to impair the general revenue fund, out of which general State activities must be financed. The result has been to diminish this fund below the necessary amount and with all of the careful management of the outgoing administration there remain at this time accumulated unpaid expense bills against general revenue in the total amount of $1,700,000. Obviously this situation cannot continue.

In the third place the people of Florida adopted at the last General Election a constitutional amendment prohibiting the levy of ad valorem taxes on property by the State for State purposes. While the reasons for this, in giving tax relief to property and in fixing responsibility for levying property taxes solely in local agencies were excellent, the operation of this amendment will nevertheless further reduce the operating revenue of the State in the year 1941 by the amount of $1,523,000, using the 1940 figures.

In the fourth place there is a strong probability of the repeal of the so-called Gross Receipts Tax, when the next Legislature convenes as the general public has indicated rather clearly its feelings that this tax is inequitable, unfair and unsound. Its repeal would, nevertheless, mean the annual loss of close to $2,000,000 from school revenue.

Surely it is not necessary to continue further the recital of the facts which make our tax situation the most grave internal problem ahead of us. I am happy to say that there seems to be in the minds of most business men a general realization of this fact. Since last September there has been underway, at the expense of many business, agricultural, labor, professional and school groups of the State, a tax inquiry which is being conducted by the Brookings Institution of Washington, the most authoritative agency in this field. The report of this tax inquiry is being eagerly awaited and I sincerely hope that it will be followed by the recommendation from taxpaying groups, throughout the State, of comprehensive adjustments of our tax structure. I shall not attempt to predict the result of this Brookings inquiry, but I will call attention to the fact that in my platform I took a firm stand for the bringing about of uniform and equal assessments of property taxes and for more drastic collection laws and enforcement thereof. I do not believe any tax recommendation can avoid these two objectives, as equal treatment in assessment and collection of taxes is the first fundamental of fairness in any tax system. My platform called for the modernization of our tax structure after thorough study, and I believe that the pending inquiry will furnish a safe basis on which to begin this work. My platform declared against any further temporizing with our tax structure. It is high time that our tax policy became relatively permanent and it must be so to furnish a safe and secure basis for continuing government.

My platform declared against new taxes and against a sales tax. I still oppose the sales tax, but my declaration against any form of new taxes does not mean that I am unwilling to seek to find substitute sources of revenue if the people in their own wisdom knock out sources of revenue without dispensing with the activities which were financed therefrom. That is what has been done by the adoption of the amendment prohibiting State ad valorem taxes, and is what will be done if the gross receipts tax is repealed. I personally favor both of these actions, but I do so with my eyes open, knowing that their repeal will mean that our government will have to look somewhere for revenue to take the place of that which is lost. I want the people to have a clear understanding of this fact and also of the substance and meaning of any recommendations that may come from the pending tax inquiry for submission to the next Legislature. I ask the press to be particularly diligent to see that discussions of proposed tax changes, and particularly of any proposed new taxes, be given fullest publicity so that the people may be thinking seriously of taxation and its vital effect upon them, as taxpayers and likewise as the ones who receive the benefits from the various governmental services which are financed by taxes. If the people will think seriously and in terms of equitable distribution of the burdens of taxation, I shall have no doubt that the outcome will be a sound one. In my tax platform I also declared for closely budgeted State expenditures, upon which I shall certainly stand, and also for greater economy in administration. I trust that the first interest of those conducting the Brookings tax inquiry, and of the public as it studies this intricate tax problem, will be the question of where savings can be accomplished without taking away service that is needed. I shall not hesitate to support any reasonable program for economy and, in fact, I propose to lead the way in such a program, as already stated some minutes ago, by insisting upon economy in those departments of government which will be under my control.

There is yet another subject which vitally touches this whole field of taxation, and at the same time bears upon the ability of the State to construct and maintain an adequate system of good roads, and that is the working out of a method of securing better value to the people of most of our counties from the use of that so-called second three cents of the gas tax which goes to the counties to apply on road bond indebtedness and to reimburse them for money they paid out in the construction or roads which are now State roads. One of our most prized constitutional provisions is that our State cannot issue bonds or borrow money and yet through the payment of State gas tax money as a gift to the counties and special road and bridge districts we have allowed, and are continuing to allow, the State to pay off out of State funds debts which were contracted on. the credit of small units of government which had to borrow at high rates of interest. Much of the money being paid out by the State for the benefit of the counties and districts is being used to pay off interest at very high rates, often as high as five and five and a half per cent. I think this is wrong in principle. It is my strong hope and aim that this situation may be corrected so as to reduce the interest burden of the counties and districts affected, and at the same time make possible the reduction of their local property taxes levied for the purpose of paying off road bonds. This gas tax question is, therefore, an intimate part of the whole picture of taxation—particularly as applied to county government—and will have to be considered and solved as a part of the whole picture. Studies in this field are going on under several different agencies and I know that I voice the hope of the people of this State when I say that we shall be earnestly hoping for good results, bringing to the people tax relief and at the same time making possible more road construction.

And now, I must mention the outstanding part which I am sure the State of Florida will play in helping to speed up and complete the national defense program. I feel absolutely certain that all Floridians will expect this State to do its utmost to meet promptly and effectively all reasonable requests from the National Government for assistance in this great undertaking. Floridians are first of all loyal Americans and they will gladly and naturally join with the people of all other states in preparing a defense so strong, so unconquerable, that none but a sheer madman would dare to spend his strength in launching an attack against us, and peace may be assured to us, if, indeed, there is a way to assure peace. And I am sure I speak for all of our citizens, and particularly for those veterans of former wars, both men and women who are here in such number today, when 1 say that we hope for peace, we pray for peace, and we steadfastly believe that peace is possible only to that nation which is so strong that none dare attack it.

Of course, we knew that our Nation must be so adequately prepared that she can defend not only against direct attack on us, but also against attack on any other portion of the Western hemisphere, for under modern warfare hemispheric defense has become a necessary part or our own national security. And so, every person within sound of my voice knows full well that, because of our strategic geographic location, Florida has become the veritable spearhead of that most vital part of the defense program which looks to the protection of the Panama Canal and the life line of communication with South America. Numerous military and naval bases are already clustered in Florida, extending in a great arc from Pensacola to Key West. The Pensacola Naval Air Training Station, the great Army cantonment at Camp Blanding, the huge Naval Air Base at Jacksonville, the Southeastern Army Bombing Base of MacDill Field at Tampa, a dozen others, all important, but which lack of time forbids me to mention, all stand as evidence of the tremendous strategic importance , to the entire Nation, of our Florida—this index finger of North America which points southward to the lands whose future is so intimately linked with ours. Tens of thousands or our American boys will train here—tens of thousands more will have their permanent stations here. And I feel that Floridians are proud of this recognition of the importance of our State and eager to fulfill the grave and unusual responsibilities which it throws on our shoulders.

Not only must we aid in the national defense program, but we must also prepare for the supplemental defense of our own State and its communities and we must likewise plan to protect and preserve Florida's business and economic life under all eventualities. Roads and bridges must be built, other bridges strengthened, housing increased, health conditions safeguarded, recreation facilities and schools enlarged, home guards organized, equipped and trained, sabotage prevented, subversive activities stamped out and a hundred other vital things effectively. All vital public services must be coordinated and protected. The civilian population must be organized to play its part in defense—an important part as shown by the experience of the civilians in all those nations where war now reigns.

All these things will require planning, work and money. To accomplish them will almost certainly require dislocations and postponements in important activities of our own internal program. In the field of road construction, for instance, who would insist strongly on the construction of a road important to the service of his own community when the army or navy staff pointed out a road elsewhere in the district of compelling importance to national defense? You can see, of course, that sacrifices will be required, in many fields and in an unpredictable number of instances. We shall seek all proper assistance from Federal sources, but I say again that I am certain that Floridians will expect Florida to do its part promptly and to the limit of its ability. Our first duty as Americans will be to hold up the hands of our great President, our Congress, the commanders of our Army and

Navy as the Nation moves rapidly under their leadership to the creation of impregnable defense.

I am pleased to be able to report to you that a strong State Defense Council has been set up by Governor Cone, consisting of outstanding citizens jointly approved by him and by me. Their activities are already underway, and will continue at an increasing pace. They are working in close cooperation with the National Defense Council and with the Federal and State Governments as well as the Army and Navy. There will be no changes in the personnel of this council as a result of the change of the State Administration.

But, regardless of how fully we may meet our collective responsibilities in carrying forward to physical completion the outward aspects of the National Defense program in Florida, I think that in Florida, as elsewhere in our Nation, there is a most vital phase of preparedness which will have to depend entirely upon the attitude of our individual citizens toward their government. No democracy can be strong and sturdy and self reliant—able to defend itself successfully against all foes, without and within—unless it commands the love and patriotic service of its citizens, as evidenced by their carrying their full share of responsibilities of citizenship. There is important work to be done by every Florida citizen, no matter what his station in life and even though large sacrifices of time and effort may be required. Complete preparedness in a democracy cannot be bought with money. Active participation in government, insisting on true information on public issues conscientious voting, paying taxes, playing fair, upholding the arms of their chosen officials, observing the democratic principle of majority rule—supporting the government instead of looking to it for support—demanding, above all things, clean and efficient government, substituting work for lip service—all these practical evidences of patriotism are far more important now than they have ever been since our Nation was founded. And we must build morale—capture anew the deep conviction that the American system of government and way of life is eternally right—that it has proved itself by the great and good Nation it has produced in such a short time, as nations' lives are measured. How could we who love Florida and claim it as our hone have anything less than the deepest conviction that the American system means everything to us—has given us every really worthwhile value that we claim as unspeakably dear. Consider Florida's history just a moment—from 1565 to 1821—256 years of dreamy lethargy under other forms of government with not enough development to be worthy of notice—120 years of American life and government, just two short lifetimes—and we have developed from a tangled wilderness into one of the beauty spots of the world—one of the most prosperous of all the States, with almost two million permanent citizens, with a definite appeal that brings millions of others here to enjoy our many pleasures and matchless possibilities and to mingle with our people—with prosperity and boundless opportunity on every hand—with individual freedom such as few spots in the world now enjoy. Can we in Florida doubt for a single moment that the American system is sound and clean and eternally right—and that it is worthy to receive our unbounded loyalty and devotion and our sacrificial service as citizens?

Over 13 months ago; on Dec. 4, 1939, when I announced as a candidate for Governor, I included in my announcement a statement of my conviction then as to the kind of government which I felt that Florida should have. That was before Germany invaded Norway, before the second World War had become really active, before our present national defense program had been started. I believe you will agree with me that the statement was true then and that its truth has been even more fully accentuated by the tragic events which, stalking across the world stage since that time, have cast their lengthening shadows even as far as peace loving America. I hope you will pardon my repeating that statement now at this hour in my life of greatest inspiration.

I believe it is appropriate here. Speaking of State government in Florida, I said then, 13 months ago: "Democracy is on trial throughout the world and Florida must have a State government which will command respect. Such a government must be honest, liberal, efficient, economical, wholly non-sectional and soundly democratic." I still have that conviction, and I hereby pledge myself to the people of Florida, who have honored me so signally, to devote myself during these four years with unceasing effort, complete loyalty and full humility to the maintenance in Florida of a state government possessing those qualities named in my statement just quoted. I respectfully request the assistance of all Florida citizens, not only for me as your Governor but for all who serve you in official positions in Federal,

State and local government. With your help and the help of each other, and relying, too, upon that divine guidance without which all human effort is so sure to be futile and ineffective, I shall endeavor with all my strength to maintain in Florida that sound and wholesome government which I know you so strongly desire.

Governor Millard F. Caldwell
Term: 1945 - 1949

In his first and middle names Millard Fillmore Caldwell (born February 6, 1897 – died October 23, 1984) bore the name of an antebellum Whig president. He was born near Knoxville, Tennessee, and attended Carson Newman College in Tennessee, the University of Mississippi, and after military service in the army during World War I, the University of Virginia. In 1924 he came to Florida and began practicing law in the Panhandle city of Milton. He represented Santa Rosa County in the state House of Representatives during the sessions of 1929 and 1931 and then won election to the national house of representatives in 1931. He represented Florida's Third District until 1941. Retiring from politics because of differences with the Roosevelt administration's New Deal policies, Caldwell moved to Tallahassee, settled with his family on the Harwood Plantation nearby, and opened a law office.

Reentering politics in 1944, he sought the Democratic nomination for governor. There were six candidates, but the campaign was relatively free of "politics" because the war was still in progress, and Floridians were more interested in ending the conflict than in rancorous state rallies aimed at attracting voters. With the fighting definitely tilting toward the Allies the state concentrated on military victory, and few states were more directly involved with the war than Florida.

Robert A. "Lex" Green, a Congressman during the 1920s, had always wanted to be governor, and was Caldwell's chief opponent. The demands of war could not totally dispel politics, and Green accused Caldwell of being anti-New Deal and an agent for big business while he, Green, was the poor man's friend. He also made a bid for the teachers' vote by pledging raises for those who labored in the state's classrooms. With an eye on the future, Green also advocated free land for returning veterans. Ernest R. Graham, father of Governor Bob Graham, was another strong contender, particularly because of his appeal in heavily populated Dade County. Caldwell wisely did not deal in personalities, and led the field in the primary with 116,111 votes, although Green received 113,300 and Graham was a strong third with 91,174 votes. In the run off primary Graham endorsed Green, but was unable to deliver his supporters' votes, and Caldwell was an easy winner. Unlike the 1944 campaign, the Republicans nominated a candidate, and Bert L. Acker spoke meaningfully of the two party tradition, chided Caldwell for his lack of support for the New Deal, and questioned the fourth-term candidacy of Roosevelt. Predictably, Caldwell won with little difficulty.

The plain spoken Caldwell faced numerous problems as governor, but carved a solid record. He inherited a treasury surplus but told his inaugural address listeners, gathered to hear the speech celebrating the state's one hundredth birthday, and other Floridians that they faced possible new taxes. These he raised by a program that increased excise taxes on beverages, cigarettes, and racing, and by taxing private and public utilities an additional ten percent–the latter proved so unpopular it had to be abandoned. One law reduced almost three hundred state funds to six classifications, and another increased state spending for advertising and authorized a full-time director of the budget and staff. Caldwell also got sixty-five full-time health units in the state's sixty-seven counties.

Significantly, under Caldwell the legislature refused to revamp its primary voting procedures so that a recent decision by the national Supreme Court declaring "white primaries" unconstitutional could be circumvented. Such efforts in other southern states proved unconstitutional. Caldwell also demonstrated regional leadership in opposing protective tariffs and freight rate differentials as harmful to the South. The 1947 legislature also increased appropriations for public buildings, especially the physical plants at the University of Florida, Florida State, and Florida A. & M. Governor Caldwell was basically conservative, but he tried (and failed) to get the state legislature realistically reapportioned. Yet, he was much more successful in the area of higher education. In 1947 the legislature passed laws that made the University of Florida coeducational and did the same in Tallahassee for the renamed Florida State University. He also made an effort to set up a system of junior colleges, although the process did not move into full gear.

Inaugural Speech
(Source: Jacksonville *Florida Times Union*, January 3, 1945)

In the year 1845, one century ago, William D. Moseley, the then newly-elected first governor of Florida, took the oath of office on the east steps of the capitol and commenced his inaugural address with these words:

> I should do in justice to the best feelings of my heart, were I not, on this occasion to express a becoming sense of gratitude for the enviable and honorable distinction, so recently conferred upon me, in elevating me to the supreme executive authority of the state—a distinction the more happily prized

from the flattering circumstances under which it was conferred. An expression of public sentiment through the suffrages of freemen, for an office within their gift …

In this year of 1945, 100 years later, I can find no more fitting language to use at the outset of my own inaugural address. And so I say, in my time, that

> I should do injustice to the best feelings of my heart, were I not, on this occasion to express a becoming sense of gratitude for the … honorable distinction … conferred upon me … by an expression of public sentiment through the suffrage of the citizens of Florida.

And just as Governor Moseley felt it incumbent upon him to express, upon that occasion, his views, his philosophy of government and his purposes, so must I now direct your attention to certain matters or vital concern to the state and to its citizens.

Ahead of us are four years—years which will bring us face to face with difficult problems that must be solved and tasks that must be accomplished. Those problems and those tasks will be of concern to and the responsibility of the people of this state. With the thoughtful assistance of Florida's citizenship, this administration can do much but without it, little. That I will enjoy your confidence and cooperation I have no doubt.

I look forward with assurance to four years of effective team work with the administration legislative, and judicial officers of the state.

The duties, powers and functions of my offices are complex. The confusions and uncertainties usually incident to a change of administration have been greatly minimized by the gracious helpfulness of Governor Holland and his official family. To them I want to say that for their many courtesies, I am sincerely grateful.

Governor Holland has given the state four years of progressive, sound and solvent administration. To me and to those who are to help me, that record of achievement is a challenge to do as much and more if we can.

Here let me restate my belief in local self-government—in government close to the people and responsive to their will. It was upon that kind of government this nation and this state were founded, upon which they have grown and prospered, and without which they will, as have other nations and states before them wither and die. The trend toward centralization of governmental powers has progressed too far and must be curbed. Government centered in remote places, in the hands of strangers, is not the kind of government the people of American and Florida established and it is not the kind of government which should be encouraged.

In our consideration of proposals for increased state aid to local units of government, we must not lose sight of the fact that control always follows the dollar. History has shown that the smaller unit of government, in seeking and accepting financial aid from a larger, inevitably surrenders a proportionate part of its freedom and independence. Thus we have seen control over state affairs moving to Washington as the federal government increased its contributions to the states, and control over county and school affairs moving to Tallahassee as the state increased its financial aid to its political subdivisions. Let those who advocate state aid to municipalities carefully read the record.

Florida, in its 100 years of statehood, has made great strides but, we, its people, faithfully execute our trust, it is just now on the threshold of its rightful place in the Society of States. By the wise expansion and development of our system of public education, by adequately safeguarding the public health, and by conservation of our natural resources, the forests, the water supply, the oil and the minerals, the wild life of the fields and streams, by the advertising to the world of the fact that ours is a sound, stable, dependable government; that we possess those things dearly prized by the home hunter, the pleasure and health seekers and by the business people of the country we will experience a growth and development which will approach the fabulous.

But these advancements are not ours for the wishing. They are to be gained only by hard, intelligently directed effort and by the judicious expenditure of money. If they are worth having, they are worth working for—and they are worth what they will cost in money.

It is my purpose to be an economical executive in the sense that I will expect no public fund to be wasted. I do not, however, propose, by false and niggardly economy, to delay or retard worthwhile development and growth.

Although, as I have previously pointed out, the state treasury is solvent and each of the funds current, it should be emphasized that the state possesses no bottomless barrel into which it can dip for new aims and new purposes.

In considering the fiscal situation we must remember that for several years Florida has experienced, because of a chaotic war, abnormal receipts from its taxes and subnormal expenditures of its funds. It is imperative that we look ahead to the postwar years when our receipts must drop off and our necessary expenses must increase.

The funds on hand and to be contemplated from existing tax sources are earmarked and obligated to presently authorized needs. The Road Department funds must be used on imperatively needed repairs and construction as quickly as labor and material are available. The margin in the General Revenue Fund over and above safe working capital must be safeguarded for emergencies. Over half the state's cash resources is represented by the $50,000,000 reserve held in Washington for payment, when necessary, to the unemployed. In the other funds, earmarked for schools, for county road bonds, for the needy aged, and for other purposes, there is small surplus, although the bills have been paid and a safe working capital is available.

It is incumbent upon me to make it plain that no money is on hand or to be anticipated from the present tax structure to pay for an adequate extension of the state's services in education, health, advertising, or conservation. They are definite needs to challenge our attention but money to finance them must be found.

In seeking more revenue, we must avoid undue, hardship. Confiscatory taxation will destroy the very foundation of the state. If business is to maintain payrolls and support the government, it must first survive.

Taxation must not only be reasonable—the tax revenue must be expended so widely as to permit business to regard it, not as a burden or a loss, but rather as a sound paying investment. Each tax dollar should earn dividends and bring permanent returns to the taxpayer. Tax revenue spent in the improvement of farming practices and marketing, in advertising our advantages, in the expansion of our public education and health facilities are sound investments.

Good health increases the productivity of our people and is an asset valuable in the attraction of new citizens. Good schools increase the earning power of each new generation and serve to bring new residents to build up our state. There are no better sales arguments than good schools and good health. There is no stronger appeal to new residents and new investors than the ability to say that Florida stands at the top of the list of states in health and education. We cannot make that claim now but we can anticipate definite progress to that end.

In our approach to these and other problems, we must apply sound principles. The state must be operated as a progressive, forward-looking business, with common sense and good judgment applied to each question as it is presented.

If we are to achieve our objective we must put first things first—single out for major attention the most pressing needs and do first those things which most need doing.

We can expect no miracles and will doubtless fall short of even near perfection in the solution of many problems but we will get results if we concentrate our efforts on the vital questions and give secondary attention to issues of lesser importance.

Some urgent needs touch the operation of certain industries, agriculture and the professions. Those with training and experience in such fields are best qualified, unselfishly and in a broad way, to prepare plans and write programs which will avoid conflict and hardships. With that in mind, I have asked those so qualified to evolve blueprints of attainable progress.

I have acted, heretofore, in concert with Governor Holland in the establishment of citizens committees to study the public school question and the problem of safeguarding the state's fresh water supply. I have acted independently in the appointment of committees to give counsel in connection with the problems of commercial fishing, operation of the hotel industry, and regulation of the potential oil industry. Other groups with plans for the benefit of the state will find me eager to counsel with them.

The only way to enhance the general prosperity is to improve the condition of industry, business and individual citizens. When an industry prospers, there is full employment and, when it falters unemployment and low wages result. It follows, therefore, as a matter of course, that industry and employment are matters of public concern and it is an appropriate function of the state to assist and encourage those activities which contributes to the general well being of the people.

During the critical times ahead, the economy of Florida, even while it is adjusted to wartime conditions and exerting every effort to make an early victory possible, must be made ready for the sudden changes and readjustments incident to the transition to peace. We must by that time have laid the foundation for a stable economy free from major unemployment and distress. The returning veterans must find their places in our communities with job opportunities in permanent employment.

That some dislocation and unemployment will follow the war is inevitable. It takes time to reconvert industries and to secure new markets. The unemployment compensation fund will, we may hope, be sufficient to substantially tide us over. The expansion of highway facilities, the construction of certain badly needed public buildings, the public works planned by the counties and cities will help provide jobs for those who otherwise would be unemployed. By such means we can cushion the shock but, at best, they constitute little more than temporary stop-gaps.

The permanent solution lies in measures to increase the flow of trade, to expand our industries, to enhance the prosperity of agriculture and to stimulate our tourist business. Stability and security in employment will never come through governmental expedients—they can only come through the normal functioning of a sound economical system.

We know that business and labor and the public have long suffered because of a wasteful squandering of natural resources, unreasonable and burdensome governmental restrictions and unwise taxation. We must do more toward the husbanding and the conservation of our resources.

We have made some progress but much more remains to be done. We have in a small way improved our practices in the use of timber and in forest fire control. We have approached the problem of conserving our wild life but there, too, we have only made a beginning. Too little has been accomplished in the proper taking, use and enjoyment of the commercial sea food supply. We have failed to take the necessary steps to conserve the fresh water supply and to protect certain of our lands from permanent damage by erosion and bad drainage practices. The time has come to anticipate the development of commercially profitable oil fields in Florida by the establishment of wise and sound measures covering the exploration and exploitation of that resource.

We must adapt to our uses the latest methods to increase production and build trade. We must speed the progress in the development of better pastures and strains of live stock. We must improve farm and grove practices through experimentation, research and extension services. We must expand travel facilities by building good roads and encouraging air, rail and motor facilities and transportation. We must stimulate the tourist trade by improving our attractions, and by speeding the development of the Everglades National Park, and the state parks, and by advertising our advantages.

In the selection of state officials, department heads and board members, I have sought to apply the principles of good business. It has been my purpose to men fitted for each place, willing to undertake the responsibilities placed upon them, at personal sacrifice, if necessary, for the privilege of rendering a pubic service. As I undertake the difficult task ahead of me, I will be surrounded by men in whom I have confidence—men or character, ability and experience, men who are attracted not by position or relatively small salaries but by the opportunity to participate in building for the future of the state. Those men have been and are in. agreement with me on the principles of government.

Ours is a great state. We can make it greater. Our opportunities are limited only by our will to accomplish.

In all the world no land is more favored by nature than America. In this land of ours, no state is more favored in natural advantages than Florida. There are no finer nor more gifted people than the citizens of Florida. We can do what we will with our assets and our opportunities.

Let it be our objective to work so well and to build so permanently that the Floridians who gather here one hundred years from today will have just cause to honor our memories. Let them say of us that we established the foundation in this centennial year upon which was erected a new era of progress raising Florida to new heights of greatness.

Florida's progress in its first century of statehood has been miraculous. It is in our power to have it said, by those who come after us, that the real start in the development of Florida's full potential was made at the beginning of its second century.

Our destiny is in our hands.

Governor Fuller Warren
Term: 1949 - 1953

Fuller Warren (born October 3, 1905 – died September 23, 1973), a Floridian, was born in Blountstown, received his elementary school education in Calhoun and Walton counties, and before entering the University of Florida Warren farmed, sold Bibles in Alabama, and went to sea as a steward. He did his undergraduate education at the University of Florida, waiting tables to help with expenses. Graduating with a law degree from Cumberland University, Warren had already been baptized in politics with his election to the Florida House of Representatives while still a college student at Gainesville. Only twenty-one, the young legislator represented Calhoun County in 1927, but in 1929 moved to Jacksonville where he won fame as a criminal lawyer. In Jacksonville the distinguished looking and flamboyant Warren served three terms in the nineteen thirties as a Jacksonville City Councilman. He was elected to the Florida House of Representatives and served two terms, but his political career was interrupted by World War II. During the war he made multi-crossings of the Atlantic Ocean while serving as a gunnery officer in the Navy.

Encouraged by his first statewide election in 1940, a confident Warren sought the governor's nomination again in 1948. In one public speech the candidate addressed himself aloud, noting that Fuller, one day you will be governor of the great state of Florida. There were nine candidates and Warren finished first. Daniel T. McCarty, a citrus producer and beef grower from Fort Pierce was the voters' second choice. He fared even better four years later. In the general election Warren defeated Bert L. Aker, his Republican opponent, with huge Democratic majority.

As Governor Warren won lasting fame for the repeal of Florida's stock law which rid the state of the long debated statute making the person who killed the livestock liable to the owner. Open range for stock was seen as unfair, dangerous, and expensive. Straying cattle was also psychologically damaging because their presence stigmatized Florida as considerably less than a modern and progressive state. Warren accomplished much more. His administration was responsible for several progressive post-war measures, including an outstanding reforestation program, the financing and construction at St. Petersburg of the Sunshine Skyway, the initiation of the Jacksonville Expressway system, preliminary planning for other important highways, and passage of a citrus code that prevented the shipment of fruit before it was ripe..

Even so, Warren had a strong, rural, Populist tint that ran counter to the usual basically conservative governors. Warren faced heavy criticism when he revealed that three friends had largely financed his election. A state furor developed over the issue and its implications. At the time the nation was concerned with crime and its political connections. The Florida situation gained national attention, increasing Warren's tenuous position. Gambling was rife in Florida and there were rumors connecting Warren with the widespread felony. Ultimately, the legislature passed a law requiring candidates to report all receipts and expenditures and limited the amount of individual campaign contributions. Warren had also opposed a sales tax. Yet, state expenses left over from Holland and Caldwell caused a serious drop in revenue, forced a special session of the legislature, and resulted in the passage of a three percent limited sales tax that the governor had to accept. It was still another setback for Warren.

Fuller Warren was a speaker of renown, and used his oratorical skills to good political and economic use. He made speaking tours of the US and various Latin American seeking investments and new business for Florida and also on behalf of Florida tourism. Warren was tireless and fully realized the importance of public relations. He wrote three books, two of them related to speaking and politics: *Eruptions of Eloquence* (1932) and *Speaking of Speaking* (1944), and, using his own credentials as evidence, *How to Win in Politics* (1949) with Allen Morris, a seasoned newspaperman and author and future clerk of the Florida House of Representatives. After his term ended Warren moved to Miami and set up his law practice there. He again sought the Democratic nomination for governor in 1956 but finished fourth to the winner, LeRoy Collins.

Inaugural Speech
(Source: Tallahassee *Daily Democrat*, January 5, 1945)

Mr. Secretary of State Gray, Governor Caldwell, Mr. Justice Thomas, Members of the Cabinet, Members of the Legislature, Ladies and Gentlemen, My Friends and. Fellow Citizens of Florida:

In his great speech dedicating the Bunker Hill monument, Daniel Webster said, "This vast, uncounted multitude before me and around me proves the feeling which this occasion has aroused."

In Webster's words, may I say that this vast, uncounted and unprecedented multitude here in the State's Capital proves the feeling which this occasion has aroused. It is reassuring that this occasion has so aroused the people of Florida. The countless thousands of citizens gathered here to witness this event shows the tremendous interest of the people in their government. An alert, active interest on the part of the people in their government is the best of all safe-guards for democracy and freedom.

Today, I take up the burden you laid upon me last May. Today, I take over the supreme executive power of our state.

Today, I enter upon four years of consecrated service to the people of Florida. Today, I assume the political and governmental leadership of a great state. Today, I begin carrying out the covenant I made with the people during the campaign.

Heavy tasks lie ahead. Florida is faced with many terrific problems.. They must be met and mastered. With the friendly cooperation of the ablest group of citizens yet to serve in the Legislature, with the solid support of citizens in all echelons of civil life, and with the guiding hand of God, we will go forward and remove the many roadblocks on the highway of Florida's progress.

At this point, I hope I may be pardoned for making a few personal remarks. It is very gratifying to me that the beloved man who kindled in me the ambition to serve Florida as its governor is here today to see finished what he started thirty years ago.

Thirty years ago, I stood in this Capitol building with a heavy heart. For the second time, I had been defeated for page in the House of Representatives. I was broke and discouraged. At 13, life seemed to hold little hope for me. I felt that I would have to go back to Blountstown and spend the rest of my life at the hard labor which had been my lot since the age of eight. But I didn't know how I could go home, for I had no money,

One of the kindest and best men who ever lived, Amos Lewis, handed me a twenty- dollar bill and told me to return to Blountstown, study hard and work hard and live right and some day I would come back here as Governor. My good friend, Amos Lewis, is sitting right over there.

It also is gratifying to see here today so many other friends who have blessed my life.

It is fitting that I should tell you of my plans for the four years ahead. I hope to make your State Government an active and powerful force for promoting the prosperity of all the people of Florida. Your State Government will not only vigorously assert its rights as a state but it will with equal vigor discharge its duties and responsibilities. In fact, for the coming four years the emphasis will be on the State's responsibilities and obligations to its citizens.

The government of this State belongs to all the people and will be administered for the benefit of all the people, and not just for a favored few. For the next four years your State Government is going to be neighborly and friendly. Every person serving in the executive branch of the government will treat all citizens with courtesy, kindness and consideration.

I am going to do my best to faithfully put into practice every plank in the platform on which I was elected. The people of Florida have approved that platform in three elections, the first primary election, the second primary election and the general election. The Honorable Perry Murray, Speaker of the 1949 House of Representatives, and the Honorable Newman Brackin, President of the 1949 State Senate, have publicly declared that the platform on which I was nominated and elected is a mandate from the people of Florida to the Legislature. Many other Senators and Representatives have said the same thing.

That platform pledges me to administer the State Government without waste. I intend to get you a dollar's worth of government for each dollar of taxes you pay. I am going to do all in my power to see that your tax money shall be spent like a wise and prudent business man would expend the funds of his firm. We are going to make the tax dollar do its full duty.

We are going to stop the killing and crippling of people on the highways of Florida. We are going to stop much of it by eliminating roaming livestock from the roads of this State. We are going to stop more of it by eliminating drunken driving. We are going to eliminate even more deaths and damage by carrying on a continuous campaign of education and instruction in safe driving. It is our aim to make the roads of this state so safe that no one will feel fear while using them. We plan to brand reckless drivers as public enemies. We hope every person in this great audience will help put this program over by driving home carefully and cautiously; and then continue to drive carefully and cautiously at all times.

We are going to build good highways for the lowest possible cost. Five of Florida's ablest men will serve as members of the State Road Department. They begin their tremendous task with heavy handicaps. The road fund is almost empty and its income for months ahead is committed by contracts already let. But we are going to get you a dollar's worth of roads for every dollar spent.

We are going to buy the state's supplies for less money. A central purchasing agency, such as 42 states already have, cannot be had until the Legislature convenes. But until the Legislature can meet and give the people of Florida this money-saving method of buying the many millions of dollars of commodities and materials used by the state, I plan by executive order to set up a central system of purchasing supplies for all the departments of state government directly controlled by the Governor. In this way, we can save many thousands of dollars of tax money before the Legislature meets, and also show the urgent necessity of a law creating a central purchasing agency to buy, at low prices, everything state agencies need.

I want to say again and again and again that I am absolutely opposed to a general sales tax. If, after practicing the strictest economy and frontier frugality, the state still must have more money to carry on the essential and indispensable functions of government, the necessary revenue should be obtained by taxing new sources, or sources which now are lightly taxed.

We are going to make a four-year, all-out attack on disease in Florida. We intend to make it the healthiest place this side of heaven. Public health should be as much the concern of the state as public order. To this end, I have persuaded Dr. Wilson T. Sowder, state health officer, who was loaned to Florida four years ago by the federal government, to stay on here and continue his winning fight against disease. It is the general opinion that Dr. Sowder is the best health officer Florida ever has had.

The old people, dependent children and the blind are going to get better treatment. They must be given kindness, courtesy and consideration at all times. The new Commissioner of Welfare and the State Welfare Board have reached a friendly understanding and will work together in harmony and good will for the benefit of all.

We are going to bring pinetree prosperity back to Florida. The millions of acres of barren land in this state are going to be green with a new growth of timber. Forest fires are going to be stopped. The busy hum of saw-mills, pulp mills and turpentine stills will be heard more all over Florida.

We are going to use the full power of the state in an all-out effort to put the citrus industry back on a profitable basis. We already have a practical citrus program to present to the Legislature.

We are going to control flood waters in Florida and conserve our drinking waters. The Water Control Committee already is working on a plan to finance the state's share of the cost of the $208,000,000 water control system engineered by the Federal government. One of my first acts as Governor will be to discuss the plan with this committee.

The public schools will be adequately financed. The schoolhouse m is as important as the courthouse. It is an integral arm of government. No free country can long remain free without education. "Education makes a people easy to lead, but difficult to drive; easy to govern, I but impossible to enslave."

I am going to make myself just as accessible as possible to the people. My time will be devoted on Tuesdays to cabinet meetings. On other days I will be glad to talk with anyone about the business of the state. When you come to see me I should appreciate it if you would transact your business as quickly as possible, so that there will be time left for me to see other people, and to attend to my many other duties.

Please remember you won't have to "see anybody to see if you can see me." Call up for an appointment, or drop in, and wait for your turn. You needn't bother about bringing letters of recommendation or introduction from any big shots.

I will be very busy during the next few weeks getting the various executive departments organized, so I should appreciate your postponing visits for awhile.

Women will be asked to serve in policy-making positions with the state government. An outstanding woman will be appointed to the Board of Control.

Labor and management will be treated fairly. Both will be encouraged to continue the cordial and cooperative relations which they have maintained in Florida.

New industries will be actively encouraged to come to Florida. For some months past, I have been working on this phase of our program.

Agriculture and the raising of livestock will be encouraged and aided in every proper way.

Conservation of Florida's game and wildlife will be an especial concern of my administration. I am determined not only to conserve what we have, but to increase and replenish it.

By every conceivable means, it is my purpose to stimulate and increase Florida's tourist business. We hope at least to double this state's tourist business during the next four years.

I also am hopeful that some way may be worked out to provide critically needed financial help for towns and cities. I am acutely aware of the almost insolvent condition of many towns and cities.

It is my earnest aim to make our state government more efficient and serviceable. Nothing will be left undone that should be done to bring that about. I am appointing the ablest men available to administer the various departments of state government. All of them will do their utmost to make our state stronger and better. They will welcome your suggestions as to how they may better serve you.

I believe Florida will enjoy the most cordial and beneficial relations with the National government during the coming four years. We are indeed fortunate that our Senior Senator, the Honorable Claude Pepper, is so influential with the National administration. Senator Pepper had a very important part in President Truman's great victory. When we three were together in Key West not long ago I realized that good things were in store for Florida during the next four years.

I look forward to the most harmonious and friendly relations with the able members of the Cabinet. For many years I have enjoyed cordial personal relations with them. Some of them already have made encouraging gestures of cooperation. I feel certain we will form an official team that will carry the ball of good government for all the people of Florida.

I cannot close without expressing my appreciation for fine and helpful cooperation Governor Caldwell has given me. He has gone out of his way to assist me in learning the routine of the Governor's office. He has been generous in letting bygones be bygones.

I renew and reaffirm the covenant I made with the people during the campaign. I will diligently devote four years of consecrated service to the people of Florida. I will energetically apply the experience 1 have gained in public service in an earnest effort to make your state government more of a blessing and loss of a burden. I will never treat the office of Governor as my personal possession, but rather as a sacred trust and a solemn responsibility which has been committed temporarily to my keeping by the people of a great and sovereign state. At all times, I shall earnestly strive to conduct myself so that at the end of my term as Governor you will still trust me as I believe you do today.

Governor Daniel T. McCarty
Term: 1953 - 1953

Daniel Thomas McCarty (born January 18, 1912 – died September 20, 1953) was born in Fort Pierce on Florida's Atlantic coast. He attended the public schools of St. Lucy County, enrolled at the University of Florida, and graduated in 1934 with a degree in agriculture. McCarty became a successful beef cattle and citrus fruit producer, but he also demonstrated a flair for politics. He served three successive terms in the Florida House of Representatives and was speaker in 1941. World War II brought him fame as a genuine war hero. He was in the D-Day Invasion in 1944. While serving with the Seventh Army he was promoted to colonel and awarded the Purple Heart, Bronze Star, Legion of Merit, and the Croix de Guerre. With such credentials and his outgoing personality, McCarty pledged honesty in government and conservatism in fiscal matters, and made a strong bid for the Democratic nomination in 1948. He was, by general consensus, the leading candidate for governor in 1952.

None of his four Democratic opponents, other than Brailey Odham, made a strong showing, and McCarty won easily. He went on to vanquish Harry S. Swan, the GOP nominee, in the general election. Unfortunately, following his inauguration, Governor McCarty served only seven weeks before suffering a heart attack.. Stricken in February, McCarty attempted to carry on from a hospital bed, but died in September 1953.

Inagural Speech
(Source: Jacksonville *Florida Times Union*, January 8, 1953)

Governor Warren, Secretary of State Bob Gray, Members of the Cabinet, Members of the Legislature, Members of the Supreme Court, Distinguished Guests, and my Fellow Citizens of Florida:

I am most humble today as I assume the duties as your Governor. I stand here fully aware of the great problems and the responsibilities of this high public office. As is the case in all types of activity, however, with responsibility, goes opportunity. To me there is no greater opportunity for service than as an elected official in the field of government. With our Democratic processes challenged on every side, the opportunity is perhaps greater today than ever before. I welcome this chance to contribute whatever may be within my power to good government for the future of Florida.

This is the first time that a Governor of Florida has taken the oath of office in this spot. We can all see from here some of the great buildings which house complex functions of our state government. These are tangible reminders that the people have entrusted state officials with vast investments of their tax funds which must be used to produce substantial returns for the good of all.

I am grateful to the many people who have had a part in making this inauguration possible. I am proud of the thousands of fine and loyal people who have helped me to achieve this high office. I want to express my appreciation to all of chose who have come here today to share with me this solemn occasion. I especially want to thank the Inauguration Committees of the Tallahassee Chamber of Commerce for the splendid job they have done in arranging all of the events of this day. No one could have provided better leadership as general chairman than my cherished friend Mr. Justice Elwyn Thomas. Mrs. McCarty and I are most grateful for the fine cooperation given by Governor and Mrs. Warren, Secretary Gray, Florida State University, Florida A. & M. College, the State Road Department, the personnel of the committees, and all others who have helped so much.

My remarks today as we begin a new administration will be devoted primarily to a statement of policy which will be followed by this administration throughout its tenure of office. I will make no attempt specifically to enumerate the various phases of legislation or matters of governmental reorganization which I shall present to the people and to the Legislature when it convenes in April.

The Constitution of Florida states in Section 1 of Article IV, "The supreme executive power of the state shall be vested in a chief magistrate who shall be styled the Governor of Florida." The Constitution further provides that the Governor shall be assisted by administrative officers as follows: Secretary of State, Attorney General, Comptroller, Treasurer, Superintendent of Public Instruction, and Commissioner of Agriculture. It gives specific duties to these officers and authorizes the Legislature to add other responsibilities. The Governor and the Cabinet serve together on many boards and commissions dealing with various phases of Florida's government. I am fully aware of the duties assigned to the elected members of the Cabinet. I am confident that our relationship will be one of harmony and will show a mutual determination to provide an efficient administration of the trust placed in us by the people.

As a former member of the Legislature, I am also aware of the problems of the Legislature and the great part which this branch of government has in our future. I am happy to greet the distinguished members of the Legislature who are here with me today on the platform. I am looking forward with pleasure to the approaching Session of the Legislature and to a friendly and productive working relationship with them.

I well realize that the effective operation of the executive branch of our government will depend largely upon the character and ability of the personnel I appoint.

There is a familiar story in the 18th Chapter of the Book of Exodus (Exodus 18:13-23) which appropriately sets an example for us. Moses, as the leader of his people, attempted to hear, and give judgment on, the individual problem of each man. Observing the great crowds of people trying to see Moses, Jethro, the priest, persuaded him to select capable men of high character to help him—and to delegate, to them the responsibility for decisions not requiring his personal judgment.

I shall have capable men and women of high character and proven ability assisting me. I will look to them for the efficient operation of their departments. I wish it were possible for me to see all who may wish to visit me, and to accept all the invitations which are graciously extended. But this is physically impossible. I, therefore, ask that the citizens of Florida allow me the maximum opportunity to do the job which they elected me to do.

All personnel on the public payroll must recognize an obligation of service in the performance of their duties. There will be no tickets issued to anyone for a gravy train ride. Honesty, efficiency, loyalty and courtesy will be primary requisites in public service. These must be maintained at all levels of government, so that public service will be, in fact, a sacred trust. Officials and individuals must be morally as well as legally honest. As Governor of Florida, I will not tolerate lax law enforcement at any level. I will remove from public office any official who breaks faith with the people and is unworthy of public trust.

I want us to have a good government housecleaning. The kind all good housekeepers know they should have at home from time to time. This doesn't mean that all the furniture and furnishings should be broken up and thrown out the window. But it does mean a good airing out and that the dirt and rust and corrosion which have accumulated in the corners and dark closets must go. All unnecessary and useless articles which may be lying around cluttering up the place also must go. In other words, I want us to get our government house in apple pie order—for our own good health and enjoyment—and for some very important company which will be dropping by to see us—the millions of tourists—and new investors—and new citizens—who will be coming our way.

The state's income during the past four years was almost double that of any previous administration. As I said many times during the campaign, I am convinced that we can meet the needs of the next four years without additional taxation on our people. I will not request the Legislature for any additional taxes except on the dog race tracks in Florida which I feel are not now contributing their fair share to the cost of government. Furthermore, I will oppose any effort to extend legalized gambling.

The humanitarian responsibilities of government have assumed new proportions during the past two decades. Local, state and federal governments share responsibility. In the fields of welfare, public health, education, highway safety, state institutions, and mental health we must assume the leadership and responsibility on a local and state level to guarantee that legitimate needs are met. We cannot continue to grow and tell the world about our achievements in other fields unless we solve these problems in keeping with our financial ability as a progressive state. We must develop additional money and effort to accomplish this end. It is my intention to appoint a committee of outstanding citizens to study our institutional problems and make recommendations for improvements in order that specific plans may be made as soon as possible.

Economic stability is fundamental to sound growth and continued prosperity. We depend primarily on three chief sources of income for our citizens in Florida—tourists, agriculture and industry. It will be the objective of this administration to foster, promote and develop these basic phases of our economy. We can thus stabilize our economic structure and meet any situation which otherwise might jeopardize the economic welfare of our citizens.

Our opportunities in the field of agriculture are unlimited but require increased research and experimental facilities. It will be my intention to offer close support and cooperation to all the agricultural interests of the state. We shall strive for maximum production, at minimum cost, favorable marketing conditions, and fair prices for the grower.

We have been blessed with climate and geographical location which attract to Florida a tremendous tourist business. Competition is increasing in this field not only from our sister states but from our neighboring countries. We must, therefore, encourage and promote our tourist business. We must see to it that Florida offers in addition to its sunshine a wholesome moral atmosphere which will encourage our visitors to return more often and stay longer.

We must realize that our tourist comes to us not as a spender I but as an investor. He must be welcomed as a neighbor and not regarded as a target for the gyp artist. He enjoys looking through glass bottom boats at what God has arranged on the bottom of our springs, but he is looking up as well to see what kind of schools and churches and law enforcement we have provided above ground. He is not content to look at the goods we polish up and put on the display shelves; he wants to know what we are carrying in the storerooms, and under the counters.

Our visitors no longer pay one-third of our state taxes without demanding to know where the money goes. They should be told the truth. We must be able to show that it is soundly spent; that it supports a government that is morally clean, rock-ribbed efficient, and at the same time dynamically progressive—a government determined to provide here in Florida security for business and labor as well as for personal health and happiness. We must let our visitors know that we want to use their brains, their vision, their civic mindedness, their enthusiasm, and not just their dollars; that we want them as partners so that together we can build better farms, and better businesses, and better communities, and a better state.

Industrial leaders and industry in general are now coming to realize what Florida has to offer in the industrial field. Our climate, transportation and natural resources invite ever expanding facilities. The investment of new capital as well as the expansion of existing industry totals millions of dollars and has added ever increasing employment to our people and stability to our year around economy.

Conservation and the development of our natural resources are essential to agriculture, tourism and industry. A sound conservation program offers a real challenge in Florida. Today we find many separate boards and agencies in existence in this field. It is my sincere hope that through reorganization and consolidation more may be accomplished in the field or conservation and better services rendered our citizens at less cost. Let us never find ourselves in the position of having wasted in a foolish way the abundance of natural blessings which God has given us. There is yet time to protect and develop natural resources if we act promptly and decisively.

I am confident that the great institutions of higher learning of the state—two or which are located here—can and must contribute materially to the economic, social and political progress of the State. In this connection, it is significant that my own Alma Mater, the University of Florida, is celebrating its 100th anniversary during 1953. It will be my pleasure very soon to issue a proclamation proclaiming 1953 as the Centennial Year of the University of Florida. I solicit the continued support of all our citizens for our institutions of higher learning in order that they may provide the greatest service to our State.

Under our Democratic process in the final analysis, the future is determined by the expressed desire of the peoples governed. I am determined to perform my duties as your Chief Executive in a manner that will clearly reflect credit not only on this administration but on all our state and its people. I believe that the words of Daniel Webster express my hope as completely as anything I know. I quote: "'Let us develop the resources of our land, call forth its powers, build up its institutions, promote all its great interests, and see whether we also, in our day and generation, may not perform something worthy to be remembered."

As your Governor, I will need your prayers and your help. And earnestly I seek then. I am determined that ours will not be an administration of "sounding brass or tinkling cymbal"; nor one tainted with any kind of dishonesty. But rather ours must be an administration of sound accomplishment by men and women of high principle, inspired in their work by a firm faith in our future. Together, with God's help, we shall succeed.

Governor Charley E. Johns
Term: 1953 - 1955

      Charley Eugene Johns (born February 27, 1905 – died January 23, 1990) was born in Starke in Bradford County. His father was a county sheriff, and was later shot to death in the line of duty while serving as a deputy sheriff in nearby Nassau County. Johns's brother, Markley, died in 1933 while president designate of the Florida Senate. It had always been Charley Johns's ambition to complete his brother's service. Johns was elected to the house in 1934, to the senate in 1936, and had been reelected in subsequent years. He achieved his goal in 1953 when he became Senate president. It proved short-lived because, according to the Florida state constitution, the ranking officer of the senate succeeded to the chief executive's office in the event of his death or incapacity. The state supreme court ruled that he would be acting governor until a successor could be elected to fill out McCarty's term. Johns took over in September 1953.

During his administration Johns pushed the expansion of Florida's highway system. He lifted the tolls from the Overseas Highway to Key West. The controversial Johns kept McCarty's policies on gambling, and followed a plan of fiscal conservatism. He did not intend this administration to be a temporary one and became a candidate in the regular Democratic nomination race for the two years remaining on the unexpired term of the deceased McCarty. The acting governor was opposed by LeRoy Collins and Brailey Odham, and won the first primary by a vote of 255,787 to second place finisher Collins's 222,791. Where Odham's first primary supporters (he received 187,782 votes) would go was crucial. Odham endorsed Collins, and many of his followers agreed. Collins was elected by over 65,000 votes.

Johns resumed his place in the senate representing Badford and Union counties, and served through 1966. When not active as a legislator, Johns conducted a longtime insurance business and was president of the Community State Bank of Starke.

Inaugural Speech
(Source: *Tallahassee Democrat*, September 30, 1953)

I have no fixed or set policy to announce at this time. I can only say that I accept, in full measure, the responsibilities placed upon me by virtue of the constitution and will exercise the powers and perform the duties of the office of governor as God gives me the light to do.

In the performance of these high duties, I solicit the support of the people of the state to sustain me in my endeavors.

Governor LeRoy Collins
First Term: 1955 - 1957
Second Term: 1957 - 1961

[Thomas] LeRoy Collins (born March 10, 1909 – died March 12, 1991), the son of a grocer, was born in Florida's state capital. He attended the Eastman School of Business at Poughkeepsie, New York, and earned a business certificate, he then received a law degree from Cumberland University. Only twenty-five when he was elected to the house from Leon County in 1934, he was reelected in 1936 and 1938. In 1940 he won election to the senate to fill the unexpired term of William C. Hodges. He was reelected in 1942 while World War II was still in progress, but resigned in 1944 to serve in the Navy. The war ended while his unit was still in training. Returning to Tallahassee, Collins was elected senator once again in 1946 and again in 1950. Having won the governorship in 1956, he ran for the four-year term in 1960 and was the first Florida governor to serve two consecutive terms.

Collins had five opponents in the Democratic primary. Among them were a past governor (Fuller Warren) and a future governor (Farris Bryant). Immensely popular statewide, Collins became the first governor to win a majority of the Democratic votes in the first primary. In the regular election he defeated the Republican William A. Washbourne, receiving 73.7 percent of the popular vote. Before he was through Collins would be the first American governor to serve simultaneously as chairman of the National Governors' Conference and the Southern Governors' Conference. He led the first delegation of governors on a visit to the Soviet Union in 1959 to compare the various Soviet states with the American states. In 1960 he served as permanent chairman of the Democratic National Convention in Los Angeles and was the first southern governor to do so.

During his administrations Collins presided over Florida's phenomenal growth and over an increasing state economy that featured industry, agriculture, and tourism. He was responsible for the creation of a State Development Commission, worked to modernize and improve the state's educational system from kindergarten through graduate school (he supported nuclear science, a statewide community college program, educational television, new schools at every level) and was twice chairman of the Southern Regional Education Board.

Collins guided the state on a moderate course during the turbulent years of Civil Rights and school integration. He is deservedly credited with sparing Florida the turmoil experienced by other southern states that attempted resistance, some times turning violent, to national Supreme Court rulings, congressional acts, and federal policies.

After ending his terms of office, Collins was president of the National Association of Broadcasters, Director of the Community Relations Service under the 1964 Civil Rights Act, and Undersecretary of Commerce in 1965. He resigned to return to Florida where he entered a law firm in Tampa. In 1968 Collins ran for and won the Democratic primary for the US Senate, but was defeated by Edward J. Gurney, the Republican candidate. He resigned from the Tampa law firm in 1969, and after a year spent in Miami, returned to Tallahassee and practiced law. During his second term, Governor Collins and his family lived in his wife's ancestral home, "The Grove", from 1955 to 1957 while the original 1907 Governor's Mansion was demolished and a new one was built on the same site.

Inaugural Address
First Term: 1955 - 1957
(Source: Florida State Library Archives, January 4, 1967)

Secretary of State Gray, distinguished present and former State and Federal officials, distinguished visitors, my fellow citizens of Florida:

I am deeply grateful to so many of you for all you have done to make this ceremony possible. The Tallahassee Chamber of Commerce and its many committees, under the leadership of General Chairman Jack W. Simmons, have done a tremendous job. I do not think we could hold an inaugural without the wise, capable, and experienced hand of Captain Bob Gray. Florida State University and Florida A. & M. University, both situated here in Tallahassee, have helped in many ways. Their bands, and the Fighting Gator Band from the University of Florida, add much to our program. I am honored that our popular and talented son of Florida, James Melton, would interrupt his contractual commitments to come here and sing for us today. I enjoyed so much, and I am sure you did also, the beautiful and inspiring song by the Glee Club of Stetson University.

Our whole nation and especially the people of Florida are saddened by the tragedy which came to our sister Republic of Panama in the loss of her great President Remon. This was a personal shock to me and my wife and the others who accompanied us on our visit to Panama recently. It seems only yesterday that we were watching a ball game together down there and between innings the President and I were talking about the future of his country and Florida. As you know, Senora Remon was on her way here with six other high ranking officials of Panama to celebrate this occasion with us when the cruel assassin struck. Our hearts and prayers are with all our friends of Panama in their great sorrow.

Our State and Nation are honored by the presence here today of delegations from our good-neighbor nations of Venezuela, Colombia, Ecuador, Haiti, Mexico, Nicaragua, Puerto Rico and Dominican Republic.

I wish I had time to call each of these visitors and friends by name. I visited in some of these countries a few short weeks ago, and the hospitality of their governments, and of their people, will never be forgotten. Their friendship, then and now, does not represent a personal feeling for me, but rather it reflects their great natural respect and admiration for our country and for our State. It is an expression of their genuine desire as friends to live with us and trade with us and work with us and, if ever necessary, to fight side by side with us for the preservation of our hemisphere. And to them I say that the people of Florida share these feelings, and are more anxious than ever before to vitalize and enrich these bonds of friendship.

But in these expressions of appreciation I leave to the last, my thanks to those whose help has meant the most in bringing about my inauguration today. I want especially to thank those mothers, and school teachers, and clerks and store owners, and truck drivers, and stenographers—all those citizens of Florida, from every walk of life, who worked so hard for my election in the campaign. Your interest was not to get a job, or to get a road. You sought in me leadership for something clean and good and wholesome. You wanted a government you |could be proud of, a government to which you would be willing to entrust your state's future, and your children's future.

The people of Florida, and not the shrewd political manipulators, put me here. You have entrusted to me your high office of Governor. I humbly accept this great responsibility—realizing full well that I can never accomplish all that you would like me to do, or all I would like to achieve. But I do solemnly commit to you and to your service a heart that loves this great State, and a mind and body that will work untiringly to advance its welfare.

Florida has come a long way over a relatively few years. It wasn't long ago when this area represented a fringe on the ante-bellum plantation system of the South. Peninsular Florida, without adequate transportation, was regarded generally then as a valueless water-logged wasteland. It is a different story today. The miracle of modern Florida is self-realization. The handicaps of nature have been defied. Wastelands have been turned fertile for crops and pasturage, cities have risen from coastal swamps, vast stretches of water have been spanned and constantly new uses are discovered for old or hitherto unknown resources. Our rate of growth in population is now exceeded only by two other states. Our total population is increasing more than twice as fast as those two other states combined. The rate of business increase in Florida far exceeds that of any other State of the Nation. Over the years our people have had the faith and the courage to bring us thus far. Many leaders in government and business have contributed substantially to this progress. Gains have been accomplished in spite of the handicap of road blocks along the way thrown up by others. Now, however, as a State, Florida stands on the threshold of greatness. Our future is limited only by the range of our vision, the quality of our leadership, and the desires of our people.

Two short years ago, we witnessed on this same spot the inauguration of another Governor. I knew him well. I had shared with him political triumph and failure. He was a fine man in every sense—high in principle and ideals—strong in his determination to serve his State well. For reasons we cannot, understand, Dan McCarty was stricken seriously ill after only 40 days in office. For seven months he fought to regain his health and to carry on his work for the people of this State. While be served nobly and with outstanding success, he lost his battle for health.

In this tragedy, Florida suffered a setback in a long and universal struggle against something I regard as dangerous and evil. It is something we must face, and face squarely, if we are to change our course, because it is a state of mind into which too many of our people are drifting. It is the attitude that the proper role of government is to take from the many and feed the faithful; that loyalty and support beget special rewards; that the giver of the rewards is making a personal bestowal of blessings and favors from the public bounty; that the receiver should accept with humble appreciation, and at the same time sing with a voice loud and clear, "For he's a jolly good fellow."

But the sad fact is that in this personalized sort of government law goes out the window. Truth and justice are lost in the shuffle. Greed takes the place of need; and while one can, on occasion, still hear the words of good government, the tune is stifled by the barking of dog-eat-dog politics.

As I accept your governorship, I accept its responsibilities and its opportunities for service as my solemn duty to you under the law. Whatever our accomplishments may be, they will be no more than you, the sovereign people of Florida, have a right to expect in the discharge of that duty. This is the way I feel, and I am sure it is the way all who will work with me feel. Any credit will be due to you, the people, and we will look for our signs of progress in your faces and in your hearts.

I so anxiously want the people of Florida to understand that progress in business, industry, and human welfare can only go so far with a ward-heeling, back-scratching, self-promoting, political system. Our progress is sure to run into a dead-end if our citizens accept the philosophy that votes can be traded for a road, or for a job for an incompetent relative, or for a favor for a friend, or for a handout through a State purchase order. The State cannot raise enough money by fair taxation of its people to finance a government of that sort very long. I pledge to the people of Florida that, insofar as the strength within me lies, government by trade, barter, and sale will be out for the next two years.

I have no feeling of hate for any man. But I do hate the things some men do. To fight for right is the easy half of the battle for progress. The hard half is to fight against wrong. But this we must do if we are to be worth our salt. Cooperation with others is essential and highly desirable, provided the cause is right. It is a sinful betrayal of the public trust in a cause that is wrong.

Over two thousand years ago, by the Sea of Galilee, Jesus taught the people that "man cannot live by bread alone." And, before that, Moses, the great law giver, hurled the same challenge in the same words before the people of Israel. How true it is that, to live, every man must have more than bread. He must be nourished in spirit by truth, and love, and unselfishness, and other virtues that are of God himself.

Government cannot live by taxes alone. Or by jobs alone. Or even by roads alone. Government, too, must have qualities of the spirit. Truth and justice and fairness and unselfish service are some of these. Without these qualities there is no worthwhile leadership, and we grapple and grope in a moral wilderness.

The job ahead is a big and challenging one. But the opportunity is just as big and challenging. I am especially proud of the large number of legislators who are here today. I predict that the next session of our Legislature will be the most constructive in all Florida's history, and that out of it will arise leadership and statesmanship of an unusual and marked degree. I firmly believe that working together we will carry Florida forward in many fields.

In the campaign last spring I offered to the people, and by their votes they approved, a progressive program for building our State. It is a program for clean, efficient, and economical government at all levels; for constitutional revision; for better educational facilities and opportunities; for improved labor, health, and welfare standards; for the conservation of our natural resources; for agricultural and industrial research and development; for highways adequate to meet proven needs; for effective highway safety; and for the proper promotion of Florida's tourist business.

To help in the formulation of the details of this program, and to do the basic research required, I have called to service more than thirty citizens' committees. These men and women, on a wholly voluntary basis, are working assiduously. They exemplify the highest type of good citizenship and devotion to civic responsibility, I am extremely proud of the progress they are making, and the State will benefit immeasurably from their efforts.

I would like also to here repeat a statement I often made in the campaign about law enforcement. We must realize that crime, regardless of where it occurs in the State, is a matter of grave statewide concern. Racketeering in any one section undermines law and order throughout our State. Under the oath which I have just taken, it is my duty, and I shall make it my business, to see that lawlessness does not prevail in any county and wrong does not go unpunished at any level.

This Florida of ours is a young State—a growing State. The doors of opportunity are wide open here. There is nothing stagnant about us. I want to make it crystal clear that the emphasis of this administration will be on the positive. To achieve our goal of building a greater State we must move forward boldly—and with an adventuresome spirit. We must not—and we will not—be deterred from our course by those of different purpose—or by those of lesser faith. We must not procrastinate—-we must not vacillate—we must not hesitate. —So much to be done—so little time.

But this new government of yours is made up of optimists and people who, if necessary, will burn the midnight oil. We have something of the spirit expressed in the lines:

> The hills have been high for man's mounting,
> The woods have been dense for his axe,
> The stars have been thick for his counting,
> The sands have been wide for his tracks.
> The sea has been deep for his diving,
> The poles have been broad for his sway,
> But bravely he's proved in his striving
> That where there's a will there's a way.

Our opportunities call for dynamic and vigorous leadership by all those in public authority. There is no place under our sun for the demagogue. We must discard the false prophets who would array little counties against big counties, section against section, and class against class. We must be united as one people seeking a common destiny in the advancement of all.

Will we have opposition to the reforms we seek? Certainly. Down through the years, all progress has been opposed. But we will not cower trembling in our tents. Live fish swim upstream. Dead fish float downstream with the current. I believe in the philosophy expressed by a former President in the words:

> Let us have faith that right makes might, and in that
> faith let us dare to do our duty as we see it.

Your Legislators, your State Cabinet, the Little Cabinet, and I—and all those working with us—will need the interest and help of the people. Government is no better than the people demand, and is just as good as the people want it to be. The right of the people to make their own political bed is inherent in any democracy.

I was told by a traveler once that over in Switzerland, high in the Alps, there is a little church in a very small village. To the casual visitor there appears nothing unusual about this church, but the close observer can note that there are no lights of any kind in it. When evening services are held, tourists behold a strange sight. Each villager, as he leaves home, carries his own lamp and finally, coming from all directions, they all converge at the church. The church then becomes brilliantly lighted with the combined force of the lights brought by all.

Politics must not be regarded by our people as some far off never-never land. Politics is everybody's business. It is your business. As Edmund Burke once said, "The only thing necessary for the triumph of evil is for good men to do nothing." For our house of government to be bright and clear and good and clean, everyone should carry his own light—and do his own part.

You and I—all of us together—have a State to build. Let us subscribe to the thoughts expressed by John Ruskin:

> When we build let us think that we build forever. Let; it not be for the present delight nor for present use alone. Let it be such work as our descendants will thank us for, and let us think, as we lay stone on stone, that a time will come when men will say as they look upon the labor and wrought substance of them—"See this our fathers did for us."

Second Term: 1957 - 1961
Source: Florida State Library Archives, January 3, 1957

Secretary of State Gray, distinguished present and former State and Federal officials, distinguished visitors, my fellow citizens of Florida:

Two years ago I addressed you from this same spot and here accepted the great responsibilities entrusted to me by the people of Florida in their high office of Governor.

Now, with greater humility and a keener insight into the responsibilities and opportunities involved, I solemnly accept your Governorship for a full new term.

I am deeply aware that this circumstance of a Governor succeeding himself is without precedent in the history of our State. Price comes with this realization, of course, but a deep feeling of gratitude comes also. I well realize I would not be here, in this unique position, without the help, the encouragement and the prayers of so very many people.

To the citizens of Florida—in every county and from every walk of life—I am grateful. Your votes, your active campaign efforts, your confidence expressed in so many ways have given me strength and the firm conviction that we have been on the right path during these past two years. And we shall stay there.

To the many who have given so conscientiously of their time and talents to assist us in advisory and often unofficial ways, I am especially grateful. I doubt if ever before any State has been able to call into public service, through committees and other processes, such an outstanding group of volunteers. Others stand ready to serve, I know. And their energies will be needed.

To those who have worked actively with me, often at personal sacrifice, I cannot begin to express my appreciation. I refer to the Little Cabinet, to the members of my office staff, to all the appointees and employees who make up this administration.

The reputation of an administration is the reflection of each part, not merely of the whole. I am proud of this team, of its record of its determination to do not simply an acceptable job, but an outstanding one. And I plan no substitutions.

To those who serve on the Cabinet with me—Secretary of State Gray, Attorney General Ervin, Comptroller Green, Treasurer Larson, Superintendent Bailey and Commissioner Mayo—I express my deep personal admiration and thanks for their generous and helpful cooperation. The accomplishments of their own departments, as well as in the fields for which we share joint responsibility, become integral parts of the record of our State government. And it is a record we are jointly determined to have measure up to the high standards the people desire.

To the members of the Legislature, I reiterate the feeling of gratitude I have so often expressed before. All Florida can be proud if of your accomplishments during the past two years. Unquestionably, the 1955 session of the Florida Legislature was one of the most constructive in our history.

An administration cannot carry forward its program effectively without the cooperation of the Legislature. And, as we plan for the future, I believe that a sound and constructive working relationship is assured.

I cannot close my specific expressions of appreciation without thanking all who have put forth so much friendly and enthusiastic effort to make this inaugural ceremony the fine occasion it is. General Chairman Jack Simmons and all the committees of the Tallahassee Chamber of Commerce have worked tirelessly and effectively. To them, to Secretary of State Gray, to others who are participating in the various events, to all of you who are here, my family and I say, Thank you.

Speaking of my family, only one who has actually served in this position can understand how much a Governor's family is called upon in the overall job, I do not mean simply in the ways you are probably thinking about, but perhaps the biggest chore of all is having to live with the Governor and endure all of his shortcomings as a husband and father, distracted as he is almost invariably by the duties of his office.

I want to say publicly that, while I am conscious of my own deficiencies, you could not have a better First Lady. I am indeed proud of, and grateful to, Mary Call and the children, my mother and father and the others. And I cannot resist the impulse to express my sentiments here.

This is not an occasion for looking backward, except to consider the foundation upon which we have to build Florida's future.

It is a foundation which has been blessed by Divine Providence and upon which men have labored for many years. I am confident that mighty improvements have been made in its stability and security in the past two years. And I believe our State government has contributed a vital share.

The contributions government has made are the cooperative works of many in public life. No one man can claim the credit; certainly I do not.

There is no doubt that Florida today is the fastest-growing major state in the Nation. How are we growing? With the question stated like that, the answer is easy. Since this time yesterday, five hundred new residents have moved in to make their homes among us. In 1950, Florida ranked 20th in population among the states; today we rank 13th; in 1965, we are likely to rank 8th.

A forerunner of this population surge—since people come back to live after liking what they see on a visit—is a phenomenal recent increase in our tourist activity.

In agriculture, Florida's growth likewise has been remarkable—a five-fold increase in income for our fanners in the past 15 years.

And, in industrial expansion, Florida has taken a firm lead over all other states of the Southeast. We are attracting new plants at the rate of one a day.

Two years ago, when I first took the oath of office, as your Governor, I said, "Florida stands on the threshold of greatness." Perhaps we were already inside the door then. But certainly we have crossed that threshold now and have felt what Florida's true greatness can be.

We as a people, are more than a State; we are a State of mind—modern, vibrant and dynamic.

We have been determined these past two years to make your government also modern, vibrant and dynamic. We have kept government in its place—not unnecessarily meddling in the lives and businesses of our people, not enriching a favored few, but acting vigorously and effectively to protect and promote the public interest and the soundness of our growth.

We have recognized that a high moral and ethical standard is basic to the proper performance of government. We have earnestly sought to make integrity the hallmark of your State government. There have been no scandals, and I am determined that there shall be none.

Our conduct has not been guided by political strategy, or opportunism looking to an election ahead, but by sincere convictions of right. It must continue to be so guided.

We have recognized, too, that government must be efficient as well as honest. Thousands of State employees are being brought under a merit system for the first time. Public employment has gained a higher level of respect; public service is becoming more attractive to the best qualified; it no longer offers a haven for the lazy or a sinecure for those who would make a business of trying to call the turn in elections.

We have well under way the great task of drafting a new Constitution to give us the tools to meet the needs of today and tomorrow.

Keenly aware that people come first, we have made outstanding advances in improving labor, health and welfare standards. Public education, the cornerstone of democratic government, has received its strongest support ever—from the kindergarten to the professional schools.

Our institutions have been expanded. Our highway, turnpike and expressway construction has given us Florida's greatest road-building program of all time—one based on need, and not on political favoritism.

Florida has been in the forefront of the States in planning the development of nuclear energy for industry, medicine, agriculture and education.

We have promoted Florida's industrial development to provide, with tourism and agriculture, a stable long-range economy. At the same time, we have taken measures to prevent the despoiling of the beauty and other natural resources of our state.

For many reasons, I would like to stop this address on this glowing note of pride in our progress and optimism about the future. But in all fairness, I cannot. We have shortcomings. I am acutely conscious of many of them as we accept the responsibility of State maturity.

We do not have the highways we need, and we must provide them in the next four years.

We do not have the public schools we need, and we must provide them in the next four years.

We do not have the institutions of higher learning we need, and we must provide them in the next four years,

We do not have the facilities needed in our correctional program, and we must provide them in the next four years.

We do not have the institutional care we need for our mentally handicapped, and we must provide adequately for them in the next four years.

In brief, our State plan falls short and must be greatly expanded to care not only for needs already upon us but also for their enormous increase brought about by our rapidly expanding population.

Our greatest challenge in government, however, is to set our own house in order. We have been making some progress, to be sure, but in reality we are just getting started. We must move forward soundly and swiftly.

We should make our government today as much improved over what it was fifty years ago as modern business is improved over what it was fifty years ago.

As we go forward, we will have growing pains. But growing pains are not nearly as bad as the aches of stagnation.

First and foremost among governmental reforms, we need a new Constitution. This is fundamental; for a State government, in philosophy, and structure, rests upon its Constitution.

Our legislators, I feel, will recognize our need for an up-to-date charter. They will take up this significant task with the benefit of months of careful work by the Constitution Advisory Commission. I feel that fair minds, conscious of their responsibility for the future of Florida, surely will settle the few areas of likely controversy.

More than this no one should ask, and those who dwell now only on the left-over feelings from a past struggle over a part of the task do a disservice to our State and an injustice to the Legislature. We will have a new Legislature with new obligations to meet and a new record to make. And it is upon this new record that it has a right to I be judged.

As we industrialize, we must be prepared to encourage labor-management harmony, and, as our State becomes increasingly urbanized, we must encourage good community planning. We must find the reasons why some communities and areas have been by-passed in our march of progress and get them in step so that Floridians everywhere will go forward and prosper.

We desperately need to make more progress in highway safety.

As I look at Florida's future, I think of the two trees growing in the same forest. One was short and scrubby. It reached just about above the underbrush and weeds. As it looked down at everything below it, it exclaimed, "My, how big I am!"

The other tree was tall. It reached all the way to the ceiling of the forest. And as it looked up at the limitless sky, the stars, the mighty space in which it could grow, it said, "My, how little I am."

With all of our growth and progress, we cannot boast and brag about how big we are. Florida is too tall for that. We look out at the limitless horizons of our future and the broad opportunities ahead and think how little we are.

I asked the question a while ago, "<u>How</u> are we growing?" and I gave statistics to prove our progress. Using the same words and in the same order but with different emphasis, I want to ask the question, "How are <u>we</u> growing?"

This is the most important question of all as we take on the work of the next four years. This is the question that strikes home, and it cannot be answered in census counts or in dollars and cents, because it deals with something more valuable and less tangible.

How are <u>we</u> growing in spirit, in moral concepts, in selflessness, in knowledge, in strength of character? These are the qualities that| determine the balance of the book of life. Without them, the pleasant jingle of the cash register is an invitation to ruin.

Rightly, we are proud of our capitalistic system. The right to own, possess and enjoy private property which bottoms it; the freedom of private enterprise which nurtures it; the opportunity to rise from "rags to riches" which vitalizes it—all have given strength and substance to a system of free government which is the finest ever devised by man.

But freedom does not in itself assure progress. It provides a climate in which we can move forward. In the same climate, however, we can slip backward if that is our will or indulgence.

To make democracy work, freedom must always be squared with the public good. Ambition, while indispensable, must have within it lofty qualities and high purpose, and must not be charged with the destructive influence of selfishness and greed.

We must not train our youth to play the part of money changers in the temple; nor to be bigots manning bastions of hate; nor to be zealots for causes they do not understand; nor to be stumble bums groping in the darkness of ignorance and indecision.

To assure that our nation will continue with vitality and that generations to come will enjoy the fruits and benefits of liberty, we must seek beauty and truth. These are our ambitions for our children. They should be no less our goals in government.

Florida's greatest resource is her people. From the people come leadership and direction, desires and fulfillment. If our people are strong, then our material gains will be meaningful and permanent. But if our people are weak, then our new material progress will lack substance and the sinews necessary to hold it together.

A problem we are facing, and one which I feel I must discuss quite frankly with you, is the matter of racial segregation about which the entire South has been upset, bewildered and confused since the 1954 decision of the United States Supreme Court in the case involving integration in the public schools.

It is important that those who would criticize us should understand that we in the South have not been a lawless people. Guided by a long line of Supreme Court decisions approving the "separate but equal" doctrine, the Southern States were under the impression they were not proceeding in violation of the United States Constitution.

We were not prepared, therefore, for psychology and sociology suddenly to be placed on the judicial scales, overturning long-established legal precedents and seeking to wipe out three generations of human attitudes, traditions and customs based thereon.

I do not know the ultimate answer. And I do not believe anyone else does. However, I am convinced that we will not find the answer in some attitudes that are being reflected in various quarters today.

In the first place, it will do us no good whatever to defy the United States Supreme Court. Actually, this Court is an essential institution for the preservation of our form of government. It is little short of rebellion and anarchy to suggest that any state can isolate and quarantine itself against the effect of a decision of the United States Supreme Court.

If such a proposal could possibly have any legal efficacy, we would have no Union and the power of the Court to protect the people in the enjoyment of their freedoms would be severely impugned and imperiled. We should frankly admit this and put the true label of demagoguery on any doctrine of nullification.

Violence and disorder in any form can never be the answer. And, as Governor, I shall use every lawful power at my command to preserve law and order, peace and harmony, for all our people.

Haughtiness, arrogance, the forcing of issues will not produce the answer,

Above all, hate is not the answer,

One may be hated and still retain his human dignity, but one who hates suffers a shrinking of his soul. We can never find the answer by destroying the human spirit. Indeed, through hate, we magnify our bewilderment and fortify our fears.

In our search for the answer, we should begin by being honest with ourselves, by recognizing realities which exist. Man's greatest failures have come when he has refused to recognize the realities of a changed situation and failed to understand that to admit the existence of a reality is not necessarily to welcome or even agree with it.

It is not easy to say, but it is nevertheless true and I feel that I should stand up and say it:

The Supreme Court decisions are the law of the land. And this Nation's strength and Florida's strength are bottomed upon the basic reverse premise that ours is a land of the law.

Now with this admitted, let us further analyze our position with equal candor.

The decisions of the United States Supreme Court, with reference to public schools, do not make the integration of our schools compulsory. They recognize to a degree local conditions and problems.

Of all the Southern States, I believe Florida has provided legislation which best will enable it to live honestly, honorably and peacefully with the two great realities facing us: the Court decisions and the social and economic conditions existing in the South.

Extremists have attacked the Florida legislation on the one hand as stepping stones to integrated schools and on the other hand as subterfuges for avoiding compliance with the Court's rulings.

It is my judgment that these laws—in line with the Court's recognition that local conditions must be taken into full account—give us assurance that there will be no integration in our public schools so long as such is not wise in the light of the social, economic and health facts of life as they exist in the various localities of our State.

Because of these laws and because of conditions in communities throughout Florida, I continue to say that our traditions and customs of segregation in the public schools can be expected to prevail for the foreseeable future.

I shall do everything in my power to see that these laws are carried out, just as I have taken the oath today to enforce all the laws of Florida.

Attitudes become increasingly important as we deal with the whole field of segregation, including those types of it outside the public schools. And we should admit that our attitude generally in the past has been obstructive all along the line.

We must be constructive and practical. White and colored citizens alike must see wrong on their side as well as right. Our strength to support the right is weakened if we arbitrarily refuse to admit the wrong.

I am convinced, for example, that the average white citizen does not object to non-segregated seating in buses—any more than he objects to riding the same elevators with Negroes or patronizing the same stores. He does resent some of the methods being used to achieve certain ends. Boycotts, ultimatums and peremptory demands can never achieve what persuasion, peaceful petitions and normal, judicial procedures can do for the Negro race.

We can find wise solutions, I believe, if the white citizens will face up to the fact that the Negro does not now have equal opportunities; that he is morally and legally entitled to progress more rapidly, and that a full good-faith effort should be made forthwith to help him move forward in the improvement of all his standards.

The Negro also must contribute by his own attitude. In the first place, he should realize that he must merit and deserve whatever place he achieves in a community. He should strive to be wanted. He should strive to avoid being resented.

To be practical about it, compulsion and ignorant interference by those without a background for understanding now only generate resistance, resistance develops hate and this defeats the Negro's own purpose. Mutual respect and confidence on the part of both races are essential.

It is folly for anyone to expect judicial dictation to compel social adjustments. The hearts and minds of people are not changed by the mere declaration of a principle. Despite the Court's great power, the hearts and minds of the people are beyond its reach and control.

And I speak not of hearts and minds filled with a sense of racial superiority or prejudice, as some would believe. These are not the attitudes of most of us.

We are, however, dealing with emotions traceable to issues of such depth that they produced a war within the lives of some still living.

We are dealing with social habits which have endured in the daily lives of millions.

We are dealing with the realities of economic handicaps which, in the aftermath of war, were made even more difficult for us to overcome.

This morning at the prayer service by which we started this inaugural day, my friend, the Reverend Harry Douglas, read my favorite hymn, "Once to Every Man and Nation." The words by James Russell Lowell have always contained for me great inspiration and challenge.

Here are the first two verses:

> Once to every man and nation
> Conies the moment to decide,
> In the strife of truth with falsehood,
> For the Good or evil side;
> Some great cause, God's new Messiah,
> Offering each the bloom or blight,
> And the choice goes by for ever
> 'Twixt that darkness and that light.

> Then to side with truth is noble,
> When we share her wretched crust,
> Ere her cause bring fame and profit
> And 'tis prosperous to be just;
> Then it is the brave men chooses,
> While the coward stands aside
> Til the multitude make virtue
> Of the faith they had denied.

As I see it, we must side with truth even though now we may share her wretched crust. History requires that we not stand aside, coward-like, waiting for the multitude to make virtue of our position.

The cause is with us <u>now</u>. It requires leadership now. not only from me as Governor but also from you as citizens.

Those who say we are incapable of this do not know the Southerners I know nor the South I love. And to those among us who might say we are sailing against the wind, let us cite the words of the poet who observed:

> One ship drives East and another drives West
> With the self-same winds that blow,
> 'Tis the set of the sails and not the gales
> Which tells us the way to go.

The people of Florida are ready to assume this kind of leadership, or I badly misjudge them. I believe I have the "feel" of this great State, and what I feel is a thrilling reassurance that the people do understand and want to rise with the occasion.

The next four years will involve for Florida transitions in many fields. We must clear out road blocks; we must do substantial remodeling, to prepare, for the limitless years ahead.

There must be change, and change usually comes hard. It takes tedious, often misunderstood, work. Change is always resisted by those who do not understand and by those who stand to lose special advantages they have long enjoyed. The true reasons for resistance are often cleverly camouflaged and obscured.

We may not achieve everything we seek, because my ambitions for Florida are not tailored by assurance of what can be accomplished on the first try. But a fight for right is never lost.

What we fail to achieve we will make easier for achievement by those who will follow.

God forbid that it shall ever be said of our administration, "They did not have the vision to see," or, seeing, "They did not have the will to try."

We must go forward, my fellow citizens, and succeed. As we climb each mountain, as we meet each challenge, we will not pause to claim credit or to celebrate.

Rather, we will see ahead a new mountain to climb. We will see in every challenge not a problem but an opportunity.

We must catch the spirit of the third verse of Lowell's hymn:

> New occasions teach new duties,
> Time makes ancient good uncouth;
> They must upward still and onward
> Who would keep abreast of truth.

This is the call of history—a history which grows impatient. Ours is the generation in which great decisions can no longer be passed to the next.

We have a State to build—a South to save—a Nation to convince—and a God to serve.

Governor C. Farris Bryant
Term: 1961 - 1965

[Cecil] Farris Bryant (born July 26, 1914 – died March 1, 2002) was born on a farm in Marion County, Florida. Bryant's undergraduate education was at the University of Florida and the Harvard Law School. In 1946 Bryant was elected to the first of five successive terms in the Florida House of Representatives, the last four without opposition. In 1953 he was elected house speaker.

In the governor's race in 1960 and the subsequent years the issues were segregation, reapportionment, taxes, education, sit-ins, and economic development in the growing state. Bryant was one of ten candidates for the Democratic nomination. He opposed the sit-ins which were used to achieve desegregation and wanted enforcement of the laws. Bryant was joined by other candidates Fred O. "Bud" Dickinson Jr., John McCarty, and Doyle E. Carlton Jr., the son of a former governor. For Thomas E. "Ted" David of Fort Lauderdale the campaign's central issue was legislative reapportionment. Of the remaining candidates Hayden Burns, mayor of Jacksonville, finished a strong third despite being a first-time candidate. Bryant was the winner, but was forced into a run off with Carlton. In the contest the citizens gave Bryant 512,757 votes, enabling him to defeat Carlton by one hundred thousand votes. Bryant easily won the general election although Republican candidate George C. Petersen received 40.2 percent of the vote.

During his term, Bryant avoided a showdown on racial segregation. Even so, the state experienced incidents involving Tallahassee, St. Augustine, and Jacksonville. Bryant favored new state universities at Pensacola and Boca Raton, but they were not established during his administration. The new governor promoted junior colleges, pointing out the services they performed and stressing that they were less expensive than four-year higher institutions. During the Bryant years higher education saw the establishment of FICUS (Florida Institute for Continuing University Studies, an off-campus degree program), there was coordination between federal and state agencies for expanded water control projects, including beginning construction on the much debated and historic Cross-Florida Barge Canal, and continued expansion of the Sunshine State Parkway, Alligator Alley, and construction of other multi-lane highways. Bryant realized that tourism and industry generated revenue and that an increased state treasury meant fewer and lower taxes. As governor-elect he visited Latin American countries promoting increased contacts, sent two traveling showcases to Europe, and had Florida participate in the World's Fair in New York. Bryant presided as Florida's chief executive during a time when the state had a role in the international friction between the United States and the former Soviet Union. In 1961, President John Kennedy ordered an ill fated military strike known as "The Bay of Pigs" in order to topple Cuban dictator, Fidel Castro. Many of the Cuban born militia soldiers were trained at the Homestead Air Force base in South Florida. In 1962, Nikita Khrushchev, Russia's leader, precipitated the Cuban Missile Crisis. Again, Florida's geographic location became a critical factor in world politics. Governor Bryant and President Kennedy (both Harvard Alumnae), coordinated Florida's role in these two events.

After leaving office Bryant lived an active life, practicing law, serving on boards of insurance companies, being active in Jacksonville's economic life, and holding appointments to federal posts. In 1970 he lost to Lawton Chiles in a run off election for the Democratic nomination to the US Senate.

Inaugural Speech
(Source: Tallahassee *Democrat*, January 3, 1961)

Governor Collins, Governor Caldwell, members of the Cabinet, the Legislature, and the judiciary, distinguished platform guests, my fellow Floridians—my friends.

This is for me a moment of deepest humility, and a moment of greatest pride: humility at the comparison of my limited abilities with the unlimited opportunities that we share; pride in the knowledge that as we grasp these opportunities there stand shoulder to shoulder with me the citizens of the finest state of the greatest nation upon which the sun has ever shone.

The political campaigning is over. For those of you who proudly and successfully proclaimed in May and in November that "It's Time for Bryant" I shall be forever grateful. But 1960—Spring and Fall—is behind us, and can be seen only if we cast our gaze behind us. It is no longer time for Bryant—it's time for Florida. It's time to forget the rivalries of May and November. It's time to remember that we are first and foremost citizens of no mean state, charged by the responsibilities of that citizenship, and by the heritage we share, to do all in our united power to make living in Florida the rich material, social, cultural and moral experience that by reason of our natural endowments it ought to be.

I glow as I drive around this lovely city and see the hospitable signs: "Welcome, Governor Bryant." How glad I am to receive your welcome! But if this day sees no more than the inauguration of a new governor, the sun will set on a day that will have been empty of meaning. This day, to fulfill its promise, must see a new dedication on the part of the people of all Florida to demand, and then to contribute to a standard of excellence on the part of all those who labor in this administration never before achieved, a standard of morality that is not only above reproach but above suspicion, a standard of achievement that uses the progress of past administrations as minimums, not as measures.

Let me make it abundantly clear that in demanding so much I do not for one moment derogate the achievements either of the administration just concluded or of those that have gone before. We take the baton in this administration where it was handed to us by the last. The blocks we lay are placed upon those that have been laid, and to expect these new blocks to reach new heights is praise of the past, not criticism.

If I have seemed to place unusual emphasis upon the part the citizens of Florida must play in the realization of her vast potential, it is not because I am unconscious of the responsibilities of leadership, nor unwilling to assume them. Rather it is because I conceive that in a highly developed democracy such as we inherit the true function of political leadership is to stimulate the people themselves so that their reach exceeds their grasp, and to so direct their efforts that they work in concert, and not in conflict. In this fashion not only do we more nearly achieve our immediate goals, but also, and more importantly, we develop our aspiration for—and our ability to reach—even higher and more significant goals.

A moment ago you heard me take the oath of office. I hope you took it with me, and that as we swore together we turned our backs on the political rivalries of the campaigns, the frustrations of the transition period, the personal jealousies to which men are subject, the misunderstandings that have divided sections and cities and citizens. With all our great wealth of talent we have none to spare. The sand, the sunshine, the sparkling waters, the soft breezes, the rich soil, support us all. The education of every child is a matter of concern to the parents of every other child. The money spent on roads in one district is collected, in part, in every other district. The living conditions, the wage scale, the moral standards, the law enforcement in one section of our State affect every citizen of the uttermost section.

I am not blind to political realities, but I am determined that the government of Florida will, for the next four years be as free from political rifts as it is possible to make it. To that end I pledge my willingness to go the extra mile. I do not plan to recognize the "Pork Chop Gang" or the "Lamb Chop Bloc." With every bit of power and influence with which you endow your governor I shall seek to fight efforts to pit a so-called "majority group" in our Legislature against a so-called "minority group." In my judgment the greatest deterrent to progressive, all-considerate legislation is the division of the Legislature, because of their stand on one or two significant issues, into voting blocs in which its members are robbed of the power of independent thought on many unrelated but equally significant issues.

The Legislature of Florida is composed of men of intelligence and good will, working toward a common goal: the betterment of Florida. It is not strange if their respective viewpoints differ. The most devoted husband and wife sometimes differ. The tragedy occurs when those differences are frozen by ill will into decisions and commitments invulnerable to logic and reason.

The interests of Miami and Madison, of Tampa and Tice, are not, I and cannot be expected to be, identical. There is no compelling reason why, however, with the help of leadership by the executive, restraint by the news media, and understanding by the people, the Legislature cannot achieve a harmonious blending of varying interests to develop equitable programs, including reapportionment. For too long we have been blocked by the fires of sectionalism blown out of control by bitterness and mistrust, fed with fuel from the political woodshed rather than quenched by a liberal supply of the milk of human kindness.

Florida faces a mighty challenge to maintain and increase in these years of great growth and sudden change the quality which has characterized the economic and social gains of which we are so proud. If there is one thought uppermost in my mind today, it is this: A Florida divided against itself cannot meet this challenge. In union alone is there strength.

Just as I yearn for a maximum contribution on the part of the citizens of Florida to the excellence of their government, and vision on the part of the members of the Legislature which encompasses all the needs of all Florida, so I shall seek for a superior effort on the part of the employees of our government. We shall seek out superior employees to reward, we shall invite and encourage, yes, and reward, suggestions for improvement, we shall try to give employees at all levels a glimpse of the larger goals for which they work, we shall encourage competition, we shall weed out incompetence, we shall seek out and punish dishonesty when and if it occurs.

If the collection of taxes is improved, I shall not have handled one account. If better roads are built, I shall not have turned one shovel. If education is improved, I shall not have taught one child. If these things are to be done, they must be done largely by employees who are now serving this state, and who will be serving the state after this administration is gone.

I know the quality of these servants of Florida, and it is good. We shall immediately and continuously seek to improve that quality through the normal personnel turnover, but the greatest opportunity for improvement lies within the employees themselves. We shall ask of them extra effort, unstinting loyalty, the dedication which sees a clock only as a warning that precious time to do the tasks that need to be done is running out.

The blot on the staff of the State Road Department revealed by the legislative investigating committee must be rubbed out. Whether the instances of dereliction brought to light are isolated instances, or symptoms of a widespread disease, must be determined immediately by a comprehensive departmental investigation. Corrective measures, designed to prevent a recurrence, to re-establish employee morale, and to start the road machines rolling, must be immediately taken. And they will be!

The necessity to which this circumstance gives rise of re-establishing the confidence of the Bureau of Public Roads serves to emphasize that Florida does not operate in a vacuum. We are part of a federal complex, and of a changing world order. Within our state itself there is a constant conflict between levels of government.

It was Woodrow Wilson who said:

> The history of liberty is the history of the limitation of governmental power, not the increase of it. When we resist concentration of power, we are resisting the powers of death, because concentration of power

is what always proceeds the destruction of human liberties.

Today these words should be especially meaningful to us, for government at every level is engaged in increasing its powers and spreading them to new fields. In some areas this expansion is proceeding at a barely noticeable snail's pace, in others at a full judicial gallop. The federal government intrudes on the prerogatives of state government, the state government intrudes on the rights of local government, and all intrude on the freedoms that remain to the individual.

There is no one who can contest the desirability of an increase in social capital, so that roads, schools, parks, and hundreds of other community needs can be met. We would all approve the proposition that in our affluent society no one should be denied a dignified minimum subsistence by circumstances over which he has no control or for which he cannot be blamed. But even these goals, high as they stand on the yard stick of the "good life," ought not and need not be bought at the cost of sacrificing those fundamental liberties of the individual which created the very affluence which make such goals attainable. The one sure way to destroy those liberties, in our haste for improvement, is to destroy the division of powers which more than any other one characteristic of our government has kept this nation free and its people independent and strong.

It will be our aim to confine the activities of the state government to the conduct of the state's business—not to the settlement of local issues best left in the hands of local officials. Similarly, we will oppose with vigor any efforts by the federal government to usurp the proper and lawful prerogatives of the state.

It is needless for me, and it is not my purpose as we take this first step across the threshold into a new quadrenium, to catalog our appointments, to specify our problems, or to prescribe a course of conduct to be followed in every situation. These are things appropriate for a campaign, and for an address to the Legislature.

Let us rather spend this brief hour in dedication of ourselves. Let us here highly resolve that, by the grace of God, we will be equal to any challenge—that we will not write the history of our time in asphalt, nor sing its epic story to the tune of a cash register. Let us come again to this historic ground as we reach the end of our appointed time confident in the verdict of history, that we as a people have highly resolved and nobly striven to do the best of which we could conceive— that each failure has been a source of learning, each success a new inspiration.

> Ever insurgent let us be,
> Make us more daring than devout,
> From sleek contentment keep us free,
> Fill us with a buoyant doubt.
> Open our eyes to visions, girt with
> Beauty, and with wonder lit;
> But always let us see the dirt
> And all that spawn and die in it.
>
> Open our eyes to music, and let us
> Thrill with spring's first flutes and drums.
> But never let us dare forget
> The bitter ballads of the slums.
>
> From compromise and things half done,
> Keep us with stern and stubborn pride,
> And when at last the fight is won
> God keep us still unsatisfied.

Governor W. Hayden Burns
Term: 1965 - 1967

[William] Haydon Burns (born March 17, 1912 – died November 22, 1987) was born in Chicago, Illinois, but because the family home was in Kentucky, he regarded himself as a native of Louisville. His family moved to Jacksonville in 1922. Burns was educated in the Jacksonville public school system and at Babson College in Massachusetts. At Jacksonville Burns attained a pilot's license and operated a flying school. He was also the owner of an appliance store. During World War II he was a Lt. (jg), USNR, and served with the office of the Secretary of the Navy. After being discharged Burns became a business and public relations consultant. With his trademark slicked back straight hair, Burns sought and won the office of Mayor-Commissioner in Jacksonville. He first election to that office came in

1949 and he was chosen to succeed himself in the next four elections. He easily held the tenure record as chief executive for the large northeastern Florida city. After his strong showing in 1960's Democratic primary for governor, Burns tried again in 1964. He faced a formidable field of five strong opponents. Florida changed its election cycle so that governors would not be elected during presidential election years, and so the 1964 election was for only two years, although victory would be a strong boost to reelection in 1970.

Burns led the field even though conservative state senator John E. "Jack" Mathews, Jr., also of Jacksonville, was a candidate. Being spokesman for the liberals fell to Robert King High, mayor of Jacksonville. All of the candidates received substantial primary votes, and there was a run off between Burns, the leader, and High. The primary victory went to Burns who defeated the south Floridian by a vote total of 648,093 to High's 465,547. The Republicans had been holding primaries since 1952, and in 1964 their choice for governor, Charles R. Holley, won. In the general election Burns scored the usual Democratic victory, although Holley won 686,297 popular votes and 41.3 percent of the total. Candidates for the Democratic nomination spent almost two million dollars on the election and Republican expenditures amounted to almost one hundred thousand dollars.

Burns's brief time in office saw advancements in water conservation, industrial development, tax reform, and progress toward industrial development. He also had the opportunity to appoint three members of the cabinet. The short term of Governor Burns was conservative and saw no new taxes. Once out of office Burns returned to Jacksonville and became a business consultant once again. He was defeated in 1971 in a race for mayor of Jacksonville.

Inaugural Speech
(Source: Tallahassee *Democrat*, January 5, 1965)

Governor Bryant, members of the Cabinet, members of the Court, members of the Legislature, other distinguished platform guests, families, friends—my fellow citizens—

It is with a sense of deep humility, as well as eternal gratitude that I stand before you, the people of Florida, today. As we pass the moment of my inauguration, I am truly cognizant that you have bestowed upon me, not only the highest honor in your power to confer upon a fellow Floridian, but also a task of great magnitude—the task to keep aglow that sacred flame on which rely future hope, progress and prosperity. In return for the confidence, my purpose will be an unrelenting determination to so serve that in the years to come you will look with pride upon the activities of this State under my stewardship.

But before we look further to the future, I should like to look to the past for a moment.

During all of my public service I have been blessed with many friends who have assisted me. And to the hundreds of loyal supporters who are here today and to the thousands throughout Florida who have given so unselfishly of their time, energy and resources in my behalf, I am grateful and there is reserved a place for you in the innermost recesses of my heart.

But, of all who have assisted and encouraged me, I would like to pay tribute to that group which blessed my life—leading always onward and upward—and that is my family—especially my wife, Mildred, who, along with our son Bill—our daughter, Eleanor, her husband, Lloyd—and my mother—have consistently provided the kind of warm, sympathetic understanding and devoted family relationships that make it possible for a man to enter and remain a part of public life. They have truly been my beacon of light—my haven of stability and serenity.

To Governor Bryant I express my best wishes. To the members of the Florida Cabinet and Department Heads, I would like to express my appreciation for their very fine cooperation in shaping the orderly transition of the state government. They have all accorded me every courtesy—and have taken every step necessary to insure a smooth path for our new administration. I am sure that as citizens of Florida you appreciate this orderly transfer as much as I do, for it is such continuity that makes for stability, orderly progress, and moreover a safe and sound system.

To the men and women who have worked so diligently to prepare and carry out this wonderful inaugural program with all of its formalities and festivities, I want to say thank you and well done. The beauty, the pageantry, and the dignity which are a part of this ceremony will long be remembered by all who are here today.

I want to express my profound appreciation for the presence today of six of Florida's most distinguished citizens of our day, former Governors Doyle Carlton, Sr., Spessard L. Holland, Millard F. Caldwell, Fuller Warren, Charley Johns, and Leroy Collins. Every citizen of this day and the future owe to these Gentlemen a lasting debt of gratitude for their great personal contributions and leadership which have brought us as a State to this great hour.

An inaugural has many meanings. This ceremony today, of course, has a deep personal meaning for me. But, more important, it has a broad meaning for all of us as beneficiaries of the past and trustees of the future. It marks a beginning—a beginning of new hopes—new dreams—new plans—new projects—the beginning of a new era in our state government. An inaugural highlights our aspirations for the future, that will be even more golden as we translate our goals into realities.

This is a majestic and magnificent country, and I am glad to say Florida is a prosperous state—a pleasant place in which to live—to study—to work—to play—to worship.

With its continual growth our State also has its problems but let us not fear—for here the people have vision and talent—energy and imagination—and sound moral values. We are a people who have a rightful place in the Space Age to which we are making real contributions. We are a people who—while keeping our feet firmly planted on the ground—focus our eyes on the broad horizon—on the stars and the moon. We are a people who are ready to move forward—joined daily by others from throughout the Nation and the world—by newcomers who want to have a part in our future, in which there are priceless opportunities.

But prosperous as we are, we realize that some of our people are not sharing as fully as they should in our general prosperity. We must exert every effort to not only bolster what we have, but to bring a soaring boost to our economy, by expanding business and industry, and attracting new enterprise, which will provide additional employment for our fast-growing population. The only limit to our realizations of tomorrow will be our doubts of today.

We are a natural location for the administrative offices of America's large corporations. Already the insurance industry has found Florida and many are moving their headquarters here in order that their employees and executives may enjoy the blessings we have. Likewise, one interstate railroad has moved its general headquarters here, and several others have regional offices.

No state in this vast Union is better suited for the manufacture and distribution of light metals and materials—chemicals—and pharmaceuticals—for furniture-making and boat-building—to name a few. These are industries that depend upon brain power—industries light and clean and wholesome, which will provide substantial payrolls and not conflict with our important tourist industry.

We do not lack the brain power here that these industries need, and we have the climate to make them flourish. We have attractive land water and utilities for their operation, and we have the kind of communities in which they want to settle. Ours is the opportunity to pursue vigorously a program of selling Florida, through a unity of spirit that cannot fail.

And let us be reminded that, in the manufacturing field, there will never be a machine made that cannot be substantially improved. There will never be developed a technique that cannot be made better. Therefore, So long as research is encouraged, we will never come to the end of the road of progress.

At one time we were almost totally dependent upon tourism and| agriculture for our prosperity. Both of these still play a vital role in our economy, but no longer is this just a winter playground—it is a year-round mecca from Pensacola to Key West, for those who seek relaxation and relief from their daily labors.

Our agricultural industry continues to expand and we expect to keep it so, as we are still the winter vegetable basket of this Nation.

Our citrus industry in central and south Florida grows by leaps and bounds. We must strive to improve the markets until these products are available everywhere on earth.

Too long neglected and too little advertised is our beef cattle industry, which is becoming the envy of our Sister states to the west. Florida beef is not just good beef—it is superior beef.

Our sugar industry in south Florida is enjoying an unparalleled development.

Our timber industry, including particularly pulp and paper, is bringing about an improved economy throughout North Florida.

One vital area of our economy to which we have devoted far too little attention is trade with the Caribbean and with all of Central and South America. Actually, we in Florida can be the keystone in an arch of peaceful relations with our sister Americans to the south of us. We can develop fruitful cultural as well as trade ties. We can help to advance the cause of peace within a free-enterprise economy.

Interama—located strategically in Dade County—is an excellent beginning in the construction of this magnificent arch. And let me point out here that although Interama is directly important to the economy of Dade County, it is important to all of Florida. It deserves the support and interest of all Floridians.

Another bright development is the growth of transportation. facilities. We now have thirteen deep water ports. We are extending business and industrial growth with water-borne commerce. The real potential in this activity awaits the completion of the Cross State Barge Canal. I pledge my every effort to the earliest possible realization of this great project. Florida today is served by a fine network of railroads and airlines. No person—no business—today is located more than fifty miles from a commercial airport.

At the same time that we are making progress with respect to water and air transportation, we must move forward with improved highways—with roads designed to move our people safely and efficiently from place to place—to move our agricultural and manufactured products—roads designed to serve the needs of our tourists. Our expressways and limited access highways now under construction must be completed without delay. I shall direct the State Road Board to give immediate attention and complete cooperation to the establishment of an Expressway Authority for Dade County to the end that we shall design and build an East-West Expressway and complete the other road systems designed for Miami and other parts of Dade County. Of paramount importance is the fulfillment and completion of Florida's entire Inter-State highway system. The new administration will put special emphasis on the completion of Inter-State 95 with major projects immediately in Dade, Broward and Palm Beach Counties, as well as the continuation of this vital highway southward from Jacksonville. Of equal importance will be the expediting of the completion of Inter-State Highway 75 from Wildwood into the downtown area of the City of Tampa, and a pronounced program for Inter-State Highway 10 beginning from the Alabama line at the Western boundary of our state and continuing the construction program from the East. These roads are all indispensable to our growth and prosperity, and while working toward these completions, we must and will be planning ahead to construct new highways where they are needed.

Related to highway construction, there are two other significant opportunities. We must continue to improve traffic safety and reduce the slaughter of people on our highways—and, while the municipal parking problem is not a direct responsibility of the State, we shall cooperate with the cities in planning their solutions.

We will be a prosperous state only so long as we have a well-trained labor supply. For this we look to our public schools—our junior colleges—our technical and vocational schools. They must be improved to the point that they are second to none.

We will be a prosperous State only so long as we have leadership. For this we look once again to our schools—and more especially to the kind of young men and women who are the products of our universities. We look to these higher institutions of learning also for the research they are doing—research that opens new frontiers of knowledge—that contributes to our economy in a variety of ways. And, although we want to graduate young people as quickly and as economically as possible, we must make certain that what we are doing is educationally sound—that we take the time and effort to produce quality as well as quantity.

In the near future I shall call for the appointment of a group of distinguished educators and laymen to study our present trimester plan and to report on their observations and recommendations. We must move forward rapidly to preserve what is good and desirable, and to eliminate that which is undesirable, in our system. Our young people are our most important resource. They must be taught by superior men and women. Their education—whether they be retarded, average or brilliant—is our most important undertaking, for our future depends on them, and our present is dedicated to them. If in the annals of history our administration can only be remembered for one contribution, then let it be said that we devoted our maximum experience, courage and labor toward helping Florida reach a peak of excellence in its entire educational system.

We want to continue our attack on diseases, so this will always be one of the healthiest states in the Nation. We are committed to a program of excellent public health, both physical and mental, in Florida. We shall not forget them.

We know that our senior citizens have provided us with a wealth of experience and wisdom in shaping the fortunes of our State in the past. As they reach the era of their golden years, we shall not forget them. Proper care, within our ability, for our aged and infirm, our blind and our dependent children—is not only a duty but a privilege and a source of joy and satisfaction.

We shall strive to keep a watchful eye over our sources of fresh water and prevent as far as possible all contamination.

With the climate, labor supply, recreational facilities, and geographical location being brought to the attention of the proper officials in Washington throughout the past years by our strong Congressional delegation, we are now the host state to many defense plants and military installations. It was a source of gratification to learn that the current plan in Washington to curtail such operations left almost untouched the ones in Florida. For a nation to maintain leadership, it must remain strong, and I pledge full cooperation with the national government in the continued operation and expansion of these facilities.

As we view our challenges, and our opportunities—we must seek the advice and assistance of all who have something to offer. We must develop constructive relationships among the branches of our government, and between all levels—local, county, state and national. Business leaders—educational leaders—governmental leaders—civic leaders—and labor—working together must develop new trust and respect for each other—must join hands in finding solutions to our problems, and thus will they be mastered.

In forming an administration of department heads under the Governor's Office, oft times referred to as the "Little Cabinet," we have been able to attract some of Florida's most outstanding citizens to accept these posts of responsibility. These distinguished citizens are dedicated to our great state, and its purposes, and I know they will serve with distinction and honor to themselves and our state.

This being a ceremonial occasion, I shall not detail the blue print for our administration, but a more comprehensive plan, with recommendations, will form a part of my executive message to the State Legislature when it convenes this year.

In conclusion, let me say that I do not have all the answers to all our problems, but I do have the will and determination to pursue with vigor every responsible avenue of solution—to seek advice from citizens both in and out of government who share my concern and devotion to this State—and I shall daily need and seek guidance from that Supreme Being from Whom all power and wisdom flow—I pledge you the full range of whatever talents I may possess.

As Mayor of the Gateway City for fifteen years, I have had the opportunity from that vantage point to observe the growth of every part of our State. In the performance of my executive duties, I shall see no East—no West—no North—no South, but one great State of Florida. My head—my heart—my hands are hereby dedicated to your service.

Governor Claude R. Kirk, Jr.
Term: 1967 - 1971

Claude Roy Kirk Jr. (born January 7, 1926) was born in California, and during his youth his family also lived in Chicago and its suburbs, and Montgomery, Alabama. He graduated at seventeen from Sidney Lanier High School in Montgomery and enlisted in the Marine Corps. After successfully completing the officers' training program, Kirk was commissioned a second lieutenant at the age of nineteen. He was in the military for three years, and returned for additional time during the Korean War. Kirk served both in combat forces and as a fire control officer. After his military service Kirk enrolled at the University of Alabama Law School and graduated in 1949. He moved to Florida, began selling insurance, and, with two other men, founded a life insurance company in Jacksonville. After serving with the company for five years he became Vice Chairman of the Board and a partner in a national investment house. He also founded the Kirk Investments Company.

As a former Democrat, he became a Republican and led that party's successful effort to carry Florida (the organization was called Floridians for Nixon) for Richard Nixon in the presidential race of 1960. Even so, Nixon lost the White House to John F. Kennedy in that election. In 1964 Kirk was the Republican candidate for the US Senate but lost the election to Spessard Holland. Nevertheless, Kirk achieved his goal of receiving statewide recognition which helped him win the governor's office in the following election.

In 1966 Kirk defeated Richard B. Muldrew and gained the GOP nomination for governor. Democrat Robert D. High won over Haydon Burns and became the Democratic standard bearer. In the general election Kirk won. The vote totals were 821,190 to 668,223. For the first time since Marcellas Stearns won in 1874, the Republicans had control of the Florida governor's mansion.

Kirk revealed his new wife, Madame X (a German born beauty, Erika Mattfeld) to the public. Both had previously been married. The unconventional governor argued with his cabinet and with Democrats and some Republicans in the legislature. An important legacy of the Kirk years was a significant revision of the 1885 constitution, and a Republican-Democratic coalition reorganized the executive department giving the governor greater responsibility. Even though the Democrats controlled the legislature, Kirk kept them off balance, and had more than enough panache to keep his agenda. For example, Kirk had pledged no new taxes and when the legislature passed a budget that would produce a deficit unless the economy turned sharply upward and produced the revenue for existing taxes, he promptly vetoed the measure. Five days after adjournment, Kirk called the legislature back into special session. Not only was the budget out of balance but, the governor charged, its educational sections were unconstitutional. Both houses, dominated by Democrats, voted to override Kirk's veto and also voted to override a companion educational bill. The legislature added fire to the governor's war against new taxes by voting itself a $12,000 a year raise (the constitution of 1968 had given the legislature that power).

Additional conflict arose over the governor's war on crime. The idea was valid but the legislature and many citizens objected to its financing by private contributions and to its being carried out by private organizations. There were also objections to the Governor's Club whose membership was secret. A hostile press and threats of lawsuits forced the revelations of the members' names. The Governor's Club had paid money to finance the governor's expenses on trips to promote the state, and, the accusers harshly charged, to promote Claude Kirk. In a time of educational strife, the governor took a stand on the efficacy of busing to achieve racial balance in Florida's schools. The governor took over the administration of the Manatee County schools in April 1969. His motive was intended to force the national Supreme Court to rule on the legality of busing. Kirk failed in his effort, and placed himself in an unfortunate position.

Under Kirk long-standing problems of state government were resolved. Despite repeated special sessions of the legislature, reapportionment had not been solved. Finally, court-ordered reapportionment of the legislature was achieved when the court accepted the plan submitted by Florida in 1967. One of the new constitution's changes was to resurrect the old office of lieutenant governor and to require both the gubernatorial and the lieutenant governor to run on the same ticket. A governor was permitted to succeed himself if he had not completed more than six years of service. Only the judicial section of the constitution of 1885 remained intact.

Kirk sought reelection in 1970, but lost to the ascendant Democrat Reubin Askew. In his later years Kirk returned to Palm Beach, and resumed his role in banking circles. He also sought political office, making unsuccessful tries as a Democrat to win the governorship and again as a Democrat to win election to the US Senate. His last effort was as the unsuccessful Republican candidate for Commissioner of Education.

Inaugural Speech
(Source: Florida State Library Archives, January 3, 1967)

My fellow Floridians:

There are those moments which live forever in the memory of man. This, to me, is just such a moment. I am engulfed by gratitude to you, the citizens of Florida, for the great confidence expressed in your selection of me as your Governor.

I am humble in the knowledge that so many people from so many walks of life gave of their time, energy, and talents to make it possible for me to stand here at this unique moment in Florida history.

Appreciation for the help, the support, the devotion of others can be expressed in many ways. It could be expressed by a simple thank you, or it could be expressed with flowery oratory.

I prefer to express my appreciation in serving you, as I have promised, by constructive action. Together we shall move our beloved state far along the pathways of progress in every field—toward our goal of making Florida number one.

We are on the threshold of a new era for Florida. Today you and I embark upon this adventure—an adventure unparalleled in our history and an opportunity that can bring greatness to our state and to our people.

Like most adventures, there will be a time for laughter and a time for tears, a time for caution and a time for valor, a tine for peace and a time for battle. To this adventure, we bring new forces.

We bring to the peoples' battle a reapportioned legislature—a legislature of the people.

We bring the beginning of a revised state constitution—a revision, which when completed, will have been done by the people.

We bring to out battle for greatness a new administration pledged to be the servant for all the people.

In looking to the future, we must review the past; review the past not only to find the solid cornerstones for growth but to cover the obstacles, the pitfalls, and the stumbling blocks we will encounter in our march toward greatness.

Some of these obstacles are well-known; others are less obvious. But in a sense, all constitute crimes against the people.

Crime has been defined as a "gross violation of human law."

To many, crime means robbery, muggings, murder, and other active violations of individual rights. Equally serious, however, are the crimes of human neglect—neglect that robs the people of their priceless heritage, of their individual freedom, of the incentive to do their best, of their faith in their government.

America and Florida have been plagued by many instances of such neglect. I brand such neglect as criminal because it robs the people of a voice. It would be a crime for us not to work for the elimination of this neglect, just as many good men have done before you.

Florida has suffered too long:

- The crime of an antiquated constitution.
- The crime of too expensive government.
- The crime of high taxes.
- The crime of inadequate educational facilities.
- And, finally, the crime of crime itself; the insidiously brutal crimes committed upon the citizens of Florida by storm troopers of the underworld, by the thugs, murderers, and gamblers.

Today, I totally and irrevocably commit myself to ridding Florida of all these crimes. I pledge to you again that in our fight against the forces, of organized crime I mean business.

The momentous battle is now joined. Today I am proud to announce to you, that I have commissioned Mr. George Wackenhut of Miami as Director of the Governor's war on crime.

Mr. Wackenhut heads the third largest private investigating firm in the United States. I am happy to say he is providing his services to the state for one dollar a year.

It will be his responsibility to marshal the forces for this great fight—the investigators, the computers, the prosecutors, the attorneys, the accountants, and the people.

Although Director Wackenhut is donating his services, I have authorized him to secure from his firm whatever manpower is needed in this campaign. The cost involved in all phases of this endeavor will be paid from funds volunteered by interested private citizens. This means that this important and crucial fight will be lead by me without additional taxes.

I hereby put our underworld adversaries on notice that this is not just another temporary campaign with a flare [sic] for publicity.

Ours will be an effective, professional, and responsible campaign—a campaign in which we push the criminal element not only from Florida but beyond national boundaries.

I have; and will continue to confer with officials of New York, Illinois, and California, as well as others who share our desire to rid America of this cancerous growth. I intend to make sure that Florida leads them in this battle against our joint enemy.

Professional crime fighters have been employed for this war— they are the reserves. Responsible law enforcement officers from all levels of state and local government will be mobilized to carry forward this campaign—they are regulars. But no war is ever won by the regulars alone. It is always the reserves who provide the margin of victory and into this fight we will throw every reserve we can muster.

When the cancer of crime is removed, the regulars can carry on without our having created another governmental division or empire. Yet these reserves can always be recommitted when and if needed.

If we are to win this war the Florida of today cannot afford the slums of yesterday—those spawning places of discontent, the breeding place for crime, the death house of initiative, the graveyard of hopes.

We will wage war on slums by marshalling the forces of free1enterprise to work as partners of state and local government. It will be a. creative program with a heart and a soul as its guide, not an unbridled federal bulldozer as its symbol.

Our forces are also being assembled as we prepare for a battle against the crime of inadequate education.

No longer can we afford to mark time while other states pursue and capture educational excellence. Florida must be number one in education. The future in this state and of our children depends upon achieving this goal. Therefore, we must have a definite program projected for excellence and a workable plan of action designed to achieve our goal at some reasonably fixed date.

Education is a disciplined activity that demands a full time commitment. With the Superintendent of Public Instruction, I plan to seek the counsel and cooperation of every citizen through a series of Governor's conferences on education. These will be working conferences. Every facet of our educational effort will be explored through these individual conferences with legislatures, educators, parents, and students.

Education also means inquiry, change, and response on a scale for which our state has no precedent. Therefore, our program must be imaginative, but it must be practical; it must have as its long range objective the creation of the best educational program in the United States. It is obvious that money alone is not the answer. The accomplishment of educational excellence means recognition of these realities and recognition that our only concern is commitment to the child in the classroom.

Florida has bean a major food source for the United States and other nations for years. We intend to accelerate by practical aid Florida's vegetable, sugar, citrus, and beef production. Agriculture is a major industry and we do not intend to stand by and see it be stifled by any federal harassment.

I will work with our Congressional delegation to make full use of Federal programs to aid in our war against high food costs and to build a greater agriculture industry.

Our road program must also have imagination, coupled with reality. The appointment of a professional engineer to the chairmanship of the State Road Board was the first step in my commitment to take politics out of road building.

Plans are now being prepared for five, ten, and fifteen year road building programs. Roads will be built according to need. Each year we will grade ourselves on the progress of this program as must future administrations.

Not only must we build our road system, but also we must strive to eliminate the slaughter on our highways. Here again, we must take advantage of every agency in government which can aid in the fight against highway "self-inflicted capital punishment."

Today we begin four years of sound business practices in the operation of your state government. Today—through the art of finance—we begin work towards guaranteeing that this administration and your economy will have directional growth fast enough to generate additional revenue to avoid any additional new taxes. Today we turn the tide against ever higher state spending.

Already the ground work has been laid for an expansive intrastate job growth program, which is dedicated to bringing new and expanded payrolls and economic benefits to Florida. There is a new vista that time and circumstance gives only now—and gives only now to Florida, if we will act.

Therefore, in several states I am now establishing a special and personal Governor's Industrial Development Committee for the sole purpose of placing the "on sight" knowledge of Florida within immediate, personal, and continuous reach of all industry. Now we can effectively concentrate our efforts in seeking new industry on a day-to-day basis.

Florida—the launching pad of the universe—roust have vision. We must look not only to the stars, but to over the sea—not only to Florida but our sister sovereignties as well. We must look to the world and especially to Europe, Africa, and South America—areas of untapped resources—areas for which Florida can serve as a conduit and a catalyst.

I will take special responsibility for realization of such projects as Interama in Dade County. This project can provide a show-case—a demonstration that Florida can become the financial and trade center of today's world.

Florida must and will become the center of world oceanography. Our vision must always include not only the beauty of field and stream, and the rolling surf, but we must see beneath those depths where in our lifetime men will plant and harvest crops, mine precious metals and discover the secrets of our universe.

Florida is now the family entertainment capital of the United States. Within the foreseeable future it will be the entertainment capital of the world. Its sun, its beaches, its rivers, its streams, its ocean, its gulf—all of these make it a natural family playground, not only for tourists but also for all our citizens.

But our natural resources must be preserved by an active program designed to combat air and water pollution. This administration shall immediately embark upon such a program.

If we are to achieve the goals that I have outlined here today, Floridians must modernize state and local government so that these governments may operate with maximum economy and efficiency.

The cornerstone of an effective government structure is a modern constitution. Florida can no longer suffer the limitations of its antiquated constitution. The Florida Constitution Revision Commission has worked hard and long to draw new guidelines for the efficient operation of our government. After months of almost continuous labor the Commission has drafted a proposed constitution. It sets the tone for returning local government to the people and serves as an example for other states to follow. It will provide a vehicle for needed governmental reorganization. It contains provisions by which the people can amend the constitution so that it will continue to be a living document. Although the proposed revised constitution may require some adjustments, it is my hope that it will be accepted by the legislature for submission to the people substantially as it has been drafted by the Constitution Revision Commission.

Constitutional revision is today's problem—not a problem of next month or next April, or next year.

For the legislature to labor sixty days next April to rewrite our laws, without, first rewriting our constitution is not consistent with good business-like procedure. Constitutional revision cannot be delayed for a long hot summer of dilatory debate. It must be tackled now while minds are fresh and courage is abundant.

With the authority invested in me by Article IV, Section eight, of the Constitution of the State of Florida, my first official act as Governor of this state will be to today sign a proclamation calling for a special session of the legislature to consider solely the critical issue of constitutional revision.

My proclamation shall direct that this special twenty day constitution revision session shall begin next Monday, January 9, 1967, at 9:30 a.m. The sole purpose of this session shall be the rewriting of Florida's antiquated constitution for immediate submission to the people for their final acceptance or rejection. It is my hope that legislators, during their special session, will provide for a special election to be held on April 18, 1967, at which time the people shall be given the opportunity to adopt a modern constitution geared to solving present day problems. I will request that the revised I constitution have an effective date of July 1, 1967.

Following the time schedule, which I have outlined above, will permit the 1967 legislature to enact during its regular session all laws necessary to the implementation of the newly adopted constitution.

My ambitions for the citizens of Florida are not limited by any city or county boundaries. In our move to greatness we together must work as one united people seeking only that which brings a new destiny for Florida.

The people of Florida are not only our native-born but also come from all states, from all regions, from all nations. Because of this we are uniquely equipped to provide a showcase of living; not only for the south, but for the nation and world—living leadership devoid of extremism, either right or left—leadership that lives in the dignity and rights of all.

Thus the many battles are joined. The objectives are clear. We will marshal every force available to make Florida number one in efficient and responsive government—education—industry—highways—agriculture—tourism—space exploration and undersea research—entertainment. Today we assault our dated and inefficient government by modernizing our constitution. We march against organized crime.

As Floridians, we must think not of yesterday's shortcomings but of tomorrow's success—believe not in yesterday's defeats but of tomorrow's victories—care not for yesterday's frustrations but tomorrow's fulfillment.

You—the citizens of Florida—have expressed your desire for a new vista in Florida's government. You have asked us to achieve for you the modernization of all practices of government.

You—the citizens—can make Florida first. But first we must do what we have now agreed to do. This is your Florida and we are your servants. We together will make Florida first.

Thank you.

Governor Reuben O. Askew
First Term: 1972 - 1975
Second Term: 1975 - 1979

Reubin O'Donovan Askew (born September 11, 1928) was born in Muskogee, Oklahoma. He moved with his mother to Pensacola in 1937. Educated at Florida State University (B.S.) and at the University of Florida (LL.B.), Askew carved an enviable record as an undergraduate and a law student. He served on important committees, was a member of several honor societies, and was a distinguished military graduate. In law school he was executive editor of the Law Review. In 1946 he became a member of the army paratroopers and served as an enlisted man. Askew saw additional military duty from 1951-1953 as a second lieutenant in the Air Force.

He began his public career in his home county of Escambia in 1956 as Assistant County Solicitor. Elected to the Florida House of Representatives in 1958 and to the Florida Senate in 1962, Askew entered the Democratic primary as a candidate for governor in 1970.

He teamed up with Tom Adams of Orange Park to oppose Earl Faircloth and George G. Tapper, Chuck Hall and Pat Thomas, and John E. Matthews and Elton J. Gissendanner. He and Adams trailed Faircloth and Tapper in the first primary by about twenty-five thousand votes, but won in the run off 447,025 to 328,038. The Republican primary had Kirk and Ray C. Osborne, Jack M. Eckerd and Robert H. Elrod, and L. A. "Skip" Bafalis and Ward Dougherty vying for the nomination. In a run off with Eckerd and Elrod, Kirk and Osborne won the nomination. In the general election the Askew team prevailed with 56.9 percent of the vote. Democrats still outnumbered their Republican opponents, but the gap was closing and future elections promised a real two-party state.

Askew was an active chief executive. He pledged tax reform during the campaign and faced strong legislative opposition. He won legislative approval of a referendum that would levy a corporate income tax, and campaigned statewide appealing to the voters for passage. The voters responded favorably by approving the measure. The vote was followed by the repeal of consumer taxes on apartment rentals and household utilities. State revenues were shared with local governments and schools, thus lowering homeowners' local property taxes. At Askew's urging the state legislature increased the homestead exemption from $5,000 to $10,000 for persons of sixty-five and older and for the disabled. Local school taxes were reduced, and the first $20,000 in intangibles were exempted from state taxes. The environmental issue became paramount in Florida as Askew led the way to the passage of the Oil Spill and Pollution Control Act (1970), and the Land and Water Management Act, the Land and Water Management Act, the Water Resources Act, and the State Comprehensive Planning Act (all in 1972). Protecting Florida's most sensitive and endangered lands was addressed by the Askew administration's land acquisition program.

When the legislature dragged its feet on a "Sunshine Amendment" requiring financial disclosures by all state officials, Askew obtained over two hundred thousand signatures to put the issue on the ballot. It was ratified by eighty percent of the voters. Strides were made by race and gender under Askew's two administrations. In 1970

Gwendolyn Sawyer Cherry became the first African American woman elected to the state legislature. In his second administration Askew appointed Jesse J. McCrary secretary of state in 1978. He was the first black since Reconstruction to be a member of the cabinet. Askew also appointed the first black to the State Supreme Court. Showing the respect that he personally had and the importance attached to Florida, Askew delivered the keynote address to the Democratic National Convention in 1972,

In the 1974 race Governor Askew's lieutenant governor candidate was J.H. "Jim" Williams because Tom Adams sought the top position himself and teamed with Burt McCormick. The other Democratic aspirants were Norman Bie and Florence S. Keen and Ben Hill Griffin Jr., and Eleanor F. Griffin. Askew and Williams were easy winners, and no run off was required. Challenging from the GOP were Jerry Thomas and Mike Thompson, unopposed in the primary. The popular Askew became Florida's first governor to receive over a million votes. Yet, the team headed by Jerry Thomas won 709,438 votes.

Askew's second administration was a continuation of the first. The first governor to be elected for a second successive four-year had been unbeatable in Florida. In 1984 he was briefly a candidate for the Democratic party's presidential nomination. Upon stepping down from the governor's office Askew joined a Miami law firm and remained before the public as a cabinet rank member of President Jimmy Carter's administration. He also taught at Florida International University and Florida State University. At FSU the university's school of Public Administration and Policy was renamed in his honor, and the University of Florida created the Askew Institute of Politics and Society.

Inagural Speech
First Term: 1971 - 1975
(Source: Florida State Library Archives)

Governor Kirk, Lieutenant Governor Osborne, Lieutenant Governor Adams, members of the State Cabinet, honorable Justices of the Florida Supreme Court, Mr. Speaker, Mr. President, distinguished members of the Florida Legislature, my fellow Floridians:

We are here today to inaugurate a new administration—the 37th in Florida's long history.

The circumstances which bring this administration to Tallahassee provide for us broad opportunities to serve the people of Florida. We are keenly aware that they impose on us even broader obligations.

We begin this administration today with the support and the strength of the people who saw in our approach to this high office a new opportunity for Florida.

<u>And we are determined to take full advantage of this opportunity</u>.

The next four years will be years of debate over such issues as tax reform, education, preserving the balance of nature, transportation and governmental efficiency. They will be years of some controversy over our programs to improve the quality of life for all Floridians. The debate is healthy; the controversy is healthy; that is the genius of the American system.

But, while we are encouraging the frank and open discussion of our programs, we are also committed to action. Talk alone will not be sufficient.

The first major test of our resolve will not be long in coming. In fact, it is with us today. I am speaking, of course, of the battle for tax reform.

I am today seeking an advisory opinion from the Florida Supreme Court on the constitutionality of a tax on corporate profits. Should the court decline jurisdiction, or should the court rule that a constitutional amendment is necessary, the special session of the Legislature, already announced for January 27, will be expanded to consider such an amendment.

Florida, for all of its virtues, has one of the poorest tax structures in the country. We have stacked burdensome consumer taxes and property taxes on middle and low income families while granting special tax favors to the politically influential.

<u>The time has come for this to end.</u>

We said several months ago that, if we were honest with ourselves, we would have to admit that this is going to be one of those years in which the question would not be whether there will be new I state taxes—but, rather, <u>who will have to pay</u>. The hard facts of the financial crisis that faces us today are now dawning on even the most optimistic among us.

Some have said that instead of closing the loopholes and requiring profit-making corporations to pay their fair share, we should once again raise the sales tax to solve our revenue problems. Let me say that for the Legislature to <u>even consider</u> increasing the sales tax in Florida to five per cent, while our tax inequities still exist, would be a complete travesty of justice. Continually turning to higher consumer and property taxes to pay for needed public services without facing up to tax inequities is the answer of yesterday.

It must not be, <u>it will not be</u>, the answer of today.

In addressing ourselves to how government raises money, we would be doing a disservice if we did not address ourselves with equal enthusiasm to the way government spends its money. We must consider the tragedy of every misspent dollar ... the tragedy of every public employee without meaningful labor. The waste is criminal because there are so many things that need to be done that are not being done simply because we do not have the money.

So, while we are realistic about the need for new revenue, we must be equally realistic about the waste in government and what it is costing each and every one of us. We must and we will examine every single program in which we are presently involved to determine if continued expenditure of public funds is justified.

When a program is not justified, we must end it without delay.

In the next four years, we also face the task of reversing the trend that is leading to the destruction of our ecological system. Florida, because of the natural beauty and value of its environment, has a larger stake than most in conservation and environmental protection.

Time is running out on us if we are to save Florida's natural heritage for ourselves and for our children. We must not take our air, water, or the beauty of our coasts and forests, for granted. We must concern ourselves with every step of the chain of life because the balance of nature is so easily disrupted.

Economic growth concerns every one of us, because jobs and payrolls are the hallmark of a healthy state. We must insure our continuing economic prosperity. But the price we pay for growth must be carefully evaluated. We must recognize that the destruction of Florida is a price too high.

In the long run, <u>ecological destruction in Florida, is nothing less than economic suicide</u>.

We must be honest enough with ourselves to admit that, not just business and industry, <u>but all of us</u>, share the blame for the damage already done. In fact, the greatest single polluters of our lakes, streams and coastal waters are governmental agencies themselves. And, too many times, what one governmental agency is trying to preserve, another is inadvertently beginning to destroy.

Our commitment to the preservation of this great state is complete. We must stop pollution and we must end the threat to Florida's wildlife. Then, we must resolve to restore those areas already polluted. <u>No less of a commitment will be acceptable during the years of this administration</u>.

At the same time, the 1970 census emphasizes what has been evident for some time in Florida. Our population is growing, and the greatest growth has been in or near urban areas. Several rural, agricultural areas have even lost population.

If the present rate and pattern of growth continues, the east coast of Florida will soon be one continuous urban area, from south Florida all the way to the Georgia border.

The question immediately arises—are we prepared for that growth?

I see in the urban areas of Florida a developing crisis, representative of all the inadequacies in our governmental and social systems.

To list the problems of our cities is not difficult. They are the problems of Florida and the problems of America, all meeting in one place—the ever-increasing incidence of violence and crime, pollution, insufficient and deteriorating housing, inadequate transportation systems, and the economic plight of many of our fellow citizens.

It is incumbent upon us to enlist the best efforts of government, industry, and all of our people to begin correcting these ills.

We, in government, can begin by examining ourselves. The great reliance we place on property taxes, for example, contributes in large measure to the poor use of land, the deterioration of buildings and the unnecessary proliferation of local governmental units.

High property taxes, which fall most heavily on low and middle income families and small businesses, make it most difficult for many of our urban citizens to rise above their existing economic conditions.

And we cannot forget that the federal government has a tax system which provides an incentive for those who build structures which can be rapidly depreciated—structures which, incidentally, rapidly become part of the urban problem.

I believe that attempts by government to remedy our urban problems will continue to be unsuccessful until government starts at the beginning and stops contributing to those problems.

In education we have perhaps our most difficult assignment. We must exercise the responsibility which has been given us by the people to accomplish reform in our educational system. And yet we must encourage and work toward that reform without making education a scapegoat for political gain. Any direction we take in educational reform will be controversial, and yet we must match the courage we have recently demonstrated in paying for quality education with the resolve to build a system capable of producing quality education.

In the past, we failed to adequately consider the unique nature of every child. But we are now beginning to understand that confronting| each child with the same educational program does not produce the same result. Children from deprived backgrounds have too often been ignored by the process, and children with exceptional backgrounds have too often been stifled by the process.

Education has, for many, been irrelevant.

Many of our teachers and educators understand this problem, but their foresight and efforts must be matched by a commitment from this administration, from the Legislature, and from the people. We must determine how to provide equal educational opportunities for every child. We must have meaningful programs of both vocational and pre-college education so that every young person, regardless of his background or interest, will leave our state-supported educational system prepared for a lifelong love of learning, living and self-discovery.

One of the greatest challenges facing Florida is in the field of higher education. Young citizens in our universities often do not realize how much the universities depend on the larger surrounding society. The outside world often does not realize how much it depends upon the universities.

The current focus on campus unrest across the country should not detract from the tremendous progress Florida universities have made during the past ten years; it should not obscure the fact that the great majority of students are law abiding and idealistic with a very real desire for constructive change; it should not make us less willing to listen to and respect those who legitimately and honestly seek to express themselves.

We must continue to strive for excellence in our state university system and, in doing so, we must be mindful to work with and to encourage strong communities of independent colleges and universities. Establishing great universities has required an emphasis on postgraduate education but, while we seek to improve graduate programs, we must not forget our obligation to undergraduate students, the backbone of our higher educational system. Undergraduate education, in our universities and community colleges, must be continually improved.

Another task which confronts us immediately is the direction and administration of Florida's Department of Transportation. I believe that the Legislature, in establishing this Department, did more than rename an old agency. It evidenced a concern for all forms of transportation, with the full realization that the construction of roads and highways alone reflected a narrow view of Florida's future.

In the next four years, it will be a tremendous task just to keep up with Florida's road needs. We hope to see the rapid completion of the interstate highway system, the expansion and improvement of our primary and secondary road systems, and the availability to local governments of greater assistance in meeting local road needs. And because roads alone will not fulfill all of our transportation needs, the early development and availability of the means for mass transportation will be given a high priority.

In our quest for a continued healthy economy, we must not neglect the needs of our two largest industries—tourism and agriculture. We will strive to strengthen our tourist flow by productive and imaginative promotional programs. This administration also intends to work with all phases of the agricultural industry to help create new markets for Florida products.

We are aware of the conditions in our prisons and migrant labor camps. When we find ourselves criticized publicly, we can take one of two approaches. We can immediately rise to our own defense and attack those who would advertise our problems to the nation. Or we can take the occasion of criticism as an opportunity to look at ourselves objectively and honestly. We can obtain the facts and, if we deserve the criticism, resolve to correct the errors. It should be understood, without any doubt, that this administration will pursue the latter course.

I have talked to you about our goals of tax reform, governmental efficiency, the preservation of our natural resources, upgrading the quality of life in our cities, improving education, and fully meeting our transportation needs. Of no less importance are insurance reform, election reform, judicial reform, and improved economic opportunities and equal rights for all of our people, rural as well as urban, black as well as white. And we must not disregard the need for protecting consumers against fraud and mistreatment at the hands of the unscrupulous.

The responsibilities before us are many—far too numerous to discuss each in detail here today. And we recognize that in meeting those responsibilities … in exercising the authority of the Chief Executive of this state … that we will make errors. But we are pledging to you today that our errors will __not__ be those of unconcern. They will __not__ be errors of inaction.

Inherent in our commitment to action is a belief that state governments can no longer wait for the federal government to solve our problems. It is now obvious that the inadequacies of our society are matters properly dealt with by government. But it has become equally obvious that the solutions are not to be found in Washington. If there is anything which has become certain in the last decade, it is that even the most well-intentioned federal program is too many miles and too many administrators away from implementation.

The Speaker of the House and the President of the Senate, when each took office, spoke of the urgent need for sharing federal income tax dollars. I share that concern and pledge our fullest efforts to see meaningful revenue sharing become a reality in the near future.

Florida is fortunate in the quality of its legislative leadership. Both houses of the Legislature and both parties are under the leadership of men who have demonstrated a long commitment to Florida and its future. I am sure that in the next four years we will have our differences. But, to you gentlemen, I want to pledge my fullest cooperation. This new Legislature is the best prepared in Florida's history, and I believe that it is equal to the task which lies before us.

I have confidence in what the future holds for this administration and for the people of Florida. We begin, not with self-serving motivations or partisan goals but, instead, as the recipients of a public trust.

I believe that we are prepared for what lies ahead. But, prepared as we are, we should make no mistake about the challenge which faces us. Our American system of government—our society—is on trial. We may well have become a nation so cynical about each other that we can no longer see ourselves clearly; so reconciled to the inadequacies of man that we no longer believe in what men can do. We mistrust our political leadership; we doubt that any group or any person serves other than the interest of greed and personal gain.

In short, we have been losing hope in the future.

The task before us at this time in our history is much greater than to simply restore confidence in our government. That we must do. But the greater task is to restore faith in ourselves.

As a people we must be aware that we are the masters of our own destiny. And we must never accept a role as servants of the institutions we have created to serve us.

In Florida, we nave a unique opportunity to achieve a rekindling of faith in ourselves. We have the opportunity to establish a spirit of vision and reform—an opportunity to reverse the tide of despair.

<u>This opportunity must not be lost</u>.

It has been said that government cannot solve all of society's problems. In that, I could not agree more. But political leadership can provide a commitment to progress and it can, by its own success, restore confidence in what can be done by individuals.

None of the responsibilities before us today will be carried out by words or platitudes. It is not enough merely to acknowledge the problems of our senior citizens—or to give pious lip service to the justifiably urgent needs of our black citizens—or to be aware of the miserable living conditions of many of the migrant workers who help bring our crops to market. The commitment to make government work will not be meaningful without the courage to face squarely and honestly the difficult issues before us. And, as we outline the goals of this administration, it should be clearly understood that we are not blind to the controversy and difference of opinion which may result. We are not blind to the fact that all will not agree with the course we are setting. But we see the responsibility of this administration to provide the leadership and the direction for this state and its people.

And, regardless of the difficulty or the controversy, <u>we will not abdicate that responsibility</u>.

The journey of a thousand miles begins with the first step. We take this step with optimism, confident that man—who has touched the stars—can reach back to this earth and solve the problems confronting us. We take this step with the realization that this is the greatest country on this earth, with a foundation built on the dignity and the highest aspirations of man.

This administration will begin with, and will always set, a tone of serious dedication to the people. It will endeavor always to be an administration of harmony and productive purpose.

With these thoughts, I pray for God's guidance that the decisions made by me and all members of government, be made in wisdom and with unselfish purpose. I pray that <u>all</u> of us in government—and all Floridians who depend upon those of us who serve them, be guided by the true spirit of man to labor to bring out the best in man so that all of us will benefit by these labors.

Inaugural Speech
Second Term: 1975 - 1979
(Source: Florida State Library Archives)

Four years ago, from this platform, I quoted the ancient proverb:
"The journey of a thousand miles beings with the first step."
With your help, we have taken that first step, and we have taken many more as well while I have been fortunate enough to serve as your governor.

We have proven, these past four years, that government <u>can</u> work, that government in Florida <u>can</u> serve the real needs of <u>all</u> the people.

Yet we have only to look around us to realize that ours is an unfinished task.

For pain and poverty still linger in the cities and in the countryside. Prejudice and waste and lawlessness still infect our lives and our institutions.

Unemployment lines are longer. Prices are higher. And hopes are fewer.

Many of us seem aimless, uncertain, and fearful of the days to come.

We denounce the causes of our discontent, but, all too often, we do not know what those causes really are, so we lose ourselves, instead, in despair.

But I cannot accept this loss of confidence … and neither can you. And we can find no consolation in despair.

The problems we face today in Florida—and in Florida government—are serious, some even critical. But painful though they may be, they are only temporary. Florida can still become what <u>we</u> want to make it.

We are not kings. We are not prophets. We are only people. Yet each of us can do something. Each of us can make some contribution.

And that is our strength, our abiding strength. For together, as <u>one</u> people, <u>one</u> people rich in experience and diversity, we can find the conviction and the greatness we have found so many times before.

But that conviction cannot come from complacency. That greatness cannot come from platitudes and idle promises.

It is not enough simply to say we are for good government, such professions are meaningful only when they are sanctioned by performance.

We have tried, in Florida, to let our performance speak for itself. We have abandoned the notion of a closed and cloistered government that trusts only itself, and we have offered, instead, a more open and more accessible government that trusts the people.

For we know that it is government's failure to trust the people that has undermined the people's trust in government. And we know that the true measure of a government's success lies not in what that government does for itself, but rather, in what it does for the people it is meant to serve.

So we have enacted positive programs of tax reform and tax relief, election reform, and consumer protection. We have streamlined our judiciary, improved our law enforcement, and cut waste in state government.

We have greatly expanded traditional building programs for highways and bridges and schools and colleges. We have equalized educational opportunities for our children and increased aid to local governments.

We have increased financial support for the elderly, the sick, the jobless and the needy. We have passed landmark legislation to protect Florida's priceless natural resources, and we have, at the same time, attracted new and clean industry into our state to supplement the agricultural and tourist industries that are so vital to our continued prosperity.

We have worked to provide equal opportunities for <u>all</u> the people of this state … and to meet the special needs of <u>some</u> of our people, such as our Spanish-speaking citizens, who, like others, sometimes need special consideration in order to obtain those equal opportunities.

All our progressive changes have made our state, and our state government, in many ways, a model for the nation.

Of these achievements, we can all be proud.

Yet they are small solace to the saddened men and women in the unemployment line.

They are little encouragement to the young couples who cannot find, and cannot afford, decent homes.

They are little comfort to the elderly who can scarcely pay their utility bills.

Our achievements are little satisfaction for those in business who are confronted by rising costs in a faltering and unpredictable market.

And they are scant consolation to the families who can no longer afford a pound of sugar or a pound of meat.

The grievances of the people remain. And those grievances, and those people, must be our principal concern as we consider the constraints of the days ahead.

The most immediate of those constraints is the nearly quarter of a billion dollar shortfall in our anticipated state revenue. Inflation and recession have combined to sharply reduce the amounts of money being received by the state. And, as each one of us must confront individually the harsh facts of hard times, so too must our government.

All the agencies and all the departments of state government will be asked to make cuts in their budgets. Those cuts will, in many instances, be substantial, because our financial problems are substantial.

But shortfalls in revenue must not bring shortfalls in compassion. Diminished budgets must not mean a diminished concern for the hopes and hardships of the people.

So the reductions we make will be selective reductions, and selections will be made with the public need in mind. They will have as little impact as possible on continued delivery of essential services ... services that are now more essential than ever.

As we seek to further reduce the costs of government, we must do everything possible to neither reduce its effectiveness nor its beneficial effects on our economy.

One of the main reasons we are having revenue problems in Florida is because we have rightfully refused to tax the essentials of daily living. We have no state sales tax on groceries, on medicines, or on household utilities.

And, in times of economic uncertainty, such essentials are what the people buy, and they stop buying those commodities that are not essential. They stop buying many of those things that Florida does tax.

And this is contributing to our shortfalls and budget cuts.

But, if we must choose between reduced revenues and increases in these consumer taxes, our choice will be the revenue reductions. And let me say once again … I oppose, and I will always oppose, a state personal income tax.

Nor will I endorse any simplistic panaceas offered as remedies for our economic problems. Simple answers, such as those offered by supporters of legalized casino gambling, are no answers at all. The social and economic costs of such an enterprise would far outweigh any possible benefits. I will actively and adamantly oppose any effort to extend legalized gambling in Florida.

Too often we have assumed, as a people, that benefits could be granted without costs being felt. Too often we have looked for simple answers.

We have been apostles of abundance, a people of plenty. We have believed in the myth of inexhaustibility. But now we are learning that it was only that, a myth.

We have believed, too, that we possessed an unrestrained right to enjoy and employ our abundance, and to exploit our plenty. But now we are learning there are limits to that abundance. We are learning that, if we do not protect our environment, we will have no environment worth protecting. And we are learning that, if we do not regulate our marketplace properly, we will have no marketplace worth having.

And, in these trying times, we are also learning that we cannot risk detachment from the misfortunes of others. For their misfortunes may soon be ours as well.

If there must be sacrifice, we all must share in that sacrifice, for, too often, in the past, the many in America, and the many in Florida, have been made to sacrifice for the few.

And, where we have hopes, we all must share in those hopes. And we all must share in the realization of those hopes as well.

We are learning, too, that while social progress may sometimes be achieved in times of prosperity, it is difficult to preserve that progress when prosperity is threatened.

Blacks, women, the handicapped, and others neglected in the past have begun to benefit from our work in this state, just as we have benefited from their involvement.

But not nearly enough. And we must prove now that they will not become the victims of our uncertainty. We must prove now that we can have an open society as well as an open government.

The task that lies before us can only be accomplished by a common effort. We know that. And we look forward to working with the leadership of the legislature, with the members of the cabinet, with all levels of government, and with the people of Florida toward our many common goals.

We know that we must work together, as we have before. We must rise above our impatience, however understandable it may be. We must rise above our frustration and our futility.

And we must summon ourselves to a happier vision for all our people. For, as it is written in the Book of Proverbs, "Where there is no vision, the people perish."

We know that we cannot find all the answers to our nagging problems of inflation and recession and growth and energy in Tallahassee. Perhaps those answers can only be found in Washington ... or at some international summit meeting on the far side of the earth.

But I do know this ... there are some things we can do.

We can work closely with the federal government in implementing federal programs. And we can be mindful, at the same time, of the impact that our state programs and state spending have on our livelihoods as a people, and especially on employment.

And, to show that we are serious in our efforts to reduce the costs of state government, we can follow the advice of Florida's business community and urge passage by the legislature of the remaining recommendations of the governor's management and efficiency study commission.

We can do our best to channel growth to those areas of Florida where it is still needed. And we can, at the same time, expand our economy and preserve the clean air and the pure water and the pristine land that are the real natural wealth of our state.

We realize that this is not easily done. But it must be done. And we must seek, at all times, a balance between the immediate public need for a better economy and the eternal public need for a better environment.

We can continues working with the nation, too, to reduce our consumption of energy, to reduce our reliance on the diplomatic whims of other nations, to find better means of transportation, and to find new and cleaner and more efficient sources of energy.

And, just as Florida played such a vital role in space research, so too can we play a vital role in the solar research that is necessary if we are to find those new sources of energy. The genius of the Kennedy Space Center that placed men on the moon can be dedicated now to resolution of the serious energy problems that afflict us all.

We can rededicate ourselves, in all that we do, to the basic principles of the free enterprise system ... to make it stronger ... to make it freer ... to make it fairer.

And we must do more, much more, to confront both the causes and the consequences of crime. For, in Florida, as in the nation, crime continues to be among our most critical problems.

At every level of government, we must provide further assurances that our people will be secure in their homes, in the streets, and in their daily lives.

We can be aware, especially in these difficult times, that misfortune often breeds crime. And we can vigorously seek solutions to the misfortune as well as the crime.

But, whatever the cause, crime is crime, and it must be faced forcefully.

We must commit ourselves anew to providing better qualified and better equipped law enforcement officers. And, while the principal responsibility for combating crime properly rests with local government, we must continue improving our efforts to coordinate law enforcement at all levels of government.

We must also recognize that one of the most forceful ways to face our crime problem is in corrections. We must continue providing the facilities and better programs that are necessary if our correctional system is ever to become truly a system of corrections.

And we must work, too, to improve our programs of parole and probation, for that is another key to combating crime.

We can make structural changes, too, in the organization of our state government ... changes in environmental agencies ... changes in health and rehabilitative services ... changes that will assure the people that they are receiving a dollar's worth of service for every dollar we collect.

Together, we can do all these things ... and much more. And, above all else, we can rid ourselves, once and for all, of the caprice and the corruption too often associated with the public realm.

We can strengthen our commitment to full financial disclosure—because the people demand, and the people deserve, such a commitment.

That commitment to the public trust must be written in law. And other laws must be enacted as well that will further diminish the degrading influences of private wealth on public elections.

Let those who have employed the instruments of privilege in Florida be warned ... there can be no special interest but the public interest.

And let those who have toyed with the public trust be warned as well ... there can be no compromise with the public conscience.

For we will not be satisfied until our system of politics is freed forever from the influences of greed and guile and conflicts of interest.

And we will not allow our system of justice to be misused. For that system must be one of fairness, and not favoritism.

And we must offer some real assurances that our system of justice will be just—for black and for white, for rich and for poor, for the powerful and for the powerless.

Our problems reflect the imperfection of our justice, the inadequacy of our compassion, and the inconsistency of our concern for the suffering of others.

Yet, even in this realization, even in this knowledge that we are not what we could and should be, we must never forget that, in all time, and in all the world, no other nation has tried longer or harder or more successfully to do right by its people that has the United State of America.

And, I submit to you today, that no other state has greater potential for giving its people a better life and a better government than has this wonderful state of ours.

And what better time for a reaffirmation of faith ... faith in ourselves, faith in our creator, faith in our country, and faith in our ability to find the truth ... than this, the eve of our nation's bicentennial?

What better time for Florida to lead the way? What better time for Florida to be the example it has been before and can be again?

I will always be grateful for the opportunity you gave me to serve as your governor. And I am especially grateful today for this second term, this second opportunity, this chance to work with Jim Williams for the people and the state we love.

We know that the future will not belong to those who are content with today, indifferent to common needs and the plight of their fellow man, fearful and scornful in the face of new ideas and new circumstances.

We know that the future will not belong to those who cannot find hope, cannot offer hope, and instead reduce the world and all its complex problems into misleading simplicities.

The future will belong to those who can fashion vision and conviction and uncommon courage into an unwavering commitment to the great dreams we have always cherished as a people.

To those dreams, and with your help, I am dedicating this new term as your governor. Together, and with divine guidance, we can continue our journey toward those dreams.

And, in our daily lives, and in our work, we can continue proving in this state, as we have so often before, that man—who has broken the bonds of this planet and touched the stars—can still reach back to this earth that gave him birth and touch his neighbor, and offer him friendship, and a helping hand.

And what we achieve here can be shared throughout this great land, our gift to America on its twentieth birthday.

Thank you.

Governor D. Robert "Bob" Graham
First Term: 1979 - 1983
Second Term: 1983 - 1987

D. Robert "Bob" Graham (born November 9, 1936), a Florida native, was born in Coral Gables. He was a Phi Beta Kappa at the University of Florida where he was active in campus activities and received his law degree from Harvard University. His father Ernest R. Graham, who founded one of Florida's largest dairy and cattle businesses, ran unsuccessfully in the Democratic governor's primary of 1944. Graham served in executive positions in his family businesses, one corporation of which developed Miami Lakes and another that had large cattle holdings in Florida and Georgia.. He entered state politics with a successful race for the Florida house in 1966, and was elected to the state senate in 1970.

In 1978 Graham entered a large field of would be governors in the Democratic primary. Besides Graham the contending candidates numbered six: LeRoy Eden, Claude R. Kirk Jr., Robert L. Shevin, Bruce A. Smathers (son of former US Senator George A. Smathers), Hans Tanzler Jr., and Jim Williams. Graham ran a strong campaign and finished second to the favorite, Shevin. Yet, in the run off election Graham won the nomination with a majority of sixty-four thousand votes. In the Republican primary Jack M. Eckerd and Paula Hawkins (later a US Senator) defeated Lou Frey Jr., and S. Peter Capua. The general election saw both candidates poll over a million votes, with the Graham led Democrats winning 4,406,580 votes and Eckerd and the Republicans receiving 1,123.888.

In 1982 the Graham-Wayne Mixson ticket prevailed in the Democratic primary as did Republicans L.A. "Skip" Bafalis and Leon Callahan. In the general election the Democratic ticket easily prevailed.

Graham's two terms as governor came at a difficult and significant time. In 1979 a truckers' strike threatened the state's economy, but Graham averted the disaster by having the National Guard protect private trucks that, on the governor's orders, transported gasoline. In the same year Florida was imperiled by two hurricanes that came within fourteen days of each other. Lives were saved and injuries prevented by the governor's effective direction of massive evacuation programs. In 1980 there was a massive influx into the state by Cubans and Haitians. There were also civil disturbances in Miami, and Graham coped with the situation by demonstrating strong leadership. He believed that capital punishment was a deterrent to crime and signed over 120 death warrants. Additionally, Graham realized that Florida's geography and location made it vulnerable to drug smuggling and illegal immigration. To help protect Florida he championed strong federal action to aid state law enforcement agencies.

Graham was a powerful environmentalist, and as governor a significant part of his legacy was the Save Our Rivers Act (it provided for the state to acquire river flood plains and water management land) and the Save Our Coasts Program which authorized a program for the state to acquire beaches and barrier islands. Other important measures were the Save Our Everglades program and the Wetlands Protection Act, both of which involved the state in restoring and protecting large areas of Florida. Key agencies in accomplishing the programs were the Department of Environmental Regulation and five water management districts. Under the auspices of Graham's elegant and energetic wife, Adele, the Governor's Mansion Foundation was founded. An addition of a family room was added to the mansion and one half of the funds were provided by the Mansion Foundation.

As governor Graham appealed to the public with a statewide "workdays" program that saw him go statewide performing at a variety of jobs: policeman, busboy, factory worker, sponge fisherman, school teacher, and so on. In 1986 he challenged the incumbent Paula Hawkins for her seat in the US Senate. In a hard fought campaign Graham won with 1,877,251 votes. Senator Hawkins got 1,551,868. During his eighteen years in the U.S. Senate, his outstanding career of public service included chairing the Senate Intelligence Committee during and after the terrorist attack of September 11, 2001.

Inaugural Speech
First Term: 1979 – 1983

(Source: Florida State Archives, R.A. Gray Building, Tallahassee, Florida)

    Governor Collins …
    Governor Askew …
    Governor Caldwell …
    Governor Bryant …
    Governor Burns …
    Reverend Clergy …
    Lieutenant Governor Williams …
    Lieutenant Governor Mixson …
    Senator Chiles …
    Senator Stone …
    Members of the Cabinet …
    Mr. Chief Justice …
    Members of the Supreme Court …
    Mr. President …

Members of the Senate ...
Mr. Speaker ...
Members of the House ...
Members of Congress...
Visiting Dignitaries ...
And, especially, some friends without whose help I would not be here today ...
I want to thank you ...
Don Morris and our students at Carol City ...
Freddie Renfro of Frostproof ...
Thomasina Griffen of Macclenny ...
Remegio Perez of Tampa ...
The Reynolds of Niceville ...
Ted Billeris of Tarpon Springs ...
Larry and Bill Daniels of Panama City ...
Johnny Denton of Deland ...
Jimmy Wright of Del Ray Beach ...
And so many others throughout Florida ...
All our fellow citizens of Florida

We stand today on this timeless hill before two capitols—symbols of the Florida that was and the Florida that can be.

Our historic capitol symbolizes the first dreams of a united Florida. It reminds us of the aspirations and the achievements of our predecessors.

Our gleaming new capitol symbolizes our own dreams. It reminds us of the challenging future we share in working for a better Florida.

As we convene before these capitols for this inauguration, we ask God to guide us as he has guided Floridians through the generations. We pray for his divine inspiration as we seek to understand and do his will.

As we make a new beginning for Florida, we must be hopeful of our future and mindful of our past. For the past and the future are intertwined with the present. The past is shaping. The future is being shaped.

And others have stood where we stand today.

In the fall of 1823, two men journeyed from opposite directions to this very site.

From St. Augustine came Dr. William Simmons. He traveled on horseback for two weeks through the piney woods and the palmetto brush of the Florida wilderness.

John Lee Williams came from Pensacola. He sailed the stormy waters of the Gulf in a frail ship in a voyage that took twenty-three days.

Their mission was to find a site for a capital for the new American territory of Florida.

The Spanish had divided Florida into two provinces. Distances and differences still divided Florida. And, in search of unity, the two men were dispatched into the frontier.

They met midway, where they had agreed to meet, at St. Marks on the coast to the south of us.

They traveled north through marshes and through meadows shaded by dogwood and pine. They passed the charred ruins of Spanish missions. They stayed one night in a Seminole village watching the haunting rituals of the rattlesnake dance.

Their search ended here. Here on this hill they found oaks and magnolias and orchards of peaches. Here on this hill they found herons and partridges and deer. Here on this hill they saw a waterfall cascading into a shining stream.

The pioneer from Pensacola wrote, "A more beautiful country can scarcely be imagined." And this place, in all its beauty, became the capital of a new Florida.

That was long ago, and much has changed in the hills of Tallahassee. The herons. The orchards. The waterfall. The stream. All have been lost.

But the hills remain. And the oaks. And the magnolias.

And this capital site remains. It remains what it has always been—a symbol of our pursuit of unity. A symbol of our desire for a common fate and a common future.

We are the heirs to the Florida which flourished so many years ago. We are the beneficiaries of all the brave dreamers of other days.

We are the inheritors of the white sands on the beaches, the mysteries of the Everglades, the secrets of the grassy savannas, and the vast silence of the forests.

And ours is a human legacy as well—a legacy of past dreams, of dreams which have been fulfilled.

A dream of a free Florida—a state in which all people of all colors and creeds can be free.

A dream of a Florida of expanding prosperity—symbolized by a railroad linking the northern border of the state to its southernmost reef in a triumph of ingenuity and enterprise.

A dream of a Florida of equal opportunity—symbolized by the lifelong struggle of Mary McLeod Bethune to educate our people.

And a dream of a sheltering Florida—a haven for the homeless in flight from tyranny.

All these dreams have come true, but we have a dream as well.

Our dream is of a once and future Florida—a Florida in which we can conserve our natural heritage, a Florida in which each of us will be treated with justice, a Florida in which all of us can earn a good living, have a decent home, and educate our children.

Our dream is of a Florida in which the oldest and the wisest among us can lead useful lives in peace and in dignity, a Florida in which the wisdom of age can be combined with the enthusiasm of youth, in mutual respect and with mutual benefit.

Our dream is of a Florida in which we can share in a renewed kinship, a Florida in which we will all be friends and neighbors and families.

But how should we pursue this dream? How can we make this ceremony today truly the commencement, truly the new beginning that it should be?

The dreams of earlier Floridians were never easily realized. Though beautiful, the Florida wilderness was hostile and foreboding. And many times the wilderness, in all its immensity, proved a formidable barrier to the fulfillment of dreams.

We are not faced with such tangible, physical barriers today. But the barriers we face are equally challenging, and they are much harder to remove, much harder to overcome, than those of the Florida frontier.

For they are not barriers of nature, they are barriers of the soul.

Ignorance, isolation, loneliness, selfishness, fear, desperation, distrust, an absence of commitment, a feeling of helplessness in controlling our own destinies. These are the most imposing, the most bewildering barriers of our modern wilderness.

But this wilderness, like the wilderness which confronted earlier Floridians, can be tamed.

For there is a vast, untapped potential in the people of Florida—a potential for work, for achievement, for service, and for generosity. There is a potential for dreaming—and for making dreams come true.

I know, I have seen it.

I have seen our potential in the curiosity of teen-age students at Carol City High School, in the artistry of the workers in a Tampa cigar factory, in the constant, daily courage of workers in a Palatka paper mill.

I have seen our potential in the strength of the oil riggers of Jay, in the resourcefulness of the fishermen of Apalachicola, in the stoic endurance of the tomato pickers of Collier County.

I have seen our potential in the dedication of policemen on night patrol in Tallahassee, in the smiles of the Cuban sandwich makers of Ybor City, in the tenderness of the aides at MacClenny State Hospital.

I have seen the boundless potential of Florida in the hopeful eyes, in the callused hands of the truck drivers, the secretaries, the desk clerks, the teachers, the flight attendants, the garbage men, the bell boys, the bus boys, the plumbers, the physicians, the factory workers, the pulpwooders, the mechanics, the homemakers, and the iron workers.

I have seen it in the loving devotion of an elderly wife in Deland who could only visit her 92-year-old husband at a nursing home three times a week—because that was as often as she could afford to pay the three-dollar taxi fare.

I have heard it, too.

I have heard it in the heartfelt words of a gentle orderly in that same nursing home: "These old folks must be good, 'cause God let them live so long."

I have heard it from a St. Petersburg delivery man in the simple expression of his faith: "There are a lot of good people out there who will help you if you will give them a chance."

And I have heard it in the plaintive question of a nineteen-year-old Pensacola worker about to be married: "Will there be a future for us in Florida?"

Yes, there is a future in Florida. There is a future for all of us, if we care for one another, if we believe in one another—and in ourselves.

We are one state, we are one people, and we will become better people in a better state when we strengthen the bonds that unite us—bonds that are far more important, far more lasting than the barriers which divide us.

For there is a commonality among Floridians which is often overlooked. There are the seeds of a finer and wiser and greater community.

I have felt the bonds among us in a semi-trailer in a feed mill in Jacksonville, where a truck driver led his fellow workers in a religious service on a hot June afternoon.

I have seen the emerging spirit of our community in Vero Beach, where people have joined together to help their neighbors participate in building their own homes.

I have seen a foreshadowing of the fulfillment of our dreams in Tarpon Springs, where people are working together to save a distinctive part of our shared and priceless heritage.

I have seen a glimpse of the once and future Florida in Margate, where the compassion and concern of her neighbors have answered the painful cry of an old and lonely woman who asked, "Will you help me die?" They gave her a new means and a new meaning for living.

Anxious, weary, perhaps discouraged, the explorers of 1823 climbed to this crest, then they stood, gazing and dreaming, at these beckoning hills.

Their dreams made our dreams possible, even as our dreams will make possible the dreams of others who will stand here in years to come.

With you, I look to the future today, to four years of stewardship, but, in looking to the future, I look also to the past. For the past has shaped me, just as it has shaped Florida. And I bring with me to this day and to this inauguration fundamental beliefs about what government should do and what government should be in this state.

I believe that ours is an endless pursuit. We will always be dreamers. We will always have dreams. Barriers of some kind will always be before us. Our task is to remove the barriers of our wilderness as we reach them, acknowledge the limits of our reasonable expectations, but striving always to fulfill our dreams by enlarging the clearing place in the wilderness for the human mind and spirit.

I believe that, in governing, we must learn when to act and when not to act. We must weigh the actions of government against the effects those action will have on the initiative and spontaneity of the people.

We must never forget that the only valid reason for the existence of government is to help people achieve their hopes and dreams. For if we forget this most basic of our beliefs, government will become a hindrance—an obstacle—a source of distrust and scorn.

So we must listen. We must be open and accessible. We must seek out people where they live and where they work to know their concerns and discover our opportunities. And we must treat all people at all times with the courtesy and respect they deserve.

We must be fair. All people—of whatever sex, age, race, creed, region, religion, handicap, or circumstance—must be treated equally. They must be given an equal opportunity to share in the bounty of the community we make.

We must be disciplined—Spartan in the ways of government. We must work, and work hard—honestly, ably, relentlessly, decisively.

I believe that the best decision is likely to be made by the people most affected by the decision. Acting upon this belief will be another form of discipline—a discipline which recognizes the need to place responsibility and trust in our communities, our schools, and our people.

And, as we govern, we must anticipate, looking beyond the moment, beyond the immediate, to the future as we establish our agenda for today's decision.

Our willingness to anticipate and to act on an agenda for the future will require sacrifice. We must be willing to sacrifice something of ourselves today for the common good of our community tomorrow.

And whatever the issues, whatever the demands of the moment, whatever our other concerns, we must never hesitate to fulfill our greatest obligation—that of teaching our children. We must educate them and prepare them as best we can to participate in the continuing community of Florida—and of the world.

We must help the sick, the hungry, the homeless, and the aged. But we must remember always the value of incentive and independence and self-sufficiency. For we do not want a helping hand to breed helplessness.

We must instill a renewed competition in our economy, among our institutions, and in our individual lives. For, through a creative combination of cooperation and competition, the fullest measure of our potential as a people can be achieved.

We must rely on both cooperation and competition to attain a lasting prosperity. To this end, state government must do all it can to keep the retired citizens and the working men and women of Florida from being impoverished by inflation, and we must be aggressive and imaginative in seeking more and better jobs for our people.

As never before, each of you must be involved personally, not only in government, but in all the rich and varied life of Florida. Government can provide inspiration and opportunity, but only with your personal participation, only with your personal dedication will we be able to find unity and fashion a stronger, happier community.

I am asking today for your help. I am asking for your wisdom. Wherever you are in this state, whatever you may have to offer, I am asking for your personal commitment.

And I am asking you to share with me today a common prayer for God's help as we accept the challenge of participation and leadership.
[prayer]

Believe that true leadership requires, not the courage, but rather the unending responsibility to do what is right—and to do so regardless of the consequences in public favor or personal misfortune.

And we must lead in Florida as we have been led by the best among us, taking as our examples the dignity, the humanity, and the statesmanship of LeRoy Collins and the commitment, the lasting achievement, and the enduring integrity of Reubin Askew.

The example of these great men, together with that of other men and women of like mind and equal dedication, will inspire me as governor, my wife Adele, our family, Margie Mixson, and Wayne Mixson as Lieutenant Governor in our service to this state.

We can all share in this inspiration. We can all rejoice in our rightful heritage. We can make that heritage last through all the generations.

The herons can fly. The orchards can bloom. The waters can fall. The streams can shine in the sun.

These hills can abide forever, and we can say of the Florida we love, as was said so long ago, "A more beautiful country can scarcely be imagined."

But first we must dream. We must dream the great dream of the once and future Florida. And we must make that dream come true..

Ours can be a Florida in which we will cherish our past, be confident of our future, and be proud to say, "I am a Floridian."

I pledge to you today that, as governor of Florida, I will summon every ounce of strength, I will employ every spark of imagination, I will exercise every proper measure of discretion, and I will use every resource and every resolve at my command, for the sake and in the service of that dream.

Inagural Speech
Second Term: 1983 - 1987

(Source: Florida State Archives, R.A. Gray Building, Tallahassee, Florida)

My fellow citizens of Florida:

Florida has always been a land of dreamers. But our Dreamers have also been pragmatic builders. They have never lost sight of the realities that would define the outcome of their vision.

We stand once more at the juncture of our dreams and our destiny. We are fully confident that we can shape the Florida we have inherited into the Florida we all envision for ourselves and for our children.

We dare to dream, but we do so with our eyes open.

We know that we cannot ignore the ever increasing demands of our inevitable growth.

We know that if our economic prosperity is to be shared by all Floridians, we must look to the future as an international state, mastering the complexities of a global economy.

We know that the pressing demands for basic services can no longer be approached with a blank check philosophy.

These are the inescapable realities we all face in one of the most dramatic decades in our state's history.

But we also know that we can make a difference in our destiny, that we can create and sustain through our own efforts a Florida that works for all, a Florida that cares about the dignity and well being of each of its citizens, a Florida that invests and plans for its future without forgetting its past.

A Florida I speak of is not a set of promises, but a set of challenges.

Two months ago the people of this state gave a mandate, not to one man, or to a team of two, but to all Floridians who passionately care about meeting those challenges.

Today, on behalf of all of you, the architects of the Florida of the future, I accept that mandate to build upon our dreams.

I am not alone in this endeavor. For the first time in history our people have chosen a lieutenant governor to represent them for a second term.

Anyone who knows Wayne Mixson knows why he makes history. This man from Jackson County is a gentleman, a scholar, a businessman, a farmer, above all a man of enormous human warmth. And Wayne has agreed to help lead our state into the future as both lieutenant governor and secretary of commerce. In this new role, he will prove invaluable to the achievement of a series of specific goals we have set for our administration.

We are the fortunate heirs of a philosophy of government for the people. The greatness of our future will not be measured by the size of faceless institutions, but by the degree of self-fulfillment, independence, and prosperity those institutions can extend to each of our citizens.

Together I am certain we can forge the proper links to anchor our ten million dreams to reality. Each of your dreams has a place here, each of you bolsters our collective strength.

Over a quarter of a century ago, a great and courageous governor stood on the steps of this historic capitol and expressed his faith in the future of our state.

Today we are at the midpoint of what Governor LeRoy Collins called the miracle of modern Florida. We are now the ones who have been called upon to usher that miracle into the twenty-first century.

I have pledged the next four years of my life to the premise that the Florida we all want can be shaped by our own hands, that, indeed, the miracle of modern Florida is self-realization.

For the sake of convenience we speak of our common goals under different categories. In reality they are all interdependent.

The goals of economic development, education, environmental protection, and responsive social services must all intersect in our path to progress. None of them stands alone. They all require a willingness to invest in our greatest resource, our human potential.

In order to fulfill the potential of each of our citizens, we must be committed to avoiding the most devastating deficit of all, the deficit of knowledge. If all Floridians are to be full partners in the achievement of our dreams, we must increase our investment in education.

Our teachers are training the workforce of the twenty-first century. Half of that workforce is already on the job. Many will have to be retrained.

We have entered an age in which our classrooms must reach out beyond the walls of traditional schools, reach out to the marketplace, to the workplace, and work in close partnership with the economic forces shaping our future.

An educated workforce is not a renewable resource unless we make it one. And we intend to do so. The next chapter of Florida's economic future will be written in its classrooms.

But jobs alone will not sustain the spirit that drives Florida. What some may call our obsession with education goes beyond economic objectives. The degree of excellence we are striving for goes beyond dollars and cents to more intangible and enduring dividends.

The power of choice that comes from learning, infuses lives with purposeful meaning.

Our driving energy stems from that power of individual choice, whether it is derived from a sonnet from Shakespeare, or from a flawlessly executed computer program, or from the understanding of how each of us as citizens can shape decisions in our democratic system.

The dream of individual choice and economic prosperity for each of our citizens is the best cure for many of the social ills plaguing our nation and our state.

Florida is fortunate to be an international state in what has become a global economy. Unlike many other states, we are not shackled to defensive strategies.

We have already launched a crucial phase of our journey of economic discovery. Our future is riding firmly and confidently on a people equipped to compete fairly and prosperously with any other state in the world.

The destination of this flight is individual opportunity, fulfillment and prosperity. The common reward for our journey will be the public funds to support education, social programs, community services and environmental protection as our state continues to grow.

Florida is a state that learns as it grows. We have learned a great deal about how to make dreams conform to reality from our experience with agriculture. The ability to maximize the product of our work in the fields and make our state's crops a staple that fees the nation and the world did not come by accident. It was hard earned through the cooperation of business, education, government, and the ultimate architects of that particular dream, the Florida farmers with the vision and courage to adapt to change.

The lessons we have learned from agriculture, a traditional economic strength, can be applied to our goal of making Florida a key state in high technology, information services, and international trade and commerce.

The enhancement of our greatest asset, our human potential, cannot ignore the wealth of experience and wisdom that our older citizens have brought to our state. We want to extend to all of them the same power of choice—the kind of support system that increases instead of smothers their independence.

Expanding the ability of our older citizens to contribute to our future is something we owe Floridians of all ages.

The investment in our human resources must also look to our young people, many of whom see their futures threatened by dead ends that foster a life of violence and crime.

We know that we must become more creative in dealing with the tragedies of drug, alcohol, and child abuse, and juvenile delinquency.

We are committed to making Florida a safer place to live because all of our dreams are threatened if we cannot live free from fear. Our intolerance for violent criminals and repeat offenders will not let up. But our sensitivity to those who can still be turned from a life of crime can and must be enhanced. The loss of even one of those young lives to crime diminishes us all.

The respect for the dignity of each of our citizens must also be extended to the beauty and quality of the environment that is our common heritage.

In our early history it was the unrestrained forces of nature that threatened the survival of men and women here in Florida. We have now come full circle. Today it is the unrestrained growth of our population that threatens the survival of the magical qualities of land and sea that have attracted so many of us here. By the turn of this century, Florida will be the fourth largest state.

The responsibility for preserving our irreplaceable and fragile natural resources rests with all the people of this state and their trustees.

Once again we must plan and act in a concerted way to achieve a proper balance between man and nature and to ensure that quantity will not destroy quality in our state. The public must be brought into this process while there is still time to plan for orderly growth, rather than react to insurmountable problems.

There is one ennobling search of the human spirit for which government institutions were initially established: The dream of justice.

A government sets up institutions to achieve this dream. But an honest government must also guard against the screens of process and procedure which can mask the denial of individual justice.

The test of justice is in consequences—in the answer to the question that must be asked again and again: Have our institutions dealt with each Floridian equally, openly, affording each self-respect and dignity?

When we can answer that question in the affirmative for each of our citizens, we will have come the distance in our realization of our dream of justice—our dream of a state worthy of our creator.

These then are the goals which will link our dreams to our future. This is the Florida we can build together. But we cannot build it without tools.

The fiscal prudence of our predecessors like Governor Collins, and Governor Askew, who honor us with their presence today, has spared our state from the problems of deficit by overspending.

We must be vigilant against another kind of deficit—those deficits created by our failures to maintain our investments in areas critical to our healthy development. We can call these the deficits of selfishness.

Each generation makes a choice, whether to squander on itself, or to build for the future.

Make no mistake, the deficits of selfishness have expensive consequences.

Our generation is still paying a high human cost for the deficit of almost one hundred years of segregation.

Our children will pay the price for each child born without hope, each older citizen denied dignity, each mind denied an avenue to self-fulfillment.

It is far more fiscally sound to invest our resources actively than reactively. Our failures to protect and expand our investments in transportation are still redeemable, but at a much higher price.

It is far, far better to invest in jobs and children now than in prisons later. We do not want to force yet another generation to devote precious resources to the upkeep of our monuments to failure.

If the resources we devote to our initiatives are to yield the maximum benefits, we must think beyond the immediate present and act as the constituency for the future.

We must be innovative, we must be bold, above all we must be courageous in facing the challenges of the twenty-first century which are already upon us.

The concrete goals I spoke of today can only be brought forth by self-realization, by our will to accept ourselves as a constituency for the future.

That constituency for the future was there in the early Spanish explorers who braved unknown perils to reach a land that held unlimited promise.

The constituency for the future was there in the settlers who came from the north and did not let the threat of wars or massacres deter them from their dream of building new communities.

It was there in the bold initiatives of a logger, farmer, fisherman, steamboat operator, soldier, sheriff, and eventually Governor Napoleon Bonaparte Broward, who led this state into the twentieth century with unrivalled dynamism.

It was there in the quiet courage of a lady, Mary McLeod Bethune, who in 1904, with a capital of $1.50, opened her own school in Daytona Beach. Today that school is Bethune Cookman College.

The same spirit was also there in the perseverance of a widow from Cleveland, Julia Tuttle, who at the turn of the century willed the construction of a magic city in south Florida by waving the promise of an orange blossom.

The constituency for the future was there twenty years ago in the wide eyed hopes of children who arrived here from Cuba without their parents or a penny to their names. Today they are teachers, doctors, lawyers, businessmen and women actively involved in the goals that bind all of us as a people and a state.

In a world that measures most things in strict material terms, dreams may not hold much weight, but the lives of such men and women underscore an irrefutable fact: All great accomplishments begin with a vision.

Florida's indomitable spirit has only been strengthened by severe tests: hurricanes, floods, social turmoil, refugees, and economic strains. Yet we have withstood such enormous challenges united as a family of families.

Not one of these crises has eroded our sense of purpose, or fairness, or generosity. We have sustained the basic values of democracy through very difficult times. We have endured, but more importantly, we have prevailed, and the Florida we all seek is now within our reach.

Let us go forth then, confidently, as dreamers and builders of our future.

Governor Wayne Mixson
Term: 1987 - 1987

[John] Wayne Mixson (born June 16, 1922) was born on his family's farm in Alabama. Upon Graham's election to the senate, he resigned as governor to take the oath of office in Washington. The Florida constitution declares that if the governor's chair becomes vacant, the lieutenant governor succeeds to the governorship, and in this way Mixson served as governor for three days–and delivered an inaugural address.

Upon his graduation from high school in Alabama, Mixson moved to Panama City and began working in a paper mill. During World War II he took advantage of the Navy's V-12 program and attended New York's Columbia University. Later, he was a student at University of Pennsylvania's Wharton School of Finance. After his military service, Mixson attended the University of Florida and graduated with honors in business administration. Governor Mixson and his family owned a large cattle and feed grain farm in Jackson County near their home in Marianna. First elected to the Florida House of Representatives in 1967, Mixson served six consecutive terms. His popularity in the Pan Handle was a solid plus in the south Florida candidate Graham's two gubernatorial campaigns.

Inagural Speech
(Source: Patricia L. Clements, Tallahassee, Florida)

Abraham Lincoln said, "the world will little note nor long remember what we do here today." Well, actually, we're **not** going to do much in the next few days.

And I don't think we'll be here long enough to grasp any nettles, Bob.

But there is just enough time to appoint a lieutenant governor—would you be interested, Bob? We could call it the Mixson-Graham administration.

Seriously, this is not a time for an inaugural address, for this is not a beginning, but the end of an administration. But I do intend to carry out my responsibilities with dignity, with joy, and with a sense of fun.

It is a great honor for me personally to preside, however briefly, over the affairs of state. I am honored to have this opportunity to recall what I consider to be some of the most important programs of this administration over the past eight years.

The Mixson-Graham legacy [isn't it amazing how soon we forget, Bob] is one of prosperity, and independence. Probably the most important thing to know about Florida today is that we are no longer a poor state.

Our per capita income, for the first time, is equal to the national average. Only Virginia, among the Southern states, can match that achievement. It has taken us many years to accomplish this feat.

Fifty years ago, during the great depression, cities in our state went bankrupt. Teachers were told by the middle of the school year that there was no more money to pay them and children were sent home. I know. My 7th grade school year lasted only three months.

Fifty years ago, our citizens lined up for the dole. Today, Florida is a leader in the world economy, not just the American economy. We are a state to which others look for leadership. And we have made strides of which we can be justly proud:

1. In the past eight years, we have created approximately 1.4 million net new jobs in our state—no other state can match that. Our growth in jobs far outpaced our growth in employable population.
2. We have brought in more than 800 new industries, and assisted thousands more to expand. Our state has become one of the most significant international trading and banking centers in the world. We are the third largest state in motion picture and T.V. production.
3. We have continued—remarkably—year after year as the world's number-one tourist destination. This is another record year, in part because of the added new international dimension of our tourism—with more than 4 million foreign visitors each year.
4. We have kept our tax structure among the lowest in America, while providing a quality of life which rivals the best in America.
5. And we have done all this because of a simple understanding of the most important element of the relationship of government to business: we don't tax them to death, we don't regulate them to death. We seek, on the contrary, to develop opportunities for cooperation.
6. We recognize that state government can only do its job of saving the environment, protecting our citizens, educating our youth, and providing for necessary social services if our economy is strong enough to support it.

Florida has a fragile environment. Protecting it is expensive. Building the right kind of economy is not in conflict with our environmental goals and commitments. Indeed, the resources generated by our economy are essential if we are to meet our other objectives.

Enforcing our laws and protecting ourselves from crime is an expensive proposition.

We must meet the needs of our elderly citizens and those unable to care for themselves.

We recognize the significance of an education system second to none in our economic development. And we have made important strides in connecting our educational system to our mission of economic development. A case in point: five years ago, we began a program to expand the number of engineering graduates. We provided enhanced resources. And today, we are graduating twice as many engineers as we did five years ago.

Our goal has been to create an economic base that will sustain and support these necessary programs.

I would like to share with you a story about a blacksmith named John who lived in New England in the middle 1800's.

For a time, John was successful, but then his luck turned. Debt piled up, fire destroyed his business.

At this point, broke and broken in spirit, the blacksmith fled. Forced to leave his family behind, he headed west in search of a new life for them. He traveled from Vermont to the frontier—central Illinois, at that time.

And there John encountered a special problem. The rich deep soil of that country made conventional plows worthless. The dirt caked on the plow blade and made it impossible to get through the field.

So John Deere, for that was his name, came up with the invention that made his name a household word the world over, the self cleaning plow.

And from that, the lesson here for us is he built the enterprise that still bears his name today. So let us remember that story. The only ultimate failure is the failure to try again. And the only ultimate success is the success that comes from persistence.

Florida is like John Deere. We have had periods of success and periods of adversity. In time of success, our role has been to seize our advantage and make the most of it. In times of adversity, the task has been to fight to change our circumstances.

And the lesson we have learned from the past eight years is that our future is in our own hands. Our persistence is what will make the difference. A major bill seldom passes the Legislature in a single year, but, rather, requires many years of consistent, patient effort to become law. So too will our dream for the success of our state, require constant vigilance.

There is no stopping Florida. In the last 86 years, we have risen from the thirty-third largest state to the sixth largest state. We have established a State University System which is on the verge of a national standard of excellence. We have raised the high school graduation requirements to a level that exceeds that of every other state. And in the past year, we have had the highest increase in the Scholastic Aptitude Test of any state in America.

It's a far cry from the day when children were sent home after only three months of school, half a century ago.

There is a reason for this progress: It is because Florida understands the importance of building the work force of the future. Tomorrow's work force is in our classrooms today. And tomorrow's business will function in an environment which we can barely glimpse today. We know only that the ability to adapt, to think, to respond to change, and to create new information and new products are the elements of success in our future.

Accepting with due humility and a sense of honor the custodianship which is mine for the next few days, I speak proudly of the future of our state, and confidently of the future of our economy.

I'm certain that the next governor, whose term will be somewhat longer than mine, subscribes to these values and will advance them ever further than we have been able to do.

Ours is a state in balance. We will work together in all segments of our economy—in agriculture, in tourism, in manufacturing, in the knowledge-driven, technology-based industries, and in the growing service segment of our economy, to produce a Florida we can all be proud of in the future.

Thank you for coming to be with us today and please share my sense of excitement and great joy in having the opportunity to serve the people of Florida at the highest possible level.

Thank you and good day.

Governor Bob Martinez
Term: 1987 - 1991

Robert (Bob) Martinez (born December 25, 1934) was born in Tampa, the son and grandson of Spanish immigrants. He earned his undergraduate degree at the University of Tampa and a master's degree in labor and industrial relations from the University of Illinois. He served as mayor of Tampa for seven years before entering state politics in 1986.

In the nominating phase of the gubernatorial race Martinez teamed with Bobby Brantley against a field of four combination tickets, but was strong enough to win without a run off. The Democrats had numerous tandems contending, but the most important ones were Steve Pajcic and Frank Martin versus Jim Smith and Marshall S. Harris. The vote was close with the Pajcic team about fifty thousand votes ahead. Smith and Harris rallied in the run off but still fell short.

The vote was 429,427 to 418,614. The general election saw Martinez and Brantley prevail as 1,847,525 ballots were cast for them. Pajcic and Martin received 1,538,620 votes,

Florida voters had chosen their first American governor of Hispanic descent, the second Republican since Reconstruction, and the first from the Tampa area in almost fifty years. The new chief executive took up the cudgels of environmentalism where Graham left off. During the Martinez administration Florida's legislature passed the Surface Water and Environment Act, the Solid Waste Disposal Act, and had a program called Preservation 2000. Governor Martinez vigorously carried forward the existing "Save the Everglades" campaign. The governor was interested in the drug problem (Florida rated high nationally in its effectiveness against illegal substances), and supported prison construction.

The republican governor and the Democratic legislature clashed over "turkeys" (expensive state programs that supposedly had little value), and he attempted to weed them out individually. They also clashed over the governor's frequent vetoes of items in appropriation bills than he disliked. The chief executive was embarrassed when he endorsed and the legislature passed a tax on services. There was a strong reaction from levies on television advertising and the services of professionals and physicians. Both the executive and the legislative branches of state government backed down and the tax was repealed. Martinez's efforts during his tenure were intentionally thwarted by Democratic opposition in both houses, resulting in the solidification of Democratic strength statewide. The result was that in the election of 1980 he and Allison DeFoor were defeated. President George W. Bush appointed Martinez director of the National Campaign Against Use of Drugs. Later, he returned to Tampa and pursued his business interests.

Martinez, like Kirk, a republican governor, was hampered in his efforts to pass important legislation with a legislature dominated in both houses by a Democratic majority. The Democrats had lost the executive office in the general election but continued to battle for power during the legislative process.

Inaugural Speech
(Source: Florida State Archives, R.A. Gray Building, Tallahassee, Florida)

I stand before you honored by the opportunity to add my efforts to the distinguished record of public service compiled by the thirty-nine men who have held the office of Governor before me. And I am humbled by the challenge of measuring up to the high standards they set in leading this great state during the last one hundred and forty two years.

Governor Mixson is here today representing that rich tradition of leadership, and I thank him—on behalf of myself for the cooperation and support he has given me in the last two months—and on behalf of the people of Florida for the last twenty years of his life, which he so unselfishly gave to all of us.

To Senator Graham, who is in the Nation's Capitol tackling a new job with his usual fervor, I say thank you for an old job well done. We will continue to be well served by Bob Graham as Florida continues to move to the forefront as a national state.

I also want to recognize and pledge my cooperation to my distinguished Cabinet colleagues—Secretary Firestone, Attorney General Butterworth, Comptroller Lewis, Treasurer Gunter, Commissioner Conner, and Commissioner Castor.

Of course, no Governor can succeed without a responsive—and responsible—legislature. President Vogt, Speaker Mills, and the Republican minority leaders. Senator Jennings and Representative Patchett, are here on the platform representing their colleagues. I thank them for their participation, and I look forward to working closely with the legislature for a better Florida.

Our judges round out the constitutional triad, and I thank Justices McDonald, Adkins, Boyd, Overton, Erlich, Shaw, and Barkett for representing all those dedicated men and women without whose vigilance a free society could not long survive.

As I said before, I am honored and humbled to be here, but I am also acutely aware of how difficult it was to get here. The journey from Tampa to Tallahassee was a long one, and I would have lost my way without the love and support of my wife of 32 years, Mary Jane, my son, Alan, my daughter, Sharon, and her husband, Neil. Whenever I said "I can't," they said "we can," and they are the reason I am here today.

Among those also deserving special recognition today are Lieutenant Governor Bobby Brantley, his wife, Patti, and their two sons, Lenny and Bobby Jr. When it comes to hard work and sacrifice, Bobby and Patti have no peers. I am fortunate to have them at my side.

To the remaining platform guests, I say welcome, and to those among you who have been selected for leadership roles in this administration I say enjoy yourself today, but be prepared to go to work in earnest tomorrow. For there is much work to do.

For the last twenty years, Florida has been growing at an accelerating rate. Just last week, Florida became the fifth most populous state in the Nation. Before the year is out, we will move into fourth place, passing Pennsylvania.

This means that eight hundred and ninety five new Floridians are arriving each day. Each day, we need another 130,000 gallons of water. Each day, there is another 111,000 gallons of wastewater and 4,200 more pounds of solid waste to dispose of, and each day we need two more miles of highway, three more jail beds, two more police officers, two more classrooms, and two more teachers to teach in those classrooms.

During the last eight years, this kind of growth resulted in a 168% increase in spending by state government, from $6.2 billion in 1979 to $16.5 billion in 1987.

$16.5 billion. A big number that will get bigger as Florida continues to be the pace setter of national growth.

No one really knows the cost of future growth, and estimates vary widely. One such estimate puts the cost of new transportation, water, and wastewater facilities needed between today and the year 2000 at thirty one billion dollars. Add the existing backlog and the number becomes forty one billion dollars. Throw in new schools, prisons, public buildings, solid waste disposal facilities, and drainage facilities and the number might climb as high as sixty billion dollars.

I cannot say whether the number is sixty billion, or thirty billion, or twenty billion, but I can tell you that whatever the number is, it has a human face. It represents endless hours of toil by countless

Floridians. These cold and lifeless numbers are actually the hopes and aspirations of a generation, an investment in tomorrow, an investments we hold in sacred trust. We can discharge that trust diligently, faithfully, and effectively, but there is little margin for error.

So, what is to be done?

First, we must not take counsel of our fears.

Second, we must realize that unlimited good intentions have to give way to the reality of limited resources.

Third, we must make hard choices about our goals, and we must reexamine and redefine those goals, if necessary.

Fourth, we must concentrate our resources to achieve the goals we have chosen and employ those resources in new and better ways.

Fifth, we must accept the fact that state government needs allies, including the private sector, and we must make local government a real partner in the business of shaping Florida's future.

Finally, we must pursue our chosen course of action with dogged determination.

Fine sounding words, but what do they mean?

When I said that we must not take counsel of our fears, I was thinking of the pronounced tendency among many politicians, editors, and other professional pundits to look for the black cloud around the silver lining.. After finding the cloud, the accepted procedure is to wring one's hands and walk around stooped by the weight of the knowledge of impending disaster, crying out "woe is me!"

At least part of the reason for this gloom and doom perspective is that there is another tendency to emphasize the liabilities of growth while ignoring the assets of growth.

I don't want to sound like a heretic, but I do want to talk about the good news for a minute.

Per capita income in Florida was just 88% of the national average ten years ago. But today it is more that 98% of the national average. Our construction industry remains strong, and tourism continues to flourish. Overall, our economy is becoming more diversified every day, and our unemployment rate is consistently less than that of the Nation as a whole.

We seem to forget that new residents mean new jobs and increased economic activity. This increased economic activity means prosperity and more revenues for government to solve the problems that must be solved. .

Most importantly, Floridians, whether native or new, are a unique blend of ethnic, racial, and age groups. This diversity has produced a spirit of independence and enterprise— a can do attitude—that is our greatest resource.

In short, the rumors of Florida's demise are greatly exaggerated. We are a growing, vibrant state on the cutting edge of national leadership. Our potential and our opportunities increase with the arrival of every new Floridian. The day they stop coming is the day we will find it more and more difficult to maintain the quality of life that has made Florida synonymous with the good life.

Until that day, there is no need to be frightened by the challenges we face. We can succeed, and we will succeed, if for no other reason than we must. I, for one, am not willing to endure the reproaches of my grandchildren for having left them a Florida that is less than the Florida that nurtured me.

I said before that good intentions have to give way to limited resources. My optimism alone cannot pave a road. That takes money, and money means taxes—a commodity limited by financial circumstances and political reality.

The reality is that state government cannot be all things to all people, because the people will not pay for anything and everything. We can do some things very well, or we can do a great many things by half measures. That is our choice, and we must make that choice now.

I believe we must put aside the false luxury of the poor results that are the product of half measures. We must make hard decisions about our priorities. In this context, I believe we must concentrate on the fundamental, historic tasks of government in America. We must return to the basics—public safety, public education, public health, and public works—and we must do these things well.

My vision of Florida is simple. I want a Florida in which all of our children are given an education that allows them to seize the very best opportunities life has to offer. I want a Florida no one need leave in order to find those opportunities in abundance. To the maximum extent permitted by the human condition, I want a Florida in which everyone can live free of the depredations of human predators who live outside the law. And I want a Florida in which everyone can breathe clean air, drink clean water, enjoy the benefits of our very special environment, and never fear that they will be denied quality medical care for any reason.

A public school system that produces quality as a matter of course. A strong, vibrant economy supported by transportation, waste disposal, and water systems that work. A criminal justice system that provides real public safety. And health care second to none.

A simple vision, but an enormous challenge.

But it is not enough just to choose the goals to which we are going apply the lion's share of our limited resources. We must also reexamine and redefine the goals themselves.

I could use examples from the fields of public works or public safety. But permit me to choose my example from the field of education, in which I worked for fifteen years and Mary Jane for twenty years. I am committed to quality in terms of funding formulas, career ladders, retirement benefits, or quartiles. To me, educational quality means students who graduate with a quality education.

Yet, since I've come to Tallahassee, all I've heard is that teachers are underpaid, that the state needs to be in the upper quartile on teacher's salaries. There isn't much said about college placements, vocational education, or dropout rates.

I believe the emphasis should be on the students who come out of our schools, not on the money we put in.

Do not misunderstand me. I happen to believe that our classroom teachers are by and large dedicated professionals who will turn out students with excellent educations if they are treated as professionals and supported as such.

Professionalism, however, is a function of working conditions, not just more money. Higher pay for our teachers is required. But so are more and better instructional materials, fewer layers of supervision at the local level, and fewer mandates and less supervision from the state level. Two of these items mean more money, and two should mean less money.

In this context, if we believe it is important that teachers be paid more, then we should make sure that the money actually goes to the teachers, not to some nebulous entity known as "education."

My point, which I apologize for belaboring, is that we must choose our goals carefully and then craft specific means to achieve them. We can no longer afford the shotgun approach to public policy. More money may be an appropriate tool in some cases, but more money is not an appropriate goal in any case.

I said before that we must concentrate our resources and employ them in new and better ways. I was referring primarily to saving money through increased government efficiency and applying these savings to the high priority areas I outlined earlier.

During my campaign for Governor, I apparently surprised some people by stating that, if elected, I could save eight hundred million dollars by better management and increased efficiency in state government. Those same people are probably sure that the last two months in Tallahassee have taught me the error of my ways. If so, I take great pleasure in surprising them again today by repeating that during the next four years I will sweat eight hundred million dollars out of state government, providing the good Lord is willing and the legislature cooperates. 1 will begin this process with the budget I will submit to the legislature in a few weeks.

These savings will come from increased efficiencies, some program reductions, some program eliminations, and a lot of changes in priorities. As a result, we will be able over a period of time to concentrate adequate resources to achieve our basic goals.

I also said we must forge a working partnership with local governments. The challenges we face are too great for state government to meet alone, and we can no longer look to big brother in Washington to help us. We are going to have to give local governments the authority and the resources to do something about wastewater treatment and disposal, solid waste collection and disposal, transportation, jails, and all of the other things that have such a direct impact on the quality of life in Florida.

This will take some radical rethinking by many. I sometimes suspect that there is a school on the road to Tallahassee that teaches those who come here that most local government officials are stupid or corrupt and the deluded people who elect them cannot be trusted to know what is good for the communities in which they live and work.

I came here by a different road, so I did riot graduate from that school, and I intend to reach out to local governments and bring them into the decision making circle.

I want to end my remarks by pointing out the obvious. Good government is an ongoing process, not a magic formula waiting to be discovered in the next legislative session. Complex problems are not solved by simple solutions, and some problems cannot be solved at all. But we must try, and the only chance we have to succeed is through hard work and perseverance. That work must be done every day, early in the morning and late at night, in the winter as well as in the spring.

It has been said that there are no great men, only great challenges. We certainly have before us challenges enough to make great men and women of us all.

For myself, I do not come before you to complain about the weighty burdens of high office. I look forward to the next four years with eager anticipation. Much has been said and written since my election about how different I am—that I am Hispanic, a Republican, and a former mayor. All of this is true. But I did not come her to be different. I came here to make a difference. With the continued confidence and cooperation of the wonderful people of this great state, I will.

Thank you and God bless you.

Governor Lawton Chiles
First Term: 1991 - 1995
Second Term: 1995 - 1999

Lawton Mainor Chiles (born April 3, 1930 – died December 12, 1998) was born in Florida and attended the Lakeland public schools. He graduated from the University of Florida in 1952 and from the institution's law school in 1955. He served in the Army as an artillery officer during the Korean war, 1953–1954. Admitted to the Florida bar in 1955, he began the practice of law in Lakeland. As a citizen he matched his outstanding record as a student at Gainesville by his activities in numerous civic and service organizations.

He was a natural politician and began his undefeated string of elections in 1958 with his election to the house of representatives, where he served until 1966. A rising Democrat, he was then elected to Florida's senate serving from 1966 to 1970. Chiles was chairman of the Florida Law Revision Commission, 1968-1970, and was elected to the US Senate in 1970. During the campaign he won the nickname "Walkin' Lawton" with his 91-day hiking trip through the state. He began in the Panhandle and ended his journey 1,033 miles later in the Keys. This brilliant and innovative campaign was designed by his wife and political partner, Rhea. He remained an important senator for eighteen years. Chiles chaired the Special Committee on Aging and was the first Floridian to served as Chair of the Senate Budget Committee (he hammered away at the growing federal budget deficit). During the Chiles years in the District of Columbia, Rhea found and purchased a property which would become known as Florida House. The funding came from private sources and the renovated historic building now serves as an "embassy house" for Floridians. Senator Chiles gained national attention by helping create the National Commission to Prevent Infant Mortality.

In the 1990 Democratic primary Chiles teamed with Kenneth H. "Buddy" MacKay to win the governorship and the lieutenant governor slots by defeating Bill Nelson (later elected US Senator) and Tom Gustafson. Their opponents, Bob Martinez and Allison DeFoor, who won the Republican primary, were no match for them in the general election. Again in 1994 the same Democratic team defeated Republicans Jeb Bush and Tom Feeney in a close and hard fought contest. The results were 2,135,008 to 2,071,068. For the first time in Florida's history each candidate received over two million votes.

Numerous important legislative acts were passed during the Chiles administration. Among them were the Florida Kidcare Act (1989) which provided health care cover to thousands of Florida children. Prenatal and infant care services were expanded, and child care services were enlarged, as Chiles's concern for protecting children from neglect and abuse and preserving families became evident and won wide public support. The governor helped business by privatizing the Florida Department of Commerce and established the Florida Tourism Industry Marketing Corporation and Enterprise Florida as private and published partnerships to support tourism and economic development. Another achievement of the Chiles tenure was a litigation victory against the Tobacco industry which provided a $11.3

billion settlement to the state which was to be distributed over a twenty-five-year period.

Chiles was within twenty-four days of completing his second term when on December 12, 1998, he died suddenly while exercising in the Governor's Mansion gymnasium. The shocked and grieving citizenry learned that the governor had suffered a fatal heart attack.

Inaugural Speech
First Term: 1991 - 1995
(Source: Florida State Archives, R.A. Gray Building, Tallahassee, Florida)

Governor Martinez—Members of the State Cabinet—Chief Justice Shaw—Justices of the Supreme Court—Madam President—Mr. Speaker—members of the Florida Legislature—my family—my friends— and fellow Floridians.

For you Governor Martinez—Lieutenant Governor MacKay and I join with all Floridians in offering our best wishes and strong support for you and Mary Jane as you move to your important new assignment in Washington. Thank you for your kind assistance in our period of transition.

To you Commissioner Conner, we express our deep gratitude for your forty years of distinguished service to our state and our warm feelings of friendship for you and Laurita as you look forward to enjoying your retirement years.

To the members of the State Cabinet—Secretary Smith—General Butterworth—Commissioner Lewis—Treasurer Gallagher—Commissioner Castor—and Commissioner Crawford —I look forward to our first meeting day after tomorrow to begin our deliberation together across our broad and challenging agenda.

To you Governor Kirk and Erika, we thank you for bringing your uplifting spirit to our ceremony.

To President Margolis, to Speaker Wetherall, and members of the Legislature who have joined us today, Buddy and I remember well our 22 years of service in your chambers and we soon join hands with you as we engage upon a future course that will test our vision and our will.

All Floridians share the honor and the privilege of the presence today of the First Lady of Florida's Natural Heritage—Mrs. Marjorie Stoneman Douglas who epitomizes the spirit of inspired individuality.

On this platform today, I'm blessed to have my closest confidant—my best friend—my key political advisor—the Love of my life—my wife and the mother of my children. Rhea fills all these roles and she is now also your First Lady of Florida.

Buddy MacKay has to be the most qualified and talented Lt. Governor this state has ever had. He also has a tremendous partner in his wonderful wife, Ann.

At the outset of our campaign, there were some who did not fully appreciate the special relationship that I have with Buddy MacKay.

Today the Chiles/MacKay people are beginning to understand the benefits to our state if we function as a team utilizing every speck of talent both of us possess.

Rhea and I consider ourselves especially fortunate to have Ann and Buddy as partners with us in this great adventure.

I am especially grateful for the presence of Governor Askew and Senator Graham
The platform today. Their extraordinary service to our state reminds us all of Florida's Governor of singular greatness—Governor LeRoy Collins.

Governor Collins is not feeling well enough to be with us today, but his spirit, his inspiration, and his soul, touch us all, as we remember what he once told us.
"God forbid that it shall ever be said of us—They did not have the vision to see—or seeing—They did not have the will to try.

Florida became a territory of the United States by proclamation of President James Monroe. Today—170 years later—we are gathered on Monroe Street in the city built upon the seven hills—for an inaugural ceremony that celebrates the endurance of his deed.

As Buddy MacKay and I have been preparing ourselves for to take the solemn oaths of office today, we have thought of those governors who have gone before us and the challenges that they faced in their time.

Florida's early Governors suffered the hardships of frontier life and bore the shame of conflicts with our native Americans.

At the middle of the last Century, Governors confronted the War Between the States and then endured the period of reconstruction.

Early in this Century, Governor Doyle Carlton, Sr. governed our state during the Great
National Depression.

Governor Spessard Holland—my inspiration to become a United States Senator—fought as a decorated hero of World War I—then governed our state during the trying years of World War II.

By the middle of this Century, facing storms of racial furor and conflict, Governor Collins was challenged to lead our state out of the bondage of racial division and hatred.

Then, twenty years ago, Governor Reubin Askew—so dedicated to his mission of governance— met his challenges:

- a severely flawed tax structure that placed harsh and regressive demands on those least able to pay,
- a flimsy environmental regulatory scheme—helpless in preventing massive destruction to our natural resources, and
- an ugly resurgence of racial tensions and turmoil.

Senator Graham—one of only three Florida Governors in our history to become a United States Senator—found his challenges in responding to Florida's exploding growth and turning our attention to the workplace.

Now <u>we</u> meet <u>our</u> challenges.

Today, I was sworn in on a Bible that was carried in the saddle bags of my Great-Grandfather Seaborn Chiles, who was a Methodist "circuit rider" preacher in North Florida and South Georgia. About his preaching ability, they said Brother Chiles was a fine worker but he was not particularly gifted as a "pulpiteer." Well, maybe that's why I sometimes have trouble behind a podium.

I was raised in the years during the depression. My father had a milk route—today you would say we were of the working poor, but that's just a state of mind, and we never had that state of mind. My mother drove into me that my folks were good and responsible people.

Politics took center stage when I was growing up. We looked up to office-holders and people felt they were responsible for electing them and they took their jobs very seriously, but they still had great fun doing it.

This campaign and this inauguration remind me of those times, and I love it.

In my life anything that I've been able to believe I could do, I've been able to do. I went to Boys State and believed that someday I could go to the Florida Legislature, and I did—I walked the state believing that I could get elected to the United States Senate, and I was. I believed we could limit our contributions to $100 and get elected, and we did.

Two years ago I left Washington after 18 years in the U.S. Senate. I was Chairman of the Budget Committee—chaired the Subcommittee of Appropriations that had all the budgets of Health, Education and Welfare—and was 17th in Seniority—I left frustrated and disillusioned and depressed.

Today I have taken the oath of office, and I stand before you, the people who elected me, as your Governor.

In spite of the problems that Florida faces, I am full of hope and feel more confident than I ever have in my entire life.

What makes the difference?

You do—you are the difference—each of you and all of you. In my office will be a book entitled "Chiles/MacKay Special Interest Group."

It will list the names of the 75,000 of you who contributed to our campaign. It does not list the thousands of you who gave—your faith—your prayers. You should also be listed. If you qualify, let me know and I'll put your name in our book.

When I left Washington, the federal government was beached on a bloated and inefficient bureaucracy, totally unresponsive to the needs of the people.

The system had become driven by the insatiable desire of the members to perpetuate themselves in office by depending on exorbitant contributions from those having special interests in legislation. Fundraising became a full time occupation.

Presidents who refused to lead and Congressional leaders who refused to dare had left our ship of state rudderless; lacking the will to deal with the deficit, or other major problems facing our country. We lost our vision. And where there is no vision the people perish.

On the surface, Florida's government seemed to be heading in the same direction. But beneath the bureaucratic crust, there was a budding of life—hope—vitality—vision—in our communities, there were evidences of our people's resolute determination to do something.

In my opportunities to travel across Florida as Director of the Collins Center for Public Policy I began to sense this. I saw other states waking up to the fact that they couldn't and shouldn't wait for Washington, they needed to move on their own.

I remembered the shade tree mechanic in West Florida who told me when I was walking late in 1970, that I should remember "government don't work." But I put that with what another West Florida Sage told me to remember—""Programs don't work, people do."

Last April, Buddy MacKay and I found that we shared the belief that people ... were better than the system that was governing them. That, in fact, the system had lost the consent of the governed. So we decided to make you a dare. We dared to trust you—that if we refused Political Action Committee contributions, limited our contributions to $100, and chose not to rely on special interest negative campaigning, you would vote for us.

We are here today because you took us up on our dare. Thousands of you supported our campaign, and we can now look forward to an administration free of indebtedness to special interests because of our 100 dollar limit.

What a wonderful feeling that is for us. How many things become possible when people win instead of money.

What's the difference in my outlook today compared to how I felt when I left Washington?

In the election campaign, we designed and built a model—based on mutual faith and trust. We tested it and it worked—we have a prototype. Our challenge is to apply this prototype in the governance of Florida.

Where do we start?

We're out of money. And we face over a billion dollar shortfall next year.

I have been reading the press pundits' comments with quotes from others in leadership roles to the effect that with the economic crisis we face, together with declining revenues, Chiles will find that the peoples' expectations far exceed our resources and this means that I'll find the honeymoon is over. (I don't even think we've kissed yet.)

If you equate "our resources" with tax revenues they would be right, but I equate "our resources" with the talent and determination of our people—with grit—your will to suck it up—and as any athlete or risk-taker knows, where there is no pain there is no gain.

I believe this crisis is our opportunity to force the bureaucracy to respond to our effort to decentralize, to cut out many of the bureaucratic layers, to bring about a community-based delivery system for services that will be more efficient, more responsive, more accountable ... in short, a system that will work better.

I know we need tax reform. I know our sales tax is too narrowly based, in many ways it is unfair and inequitable. I doubt our present tax situation can generate enough revenue to take care of Florida's needs.

However, I know you don't believe we are getting our money's worth from our present spending. I know that you are right. We are also not holding ourselves accountable for the money we're spending.

I do not believe given the current top-down management in HRS and Education, that we could improve the delivery of services even if we increased taxes now.

We are not going to seek new taxes now.

After we have earned your confidence by being more efficient, effective and accountable in our method of managing your tax money, we will turn our attention to tax reform, and then we will tell you if we need to raise taxes. But not this session.

This session we will seek ethics reform, better lobbying disclosure and campaign finance reform; and take all the steps to restore your faith and trust in your state government. Hedrick Smith said in his book, *The Power Game*, that if a leader expects his troops to follow he must be willing to place himself way out on the point, so everyone knows he will stand or fall on whether or not his troops follow and he is able to produce.

President Gwen, Speaker T.K., I want you to see Lawton is way out there on this one.

I know because you each have told me and so many of your members that we, the Legislature and the Executive branches must regain the trust and confidence of our people—for without it, even if we find the perfect solution, it will not work—for people must believe in us ... to believe and accept our solutions.

We can pass some laws and write some rules, but laws do not regain the people's trust We regain the people's trust the old-fashioned way ... we earn it.

This session of the legislature we shall see the creation of a Department of Elderly Affairs. The people voted to have such a Department. We can do this without spending more money. We will use this as a model law to decentralize, empower and provide more community participation and control of services.

We have appointed task forces to study HRS (Social Services), Criminal Justice, General Government, the Environment and Growth Management, Education, Transportation and Economic Development. They will report to me before the legislative session begins. We will use their reports as our basic plan for making these areas more responsive and more accountable.

Tomorrow I will announce the appointment of a new Commission to explore and provide the road-map of right-sizing our government, to provide more competition in our government services, to show us how to measure outcomes, to give money on the basis of these measured results rather than on the size of legislative inputs, so that we can properly evaluate whether state government is providing services that result in customer satisfaction.

There are 13 million of us, old and young, wealthy and poor, Black and White, Hispanic and Asian, and Native Americans. I'm not trying to create a new community spirit throughout Florida—it's here, I've seen it and felt it. I want to break the fetters of "business as usual", to unbar the doors of government and open wide the system to let all our people in.

Governor Collins in his second inaugural address said that:

"Government must have qualities of the spirit. Without the qualities of truth, justice and unselfish service, there is no worthwhile leadership and we grapple and grope in a moral wilderness."

This time the people won, and this time, the people will celebrate. That is why we have called our inaugural event a Jubilee. Jubilee means to proclaim a celebration. In the book of Leviticus in the Old Testament we are told that when the Lord spoke to Moses on Mount Sinai he told him to tell the children of Israel that there was to be the year of the Jubilee every 50th year. The beginning of that Jubilee year was to be proclaimed by loud trumpets. Liberty for every inhabitant was to be proclaimed throughout the land.

Every slave was to be freed and every man was to have returned possessions of his that had been sold. Every man was to return to his family.

We seek to make this a time of Jubilee—to have the return of our most valued possession, our sense of family, our sense of belonging. To assure every person that they have great worth—to empower individuals to help themselves—to establish beneficial partnerships with people and their government.

Another ancient ritual is that of the covenant. The cutting of the covenant or the blood covenant was practiced in many civilizations—such as tribal Africa and our Native American Indians—In the Old Testament there was a covenant between the Lord and Abraham. In the New Testament, Christians celebrate a covenant made between God and Jesus for the people. These covenants are agreements one with another. They are agreements of mutual aid. They rest upon the principle of life that to secure our own help and protection, we must agree to help and protect others. This principle, if acted upon, has great power.

The difference between a crowd and a community is that in a crowd there is no covenant People are standing next to each other but they are looking out only for themselves. In a community, people have entered into a covenant to help one another. They recognize that all are diminished when one person suffers, and that one cannot be deprived without depriving all. We are, at last, our brothers keeper.

The covenant that we made together during the campaign is still in force and our task has just begun. Washington will not solve our problems, nor will Tallahassee. But you and I have proved that when we covenant together, we can overcome the odds.

I have decided that I am going to be a mentor to an at-risk student, one in danger of becoming dependent on the welfare system. I'm going to volunteer to teach this summer to take up some of the slack caused by cuts in the Education budget.

If you'll join with me in a covenant to help our State become a community. I would like you to stand and reach out on each side of you and join hands as we ask our Father to bless us.

Prayer:

Now Father, we acknowledge that we are totally dependent upon you. We of ourselves can do nothing. We also confess that we need one another. Give us the wisdom and will to share our blessings with others. Show us how giving will bring meaning and purpose to our lives. Thank you for your faithfulness and for your forgiving spirit.
We thank you that you are the Father of Abraham and Jesus. Bless our State and our Country.

And now let us go forward together.

Inaugural Speech
Second Term: 1995 - 1999
(Source: Florida State Archives, R.A. Gray Building, Tallahassee, Florida)

Members of the Cabinet; Chief Justice Grimes—and distinguished members of the Supreme Court; Speaker Wallace, President Scott. members of the Senate and the House of Representatives; my teammate and partner. Buddy MacKay; my family, my friends, and my fellow Floridians.

My good friend, Governor Askew, whose service to Florida involved courageous leadership, thank you for presiding over these ceremonies today.

For you Commissioner Lewis, Secretary Smith. Treasurer Gallagher and Commissioner Jamerson, on behalf of all Floridians, thank you for your distinguished service to our state. I wish you good luck and continued success in the new challenges that await you.

To the newest members of the Cabinet—Comptroller Milligan, Treasurer Nelson, Commissioner Brogan, Secretary Mortham—I look forward to our first meeting as we work together to make Florida a better place to live and raise families, work, and visit.

To President Scott, Speaker Wallace and members of the Legislature: let today mark the beginning of a new era of cooperation—with our commitment to put the people before the special interests.

Together, let's lead Florida to the highest common ground. We have great challenges ahead of us and we must pull together to meet them.

Surely, there will be times when we will disagree. That is what our democracy is all about. But I pledge to you my best efforts to make this a time when gridlock becomes old history in Florida.

I am blessed to have the love of my life—my partner, my key advisor, my best friend, my wife and the mother of my children with me today.

Rhea—you are always my First Lady and you have excelled in your role as Florida's
First Lady.

And to my political partner, my sidekick and right hand, Lt. Governor Buddy MacKay, and his wife Anne—thank you for your strength, determination and wise counsel.

Buddy, you are the true definition of "public servant"— and I'm proud to serve with you.

Today we stand on Florida's front porch—in the shadow of our Capitol. In March, we will officially observe the 150th anniversary of Florida's statehood. As we look back to celebrate Florida's history, we also must have vision to look ahead—to secure Florida's future.

There is nothing like a campaign to put you in touch with reality. A landslide like mine puts you even closer in touch.

Since November 8th, I've had a chance to walk in the woods and ponder the mood of the people. I have never seen the anger—the distrust—the cynicism toward government and its leaders.

The paradox was most of the issues that people were most concerned about—we are now in the process of addressing. It's a real failure of communication on our part. Fortunately for us, there were hundreds of people like you who were involved in the changes we were addressing—and you told enough people to get us reelected.

We got elected. But how do we restore some level of confidence in our government so that people will participate and work with us?

When I walked the state 25 years ago, an old cracker told me the walk would get me elected senator—but he wanted me to always remember that "Government don't work."

I've puzzled this over the years ... now I know he was right. Government don't work. Government can't work. People work. Government is the framework through which people work. Government is neither bad nor good. It's neutral.

Our problem is when we expect "government" to solve our problems—it can't. But our unique and wonderful constitution gives us the opportunity to design a framework whereby people can participate—to solve problems. State government should be a catalyst—to bring together people, local governments, not-for-profits.

There are two major changes we need to make to our framework. First, in the old, top-down way, all services were delivered vertically. Life and its problems occur horizontally.

In the environment, we looked at the single problem of how to de-channelize and restore the Kissimmee River to its old boundaries. Each government agency said "we're only responsible for this slice." Now, we will look at an entire ecosystem—and the Kissimmee Basin starts just south of Orlando ... but it also encompasses Lake Okeechobee, the Everglades and Florida Bay.

So, we look at the entire system and bring together a plan and the agencies to deal with all of the problems, horizontally, like the river flows.

We must look at neighborhoods the same way. What are all the pieces and players necessary for the health of a neighborhood?

First, there must be a core of stakeholders—people who live there, who want to work and improve their quality of life. They work up a plan of the help they need. The state acts as the catalyst—and it says to the banks, local governments, businesses, stakeholders: "If you come to the table and bring your assets, we will participate with you. We'll use the leverage of our programs and help to make it happen."

Buddy will be working to make this happen in economic development and trade, which will include job training, capital, education and regulations.

The stakeholders—businesses, communities—must come to the table with their chips. They must draw the plan and furnish the leadership. We will be a partner.

The second redesign is to drastically change our bureaucracy. To bring about fairness and equal treatment, we decided we needed to prohibit any official from acting in an arbitrary manner—so, through rules and regulations we deprived our officials of all decision-making authority.

Now, there are thousands of rules and regulations that take away all discretion of an official to make a decision based on common sense and then be held responsible for it.

We must set the goals—the public policy we wish to accomplish -but we must restore sanity to how we accomplish this. This is the fundamental change that must be made—to restore confidence in our government.

I have 200 acres of woods north of Tallahassee where I have an old log cabin. I wanted to build a cook shack out back—wood poles, tin roof, screened sides, and an old stove.

I've been trying to get a permit for over a year. "You must have plans," they say. But, a cook shack is unusual; there are no regulations for one. So they ask: "Does it have a stove?" YES. "Does it have a toilet?" YES.

"Well, the closest thing we have is a single-family residence; so it needs steel tie-downs; it must withstand Andrew-type winds, etc."

The cost went from $15,000 to $65,000.

I've concluded the Lord gave me this problem so I could understand why people hate government so much.

Mr. Speaker—Mr. President—every member of the Cabinet, I respectfully request your help in this. Let's set as a goal to reduce the present rules and regulations by 50 per cent within two years.

But it is just as important to change the current philosophy that removes decision-making authority and responsibility from ourselves and our state workers.

I've always heard the best way to lead is by example. So, as an example of how this new—or really old—philosophy would work. Buddy—I charge you to make this happen: delete 50 percent of the rules and regulations within two years. Good luck.

And Buddy—when you slay this dragon, I want you to help me with my cook shack.

Remember—government don't work; PEOPLE work.

There also are thousands of examples of the how our people are working. It's the Power of One: individuals—from all parts of Florida whose hard work, dedication and commitment are truly making a difference.

Today, as we celebrate the strength of Florida's people—and the diversity that is key to our strength—I'd like for you to meet some of our fellow citizens—neighbors who are making a difference.

For these ceremonies that demonstrate our democracy truly reflect the power not of government—but of the people.

MARILYN HOLIFIELD is a native of Tallahassee. She's a brilliant lawyer who is a senior partner in the firm of Holland & Knight. But her greatest accomplishments can be measured by the positive influence she has on others—and through the civic work in which she is so deeply involved. Marilyn?

[MARILYN HOLIFIELD presentation]

JOE GREER is a Cuban-American doctor from Miami who gives new meaning to the phrase "public service." Several years ago, he heard there were homeless people with serious medical problems living under Miami's bridges and expressways. He took his medical bag to begin the equivalent of thousands of house calls—the first steps to establishing clinics for the homeless.

Today, he is one of America's leading experts on the homeless. That's why *Time* magazine named him one of the country's most important leaders under the age of 40.
Meet Dr. Joe Greer—one of our neighbors.
[JOE GREER presentation]

VIRGIE CONE is 86 years old—but her energy, enthusiasm and dedication to serving others are an example of the important contributions every individual has to offer. This Jasper resident is a retired teacher—but we continue to learn lessons from her in her role as a tireless advocate for the rights and needs of Florida's elders. Meet one of our neighbors—Virgie Cone....
[VIRGIE CONE presentation]

These three citizens are representative of the many others who give of themselves, every day, to help build a brighter future for our state. Don't they make you proud to call Florida home?

I'd like you to meet some other Florida neighbors whose own lives have been touched by government working as it should ... as a partner and a catalyst.

Making sure that every child has a good beginning in life is a principle to which we are committed. Prenatal care—for mother and baby—makes all the difference.

Our Healthy Start program is a national model—providing screening to every pregnant mother.

KELLY DISLA, from Riverview, has three children, including Aramis, a three-month-old she considers a "miracle baby." And it's a miracle she credits to Healthy Start. Kelly?
[KELLY DISLA presentation]

JAIME MILLER and his wife LORI, own a small painting business in West Palm Beach. Like thousands of other Florida businesses, they feared for the security of their employees and their future because of soaring workers' compensation insurance rates.

This was a critical problem—and business people raised their voices together demanding help.

Jamie and Lori Miller can tell you what happened ...
[JAMIE and LORI MILLER presentation]

Nothing is more important to our future than the ability of Florida's two million public school students to get the tools they need to succeed in life. But for too long, Tallahassee pretended to have all the answers about improving neighborhood schools.

Today, parents and teachers have the power to decide what needs fixing in their own neighborhood schools. Our Blueprint 2000 reforms have moved the decision-making to local communities.

SUSIE HENDERSON, of Tallahassee, is one of more than 50,000 parents who actively serve on local school advisory councils. They're making a difference for our children. Susie served last year as Chairman of the advisory council at Leon High School. Susie?

[SUSIE HENDERSON presentation]

Affordable health care should be the right of all people, not the privilege of the few. But the cost of coverage prevents so many businesses from being able to extend coverage to their employees.

Our reforms have made it possible for competition that is resulting in affordable rates—improving the bottom line for businesses and the peace of mind for their workers.

BLA1R HOWARD owns a small wholesale grocery in Orlando—a business started by his grandfather more than 80 years ago. But the business could not afford to cover health care costs for employees.

It's a different story today—and Blair can tell us about it.

[BLAIR HOWARD presentation]

Fighting crime involves punishing people who break the law. But it also means preventing children from going astray of the law, and intervening in the lives of young people who will respond when given discipline and direction to get on the right path.

KEITHAN BROWN, from Crestview, is 16 years old. He's been in trouble with the law—but today, he's turning his life around at a Department of Juvenile Justice halfway house.

Next week, he completes a successful program at Pensacola's Boys' Base, where he serves as a peer counselor helping others at the Base. He has been honored as "student of the week" and "resident of the month."

[KEITHAN BROWN presentation]

These Floridians demonstrate the difference our government can make when it works as a partner—and as a resource. They prove that when people are trusted with the power to make a difference, they can.

This is our time to rededicate ourselves—and to seize the future through our actions. We'll need the help of each other to get there. But we'll also need the help of God.

I'd like to ask DR. HOWARD ADDISON, of Temple Beth Israel, in Fort Lauderdale, to give today's benediction ...
[DR. ADDISON benediction]

This has been a glorious morning. It is filled with the possibilities of the future—and the excitement of choosing the path to our future. Every individual has the ability to make a vital contribution as we find our way on that path.

And all of us together can raise our voices and lend our efforts to making the community of Florida better and stronger. We can solve difficult problems. We can embrace the challenges before us. We can walk the walk together—and we truly can make a difference.

We're only here for a little while. So let's use the time we have to build the Florida of our dreams.

A son of Florida, BILLY DEAN, captured the spirit I'm talking about in his song—"ONLY HERE FOR A LITTLE WHILE."

He's going to sing it for us now—and we all can lift our voices with him .... BILLY?

Governor Kenneth H. "Buddy" McKay
Term: 1998 - 1998

Kenneth Hood "Buddy" MacKay (born March 22, 1933) was born in Marion County. He became governor following the unexpected death of Lawton Chiles. MacKay earned two bachelor's degrees at the University of Florida in 1954 (he had an outstanding record as an undergraduate). Following graduation, he served as a captain in the Air Force 1955-1958. He returned to his alma mater, the University of Florida, enrolled in law school, and graduated in 1961. He became a lawyer in Ocala (and also in Miami) and was a citrus grower.

MacKay entered politics with powerful credentials. He represented Marion and Alachua counties in the legislative house from 1968–1974, when he was elected to the senate from the Sixth District (a sprawling district in north central Florida). In 1980 MacKay lost in the Democratic primary for a US Senate seat, but won in a race for the national house and served three terms beginning in 1983. In 1988 he won the Democratic nomination for the US Senate in opposition to the Republican Connie Mack. In an especially close contest Mack emerged as the victor with 2,049,329 votes and the unlucky MacKay got 2,015,717. Their percentages were Mack 50.4 and MacKay 49.6.

MacKay proved to be a strong part of Chiles's two successful wins as governor. He did not make an inaugural address, but he did seek the popular election to succeed Chiles. He and Rick Dantzler, candidate for lieutenant governor, faced no candidates in the primary. Their Republican opponents were Jeb Bush and Frank Brogan, who also had no opposition in the primary. As the son of George H.W. Bush, former president, and as a close loser to Lawton Chiles in 1994, Bush was in a strong position and won the election. Once again the GOP was triumphant.

During the twenty-four days following Chiles death, and just over one month since his own political defeat in a bid for the governor's office, MacKay led the state through a smooth transition period. He took the oath of office at 12:30 am on December 13, 1998 in his private office at the capitol. Justice Charles Wells presided over the two minute ceremony that was attended by MacKay's wife, Anne MacKay and a small group of family and friends. MacKay issued a brief statement regarding the death of his friend, the late Governor Chiles.

Buddy MacKay was the first Lieutenant Governor to serve as governor because of a sitting governor's death while in office. The last governor to die in office previous to Chiles was Daniel McCarty in September 1953. At that time Florida did not have a lieutenant governor. The following comments were made by MacKay upon being sworn in as Florida's governor. It consisted of two brief sentences:

God has called a great man home today. There will never be another like him.

Governor John Ellis "Jeb" Bush
First Term: 1999 - 2003
Second Term: 2003 - present

    John Ellis "Jeb" Bush (born February 11, 1953) was born in Texas, the scion of a politically powerful family, he was the son of President George H.W. Bush (41st president) and his wife Barbara. His older brother George W. Bush (43rd president) was elected president in 2000. Jeb Bush was educated at Phillips Academy in Andover, Massachusetts, and received his college education in Austin at the University of Texas. He majored in Latin American Studies and graduated with a Phi Beta Kappa key. He entered the banking business in Houston, worked for a time in Venezuela, and then returned to Texas. While campaigning in his father's presidential race in 1979, Bush met a South Florida builder named Armando Codina who persuaded him to move to Miami and become his business partner. In 1991 Bush co-founded a new real estate development company called the Columbia Group which became successful and grew rapidly.

Bush became active in South Florida: he was a volunteer worker for the Miami Children's Hospital, the United Negro Fund of South Florida, the United Way of Dade County, the Dade County Homeless Trust, and chaired a foundation that co-founded with the Urban League the Liberty City Charter School. In 1994 he ran on the Republican ticket for governor, and, although narrowly defeated by Lawton Chiles, received statewide and national attention. Bush authored a book in 1995 entitled *Profiles in Character*. The work honored fourteen of Florida's civic heroes.

In 1998 Jeb Bush and Frank Brogan won the Republican gubernatorial primary without opposition, and, using the same script, so did Democrats Buddy MacKay and Rick Dantzler. Bush's beautiful Mexican born wife, Columba, was a political asset among the Hispanic population of the state. As a candidate, Bush campaigned using his fluent Spanish. The showdown came in the general election (its results had national implications for George W. Bush's bid for the Republican nomination in 2000). The results of the governor's race were a demonstration of Jeb Bush's popularity, how numerous Republicans were in Florida, and the advantages of an efficient party organization that got out the voters. Bush and Brogan received 2,192,105 votes to their opponents' 1,773,054.

In his inaugural address Bush stressed family and family values perhaps more than any of Florida's previous governors. In 2002 he ran unopposed in the Republican primary (and once more with his lieutenant governor Brogan). The question was could he repeat his victory of 1998? The Democrats had a tough primary fight that featured a three-way race among Daryl L. Jones, an experienced African American legislator; Bill McBride, a highly respected trial lawyer with limited experience in government, and the well known Janet Reno, who had served as attorney general in both of President Bill Clinton's two administrations. In an extremely close contest McBride won with 44.4 percent of the vote to Reno's 44 percent (Jones got 11.6 percent). In the general election Bush and Brogan contended against McBride and Tom Rossin. The result was a solid victory for Bush and the Republican party. Bush defeated McBride 2,856,845 to 2,201,427 and garnered 56 percent of the popular vote. Soon after the election, Brogan resigned to become president of Florida Atlantic University. Bush then appointed Toni Jennings, a former two-time president of the Florida Senate to be his Lt. Governor. The governor's appointment gave the state its first woman Lt. Governor.

As governor, Bush instituted changes in state government and new laws that had far reaching impact. Some of his plans were successful while others were less so, although the Republicans controlled not only the governor's chair but both houses of the legislature as well. Bush's time as governor was in part determined by forces outside his control, and none more than the presidential election of 2000. His brother contended against the sitting vice president Al Gore, and in one of the nation's most contentious elections George Bush, who lost in the popular vote, won in the electoral college. The Florida Supreme Court as well as the national Supreme Court issued rulings regarding conflicts relating to the election in Florida. As an outcome of these rulings, the Republican party carried Florida by 537 votes. Once again, as in 1876, Florida's electoral vote played a major role in deciding the presidency.

In general, Governor Bush's program adhered to the Republican policy against higher taxes. A compromise between trial lawyers and the medical profession remains a work in progress. Another remarkable first involved education and the governor's restructuring of the governance of the state institutions and his bringing an end to the policy of affirmative action and a policy of holding individual schools responsible for their students academic progress. Bush inherited the problem of deciding on water use from the Apalachicola-Chattahoochee-Flint river system. In a series of talks among representatives, including the governors from Florida, Georgia, and Alabama stretching over years, no agreement was reached. Florida was basically concerned with protecting the future of the Apalachicola River and Bay, while the other states concentrated on industry, agriculture, recreation, and the growing demand for water in the Atlanta area. Failure to reach an agreement opened the way for the national Supreme Court to hear the evidence and probably appoint a mediator. Public opinion was also affected by amendments to the constitution such as one limiting the size of classes in Florida's public schools. Obviously needed, the amendment also imposed an expensive demand on the state budget.

Everything in Florida and across the country was affected by the terrorist attack of September 11, 2001 and the following national economic situation which forced state governments to cut back drastically on most of their operations. Compounding the situation was the commitment of the US to expensive military operations overseas. Immensely popular (he had an 80 percent approval rate) during his second term, Bush guided Florida through this financial crisis and returned the state budget to solvency in record time. The effects of the Bush administrations on Florida could not be foretold immediately, although it is certain that a large part of Bush's legacy will rest on his innovative approach to improving public education throughout the state. Bush's A+ Plan during his first term provided a three year increase in K-12 funding. By the beginning of his second term, his accountability system of measuring a student's progress as well as assigning ratings to public schools, had measurably improved standardized test scores throughout the state.

In the summer of 2004, Florida was hit with four hurricanes. Property damage was at a historic high, and thousands of homes were destroyed. Traveling throughout the state, Bush took a hands on approach to disaster aid, restoring utilities and water to storm victims while designing a plan to revitalize tourism, vital to the state's economy.

First Inaugural Speech
(Source: State Library of Florida, January 5, 1999)

I thank God for the opportunity to be here today and for the blessings that have been bestowed upon us all. You have honored me beyond measure by asking me to lead Florida forward into a new millennium. At the turn of a new century, I think it wonderfully fitting to stand here in front of Florida's beautiful Old Capitol. It is a noble, yet modest symbol of our common heritage and a timeless reminder of our shared history.

When this beautiful building was restored nearly 100 years ago, Florida was at the untamed reaches of the American map—a frontier and home to a half-million people—forerunners courageous who fought the heat and the isolation to wrest a living from the land.

Our most populated county had fewer than 40,000 people. Roads were primitive and travel slow. In 1902, Florida public schools produced 136 high school graduates statewide. Think about that: In one school year, one hundred and thirty-six high school graduates in the entire state. The state made more by selling the services of its convicts than it spent on salaries in the executive branch, a ratio that might still appeal to some of us today.

Look at us now. Look at what we have become today. From our shores, men have traveled to the mountains of the moon. Our population has increased more than 25-fold, and we have an economy that is the 16th largest in the world, ahead of entire countries such as India and Argentina. Last year, we graduated more than 110,000 young people from public high school, and through the leadership of people like Chancellor Adam Herbert and our incoming Lieutenant Governor Frank Brogan, our university system is becoming the envy of the nation.

But change has not been all for the better, even in a state as seemingly blessed as ours. There are still immense challenges for Florida, great challenges calling forth courage and leadership. While our cities have grown larger, our communities have grown weaker and our natural treasures more exposed to harm. While more children graduate from high school, many have not learned the lessons that will make them better adults. And while our government has grown larger, so too has the crushing weight of taxes, regulations and mandates on Florida's families and entrepreneurs.

As we address these great challenges into the next century, we need not only ask "What's new?" we should more often ask, "What's best?" For the things that are best will endure, and the things that are merely new will soon become old and discarded.

And so today I ask: What is best? What endures? At the core of our understanding must be a fundamental humility born of the recognition that we owe all to our Creator. People like Dr. Billy Graham have changed the course of this century by reminding us that we have been given an unearned gift of incomprehensible generosity. We have been given life and through our living the opportunity to know the Divine Giver. This is not a relationship based on rigid dogma or divisive thinking, it is based on acceptance and love of others, despite their faults, just as we have been accepted and loved, despite ours. This very private relationship is the wellspring from which goodness flows, and combined with the goodness of others can be the torrent that changes our society.

Our devotion should also extend to our families because it is here that most of life's principles are forged. Loyalty, empathy, generosity, and caring are cords of a rope that bind us together into something far stronger than we can ever be individually. Today, looking at the faces of my parents, my brothers and sister, and my own precious wife and children, I am reminded of the strength they have given me and the debt I can never repay. But just as our parents have made a better world for us, we must try to create a better world for our children. If we leave no other legacy than to make our children better than ourselves, we have accomplished far more than we can ever imagine.

And finally, there are our friends, our neighbors, and our communities. Little could be accomplished without the shared vision and triumphs of those people with whom we choose to share our lives. Friends beget friends, and from these personal connections communities flourish.

Faith family friends These are what's best. These will endure. We should trust in these more than we trust in government. State government, now and forever, must respect and nurture and rely on these enduring institutions so that we can unleash their amazing potential.

And so, let state government give families and individuals greater freedom—more freedom to exercise compassion, to keep more of what they earn, and to make the choices that will improve the lives of their loved ones. True compassion invariably begins with a single person, not with sections hidden within bureaus nestled within divisions placed within agencies.

Let state government trust Florida's communities to confront their everyday challenges, to advance the ideas that will shape our state.

The best and brightest ideas do not come from the state capital, but from the untapped human capital that resides in our diverse communities.

And, let state government touch the spiritual face of Florida. Let us not be afraid to engage our churches and synagogues and spiritual entrepreneurs to enhance care for the needy and to fill the hollow hearts. State government can draw much from these reservoirs of faith. In his own inaugural address 44 years ago, Florida Governor Leroy Collins said, simply, "Government cannot live by taxes alone or by jobs alone or even by roads alone. Government, too, must have qualities of the spirit. Truth and justice and fairness and unselfish service are some of these. Without these qualities there is no worthwhile leadership, and we grapple and grope in a moral wilderness." So, too, Lawton Chiles was one of those rare leaders who used his faith as a compass in his public life. He not only understood what his friend, LeRoy Collins said, he lived it and practiced it. Florida will be eternally grateful for his goodness and for his appreciation of the qualities of the spirit.

Public servants must have the humility to listen to and trust Florida's head, heart and soul. Only then will the body be strong. Government well be unencumbered to make a true difference where it is most needed and where it can be most effective: Education, public safety, public works, and the protection of the frailest and weakest among us. Give to Floridians a state government that makes these few precious things the core of its being, and we can match the lofty challenges illuminated by the wonder of a new tomorrow. We can see that children learn a year's worth of knowledge in a year's worth of time, and work with unbridled determination to ensure that no child in our education system is left behind. We can make the tragedy of child abuse an exception, not an expectation. We can comfort Florida's families so that their loved ones dwell in safety, not fear. We can bring opportunity and growth to our urban cores, and in the process, sustain our natural environment. And, we can restore respect for our elderly, allowing them to reap the benefits of expanded choices in care and health decisions.

For these are the principles that will guide us. I want state government to be an ally, not an adversary of positive change within each community. I want to protect people, not bureaucracies. I want state government to be more respectful of the earnings of Florida's families, not more desirous. I want our leaders more trustful of the choices of our citizens, not more suspicious. And, I want to rely on the rich debate afforded by diversity, not the sterile monologue of insular politics.

If we do these things we need not wait a hundred years to see their benefits. In five years, our state can be transformed. Such is the power of our shared vision.

So today, I want to thank you for giving me the opportunity to serve and to lead us in this greatest of undertakings. This is your journey as well as mine. This is our call to arms. I ask you to join with me to make Florida not only a magnificent engine of commerce that defines the economy in the post-Information Age, but something that is far simpler, and far more elusive: It should also be a better neighborhood, a nicer place We should be known for the compassion of our dreams as much as their grandeur.

Our success in this great endeavor will not be measured by the quantity of our accomplishments as it has been in this century, but by the quality of our lives in the next. And so, let us begin the journey, not with what we can carry on our backs, but with what we carry in our hearts. Let the capacity of our courage and caring be the measure by which we are judged, and let us take the first step on a path that begins here in the scattered light under these ancient oaks to a Florida that glimmers now beyond time's horizon

Thank you and God Bless Florida forever.

Second Inaugural Speech
(Source: Governor's Office)

I thank Almighty God for the opportunity to be here today, and for the colleagues, friends, and family who have gathered to celebrate our common purpose. I also thank the people of Florida who have honored me with a second term as Governor. I am humbled and grateful for the trust you all have placed in me.

Can it be that only four years ago we paused under these oaks to talk about the future with an enthusiasm and, in hindsight, an innocence, that was unique to that day? Only four years, yet a generation's wisdom learned in that time.

Through goals achieved and hardships endured, we have seen the world change in ways that were then unimaginable. It is fitting and good that we, as Floridians, return here today wiser and more resolute, with the energy and commitment to continue our journey forward. But most important is this: That we come here today as a people; as a community; as a state that has for the first time in our modern experience united behind common goals that elevate all of us and the least of us.

And how will we realize our destiny? We will do it with the grace of God a fierce determination, and the lessons we have learned.

Those of you who were here for the last inaugural may remember the warm tropical breeze that enveloped our capital city. I hope you also remember my message that day. I said that government is not the answer; that we must build a life centered on faith, friends and family. Four years later, I am more convinced than ever that if we remain true to this focus our lives will be fulfilling and meaningful.

Faith is grounded in humility, gratitude, and generosity; an acknowledgment that through life we have been given a gift that is wholly unearned and never fully understood. It requires the difficult acceptance that we are loved, despite our flaws, just as we should love others, despite theirs. In our darkest hours, it is what sustains us. In our final darkness, it will bring us light.

Friends, too, sustain us. Through laughter and loyalty, they fill our lives through a bond made all the more extraordinary because it is freely chosen. This, too, is a priceless gift, and many listening today have blessed me with their friendship. Through these relationships a life is made rich; and through the web of relationships that spring from friendship a society emerges and flourishes.

And then there is family. It is family that taught me the importance of faith and friends. These weren't conclusions I drew based on reading or research, but on seeing my own parents make these their priorities. My mom and dad are here today, and each remains for me a very personal and compelling example of a life fully lived; of people who have experienced both the triumphs and pain that come from giving themselves over to the vibrant core of human experience and to the service of others. God Bless you both. To this day, I call my dad for advice, and his response is always as gracious as it is wise. He is now and forever my greatest hero.

Now my mother, she doesn't usually wait for my call. She calls me. And what she lacks in coddling, she more than makes up for in smaller phone bills by keeping her comments short, to the point, and right on target.

At any rate, my parents have shown me that when we accept personal responsibility for ourselves and those we love, we don't have to invent government programs that apply complex rules to matters better addressed by profound human caring. What is a checklist compared to kindness? What is agency procedure compared to compassion?

But without a caring society, without each citizen voluntarily accepting the weight of responsibility, government is destined to grow even larger, taking more of your money, burrowing deeper into your lives.

Consider the mathematics of the tragedy: Each year in Florida, 80,000 children are born without a father in the home. Each year, there are 85,000 abortions. And each year, 80,000 marriages are dissolved. Sadly, today, almost 50,000 children are in the custody of the state, and hundreds of thousands more aren't receiving the child support they are due. The numbers are so staggering, the implications so bleak, that we can become numb to the human toll they exact.

In the past, our response has been to raise more taxes, grow more government, and embrace the thin fiction that if only we can hire one more social worker or complete one more form then we can somehow reverse these corrosive trends and salvage these lives. But while these intentions may be noble these methods are folly. Government will never fill the hollowness of the human heart. It can only be filled by a like-kind substance. It can only be filled by another human heart.

So in the end, while I am the one who takes this oath today, when we leave this place your responsibility is as sacred as mine: Through our example and our deeds we should strive to shape our society through kindness and caring. In our businesses, we should give moms and dads time to be parents with their children. In our hectic daily lives, we should fiercely guard a time for selflessly helping the most vulnerable and needy. In our most private moments alone, we should reflect on our unearned gifts and rededicate our lives to those around us. In a thousand ways we can be more accepting, more giving, more compassionate.

And if we are, we can embed in society a sense of caring that makes government less necessary. There would be no greater tribute to our maturity as a society than if we can make these buildings around us empty of workers; silent monuments to the time when government played a larger role than it deserved or could adequately fill.

But this is a distant destination, and there are many steps in the journey. I am reminded of the wisdom of Gov. Leroy Collins, the man I consider to be Florida's greatest governor. When describing his leadership, Gov. Collins said that the proper role of the chief executive is to make sure we navigate the ship out of the harbor but not beyond the horizon where it can no longer be seen by those on shore.

So we should pause and reflect on the visible. In my first term, with your help we set and achieved some remarkable goals. We dramatically reduced the rate of violent crime by imposing swift and certain justice on those who illegally use guns and punished to a greater extent repeat violent offenders. We signed an historic accord to save the everglades. We significantly increased resources for the developmentally disabled and made them a focus of this administration.

But at the pinnacle of our achievements sits education, and appropriately so. Better education is the fundamental mechanism by which a society is elevated and transformed. Every small accumulation of knowledge and skill in each person is amplified to huge effect over a lifetime.

We have done nothing less than revolutionize education in Florida. We have built a school system that is accountable to our students and parents. It has not been painless, and the protectors of the status quo have resisted every step of the way. In the end, we have prevailed -but it is our students who are achieving victory.

The changes we have made will not be undone because the people of Florida understand their power. Can it be that just four years ago parents were left to guess whether their children's school was giving them a good education? How is it possible that we tolerated a bureaucracy that was indifferent to the success or failure of a child? We will never, never, never go back!

We will only go forward. If education is the most important function of government, then reading is the most important skill to be derived from education. That is why it is my goal over the next four years to make reading an enduring core value of our state. This means showing the way for all to be involved. It means making sure that our early childhood programs have reading as their highest priority and that our teachers are fully skilled to teach reading. It means that parents and mentors have our full support in their selfless campaign to instill in our children a love of the written word.

And that is why we have developed a battle plan that is aggressive and bold, committing massive resources to nurture the skill that is the basis of productivity and understanding.

Just as we will be equipping citizens with the tools to thrive in an increasingly complex world, it is my goal in the next four years to help grow an economy that will give our people the opportunities they deserve. Already we have seen the wisdom of cutting taxes and red tape. While other states have languished in our national economic downturn, Florida has been a national leader in the creation of new jobs.

As the great inventor Thomas Edison said, "Restlessness and discontent are the first necessities of progress."

We must never be merely content with the progress we have made in Florida we must always be restless. We must always strive to do better.

We need to build an economy that creates not just new jobs, but better jobs; careers that enhance the quality of our lives, and protect the integrity of our natural environment. I will make it my calling to bring these jobs to this great state.

And finally, it is my most ambitious goal to provide the catalyst, in small ways and large, that will bring our families closer together. I, for one, intend to begin with my own family. Although it is an intensely private—and, at times, painful matter—you should know I have rededicated myself to being a better father and husband. Looking today at the faces of my wife and children, all three of them, I realize that any sense of fulfillment I have from this event is meaningless unless they, too, can find fulfillment in their lives. They have sacrificed greatly for me, and I love them dearly.

And so that their sacrifices and yours have not been wasted, and that our hopes and dreams for our beloved Florida are fully realized, I leave you with this thought: In my first inaugural address at the dawn of this new century, I talked about how the forces of the previous hundred years would shape my first four years in office.

Today, I want you to consider how we may, in the next four years, shape the hundred years that come after.

In a mere 48 months, another person will be standing on this spot, placing his or her hand on the Bible, taking the oath of office and becoming our next governor. Our principles must endure beyond that person and those who come after. They must be intractably rooted in a culture that demands excellence, not adequacy; that exalts in the individual, not government; and that through compassion, rather than compulsion, provides solace and support for the most vulnerable among us.

This can be our legacy. This can be Florida.
And it begins today.
It begins now.
It begins with you.
God bless you all, and God bless Florida.

Bibliography

Brown, Canter Jr. Ossian Bingley Hart: Florida's Loyalist Reconstruction Governor. Baton Rouge: Louisiana State University Press, 1997.

Caldwell, Millard F. The Administration of Millard F. Caldwell as Governor of Florida, 1945–1949. Tallahassee: Rose Printing Company, 1949.

Cash, W.T. History of the Democratic Party in Florida. Live Oak, Florida: Democratic Historical Foundation, 1936.

Church, George B. Jr. "Henry Laurens Mitchell." Master's thesis, University of Florida, 1969.

Day, Edith Hansen, "A Rhetorical and Contact Analysis of Florida's Gubernatorial Inaugural Addresses, 1845-1971, Ph.D. Dissertation, Florida State University, 1971.

Deal, John R. Jr. "Sidney Johnson Catts, Stormy Petrel of Florida Politics." Master's thesis, University of Florida, 1949.

DeToledano, Ralph and Brennan, Philip V. Jr. Claude Kirk–The Man And The Myth. Moonachil, New Jersey. Pyramid Publications 1970.

Flynt, Wayne. Cracker Messiah Governor Sidney J. Catts of Florida. Baton Rouge: Louisiana State University, 1997.

"Four Fruitful Years: The Administration of Spessard Holland as Governor of Florida." Florida Highways, XIII (December, 1944).

Jacobstein, Helen L. "The Segregation Factor in the Florida Democratic Primary of 1956." Master's thesis, University of Miami, 1964.

Kabat, Ric A. "Albert W. Gilchrist: Florida's Progressive Governor." Master's thesis, Florida State University, 1987.

Kalina, Edmund F. Jr. Claude Kirk and the Politics of Confrontation. Gainesville: University of Florida Press, 1993.

Gammon, William Lamar. "Governor John Milton of Florida, Confederate States of America. Master's thesis, University of Florida, 1948.

McDonnell, Victoria H. "The Businessman's Politician: A Study of the Administration of John Welborn Martin, 1925-1929." Master's thesis, University of Florida, 1968.

Proctor, Samuel. Napoleon Bonaparte Broward: Florida's Fighting Democrat. Gainesville: University of Florida Press, 1950.

Staid, Sister Mary Elizabeth. "Albert Walker Gilchrist, Florida's Middle of the Road Governor." Master's thesis, University of Florida, 1950.

Vance, Linda D. Mary Mann Jennings, Florida's Genteel Activist Gainesville: University of Florida Press, 1985.

Wagy, Thomas R. Governor LeRoy Collins of Florida, Spokesman of the New South. Tuscaloosa: University of Alabama Press, 1985.

Warren, Fuller, and Morris, Allen. How to Win in Politics. Tallahassee: Peninsular Publishing Company, 1949.

Williamson, Edward C. Florida Politics in the Gilded Age, 1877–1893. Gainesville: University of Florida Press, 1976.

Index

A
A+ Plan, 406
Academies and High Schools 25
Acker, Bert L. 250, 260
Adams, Thomas 330, 331
Adkins 375
Adkinson, D.C. 219
African-Americans 184, 331
Agricultural Department 115
Air Force 329, 401
Allen, George W. 146
Allies 250
Alligator Alley 302
Allison, (A.K.) Abraham Kurkindolle 32, 33
American party 23
Amnesty Proclamation 38
Andrews, Charles O. 198, 234
anti-New Deal 250
Apalachicola-Chattahoochee-Flint river system 405
Army 245, 383
Askew Institute of Politics and Society 331
Askew, Reubin O'Donovan 321, 329, 330, 331, 359, 387
Atlantic Gulf Coast Canal 126
Attorney Generals
    Butterworth 375
    Ervin 288
    Gibbs 236

B
Babson College 309
Bafalis, A.L. "Skip" 330
ballot-box 72
Banquo's ghost 151
Barbour, P.P. 46
Barkett 375
Battle of Natural Bridge 89
Bethune Cookman College 365
Bie, Norman 331
Bill of Rights 114
Billeris, Ted 352
Black Codes 36, 44
Black Republicans 28
Blackstone 75
Blair 399
Bloxham, William D. 64, 75, 76, 77, 100
Blueprint 2000 reforms 399
Board of Control 108, 237, 265
Board of Instruction 25
Board of Public Welfare 198
Board of Visitors 119
Book of Proverbs 344
Booming Twenties 184
Bourbon 76
Bourbon Democrat 76
Bourbon Democrats 71
Boyd 375
Boys State 388
Brackin, Newman 263
Brantley 374
Brantley, Bobby 373, 376
Brogan, Frank 404, 407
Brogan, Frank 402, 404
Bronze Star 269
Brookings 242
Brookings Institution of Washington 241
Broome, James Emilius 15, 16
Brother Chiles 387
Broward 107, 108, 120

"Broward Era" 108
Broward, Napoleon Bonaparte 98, 107, 365
Brown, Keithan 399
Brown, Thomas 9, 15, 32
Bryan, William Jennings 97
Bryant, Ferris C. 280, 301, 302, 310, 311, 351
Buckman Act 108
Bunker Hill monument 261
Bureau of Public Roads 306
Burns, W. Haydon 302, 309, 310, 320, 351
Bush, Columba 404
Bush, George H.W., 403, 404, 405, 406
Bush, George W. 374, 404
Bush, John Ellis "Jeb" 384, 402, 403, 404
Butterworth. Bob 385
Buy Now campaigns 198

C

Caesar 148
Caldwell, Millard F. 234, 249, 250, 251, 260, 261, 266, 303, 312, 351
Call, Richard Keith 1
Call, Mary 289
Callahan, Leon 350
Callaway, Elvery E. (E. E.) 210, 220
Camp Blanding 244
Capua, Peter, S. 350
Carlton, Doyle E., Jr. 301
Carlton, Doyle E., Sr., 197, 198, 302, 312, 387
Carol City High School 355
Carolina Military Institute 119
Carpetbaggers 59
Carson Newman College 249
Carter, Jimmy 331

Castro, Fidel 302
Catts, Sidney J. 145, 146, 197
Centenial Year 275
Cheney, John M. 120
Cherry, Gwendolyn Sawyer 331
Chief Ploughman of the State 1
Chiles, Lawton M. 303, 351, 383, 384, 385, 390, 391, 401, 402, 404, 409
"Chiles/MacKay Special Interest Group." 388
Chiles, Rhea 384, 386, 394
Chiles, Seaborn 387
City Hotel 9
Civil Rights Act 280
Civil War 16, 32, 89, 93, 113
Civilian Conservation Corps 210
Clay, Henry 46
Clinton, President Bill 404
Codina, Armando 403
Collins Center for Public Policy 389
Collins, [Thomas] LeRoy 261, 279, 280, 303, 312, 351, 359, 361, 364, 386, 387, 391, 409, 413
Columbia Group 403
Columbia University 197, 367
Commissioners
　Brogan 394
　Castor 375, 385
　Conner 375, 385
　Crawford 385
　Jamerson 394
　Lewis 385, 394
　Mayo 288
Commissioner of Welfare 264
Common Schools 7, 16
Community Relations Service 280
Comptrollers
　Green 288
　Knott 146
　Lewis 375

Milligan 394
Cone, Fred P. 219, 220, 235, 236, 245
Cone, Virgie 398
Confederacy 24, 32, 39
Confederate States of America 31
confiscation laws 39
Congressional Reconstruction 44
Conover, Simon B. 76
Constitution Advisory Commission 292
Constitution Revision Commission 327
constitutional convention 36
Constitutional Secessionist 46
Constitutional Unionist 32, 43
convict lease system 134, 184
Cox, Thomas W. 134
Croix de Guerre 269
Cromwel, Oliver 31
Cromwell 147, 148
Cross-Florida Barge Canal 302, 314
Cuban Missile Crisis 302
Cumberland Law School 133
Cumberland University 145, 259, 279

D

D-Day Invasion 269
Dade County Homeless Trust 404
Daniels, Larry and Bill 352
Dantzler, Rick 402, 404
David, Thomas E. (Ted) 301
Davis, Jefferson 31
Day, Samuel T. 60
Dean, Billy 400
death warrants 350
Declaration of Independence 47, 147
Deere, John 370
DeFoor, Allison 374, 384
Democratic National Convention 280
Denton, Johnny 352
Department of Agriculture 141
Department of Elderly Affairs 391
Department of Environmental Regulation 351
Department of Juvenile Justice halfway house 399
Dickinson, Fred O. (Bud), Jr. 301
Disla, Kelly 398
Disston, Hamilton 76
Disston Land Purchase 76
Distinguished Service Cross 233
District of Columbia 384
District of Florida 44
Dougherty, Ward 330
Douglas, Marjorie Stoneman 386
Drew, George Franklin 70, 71, 79
Dr. Addison 400
Dr. Sowder 264
"due process of law" 126

E

East Coast system 127
East-West Expressway 314
Eastman School of Business 279
Eckerd, Jack M. 330, 350
Eden, LeRoy 350
Edison, Thomas 414
Elliot, Fred G. 98
Elrod, Robert H. 330
Elwyn, Justice Thomas 271
"embassy house" 384
Emory College 233
environmentalism 374
Eruptions of Eloquence 261
Evans, Christmas 148
Everglades 76, 108, 113, 114, 116, 126, 127, 134, 140, 149, 154, 189, 195, 205, 353, 395
Everglades National Park 234, 238,

257
Expressway Authority for Dade County 314

F

Faircloth, Earl 330
Farmers' Alliance 90
Federal Emergency Relief Administration (FERA) 210
Feeney, Tom 384
Florida Institute for Continuing University (FICUS) 302
Fifth Congrssional District 145
Fighting Gator Band 281
Fillmore, Millard Caldwell 249
Firestone, Secretary 375
first National Bank 4
Flagler, Henry M. 76
Fleming, Francis P. 89, 90
Florida A. & M University 108, 251, 271, 281
Florida Agricultural College 220
Florida Atlantic University 404
Florida Citrus Commission 237
Florida Constitution Revision Commission 327
Florida Department of Commerce 384
Florida East Coast Railroad 194
Florida House 384
Florida International University 331
Florida Kidcare Act 384
Florida Law Revision Commission 384
Florida Naval Militia 99, 113
Florida State Board of Health 108
Florida State Chamber of Commerce 198, 209, 211
Florida State Troops 99, 113
Florida State University

251, 271, 281, 329, 331
Florida Tourism Industry Marketing Corporation 384
Florida's boom and bust 193
Florida's Department of Transportation 336
Florida's highway system 278
Florida's Internal Improvement Fund (IIF) 76
Florida Second Regiment 89
Florida's state election law 146
Florida's stock law 260
Florida's Third District 249
Foster, General John G. 36
Fourteenth Amendment 44, 184
Freedmen's Bureau 69
French Revolution 147
Frey, Lou Jr. 350
Fuller's earth 129

G

Game and Fresh Water Fish Commission 234
Gateway City 317
Gay, George E. 183
Generals
    Foster 57
    Grant 148
    McCook 33
    Pierce 20
    Taylor 12
    Washington 46
General Revenue Fund 254
Gibbs, Mrs. J.B. Gibbs 120
Gilbert and Sullivan opera 90
Gilchrist, Albert W. 119, 120, 144
Gissendanner, Elton J. 330
Gleason, William H. 60
gold of Ophir 57
Gore, Al 405
Governor's Club 321
Governor's Industrial Development

Committee 326
Governor's Mansion
 108, 281, 385
Governor's Mansion Foundation
 351
Governor's war on crime 323
Graham, Adele 351, 359
Graham, Ernest R. 250, 349
Graham, Robert (Bob) 250, 349,
 350, 351, 367, 368,
 374, 375, 386, 387
gravy train ride 272
Gray, Robert (Bob) 261, 270, 271,
 281, 287, 288, 289
Great Depression 184, 197, 210,
 234, 387
Great Seal of the State 114
Greeley, Horace 46
Green, Robert A. "Lex" 250
Greer, Dr. Joe 397, 398
Griffin, Ben Hill, Jr. 331
Griffin, Eleanor F. 331
Griffen, Thomasina 352
Gross Receipts Tax 240
Gunby, Edward R. 76
Gurney, Edward J. 280
Gustafson, Tom 384

H

Hall, Chuck 330
Hardee, Cary Augustus 183, 184,
 209
Harris, Marshall S. 373
Harry, Reverend Douglas 297
Hart, Isaiah David 63
Hart, Ossian Bingley 63, 64, 69,
 76
Harvard Law School 301
Harvard University 349
Harwood Plantation 250
Hawkins, Paula 350, 351

Hayes, Rutherford B. 72
Healthy Start Program 398
Heflin, J. Howell 145
Henderson, Susie 399
Herbert, Chancellor Adam 407
High, Robert D. 320
Holifield, Marilyn 397
Holland & Knight 233, 234
Holland, Spessard L. 233, 234,
 252, 255, 260, 312, 320, 387
Holley, Charles R. 310
Holloway, W.M. 126
Homestead Air Force Base 302
homestead exemption 330
Hoover, Herbert 198
Hopkins, Edward A. 32
How to Win in Politics 261
Howard, Blair 399
Howard, Dr. Addison 400
Howie, W.J. 197
Hulley, Lincoln 183

I

illegal immigration 350
impeach 60
"Imperial Polk" County 233
Independent party 146
Indian boundary 18
Indian Corn 26
Indians 18, 19, 219
indirect revenue 5
initiative referendum 134
Interstate Highways
 9 314
 10 315
 75 315
Interama 314, 326
Internal Improvement Fund (IIF)
 26, 76
Internal Improvements 4, 19
"It's Time for Bryant" 303

J

Jackson, Andrew 35, 146
Jasper Normal College 220
Jefferson, Thomas 104, 116, 147
Jennings, May Mann 97
Jennings, Toni 404
Jennings, William S. 97, 98, 108
Jennings, Senator 375
John the Baptist 148
Johns, Charley E. 277, 278, 312
Johnson, Andrew 33, 35, 36, 44
Johnston, Sidney Catts 145
Jones, Daryl L. 404
Judge Lynch 40
Judge McKean 46
judicial tribunal 72
Justices
    McDonald 375
    Thomas 261

K

Kansas-Nebraska Act 27, 28
Keen, Florence S. 331
Kempt, Georgianna Carolina
    (Carrie) 107
Kennedy, John F. 302, 320
Kennedy Space Center 345
Khrushchev, Nikita 302
King, Robert High 310
Kipling 154
Kirk, Claude R., Jr. 319, 320, 321,
    330, 332, 350, 374, 385
Kirk Investments Company 320
Knott 146
"Know Nothing" party 23
Knox, John 148
Korean War 319
Korean War 383
Ku Klux Klan 60

L

Labor party 90
"Lamb Chop Bloc." 305
Land and Water Management Act
    330
Lane, Prof. Benjamin Benson 153
Latin American Studies 403
Law of the Wreck and Salvage 35
Law Review 329
Lee, Robert E. 128, 129, 148
Legion of Merit 269
Legislative Council 9
legislative reapportionment 302
Lewis, Amos 262
Lieutenant Governor Adams 332
Lieutenant Governor Osborne 332
Lincoln, Abraham
    24, 128, 129, 368
Little Cabinet 288, 316
"Little" New Deal 210
Lowell, James Russell 297

M

MacClenny State Hospital 355
MacDill Field at Tampa 244
Mack, Connie 402
MacKay, Anne 402
MacKay, Kenneth Hood (Buddy)
    384, 385, 386, 389, 393,
    394, 401, 402, 404
Macon, Nathaniel 46
Madame X 320
Madison, James 119
Marine Corps 319
Martin, John W. 193, 194, 209,
    220, 374
Martin, Frank 373
Martinez, Robert (Bob) 373, 374,
    384, 385
Marvin, William 35, 36
Martinez, Mary Jane 375, 379,

385
Mason 9
Mattfeld, Erika 320
Mathews, John E. (Jack) 310, 330
McBride, Bill 404
McCarty, Daniel T. 260, 269, 270, 277, 278, 283, 402
McCarty, John 301
McCormick, Burt 331
McCrary, Jesse J. 331
McFarlane, Matthew B. 97, 98, 108
McLeod, Mary Bethune 354, 365
McLin, Hon. B.E. 124
Mediterranean fruit fly 198
Melton, James 281
Meuse-Argonne campaign 233
Miami Children's Hospital 404
migrant labor camps 337
Military Rule 44
Miller, Jaime 398
Miller, Lori 398
Milton, John 31, 32
Milton, Virgil Homer 31
Minimum Foundation Program 234
Mitchell, Henry L. 93, 94, 108
Mixson, Margie 359
Mixson, John Wayne 351, 359, 360, 367, 368, 375
Model-T Ford 146
Monroe, James 386
Morris, Allen 261
Morris, Don 352
Mortham, Sandra 394
Morton, B.A. 98
Moseley, William D. 1, 2, 9, 251, 252
Muldrew, Richard B. 320
Murray, Perry 263

N

Napoleon 71, 148
National Association of Broadcasters 280
National Campaign Against Use of Drugs 374
National Commission to Prevent Infant Mortality 384
National Defense Council 245
National Governors' Conference 280
National Guard 350
National Recovery Administration 210
National Youth Administration 210
Native American Indians 392
Naval Air Base at Jacksonville 244
naval stores 26, 116
Navy 245, 260, 279
Navy's V-12 program 367
"Negro Rule," 85
negro suffrage 56
negro suffrage 54, 56
Nelson, Bill 384
New Deal 210, 249, 250
New York World's Fair 220
Nineteenth Amendment 146, 184
Nixon, Richard 320
"noblesse oblige." 120

O

Odham, Brailey 270
Oil Spill and Pollution Control Act 330
Okeechobee Land Company 126
"Old Swanee," 220
"Once to Every Man and Nation." 297
O'Neal, William R. 134, 193
Only Here for a Little While 400
Overseas Highway to Key West 278

P

Pacific territory 77
Pajcic, Steve 373, 374
Panhandle 249, 368, 384
pari-mutual betting 198
Patchett, Representative 375
Pensacola Naval Air Training Station 244
Pensacola's Boys' Base 399
Pepper, Claude 219, 266
Perez, Remegio 352
Perry, Edward Aylsworth 23, 24, 85, 86
Perry, Madison Stark 23
Petteway Raleigh W. 220
Pettigrew, A.J. 120
Phi Beta Kappa 349
Phillips Academy 403
Plant, Henry B. 76
Plant Railroad 77, 93
Political Action Committee contributions 389
Polk, Frank 85
Populist party 76, 85, 90, 93, 98, 134, 260
"Pork Chop Gang" 305
power-loom 5
Preservation 2000 374
Presidential Reconstruction 44
Profiles in Character 404
Progressives 98, 134
prohibition 146, 151
Prohibition party 90, 146
Public Domain 4
"pulpiteer." 387
Purple Heart 269

R

racial segregation 302
Racketeering 285
Radical 59
Railroad Commission 111, 112, 141
Randolph, John 46
rattlesnake dance 353
Reconstruction 24, 65, 75, 85, 331, 374
Reconstruction Finance Corporation 198
Reed, Harrison 59, 60
Remon, Senora 281
Renfro, Freddie 352
Reno, Janet 404
Republic of Panama 281
Revolutionist 46
Road Department 254
Rock of Gibraltar 203
Roosevelt, Franklin D. 134, 210, 220, 223, 249, 250
Roosevelt, Theodore 134
Rossin, Tom 404
Rothschild 147
Ruskin, John 287

S

Sanford, Henry S. 76
Save Our Coasts Program 350
Save Our Everglades Campaign 350, 374
Save Our Rivers Act 350
Scalawags 59
Scott, George W. 59
Second Seminole War 31
Secretary of the Navy 309
Section 1, Article 9 103
Section 1 of Article IV 271
section 4, article xii 126
segregation 364
self cleaning plow 370
Seminole Indians 17
Senate Intelligence Committee 351
Sentinel 2

"separate but equal" doctrine 294
Seventh Army 269
Seventh Florida Regiment 24
Shafter, General William 77
Shakespeare 362
Shevin, Robert L. 350
Shipman V.J. 90
Sholtz, David 209, 210, 219
Sidney Lanier High School 319
Simmons, Eugenia 219
Simmons, Jack W. 281, 289
Simmons, Dr. William 353
Sisal Hemp 17
sit-ins 301
Sixth District 401
slave state 28
Smathers, Bruce A. 350
Smathers, George A. 350
Smith, Hedrick 390
Smith, Jim 373, 385, 394
Socialist 120, 134, 146
Society of States 253
Solid Waste Disposal Act 374
Southeastern Army Bombing Base 244
Southern Governors' Conference 280
southern progressive 107
Southern Regional Education Board 280
Soviet Union 280
Sowder, Dr. Wilson T. 264
Spanish Tobacco 17, 26
Spanish-American War 77, 120, 133
Speakers
  Mills 375
  Wallace 393, 394
  Wetherell 385
Speaking of Speaking 261
Special Committee on Aging 384
spinning-jenny 5

"spoils system" 146
Sprague, Colonel John T. 44
St. Augustine *News* 2
State Board of Education 86
State Board of Equalization 103
State Board of Health 90, 103, 237
State Canvassing Board 76, 146
State Comprehensive Planning Act 330
State Defense Council 245
State Development Commission 280
State Highway Commission 134
State Militia 113
State Racing Commission 198, 225
Sstate Reform School 143
State Road Board 314, 325
State Road Department 225, 227, 263, 271, 306
State Seminaries 25
State Tax Commission 134
State Treasurer Knot 236
State Treasury 224
State University System 371
State Welfare Board 210, 264
state's rights 2
States Rights Democrat 32
Stearns, Marcellas L. 69, 70, 320
Stetson University 183, 197, 209
Stone, Senator 351
Sullivan, John L. 108
"Sunshine Amendment" 330
Sunshine Skyway 260
Sunshine State Parkway 302
Superintendent Bailey 288
Surface Water and Environment Act 374
Swan, Harry S. 270

T

Taft, William Howard 134
Tallahassee Chamber of Commerce 281, 289
Tampa Bay Hotel 77
Tanzler, Hans Jr. 350
Tapper, George G. 330
Temple Beth Israel 400
terrorist attack of September 11, 2001 405
"The Bay of Pigs" 302
"The Grove" 281
The Power Game 390
The Water Control Committee 265
Third Florida Volunteer Infantry 119
Thomas, Jerry 331
Thomas, Pat 330
Thompson, Mike 331
Tilden, Samuel J. 72
Time 398
Tobacco industry 384
Trammell, Park 133, 134, 145, 193
truckers' strike 350
Truman, Harry 266
"turkeys" 374
Tuttle, Julia 365
Twenty-First Amendment 210
Twenty-Fourth Flying Squadron 233

U

Unionism 23
United Negro Fund of South Florida 404
United Way of Dade County 404
University of Alabama Law School 319
University of Chicago 197
University of Florida 233, 251, 259, 269, 275, 281, 301, 329, 331, 349, 368, 383, 401
University of Illinois 373
University of Mississippi 249
University of North Carolina at Chapel Hill 1
University of Pennsylvania 368
University of Tampa 373
University of Texas 403
University of Virginia 249
US Department of Agriculture 98
US Military Academy 119
USNR 309

V

Vanderbilt 133
Vicksburg siege 93

W

Wackenhut, George 323, 324
Walker, David Shelby 27, 28, 29, 43, 44
"Walkin' Lawton" 384
War Between the States 387
War of 1812 9
Ward, George T. 15
Warren, Fuller 234, 259, 260, 261, 270, 271, 280, 312
Washbourne, William A. 280
Washington, George 12, 119, 128, 129, 148
Water Resources Act 330
Webster, Daniel 46, 261, 275
Weeks, William W. 76
Wellborn, John Martin 193
Wells, Charles 402
Wesley, Charles 148
West Point 119
Wetlands Protection Act 350
Weatherell, T.K. 391
Wharton School of Finance 368

Whig party 15, 23, 43, 249
Whitehair, P. Francis 234
White House 134
"white primaries" 251
William and Mary College 75
Williams, John Lee 353
Williams, J.H. (Jim) 331, 350, 351
Williams, Colonel William F. 77
Wilson, Woodrow 134, 306
"workdays" program 351
Works Progress Administration 210
World War I 146, 209, 233, 249, 387
World War II 210, 233, 260, 269, 279, 309, 367, 387
World's Fair in New York 302
Wright brothers 204
Wright, Jimmy 352

Y

Yale 209
Yankee 219
yellow fever epidemic 90, 103
yellow gem citrus fruits 154